Informal Cities

Informal Cities

Histories of Governance and Inequality in Latin Europe, Latin America, and Colonial North Africa

EDITED BY CHARLOTTE VORMS
AND BRODWYN FISCHER

The University of Chicago Press
Chicago and London

The University of Chicago Press, Chicago 60637
The University of Chicago Press, Ltd., London
© 2025 by The University of Chicago
Published 2025

34 33 32 31 30 29 28 27 26 25   1 2 3 4 5

ISBN-13: 978-0-226-83599-0 (cloth)
ISBN-13: 978-0-226-83601-0 (paper)
ISBN-13: 978-0-226-83600-3 (e-book)
DOI: https://doi.org/10.7208/chicago/9780226836003.001.0001

This book was published with the support of Université Paris 1 Panthéon-Sorbonne
and Centre d'histoire sociale du XXème siècle.

Library of Congress Cataloging-in-Publication Data

Names: Vorms, Charlotte, editor. | Fischer, Brodwyn M., editor.
Title: Informal cities : histories of governance and inequality in Latin Europe, Latin
    America, and colonial North Africa / edited by Charlotte Vorms and Brodwyn
    Fischer.
Description: Chicago : The University of Chicago Press, 2025. | Includes bibliographical
    references and index.
Identifiers: LCCN 2024053466 | ISBN 9780226835990 (cloth) |
    ISBN 9780226836010 (paperback) | ISBN 9780226836003 (ebook)
Subjects: LCSH: Squatter settlements—Latin America. | Squatter settlements—
    Africa, North. | Squatter settlements—Europe. | Urbanization—Latin America. |
    Urbanization—Africa, North. | Urbanization—Europe. | Equality—Latin America. |
    Equality—Africa, North. | Equality—Europe.
Classification: LCC HD7287.95 .I537 2025 | DDC 363.5/8—dc23/eng/20250118
LC record available at https://lccn.loc.gov/2024053466

Contents

Informal Urbanism as History

BRODWYN FISCHER AND

CHARLOTTE VORMS

At some point during this millennium's first decade—in 2007, according to the UN's *World Urbanization Prospects* report—the balance of Earth's population tipped toward cities.[1] The certainty that "the future of the world's population is urban" generated hope in the "urban ability to create collaborative brilliance."[2] It also sparked dread that contemporary urbanity is not up to the intersecting challenges of late-stage capitalism, climate change, mass migration, technology-driven surveillance regimes, racial exclusion, and extralegal defiance of state legitimacy.

At the crossroads of utopia and dystopia—or perhaps in their crosshairs—we often find the so-called informal city, a wide range of geographies and morphologies united by their uncertain legal status, precarious access to public infrastructure, and systematic marginalization. This urban form is conceived by turns as a "planet of slums" that dissolves the shimmering mirage of urban modernism and a "commons" that holds within it the promise of actualized rights to the city.[3] The informal city is home to a significant portion of the world's urban population—around a quarter if we consider only UN-denominated "slums," more if we include other iterations of informal housing—and it often seems that urbanity's very future hangs on its fate.[4]

Given all that, it is not surprising that informal urbanism has generated an enormous outpouring of research, art, commentary, and policy initiatives. Some of this recent work shares with previous waves of "slum studies" a tendency to understand informality as a holdover from the developmental past. Other authors conceive informality mainly as a symptom of contemporary crisis, attributing to neoliberalism or democratic erosion or climate change the same phenomena that previous generations might have attributed to racial defects, underdevelopment, populism, authoritarianism, or state overreach.[5] These, however, are only two currents within broad and heterogeneous debates, which are often significantly attentive to issues of local agency and rights to the city and have had a substantial impact on the global policy agenda.[6] Recent work has also begun to break down long-standing paradigms that identify informal urbanism entirely with the form of the shantytown or slum, site it only in the Global South, minimize its importance to state building and governance, and fail to recognize its centrality to urbanism across divisions of class, race, or ethnicity.[7]

In the flux of these debates, history often looms large. Sometimes, the informal city is defined as a historical anachronism—an atavistic modern iteration of a way of life that rightly belongs in the distant past. Elsewhere, history intersects with informality as a narrative or political strategy, or as substantiation for myriad legal and ethical claims. Yet "history" in these contexts rarely digs too far beneath the surface of widely accepted origin stories. Social scientists, activists, and policymakers often invoke received wisdom about the distant past as a kind of origin point that leads directly to present-day dilemmas; many also cite well-established historiography about politics and urbanism that provides context and background for their arguments about the informal city. But analysts of contemporary urbanity do not generally understand history as a research field or an analytical method that might yield new insights into the nature of informal urbanism, in part because they often confuse the emergence of the term *informality* in the 1970s with the origins of the practices that constitute it.[8] Historians, for their part, have generally treated informality as a niche topic—marginal to the historical field more broadly—or as a recent development that can be traced only anachronistically in the past. While historians sometimes acknowledge the presence of informal urbanism's integral elements in certain historical contexts—especially in the Global South—they rarely recognize informality as a historically constructed phenomenon or conceive its dynamics as constituent of broader genealogies of urbanism, governance, politics, or inequality. As a result, social scientists, policymakers, and activists give little creed to how informality has been created, sustained, and transformed over time, and historians know less than they might about informality's role in forging the past. When compounded by the fact that global urban debates are still structured by North Atlantic traditions in which informal urbanism rarely figures except as an exceptional disjunction of the Global South, these lacunae create important omissions and distortions in urban policy, theory, and history.[9]

Based on three years of collective work as part of the Paris-based La Ville Informelle au XXe Siècle project, and with the aim of highlighting recent historical work that has bucked the previously mentioned trends, this volume seeks to spark further debate by exploring the local, transnational, and comparative history of informal urbanization processes that have been integral to cities, economies, politics, and governance practices around the world.[10] Informal urbanization, in this context, refers to the specific realm in which urban space, housing, and public resources are claimed, occupied, negotiated, created, and policed beyond the formal sanction, regulation, or protection of laws or legally bound institutions.[11] Our geographical reach—spanning Western Europe, French colonial North Africa, and Latin America—substantiates our claim that informality was vital to urbanization processes across the divides of north and south as well as colonized, free, and colonizing, in a range of political, social, and economic contexts. At the same time, the countries and cities we analyze were nodes of common global networks, and (as inheritors of Roman law and European political traditions) they shared crucial features of law and governance that render our transnational and comparative analysis more legible.

By historicizing informal urbanization as it occurred in these places from the late nineteenth to the late twentieth centuries, these chapters demonstrate that it is neither an atavism nor a new or contingent phenomenon specific to the transition from rural to urban life or produced as a temporary externality of political and economic development. It is not unique to the Global South, nor should it be understood as the product of contemporary neoliberalism or deregulation. Rather, informal urbanization is created by the very processes of legal, political, and economic modernization that it is often said to undermine, co-constructed by actors across the socioeconomic, ethnic, and racial spectrum, and constitutive of forms of power and marginalization that are integral to modern urban life. Understood historically, informal urbanization emerges as an intrinsic feature of urbanity, capable of illuminating global processes of state formation, socioeconomic stratification, and political struggle. It also appears as an underappreciated constitutive element in national, regional, and local histories of power and resource distribution, adding new layers to our understanding of seemingly disjunctive social configurations and modes of governance that shape the modern experience of citizenship and the city.

Informality, Informal Urbanization, and History

Informal urbanization derives from the concept of informality, a term that often confuses as much as it clarifies. First coined by Keith Hart in 1973 to describe unregulated economic activity in Ghana and the developing world,[12] informality soon evolved to describe myriad phenomena that had long been integral to urban life around the globe, from street commerce and shanty-towns to unregulated construction and service work and unsanctioned movement across borders.[13] This wide range of activities is often too divergent for fruitful comparison, and the cacophony of descriptive terms such activities have generated over time and space also complicates global historical analysis. The binary way in which informality has been opposed to formality has rightly been called out for its distorting effects, and the concept has also suffered from misleading elision with the experiences of poor communities and cities of the Global South, despite the fact that the phenomena it describes consistently transcend borders and social distinctions.[14]

Informality's moral and political implications have also provoked considerable debate.[15] As vernacular urbanities have become central to postcolonial politics, and as residents themselves have claimed increasing space as knowledge producers and policymakers, the concept of informality has invited significant criticism as a demeaning and marginalizing designation that lends a normative quality to the legal order and stigmatizes poor neighborhoods as illegal and criminal. Thus entangled in debates about epistemology and power, informality is often understood as a colonizing concept.[16] But the opposite perspective is also common among those who celebrate informality as creative, "kinetic," or vernacular, in perennial opposition to colonial and capitalist hegemonies.[17] In political terms, analysts have variously identified informality with an insurgent demand for rights to the city, a corrupt and clientelistic hollowing of democratic forms, or a hybrid of both.[18] In the face of such contradictory interpretations, the concept of urban informality emerges as a terrain of moral, political, and epistemological dispute, where the informal city itself—as a place where real people make urbanity and drive history in real time—is often abstracted, effaced, or fractured.

Despite informality's polysemy and contradictions, however, we believe that a precisely delimited version of the concept retains the capacity to anchor transnational and historical analysis. Informal urbanization, understood as any urban practice that occurs in the conflictual or ambiguous space on or outside the margins of formal law and regulation, can be an especially vital lens for understanding the evolution of spatial configurations, legal processes, and power relations that shape the urban form and society. It can also reveal much about the histories of broader phenomena such as institutional liberalism, citizenship, and enduring economic and legal inequalities. We can follow the history of informal urbanization in a wide variety of contexts, in many forms and equally varied geographies. In so doing, we can come to understand informality not as a moral abstraction, a political stance, or a conjunctural crisis, but as a particular articulation of power and resources that has been integral to economy, society, governance, politics, and social change wherever it has occurred.

Throughout this volume, we take it as a given that informal urbanization has occurred in the Global North as well as the Global South, and that it has been generated by members of all social classes and racial and ethnic groups; even the most seemingly marginalized spaces have been cocreated by the powerful and the dispossessed. Informal urbanization has manifested itself not only as a range of specific urban forms—the self-built shack, the unserviced cinder-block home, the multifamily structure that does not conform to sanitary or building regulations, the neighborhoods characterized by these kinds of structures—but also as the basis for and expression of a mode of governance. As such, it has helped ensure a perennial unequal distribution of public resources and has reinforced forms of power that are not subject to institutional constraints. While informal urbanization has allowed poor and marginalized people to create vital spaces for survival, autonomy, and city making in the face of constrictive legal regimes, its emancipatory possibilities have always been constrained by inherent vulnerabilities and exclusions.

Thus defined, informal urbanization has much to contribute to history, just as history has much to contribute to the study of informality. Yet the task of historicizing informal urbanity has its challenges. Beginning in the mid-twentieth century, previous waves of "slum studies" began to document the dynamics they witnessed and the histories their informants articulated, establishing a series of flash points that structure powerful but incomplete ideas about informality's historical evolution. The most important of these have become so ingrained that they are difficult to dislodge, from quasi-mythological community origin stories to the argument that informal urbanization emerged with midcentury underdevelopment, decolonization, rural crisis, or leftist mobilization, to the more recent understanding that informal urbanization has resulted from state overreach, neoliberal state breakdown, or environmental crisis. These accounts all have elements of empirical accuracy, and the memory that generates them merits study and respect. But recent research suggests that they also significantly distort our ability to understand how informality has developed over longer periods of historical time in coevolution with broader phenomena such as colonialism, liberalism, fascism, the welfare state, urban modernism, or developmentalism. Old habits in the field of history (which still struggles to provincialize hyperreal European historical templates) also hinder our understanding of informal urbanization as a transregional phenomenon integral to global urban history.[19] Even when such research does advance, it often remains enclosed within the bounds of the academy, either because historians fail to explain its theoretical and policy implications to a broader audience or because the narratives thus produced fit uncomfortably with current political imperatives.

This project originated from these tensions. By placing highly localized historical processes in transnational and comparative context, we aim not only to show that informality has a history but also to demonstrate that informality is a product and component of history. In hopes of balancing coherence and diversity, we focus on an interconnected range of local and regional contexts spanning Latin Europe (mainland France, Italy, and Spain), Latin America (Brazil, Chile, Venezuela, and Mexico), and French colonial North Africa (Morocco and Algeria). These places share some core structural similarities: the civil law tradition in national or colonial law,[20] a strong Catholic influence, the normative importance of the nation-state, certain ways of organizing the interaction of public and private power, similar conceptualizations of the welfare or social state, shared participation in Western traditions of urban planning, and common experiences of twentieth-century authoritarianism and the Cold War. Yet each case and each region also present sharp particularities; these divergences emerge especially clearly with regard to their colonial trajectories and geopolitical positionalities, their relationship to economic and urban development, and their role in the generation of global norms and structures. This balance between common history and local variations allows us to explore a wide range of ways in which informality has existed historically and acted within history while also identifying its constitutive role in shaping cities, polities, economies, and societies on both sides of the Atlantic.

Informality in History: Regional Trajectories

There are global continuities and connections both in the history of informality and in informality's role within broader histories. Yet understandings of informality have generally emerged from regionally distinct academic, intellectual, and political traditions. Although we ultimately aim to break down these geographical silos, it would be difficult to build on the trajectory of previous scholarship without acknowledging its heavily national and regional character. For that reason, we begin our analysis with a brief synthesis of the histories and historiographies of informal urbanization as they have developed along occasionally intersecting tracks in Latin America and Latin Europe (mostly France, Spain, and Italy). To facilitate comparison, we focus in each regional account on the history of the phenomena that constitute informal urbanization, the history of informality's construction as a problem in the public sphere, and the historiography of both. Considered together, these three strands allow us to set an agenda for the sort of historicization we aim for in this volume.

As elsewhere, in Latin America the history of informal practices is largely one of continuity, whereas the history of informality's problematization is one of rupture. The former has been studied only sporadically, while the latter has organized politics and knowledge production for well over a century.

If we understand urban informality through its composite practices—all the urban processes that occur partially or entirely outside the sphere of institutionalized law, regulation, and protection—then it has been a vital feature of Latin America's cities since their colonial origins.[21] While urban historians have traditionally emphasized Iberian planning traditions and the *ciudad letrada*,[22] elite urbanites frequently evaded legal constraints and always relied heavily on majority Black, Indigenous, and mixed-race populations whose relationships to property, construction norms, and urban statutes were largely governed by extralegal forms of power. For the entire colonial period and well into independent nationhood in the nineteenth century, the elaborately planned central regions of cities such as Mexico City, Bogotá, Quito, Lima, Buenos Aires, and Salvador were built, traversed, and staffed by people who lived in modest, self-built homes outside that core or who fashioned urban space for themselves by extralegally subdividing extant structures or building crude dwellings in the basements, backyards, and interstices of the legally regulated city.[23]

For centuries, these early auto-constructed cities were not considered properly urban by elite classes, who associated the city with well-defined morphological, cultural, and racial characteristics. But neither were they generally considered a specific, urgent public issue.[24] It was only in the second half of the nineteenth century that several factors converged to render ordinary vernacular urbanities problematic and thus necessarily strange. In these years, expanding state and sanitary capacities coincided with Latin America's emergence as a major supplier for the Second Industrial Revolution and with the invention of a hyperreal, Belle Époque urban ideal. At the same time, the dissolution of legalized slavery, transformations in other systems of forced labor, and the disruption of rural economies sparked urbanization and called into question private and patriarchal forms of social ordering. In that context, the ambiguous property relations, improvised huts, dirt streets, gerrymandered water and waste provisions, and general "rural" or "backward" aspect of self-built urbanity emerged as a public emergency in need of governmental solution. Projected as a threat to public health, an emblem of Black or Indigenous culture, an obstacle to real estate development and rational urban planning, or a stain on the postcard cityscape, self-built homes and neighborhoods came to be understood as impediments to what Belle Époque elites understood as the urgent projects of civilization and progress.[25]

Although the term was not used at that time, in many countries this was the moment when city authorities invented *informal urbanization*. It was forged in the public sphere not by the existence of the self-built city, but by reams of laws that sought to achieve on paper the hyperreal European forms of urbanity that they could not grasp in practice.[26] Informal urbanization materialized when urban forms that had previously existed in an ambiguous state—not endowed with legal status, but not necessarily treated as properly illegal—were defined out of the legally constituted city without any adequate measures for their replacement. Sanitary codes outlawed wells and latrines, building codes mandated specific materials and spatial configurations, ambitious urban plans banned rustic shacks from increasing swaths of major municipalities, and real estate developers sought to redevelop urban outskirts or interstices by expelling families who resided on lands without legal title. It mattered little that inhabitants of poor, self-built dwellings had no alternative or that promises of mass affordable housing went unmet: the legal city had become the normative city, regardless of the texture of the actual urban fabric, and a process of legal enclosure relegated self-built urbanity to the realm of informality.[27]

It is difficult to know with precision how Latin American urban informality's demographic and spatial dimensions changed in the twentieth century.[28] While it certainly expanded rapidly in response to dramatic upticks in rural-to-urban migration or economic crises, formal-sector housing also grew quickly, and we generally lack the kind of data that would allow us to know how much these periods of rapid acceleration altered the formal-informal balance in the urban landscape as a whole. Statisticians quantified informal urbanization rarely and incompletely among the poor and not at all among the wealthy. The spatial and demographic studies that do exist define their objects and categories very differently over space and time. Some counted all homes that departed from building and sanitary codes; some focused only on homes built of "rustic" materials. Some sought out homes on land to which residents had no legal claim, or homes without city services, or homes with these characteristics occupied by low-income people. Others targeted only clusters of homes with informal features, ignoring the dispersed informality in backyards and interstitial urban spaces typical of many cities. In some cases—most notably Recife, Brazil, which carried out the region's first published census of informal dwellings in 1939—the geography of informality was entirely ignored in favor of surveys analyzing the people who occupied informal neighborhoods. Given this inconsistency and incompleteness, any claims regarding change over time are necessarily tenuous.

All the same, a few general trends do seem apparent. As poor people's self-built housing was rendered informal by restrictive laws, it tended to be channeled away from the backyards and interstices of formalized neighborhoods and concentrated in increasingly marginalized urban geographies (hills, swamps, peripheries, regions beyond official municipal boundaries); counterintuitively, in many countries, the legal enclosure of central and prosperous neighborhoods contributed directly to the growth of larger so-called shantytowns. These denser, more visible neighborhoods—which received disproportionate attention within the informal landscape and were quickly labeled with terms such as *favela, colonia proletaria*, and *villa miseria*—grew quickly with accelerating rural-to-urban migration, which began as early as the late nineteenth century and peaked in the three decades following World War II.[29] In larger cities, corporatist, populist, and revolutionary governments attempted with some frequency to destroy, resettle, or "urbanize" informal neighborhoods, with varying degrees of success.[30] Yet at the same time, although authorities only rarely admitted it, both the region's political structures and its economic development strategies increasingly depended on the existence of cheap, self-built neighborhoods where precarious legal and material conditions fortified clientelism, where low costs allowed employers to pay lower salaries, and where a lack of civic rights relieved the government of responsibility for basic urban services.[31] This, combined with the fact that a wide range of left-wing social and political movements began as early as the 1920s to organize around issues involving housing, property, and what would later be known as the right to the city, ensured that informal urbanization would prove strikingly resilient. Even in industrial and political capitals, and especially in smaller, less-resourced regions, informality remained a semipermanent feature of the urban landscape, ebbing and flowing with economic trends and authoritarian removal campaigns but generally providing urban homes for anywhere from around 10 percent to the vast majority of urban residents. The degree to which governments have incrementally legalized informal urbanization varies widely; as the chapters in this collection show, in Mexico such incorporation was de facto state policy for much of the twentieth century, while Brazil tended more toward a politics of extralegal tolerance. But most Latin American cities arguably contain centenary communities, often located on what has become valuable land, that were originally born of informality.

This history of informal city building as an urban process was necessarily entwined with (and often overshadowed by) the history of informality as an urban problem. The definition of that problem, rooted in local variations of transnational trends, shifted significantly over time.[32] Nineteenth-century preoccupations with racial whitening, sanitation, and legibility on a range of transnational stages never faded, but across the twentieth century, they came to be layered with other paradigmatic preoccupations. The informal city was said to undermine the legitimacy of self-denominated revolutionary governments across the political spectrum; to threaten the project of state-led development by siphoning resources from capital investment; to erode the city's ability to serve as a beacon of economic and cultural modernity; to serve as a laboratory for social "marginality"; to incubate political radicalism; to negate the rule of law and the meaning of citizenship in democratizing societies; to threaten environmental equilibria; and to epitomize the failings of corporatism, socialism, authoritarianism, developmentalism, capitalism, and eventually neoliberalism.[33]

Each of these cycles of problematization deserves its own exploration, but they hold certain key features in common. In each case—with some partial exceptions, most notably in postrevolutionary Mexico and Chile—observers mostly took for granted the assumption that urban informality was an atavistic aberration that undermined a hyperreal version of normative urbanity.[34] Once problematized, informal urbanization emerged as a kind of externality of other historical processes, lacking its own history and devoid of any substantial historical role. In each case, problematization politicized informal urbanization by focusing public sphere debates on informality's intersection with the hot-button issues of the day. And in each case, problematization fostered alarmist exposés that overshadowed the agency and ordinary life at the center of most informal communities. While plenty of community members, policymakers, activists, and scholars pushed back against simplistic demonization, successive cycles of problematization organized public conversations in such a way that the self-built city was mainly visible to outsiders as a fractal emblem of crisis.

Equally importantly, the problematization of informal urbanization organized knowledge production at local, national, and transnational scales. On the one hand, particularly as Latin American urbanization crested and attained transnational attention, the perception of crisis generated research. In the first half of the twentieth century, public officials, engineers, and urbanists—spurred by fears of infectious disease and the desire to install urban amenities and secure urban investment—began for the first time to count and even map self-built cities. By the 1920s and 1930s, urbanists and social service agencies—seeking to know populations in order to relocate or govern them—had begun to conduct, if not always to publish, in-depth studies of the people who lived in informal dwellings and neighborhoods.[35] With the rise of communism and radical populisms, as well as the advent of the Cold War, journalists, novelists, photographers and filmmakers from across the political spectrum began to publish extensive exposés of urban shantytowns.[36] By midcentury, anthropologists and sociologists had begun to explore shanty-towns for their field studies, creating ethnographic records but also bringing with them transnational frameworks running the gamut from the Chicago School to Catholic social doctrine to modernization and development.[37] In the 1960s, progressive architects such as John Turner studied vernacular urbanisms; from the 1970s forward, scholars focused on the intersections of informality, democracy, gender, social movements, the environment, and the right to the city;[38] from the 1980s, the policy focus turned to Hernando de Soto's ideas about property titling as a neoliberal panacea for urban poverty; at the turn of the twenty-first century, attention turned to issues of race, social exclusion, and the production and reproduction of violence and illegal orders.[39]

These successive waves of study established a steady stream of data, creating an intentional archive of the informal urban experience, rendering urban informality increasingly visible, and recording crucial self-narrations of informality's lived experience. Yet, like all archives, these sometimes shadow as much as they reveal. Scholars and policymakers produced information in response to the political and academic paradigms and controversies of their time, which often led them to downplay or ignore questions that historians now consider vital. Surveys, documents, maps, interviews, photographs, and films all reflected the biases and priorities of their creators; now that those items have become a historical archive, they risk projecting those distortions onto our understanding of the past.

Just as importantly, because the assembly of urban practices that we now call informal urbanization received relatively little attention before the mid-twentieth century, scholars have often confused the emergence of informality's archive with its origins; the memory and historical knowledge that was captured by postwar researchers became, in essence, the entire recorded history of informal urbanization. Across Latin America, on the basis of this first draft of history, a narrative emerged in which urban informality was the product of twentieth-century hyperurbanization and underdevelopment; mainstream informal politics were the creation of revolution, populism, or corporatism (often involving corrupt clientelism practiced among politically naïve rural migrants); and the informal social movements that contested marginalization and oppression were the outgrowth of leftist vanguard politics that began to emerge only in the mid-twentieth century.[40]

In narrating the historical background of urban informality, social scientists sometimes refer to widely recognized touchstones, etched in memory by a few early analysts and transformed across the decades into a kind of palimpsest. In Brazil, these histories often include a series of landmark events in Rio de Janeiro: the emergence of the Providencia favela in the wake of the Canudos War, a series of well-known urban reform and favela removal campaigns, the emergence of samba, and the founding of the first citywide federation of favela residents in the 1950s.[41] Other countries have their own touchstones. In Mexico, social scientists remember postrevolutionary tenant strikes, early experiences with *colonias proletarias* during Lázaro Cárdenas's revolutionary presidency (1934–1940), debates about urban "cultures of poverty" sparked by Oscar Lewis in the 1950s, and the paradigmatic history of Ciudad Nezahualcóyotl in greater Mexico City.[42] Argentines might highlight the Depression-era origins of Buenos Aires's Villa 31 settlement; Chilean social scientists refer to the *tomas* (land invasions) of the mid-twentieth century, especially in Santiago's La Victoria; Venezuelans recall the occupation and informalization of Caracas's 23 de Enero superblocks in 1958; Cubans remember Havana's Las Yaguas shantytown, which grew exponentially under Fulgencio Batista before being finally razed after the 1959 Revolution.[43] But these are atomized touchstones, not histories; the *favelas*, *colonias proletarias*, and *poblaciones* do not generally emerge in these accounts as places that are integral to any larger historical processes.

With few exceptions, it was only in the 1990s that historians across the region began to dig deeper to try to understand the longer trajectory and influence of urban informality. Since then, in multiple countries, historians, historical sociologists, and legal scholars have begun to carefully reconstruct a more complex picture of how and why the self-built city evolved as it did.[44] This work has been especially useful in establishing a continuous trajectory of self-built urbanity; in analyzing informality's intellectual and policy history; in arguing that informality evolved with Latin American cities rather than constituting a rural invasion of a seamlessly civilized urban space; in substantiating the argument that informality was a condition created by law and thoroughly entwined with the history of formal economies and institutional power; and in tracing the history of urban social movements to the early twentieth century. In some cases, historians have also begun to break out of informality's historical silo and explore the ways in which informality's history contributed to larger more widely recognized historical processes involving citizenship, state building, socioeconomic inequality, the rule of law, revolutionary politics and governance, authoritarianism, Catholic social doctrine, and race. Such work is still marginalized within mainstream historical scholarship, and it only rarely offers a transnational perspective. But the very existence of this new historiography, in many cases authored by contributors to this volume, has begun to open new dimensions within theoretical debates about the causes and consequences of informality in contemporary Latin America.

LATIN EUROPE

Latin Europe followed a similar chronology, and the mechanisms through which vernacular urbanization was informalized also resembled Latin America's. The two regions diverged sharply, however, when it came to scale. In Latin America, informal urbanization often constituted the lion's share of urban housing, while in European cities it encompassed less space, housed fewer people, and had less economic impact. Latin Europe also experienced an even greater midcentury rupture than Latin America did in terms of informality's problematization. Because the postwar shantytowns were so far from Western Europe's dramatically changed standards and urbanistic norms, their perceived deficiencies stood in much sharper relief. In the context of transnational Cold War dynamics, Europeans also increasingly associated shantytowns with Latin America and the colonized and decolonizing expanses of Africa and Asia, understanding them and their residents as emblems of underdevelopment with no place on the Continent. Consequently, Europeans viewed the shantytowns of the 1950s—newly labeled *bidonvilles* and *chabolas* in mainland France and Spain—as qualitatively different from the vernacular urbanization that had existed on the Continent since the nineteenth century. Historians, following suit, have generally considered the two separately.

Pushing against the current of these perceptions, we contend that it is possible to understand the region's nineteenth-century peripheries and 1950s *bidonvilles* as avatars of common historical phenomena. By this we do not mean to suggest anachronistically that the same material construction practices have the same meaning regardless of their social, architectural, or legal context. But we believe that, just as in Latin America, a view that balances recognition of distinctions with an awareness of continuity can render Latin Europe's urban history more intelligible, helping us to understand informalization as a phenomenon that is predictably created by the same laws, politics, and real estate dynamics that forge the formalized city. While the terms shaping Europe's informal urbanism have varied greatly, the actual phenomena that such words describe—vernacular and publicly underresourced urbanisms whose practitioners use cheap or fragile building materials and act either out-side the law or in zones of loose regulation, producing neighborhoods that urban authorities regard as inadequate—are as old as urbanism itself.

For as long as we can trace, phases of rapid urban growth resulted in the densification and the extension of Europe's urban fabric. Historians of the seventeenth and eighteenth centuries have mainly focused their attention on new aristocratic developments (*lotissements*), but poor and working-class settlements also grew, whether they took the form of poor shacks and huts in existing estates or new rustic construction in the urban outskirts.[45] The growth of these nuclei outside the city walls persistently preoccupied authori-ties: to give just one example, in Paris, the Crown attempted to prohibit their expansion in 1724.

Between the late eighteenth and the late nineteenth centuries, when many countries released property from mortmain status, peripheral urbanization accelerated as part of a broader wave of urban growth. In this context, cities expanded through vernacular construction, carried out by modest develop-ers or buyers on subdivided agricultural land. These landholders could act in concert or not, and their settlements were urbanized or not depending on the buyers' profiles; even where urbanization became theoretically mandatory (as in Madrid after 1892 or in France after 1924), owners or developers inevitably broke the rules.[46] This was the story of most of Latin Europe's nineteenth-century urban peripheries—France's *faubourgs* and suburban self-built *ban-lieues*, Spain's *arrabales* and areas beyond the *ensanche* zones, Rome's extra muros suburbs. These spaces often grew from private interests and private regulation, producing layouts quite distant from modern urbanism's ideal-ized rationality.[47]

Enduringly eclectic juxtapositions thus developed in many Belle Époque urban outskirts. Before the late nineteenth century, part of Paris's Montmartre was covered with fragile buildings that strongly resembled both midcentury *bidonvilles* of the 1950s and 1960s and the contemporaneous "Zone."[48] Simi-larly, in early twentieth-century Chamberí—Madrid's largest *arrabal* in the 1850s—"good" streets occupied by local notables coexisted alongside others lined with tiny, precarious shelters.[49] This eclecticism would remain typical in the mid-twentieth century.[50] Most 1950s *chabolas*, *barracas*, and *baracche* in Madrid, Barcelona, and Rome were made of brick, and many were covered with tiles. Even if authorities, experts, and activists found the gap between vernacular urbanism and the sanctioned city much more problematic in the mid-twentieth century than they had in the nineteenth, the continuous dual-ity of European urbanization was striking.

Also in the nineteenth century, the extension of urban planning and policing (broadly conceived as the enforcement of urban order) increasingly relegated vernacular urbanism to the realm of illegality. In Paris, stone progressively displaced wood as the only legitimate building material, while the conception of the city as monumental and eternal drove the elimination of small, temporary buildings. The *échoppes*—small, foundationless wooden structures, largely commercial and commonly constructed near busy streets or monuments in the early nineteenth century—were disallowed. The imperative of circulation and the idea of a timeless city, which artists and planners rendered as made from stone and free of people, progressively emptied public space.[51]

In the second half of the nineteenth century, urban planning further entrenched a gap between two cities—one regarded by elites as proper and modern, another supposedly archaic, inadequate, and poor. From the 1860s on, Spanish planners created *ensanches de población*, planning strictly regulated urban extensions in a chessboard pattern just beyond the central cities.[52] Yet in the process they also created extra-*ensanche arrabales* (urban outskirts), because demand for cheap housing found its outlet beyond the regulated zones. Far from the city center, and separated from it by a large empty zone earmarked for future urbanization, these extra-*ensanche arrabales* would lodge more homogeneously poor people whose connection to urban services had become much more difficult and expensive, giving rise to huge insalubrious zones.[53] Likewise, Paris's Haussmanization went hand in hand with the contrasting urbanization patterns of the more loosely regulated *banlieues*.[54] During the first half of the twentieth century, planning legislation—such as France's 1919 Cornudet Act—also played a role in developing a new class of poor peripheral neighborhoods, this time labeled "defective subdivisions."[55]

Regardless of their moniker, form, or modality of production, these poor and insalubrious peripheries grew quickly in the context of the rapid urban growth that characterized the 1920s across Europe. In Rome, fascist imperial plans for the capital, which pushed popular households out of the inner city, provoked the multiplication of *baracche* outside the walls.[56] Around 1930, 17 percent of Madrid's 825,000 residents lived in these extra-*ensanche arrabales*, while around 12 percent of the 6 million people living in the Paris agglomeration lived in *lotissements défectueux*.[57]

Between 1910 and 1950, master plans, zoning laws, and building license requirements became generalized across Europe, in tandem with a transnational development of urban planning. In the context of Southern Europe's great rural-to-urban migration wave and economic boom of the 1950s and 1960s, a new generation of "inadequate" peripheries grew—now called *bidonvilles*, *barrios de chabolas*, and *borgate* and rendered fully informal by the new regulations.[58] The scale of these illegalized cities differed and, as before, the categories that shaped quantitative analysis of informal urbanization varied across time and space, making comparative analysis very uncertain.[59] Still, public administrators everywhere had their ways of counting, and their estimates give us some sense of the scale of what authorities perceived as the informal city. In 1960, *bidonvilles* lodged around 0.6 percent of the 9 million people of the Paris region, while around 10 percent of Madrid's 2 million inhabitants lived in *chabolas* and (in 1957) around 2.5 percent of Rome's more than 2 million residents lived in *baracche* and other forms of precarious housing.

The long history of Latin Europe's informal urbanization—in the term's broadest sense—thus encompasses all the ways in which poor, precarious, and vernacular cities have developed in tandem with wealthy ones, excluded from the sphere of legality by successive waves of rules and requirements associated with urban modernity. New rules have created new infractions; whenever planners have created geographically bounded regulations, they have also incentivized unregulated settlements beyond that frontier. Public authorities have tolerated these with varying degrees of benevolence, but at each step, modernization—with its new norms in terms of public spaces, building, street patterns, and services—was possible only because it included neither all inhabited urban space nor all urban people. The greater the distance between the realities of an urban society and its regulatory demands, the more important the city outside of regulatory bounds has become. Over more than 150 years, these dwellings and neighborhoods have been characterized as archaic remnants, yet they were in fact the flip side of modernization. Although the mid-twentieth century is often pinpointed as a foundational moment in European informal urbanization, what was new in the 1950s was not the phenomenon itself, but its distance from concurrent official urban norms, its level of illegality, and the ways it was perceived and constructed as a problem.

This continuous history was closely linked to the ways in which Western Europeans problematized vernacular urbanization, a process closely entwined not only with sanitarism, social reform, and state intervention but also with politics and capitalism. Throughout Europe, as in Latin America, the specific ways in which authorities defined the problem of vernacular urbanity depended on local conjunctures.

Belle Époque and interwar observers of *faubourgs*, *banlieues*, and similar peripheries emphasized sanitary and urbanistic issues.[60] They deplored their cities' disorganized character and irrational traffic patterns, urban services, and amenities, as well as haphazard use patterns that enabled industrial and residential spheres to intermix. These characteristics, related to the poverty of the built environment, were also thought to pose a health risk. The discipline of urban planning was built upon this diagnosis of insalubrity and irrationality, which was especially associated with poor and peripheral spaces and their faceless inhabitants.

After World War II, social scientific and developmentalist frameworks increasingly shaped understandings of informal urbanism. Europe's post–World War II shantytowns burgeoned just as the region experienced a dual shift involving both urbanization and unprecedented economic growth, which led to better living conditions and transformed the urban landscape. *Bidonvilles*, in this new context, embodied the other side of the developmental coin, their misery all the more unbearable because it defied the general trend. The settlements' inhabitants—mainly colonial or foreign immigrants in France and national migrants from the poorest rural regions of Italy, Portugal, Spain, and Greece—were described as having been left out of Western Europe's general prosperity. In Southern Europe, contemporary analysts understood poor self-built areas both as a symptom of sharp internal developmental disparities and as a sign of cities' incapacity to absorb poorly controlled migratory flows.[61] As was noted before, midcentury conceptions of the *bidonvilles* were also shaped by paradigms generated by Cold War and colonial politics.

Throughout this long period, as in Latin America, the problematization and treatment of informal urbanism varied widely but proved consistently responsive to political exigencies. In fascist Italy, and especially in Rome—a capital showcase under pressure to measure up to the New State[62]—an ambitious urban renewal program displaced residents from the historic center; when they sought shelter in swelling *borgate* (shantytowns), the government sought to solve the problem by demolishing homes and regulating migration.[63] Twenty years later, in Franco's Spain, a similar trajectory played out. Before the war, Spanish authorities had tended to incorporate areas of informal urbanization through punctual and exceptional public action. But after the Spanish Civil War ended in 1939, Madrid echoed Rome's role as a national showcase, and Franco's regime also regarded Madrid and Barcelona's working-class peripheries as Republican hotbeds. These circumstances, together with the workings of an expanding real estate market that dealt in peripheral land valorized by state development policies, led the Francoist regime to problematize the *chabolas* and elaborate a legal arsenal that placed working-class residents at the mercy of severe but discretionary repression involving forced removal and rehousing.[64]

In France and its North African colonies, pre- and postwar patterns also proved divergent. Through the 1920s, mainland authorities had generally upgraded and regularized vernacular settlements as part of a national public policy. But in the mid-twentieth century, the politics and security imperatives of decolonization added an additional dimension to informal urbanization's problematization. Unlike mainland France's early twentieth-century *lotissements défectueux*, populated by Europeans, midcentury *bidonvilles* carried in their very etymology a history of colonialism and ethno-racial segregation. The term *bidonville* was first coined to describe a single neighborhood of Casablanca; its use then extended across the urban Maghreb to denote new indigenous quarters.[65] Europeans conceived the North African *bidonville* as a health problem that threatened the European-populated city and had to be dealt with for reasons of safety and civilization. At the same time, the stigmatization of indigenous neighborhoods sharpened the ethno-racial distinctions critical to the maintenance of European power. From the 1950s forward, as North Africans, and especially Algerians, migrated en masse to metropolitan France, their settlements were also termed *bidonvilles*, the word practically traveling in the suitcases of the colonial officials who regarded the mainland *bidonvilles* they were often called upon to govern after their stints abroad through a colonial lens. In the context of Algeria's war for independence, the perceived need to control *Français musulmans d'Algérie* put rehousing policies on the agenda in both colonial and metropolitan territory.[66]

These frameworks of problematization still disproportionately shape Latin Europe's urban historiography, where informal urbanism has been marginalized to an even greater degree than in Latin America. While social and cultural historians have often sited their studies in poor districts, they began to really focus on issues of space and the urban fabric only in the 1980s.[67] Histories of European urbanism per se have focused mainly on large-scale developments, with particular emphasis on the highly visible intersection of real estate, capitalism, and public policy.[68] Historians of urbanism have generally represented areas of informal city building either as margins still untouched by urban development or a manifestation of modernization's policy shortcomings.

As in Latin America, mid-twentieth-century research on Western Europe's poor peripheries was part of a burgeoning transnational debate focused on urban poverty, uprootedness, and the supposed challenges that rural people faced in integrating themselves into urban society. On both sides of the Atlantic, social scientists developed similar arguments, which international organizations under US influence also diffused in the context of the Cold War. Religious sociology, seeking above all to measure and explain societal secularization, also found in the poor peripheries one of its favorite research arenas.[69] Regardless of their religious leanings, most European geographical and sociological studies from these midcentury decades approached the shanty-town through the theoretical lenses of marginality and cultures of poverty,[70] although left-wing analysts from the generation of 1968 (Catholic or not) also often analyzed shantytown residents as subjects of domination by a capitalist-state alliance.[71] Members of this midcentury European generation—unlike their Latin American counterparts—understood the rural exodus mainly as a problem for the cities; rural depopulation, the other facet of the phenom-enon, received less attention.

Between the 1960s and the 1980s, as intellectuals became critical of top-down readings that interpreted popular urbanism through external cultural and political imperatives, a more communitarian and grassroots approach gradually emerged. Architects and social scientists began to engage more closely with resident associations in designing and developing their neigh-borhoods, giving rise to a new generation of research that focused on ar-ticulating the communities' morphologies, settlement patterns, and usage arrangements.[72] With the aim of conceiving urban reforms that would be relevant to local residents, these architect-urbanists analyzed the forms of property division and construction that gave origin to what Barcelona ar-chitects called "marginal urbanization."[73] As John Turner did in Peru, they sought to reveal its use value for the populations it housed, emphasizing its location and adaptability to the vagaries of family life. Social scientists inter-ested in national and international migration sought in these neighborhoods evidence of migrants' lifeways, experiences, and treatment by host societies.[74]

Historians began to contribute to these debates only later on—beginning in the 1980s in France and Italy, later in Spain—and their early works fo-cused on the period before World War I. Structuralist and Marxist leanings had previously led many scholars to de-emphasize the historical significance of informal urbanization.[75] But in the 1970s and 1980s, France's communist suburbs and other left-wing industrial cities began to unravel and deindus-trialization and the recomposition of the working and popular classes went hand in hand with both the French Communist Party's disintegration and the beginnings of democratization in Spain, Portugal, and other previously authoritarian countries. In that context, historians looked to popular culture, urban settlement patterns, and modes of urbanization to bring to light the genesis of working-class neighborhoods, bastions of a labor movement that was radically transforming before their eyes[76] Beginning in the late 1990s, the development of French colonial studies and the reading of French his-tory through the colonial prism also led historians and political scientists to closely reexamine the politics of the *bidonvilles*.[77]

From the 2000s on, a new generation of historians has amplified these trends. Approaching poor suburban and peripheral spaces in the context of growing critiques of the framework of modernity and in recognition of the social and ecological impacts of industrialization and economic growth, they question the notion that poor and vernacular spaces are historical vestiges somehow left out of the modernization process. In works that began by reconsidering nineteenth- and early twentieth-century peripheries and are now stretching into the second half of the twentieth century, historians have incorporated both microhistorical and transnational lenses, emphasizing the ways in which global historical processes are articulated through local urban dynamics. In line with transnational historiographical trends across Latin America, South Asia, and Africa, historians of urban Europe have recognized peripheries as spaces of entrepreneurial opportunity, social mobility, and working-class political culture; they have also increasingly highlighted forms of resistance and mobilization that have emerged among subaltern populations long understood by outsiders as too dominated to be capable of agency.[78] Other scholars, incorporating the contribution of political sociology, have explored how informality can comprise a system of governance in certain sociohistorical contexts.[79]

Valuable as they are, these local renewals of the historiography have not yet come together to comprise a comprehensive understanding of European urban informality. Even in the narrower region we call Latin Europe, it is still rare for historians of Spain, Italy, France, and the French colonies to overcome the view that the *bidonvilles* were specific to the French colonial context and render the transregional experience of informal urbanization as a common history, one from which we might understand deeper dynamics of urbanization, power, and inequality.[80]

Toward a History of Informal Urbanization

As these synopses make clear, Latin America, Latin Europe, and French colonial North Africa have often experienced and understood informal urbanization in divergent ways. Colonies frame and live informality differently than independent nations do, and informal phenomena develop distinctly depending on a city's proximity to the centers of capitalist modernization and development. The scale of informal urbanization in Latin America and North Africa is generally greater than in mainland France, Italy, or Spain, and that difference has had a significant impact on policy, politics, and conceptualization. Informalization interacts differently with racial and ethnic prejudice and segregation in each context, and the experiences of Morocco, Algeria, and France in the mid-twentieth century are particularly distinct because urban informalization was part and parcel of France's colonial marginalization of Indigenous peoples. The systems of power created by informal urbanization vary with the normativity and hegemony of institutional law, which tends to be somewhat less paramount in Latin America. It is also quite significant that Latin America as a region was recognized in the mid-twentieth century as a social scientific laboratory for the study of informal urbanization, a fact that had enormous implications for knowledge production and the creation of informal imaginaries.

At the same time, the commonalities among these regional histories reveal a great deal about informal urbanization as a process, a problem, and an object of historicization. While the historiography of informality is still very much a work in progress, recent research suggests something of a paradigm shift. On both sides of the Atlantic, informal urbanization—identified chiefly with shacks and shantytowns—was long understood as an invasive anomaly, a process through which strangers to the city migrated en masse from the countryside or from abroad, challenging or threatening fully formalized urban spaces with their unbridled vernacular construction. This definitional model hinges on a number of key assumptions, among them that the preexisting city was fully formalized, that poor migrants act alone in establishing settlements outside of the law's bounds, and that informal residents are fundamentally ill adapted to and marginalized from a modern urban environment. Close attention to history undermines each of these arguments. The urban forms that would later be classified as informal have long been integral to cities; the novelty was not shacks and shanties but rather the onset of normative ideologies of urbanity that rendered vernacular city building problematic, for reasons that had little to do with the ways informal residents experienced it. Seen in this light, while informal urbanization becomes considerably more visible in eras of mass migration, it is best understood as the product of urban legal standards and regulatory practices imposed in a society that does not have the resources or will to uniformly enforce them. Actors across the full spectrum of class, ethnicity, nationality, and race participate in and benefit from the process of informal urbanization, which is itself central to the ways that cities develop over time.

Historical research has also revealed the extent to which the problematization of vernacular city building and the people who practice it has driven informalization, helping to shape and justify exclusionary urban law, the lopsided distribution of public resources, and deepening patterns of socioracial inequality. In Latin Europe, French colonial North Africa, and Latin America, informal urbanization has been understood as a symptom of a wide range of crises, from the racial and civilizational anxieties of the Belle Époque to the specter of social disorder in the era of modernization and mass migration to the challenges of underdevelopment and decolonization in the mid-twentieth century to the mutually incompatible perceptions of state overreach and state abandonment in the age of neoliberalism. While these forms of problematization can be highly localized, they are also transnational—emerging from shared paradigms, anxieties, and challenges and developing in international conversation. Domestically and transnationally, vernacular urbanization's construal as a problem has played a significant role in stigmatizing both informal residents and their settlements, thus justifying and exacerbating the process of informalization and rationalizing ever-wider gaps between formalized and informalized urban regions.

Scholars are only beginning to appreciate how these histories of informal urbanization are part of broader historical processes. Extant historiography already allows us to appreciate the degree to which informality has coevolved with the modern regulatory and welfare states, constituting one of the many mechanisms through which modern governments have segmented and fragmented seemingly universal commitments to welfare, economic development, and social peace. Informality is a powerful bogeyman for populist and authoritarian leaders, and the forms of unregulated power it sustains and creates temper formal governance, speaking to many of the disjunctures of modern liberalism. For the Catholic and other churches, as well as civil society more generally, informality has helped to incubate new and significant ways of conceiving political mediation, social justice, and social activism, especially in spaces where dictatorship has restricted other channels for political agency.[81]

It is also clear that informal urbanization has been a significant element in the economic histories of cities around the world, helping to underwrite industrial development, catalyze urban land speculation, and even seed capitalist accumulation. Colonial, racial, and social prejudices have both driven and derived from informal urbanization's stigmatization, contributing to the dynamics of inequality on both local and global scales. Research on informal urbanization can break open consecrated teleologies of urban history, and the knowledge and networks generated by the study of informal urbanization are important to the global history of social science, social action, architecture, and even religious thought.

The chapters in this volume are authored by scholars who are helping to shape this new wave of historicization in Latin America and Europe. Their content can be divided into three broad sections: a first that explores the ways in which legal and governance regimes create and govern informality over the *longue durée*, a second that examines informality's intersections with major political moments and ideological frameworks of the twentieth century, and a third that interrogates informality's place in the histories of race and coloniality.

The first part begins with Antonio Azuela and Emilio de Antuñano's "Four Regimes of Informality," which focuses on the legal and ideological foundations of informalization over the *longue durée*. Situating Mexican informality within broader currents of legal, political, and revolutionary history, Azuela and Antuñano demonstrate how successive generations have engaged vernacular city building through the juridical logics of sanitarism, urban planning, land reform, and environmentalism. Francesco Bartolini's "From Insalubrious Housing to Unauthorized Neighborhoods" pursues a similar model of historical analysis for Italy, tracing the problematization of informality from its origins in hygienic concerns about insalubrious housing to mid-twentieth-century alarm about rampant *abusivismo*, or lack of respect for the urban rule of law. Continuing the *longue durée* perspective with close attention to the legal and political processes surrounding informal urbanization in Spain, Charlotte Vorms's "A Century of Governing with Informal Urbanization in Madrid" demonstrates the interdependence of formal and informal urbanization processes across a century, showing the evolution of governance from a nineteenth-century era of gray-zone tolerance to an age that paired outright legal exclusion with the discretionary use of temporary tolerance, repression, and rehousing in the postwar Franco years.

The next group of chapters focuses on briefer periods from the mid-twentieth century, emphasizing informality's significance in moments of political transformation and conflict and its relevance to political movements and ideologies such as communism, fascism, and Catholic social thought. Luciano Villani's "The Order Came from Above" delves into the significance of Rome's precocious and often violent process of expulsion under Mussolini, exploring the ideological stakes of urban modernization for the fascist New State. Rafael Soares Gonçalves's "Carioca Favelas and the Catholic Church after World War II" details the grassroots history of the Catholic Church's social action projects in Rio's mid-twentieth-century favelas, exploring not only the church's participation in the construction of precarious state tolerance vis-à-vis informal urbanization but also the intersection of Catholic social doctrine with midcentury social science and professional social service. Serge Ollivier's "Democratizing the Republic" demonstrates how the politics of informal urbanization intersected with the rise of populism and the acceleration of grassroots activism in midcentury Venezuela. Emanuel Giannotti and Boris Cofré Schmeisser's "The Invention of the *Toma*" analyzes Chile's midcentury transition from silent to politically performative modes of informal urbanization, documenting the genesis of Santiago's urban popular movements in the context of the city's Cold War–era migratory influx.

A final cluster of chapters emphasizes informal urbanization's intersection with the politics of race, empire, and decolonization. Brodwyn Fischer's "Informality, Racialized Governance, and the *Cidade Negra*" examines the intersection of slavery and informality in Brazil, arguing that both the practice and the problematization of informality emerged from patterns ingrained during slavery, and that these historical entanglements deeply affected Brazil's twentieth-century racial dynamics. Françoise de Barros's *"Bidonvilles* in France: A New Term for an Old Phenomenon?"* explores the link between colonization and informality in mainland France, arguing that French perceptions and understandings of *bidonvilles* were heavily influenced by France's colonial history. Jim House's "Urban Risk?" shows how a range of European actors in Algiers and Casablanca constructed shantytowns and their inhabitants both as a problem of public health, migration control, colonial urbanism, and urban poverty and as a social, political, and security "danger." House thus demonstrates how large-scale state intervention in the shantytowns was connected to larger dynamics of colonial governance and security.

The authors assembled here would be the first to insist that these chapters are by no means an end point.* Although the first historical works on informal urbanization began to emerge decades ago, the field is still young. At this stage, precisely because we lack the dense historiographies of other fields of urban inquiry, our authors build general knowledge inductively, from careful engagement with specific geographies and historical processes, rather than jumping to sweeping conclusions about global histories. All the same, read together, these histories are crucial building blocks that have much to tell us about how historical methodologies can inform our understanding of informal urbanism and about the ways informality has entwined with broader arcs of urban, political, racial, and colonial history in Latin America, Latin Europe, and French colonial North Africa. We hope that our findings will spark debate and exchange with emerging historiographies of informality rooted elsewhere around the world, united in the common aim of historicizing a phenomenon so crucial to our global urban future.

---

* For a full sense of the collective scholarship that informs this volume, readers can consult our bibliography at https://press.uchicago.edu/ucp/books/book/chicago/I/bo249481119.html.

PART I

Law, Governance, and the Invention of Informality

Four Regimes of Informality:
Legal Practices and Revolutionary Politics
in Twentieth-Century Mexico City

ANTONIO AZUELA AND

EMILIO DE ANTUÑANO

This chapter offers a typology and a history of informality in twentieth-century Mexico City. By "informal," we mean the condition that results when public actors define a space, or a group that occupies it, as something that exists outside the law. These public actors then wield this legal definition to govern a territory or a population with an unusual degree of discretion; for example, by granting or denying public services to neighborhood inhabitants, or by evicting them, tolerating their occupation, or negotiating with them the provision of property titles. While these actions have a legal justification, they are, in essence, government decisions that have a political meaning. Discretionary law enforcement—what some authors call "informal governance"— has been, since the late nineteenth century, a fundamental tool of government.[1] In various cities, and certainly in the case of Mexico City, what was at stake in deciding whether or not the law would be enforced—or in deciding how or against whom it would be enforced—was the symbolic, political, and physical place that the poor would occupy in the city.

In this chapter, we ask two questions: What laws were used to impose urban informality? Who used the law, and with what results? In answer to the first question, we offer a legal typology. In response to the second question, we offer a history of how public authority governs the city and how the urban poor claim a space within it. This relationship between authorities and

This work is the result of a very stimulating dialogue with members of the research group La Ville Informelle au XXᵉ Siècle. We thank all the members of the group for their comments. We also thank Ernesto Aréchiga Córdoba, María Soledad Cruz, Andrew Konove, and Rodrigo Meneses for their invaluable comments and critiques when we presented a preliminary version of this chapter as a paper at the seminar "Urban Informality in the 20th Century: Intersecting perspectives," held in Mexico City on July 15–16, 2019.

people is mediated by law but is determined by many other political, social, and ideological forces.

Urban informality is often spoken about as if it were a homogeneous and immutable reality, as if it were an intrinsic attribute of specific urban areas. Such a belief is problematic for at least two reasons. First, while present-day observers might emphasize that certain areas of the city are outside the law, in line with the dominant discourse on the rule of law,[2] historical analysis reveals that this was not always the case. For a long time, the socially dominant definition of the neighborhoods inhabited by the poor emphasized their material deficiencies with respect to the predominant models of what was an acceptable urban space (encapsulated in the ideal of the modern city). Such portrayals were often accompanied by a social stigmatization of the neighborhood's inhabitants. Second, modern observers also often insist that a lack of property titles is the specific quality that places inhabitants outside the law. It is true that property conflicts have been part of popular urbanization processes since the beginning. However, other legal definitions have also left an indelible mark on the way in which the habitat of the poor is defined.

To elucidate those, in this chapter we identify four legal logics that constituted the informal city in twentieth-century Mexico: sanitary, urban, agrarian, and environmental. *Sanitary informality*, dominant between the 1880s and the 1920s, placed the occupants of the *vecindades* (*conventillos*, *cortiços*, or *tenements*, in other countries) in a legally tenuous situation that could be overcome only through access to other forms of housing that complied with models of security and hygiene inherited from the nineteenth century. *Urban informality*, predominant between the 1920s and 1950s, derived from the imposition of models of spatial organization associated with urban planning. *Agrarian informality*, the most important form in Mexico between the 1950s and 1970s, was the result of the urbanization of land originally granted or recognized as belonging to "agrarian nuclei" (ejidos and *comunidades*) as part of the nation's ambitious postrevolutionary agrarian reform. Finally, *environmental informality* was the result of zoning regulations that demarcated "conservation land," which, according to environmental language, performs such important environmental functions that its urbanization is unacceptable. Environmental informality became dominant in the 1980s and remains so to this day. All this does not mean that when one type of informality appeared, the previous ones disappeared completely; although each was dominant or characteristic of a particular historical period, the dimensions and complexity of the metropolis have made it possible for them to coexist.

The existence of a city outside the law, as opposed to an ideal or "lettered" city, has a long history in Latin America that goes back to the colonial separation between the Spanish *traza* (central grid) and the *repúblicas de indios* (Indian republics) surrounding it. The latter were legally and architecturally distinct from the former and were frequently made invisible in colonial representations of the city. In fact, this opposition between the Spanish *traza* and the surrounding republics is one of the singularities that, according to several historians, allows us to speak of a Latin American city.[3] Following these interpretations, some authors suggest that informality in Mexico and Latin America still shows a colonial matrix, which makes it distinct or Latin American.[4] Mexican architects and urban planners have certainly often thought of themselves as part of a tradition that goes back to the urban ordinances of the colonial period. From our perspective, however, informal governance in the twentieth century is different from its colonial counterpart to the extent that it turned the poor and their position in the city into a public problem.

The relationship between public authorities and the urban poor, mediated by law and marked by a sense of crisis, is visible in Latin America and other regions explored in this volume. The cultural construction of this public problem (perhaps, at certain times, crisis) and of the category of "the urban poor," as well as the political relationship between them and public authorities, has changed from country to country and at specific historical junctures. Unlike in colonial North Africa, residents of informal neighborhoods in Mexico were not construed as a racialized "other." As Jim House argues in this volume, urban informality in Casablanca and Algiers went as far as becoming a military concern in the context of decolonization. And, unlike in cities like Santiago and Buenos Aires, where informal neighborhoods were viewed as revolutionary hotbeds, particularly during crises punctuated by the Cold War, Mexican authorities saw them as a political resource, amenable to integration rather than eradication.[5] In Mexico, of course, a revolution had already taken place: the urban poor thus became a distinct kind of public problem.

What makes Mexican informality distinct is not its colonial past but its revolutionary origin. The Mexican Revolution (1910–1920) introduced a language of social justice that advocated the extension of rights to the popular classes and stimulated a massive popular mobilization in the countryside and the city—a popular mobilization that postrevolutionary governments channeled with greater or lesser success. In Mexico, the relationship between public authority and the urban poor has been mediated by the law—often emanating directly from the revolution—and influenced by political, cultural, and ideological factors that are also, to a large extent, revolutionary in origin.

Historical Introduction

In twentieth-century Mexico City, informality took shape and political significance in the context of three historical processes: the city's population growth, its territorial expansion over the towns and agrarian communities of the Valley of Mexico, and the Mexican Revolution. The Mexican capital barely grew during the first decades of the nineteenth century: between 1790 and 1864, its population increased from 117,000 to 133,000 people, and in 1910, when the Mexican Revolution broke out, there were 470,000 inhabitants. Yet by 1930, the city had reached 1 million inhabitants, and in 2010, it had a population of 9 million (22 million if we consider the entire metropolitan area).[6] Naturally, this demographic growth transformed the relationship between the city and its hinterland in the Valley of Mexico. During the colonial period and the nineteenth century, this valley was occupied by a group of towns and communities that, although they had an economic relationship with the city, also enjoyed political and legal autonomy. This autonomy eroded throughout the twentieth century, when towns and communities were incorporated into the city, becoming part of the urban sprawl. Finally, the Mexican Revolution introduced a language of social justice that had a profound impact on the city. Beyond its ideology and discourse, the revolution enabled the mobilization of millions of people, not only in the countryside (this was originally an agrarian revolution) but also in the city. In the decades following the revolution, hundreds of organizations of settlers and tenants successfully claimed a place in the city.[7] The analysis of informality as a practice of governance—of how public power delimited the uses of law and its application or inapplicability—must be approached in the context of these geographic, demographic, social, and political transformations.

These changes began to take shape in the last decades of the nineteenth century, when the dictatorship of Porfirio Díaz (1884–1911) promoted the growth and modernization of the capital, after the decades of civil wars and economic stagnation that had followed Mexico's independence in 1821. Beginning in the 1860s and 1870s, the city's first "modern" neighborhoods were created through the subdivision of land and the provision of public services such as water and sewage.[8] The city grew and modernized following transnational architectural, urbanistic, and technological guidelines, and in the process, it became an endless business for real estate developers. These architectural, urban, and hydraulic works shaped a city segregated by class divisions and access to public services.[9] Sanitary informality took shape in this context, becoming a key factor in the city's segregation.

The hydraulic engineering works of the Porfiriato were designed by an elite cadre of doctors and engineers who, during the second half of the nineteenth century, assumed control and authority over the "urban question," which was defined by the problem of public health. Several members of this elite formed part of the Superior Sanitation Council (SSC), created in 1841 by the federal government and with authority over the Federal District, the larger jurisdiction in which the city was located. During the following decades, the SSC would gain strength at the expense of the municipal city council (the Ayuntamiento), a process justified by the urgent public health crisis. During these years, the public health–inspired legal devices that would mediate the relationship between the government and the urban poor multiplied.

In 1891, Congress decreed the Código Sanitario (Sanitary Code), a fundamental legal device for the genesis of sanitary informality.[10] Drafted by the SSC, the Código Sanitario included items that in later decades would be regulated by other provisions and government offices, from homes and schools to temples, factories, and slaughterhouses. Its influence lies in the fact that its hygienist principles would be codified in regulations that would govern urban growth and the construction of new subdivisions. For example, one of the first regulations to regulate the expansion of the city—the Acuerdo Que Fija las Reglas para la Admisión de Nuevas Colonias y Calles en la Ciudad de México, decreed in 1903—adopted several articles of the Código Sanitario.[11] The Acuerdo was a response to the "anarchic expansion" of the city and the multiplication of houses and neighborhoods lacking "gutters," "potable water," and "good pavement";[12] among other stipulations, it dictated that subdividers had to comply with a series of obligations, including the construction of gutters, potable water supply, and street pavement.[13] *Colonias* (neighborhoods) that did not comply with these requirements would not be recognized and, consequently, would not be entitled to public services.[14] The conflict between developers, government, and settlers over who was responsible for providing these public services would shape the political field of informality throughout the twentieth century.

The sanitary regulations set forth in the Código Sanitario were not enforced, but they did (ironically) prevent much of the city's population from having access to water and sewage by defining areas settled outside the law as beyond public responsibility. In the 1890s, for example, government notices became common, posted on walls and posts in "unrecognized *colonias*," informing that these areas would not receive public services and that their homeowners, "to comply with the provisions of the Código Sanitario, would have to provide their houses with sewers, drinking water, and other conditions, at their exclusive expense."[15] Although water and sewage services were a novelty, access to them began to be understood as desirable and perhaps necessary, sometimes as a right, sometimes as a government handout.[16] At the same time, urban regulations, together with the increasingly widespread belief that water and sewage were a necessary feature of city life, contributed to the stigmatization of those who lacked them. This stigmatization of the working classes always existed, but the growth of the city produced a process of spatial segregation—visible in cities around the world—that naturalized certain spaces as unhealthy and outside the law. For example, reports collected by sanitary inspectors charged with enforcing the Código Sanitario described tenement inhabitants as "the most wretched but also the most uneducated people [of] the town," lacking "sustenance and [cleanliness], that domestic virtue."[17] While inspectors thus blamed the inhabitants for the conditions of their dwellings, the government also recognized the culpability of the *fraccionadores* (speculators who sold unserviced lots), as well as its own responsibility for having allowed the establishment of several neighborhoods in breach of the law.[18]

By 1910—the year of the outbreak of the revolution—the cultural construction of a city divided in two, one modern and hygienic and the other poor, unhealthy and outside the law, was already complete. Less clear, however, was the solution to the problem of insalubrity. In a report published in 1922, the government explained that the origin of the problem lay in the "carelessness and leniency" of past administrations, "which left such complicated situations, that their resolution, without hyperbole, constitutes the unraveling of a skein, of municipal and sanitary infractions, and of vested interests, which can no longer be attacked or destroyed. . . . [A]lthough populated and full of constructions that are more or less solid and adequate for life, [the *colonias*] have not been authorized, nor urbanized, nor recognized by the Ayuntamiento, which is in the position of knowing for certain that their existence is totally irregular and even harmful."[19]

Attributing legal responsibilities did not represent a solution to the lack of services. On the contrary, the answer to the question of who would pay for the distribution of public services was essentially political; it depended on the organizational capacity and legitimacy of different groups—government, tenants, landlords, and developers—to pursue their interests in a political field shaped by law. This political field would be profoundly transformed by the outbreak of the Mexican Revolution.

The Mexican Revolution and the Political Field of Sanitary Informality

The origins of the Mexican Revolution lie in agrarian tensions and grievances; its most visible effects are found in the Mexican countryside. Nonetheless, the revolution also had a profound, though not immediately palpable, influence in the cities. With respect to urban informality, the revolution had both short- and long-term consequences. On the one hand, the postrevolutionary regime offered the city's popular classes greater legitimacy and resources (discursive, institutional, and legal) to claim what we could anachronistically call their "right to the city." During the 1920s, hundreds of tenant and neighborhood organizations formed to demand land, public services, and protection from landlords and developers from the government.[20]

Before describing this popular mobilization, however, it is worth noting one of the most important effects the revolution had on the city: the distribution of ejido land to the *pueblos* (communities) on the outskirts of the city.[21] In Mexico City, most of these *pueblos* were located in the hinterland, in municipalities such as Ixtapalapa, Iztacalco, and Xochimilco. During the Mexican Revolution, beginning with the Law of January 6, 1915, dozens of *pueblos* requested and received land endowments and restitutions. Some had lost their political autonomy and communal lands during the Porfiriato as a result of liberal laws that made possible the privatization of communal lands and the creation of a land market in and around the city. The distribution of land to these *pueblos*—reconstituted as ejidos, or communal landholdings that were privileged in postrevolutionary land reforms—was accomplished by means of a specially created agrarian bureaucracy and would have profound consequences. We describe these later in more detail; in a nutshell, although rural communities did not recover their political autonomy, they received land under a new property system that brought with it strict control by the new agrarian bureaucracy, as well as a dissociation from the rest of the city's real estate market and urban legislation. The problem would come when the expanding city reached the ejidos that had been created only a few years earlier as rural areas regulated by the Agrarian Code.[22]

We will return to this clash between the city and the ejidos, but now let us return to the story. As a growing historiography has analyzed, resident and tenant organizations in Mexico City appropriated the hygienist discourse of the Porfirian elite to denounce developers and property owners as the culprits of urban insalubrity.[23] Thus, the stigmatization suffered by these groups during the Porfiriato was politicized, becoming a resource for mobilization. Perhaps the most representative example of this appropriation of the hygienist discourse is the tenants' strike of 1922, when thousands of tenants refused to pay their rent in order to denounce the abuses committed by landlords, particularly the absence of water and sewage.[24] It would be, however, in the city's peripheral neighborhoods—whose residents were not tenants but buyers—where the political field of informality would be most clearly articulated and would have the most lasting effects. The Colonia Portales, in the then municipality of Mixcoac, offers an example of this field and of how the inhabitants of popular neighborhoods used hygienist legal devices to vindicate their right to housing.

Colonia Portales was subdivided by the Compañía de Terrenos SA, which purchased the land in the southeast of the city from the American Herbert Lewis. The subdivision and sale of the lots were carried out in haste in the 1910s, in the midst of the revolution, as the company sought to avoid expropriation. Numerous agrarian communities had requested land after 1915, when the first law of agrarian reform was decreed. The Law of January 6, 1915, prompted landowners in the Valley of Mexico to subdivide and sell their land as a preemptive strategy against possible expropriation. The Compañía de Terrenos carried out a fraudulent sales strategy, "hallucinating" buyers with "propaganda . . . and illustrative brochures and plans of the *colonia*, even painting an electric streetcar line . . . in addition to which the daily press published attractive advertisements . . . inviting the public to visit the *colonia*."[25] Despite these promises of a modern and hygienic neighborhood, conditions remained extremely poor over the 1920s, as evidenced by a 1930 municipal report that described the situation in Colonia Portales as "truly serious, since the subdivision company . . . in no way bothered to provide it with any urbanization services."[26] The same report included a map of the city depicting "subdivisions without public services or with very deficient services," an area totaling thirty-six square kilometers.

In 1937, buyers of land in the neighborhood organized themselves into the Sindicato de Colonos y Vecinos de Portales and sued the company for selling them *potreros por colonia*, that is, wild fields instead of the fully urbanized neighborhood promised and contracted. That same year, the buyers demanded a new law "regulating relations between land purchasers and subdividers," a petition suggesting the ineffectiveness of existing regulations.[27] They also argued, in a letter to the president of the Republic, that the Sanitary Code in force when Colonia Portales was subdivided obliged the developers of the neighborhood to provide "drinking water and sanitation and drainage works."[28] This is the same "skein of municipal and sanitary infractions" referred to earlier. The difference is that the revolution made possible the creation of organizations and federations that demanded hygienic housing conditions. In the 1930s, the Sindicato de Colonos y Vecinos de Portales formed an alliance with similar organizations grouped under the Frente Único de Colonos de la República. This Frente Único, along with the Federación de Organizaciones del Distrito Federal, the Confederación Mexicana de Colonos Proletarios, and the Confederación de Colonos de México were some of the federations that in the 1920s and 1930s grouped together around sixty neighborhood organizations.[29] Thus, public officials and experts were not the only actors present in the process of sanitary informalization; the inhabitants also made themselves heard, grouped into organizations that deployed claims consistent with the dominant discourse of the postrevolutionary era. During the following decades, the government would struggle to mediate between these groups and the city's urban developers.

Urban Informalization

From the 1920s onward, demands for "sanitary citizenship" were inserted into a more complex legal and political field, administered from 1930 by the Departamento del Distrito Federal (DDF), the entity in charge of the city's government once the elected city council was dissolved in 1928.[30] The legal and political conflicts that had been articulated around compliance with the Sanitary Code in the 1920s and 1930s changed in character during the 1940s, although the heart of the problem remained the provision of public services. The change was brought about by the importance that the Public Works Directorate (DOP in Spanish) acquired within the DDF and by the logic of the legal arguments it used to justify this position. Hygienist principles did not lose importance, but they were integrated into a much broader discourse: urban planning.

The discourse of urban planning had justified the disappearance of Mexico City's municipal government and its replacement by the DDF, a technocratic government whose creation followed a clear political logic: to liquidate the power of the municipalities and place the capital under the authority of a government appointed by the president. But the change also obeyed a technical logic: to eliminate the municipalities—representative of local interests—and create a regional government capable of regulating the city's growth. For many architects and urban planners, the loss of a free and democratic municipality was a small cost to pay in exchange for a more rational and powerful government. Urban planning also inspired and justified the city's main legal devices from the 1920s onward, a list that includes, among many other laws, regulations and codes, the Reglamento de Colonias of 1920, the Federal District's Ley de Planificación y Zonificación (Planning and Zoning Act) of 1933 (replaced by a new one in 1936), the Reglamento (bylaw) that regulated parts I, V, and VII of that same act's third article, the Reglamento de Fraccionamientos (Subdivisions Bylaw of 1941), and the Ley de Planificación y Zonificación (Planning and Zoning Act) of 1953. These legal provisions were drafted by a generation of urban planners who during the 1920s and 1930s edited magazines, organized congresses, and occupied positions in the DDF government (especially in its DOP), consecrating planning as the dominant legal argument between the 1920s and the 1950s.[31]

There are indications that the rise of the planning movement generated conflicts with physicians, whose power was to be shared with another, and sometimes rival, professional group. For example, the drafting of the Reglamento de las Construcciones y de los Servicios Urbanos en el Distrito Federal in 1942 provoked the Health Department to claim that the DOP was "invading its attributions," since the new regulation included sanitary regulations. The DOP argued that it was natural for a building regulation to include sanitary provisions, which should be considered in building design.[32] The conflict did not escalate, but it reveals two dynamics that are important to note. First, as government offices multiply, it becomes more complex to specify what the informal city is, as there are countless laws that define it in one way or another. Second, the primacy of urbanism in defining the meaning of urban informality between the 1930s and 1950s is a consequence of the growth of this discipline throughout the world; that is, this preeminence is a result of the dissemination of a series of assumptions and ideas about what a city should be and what role government should play in achieving this idea of a city. As we will see, the environmental movement would reach a similar position of influence in the 1980s.

Starting in the 1940s, subdivision permits and official plans (signed by the DOP) became the legal devices that defined the informal city in practice, almost like a photographic negative. Permits were denied and plans rejected because, among other reasons, they did not comply with the Subdivisions Bylaw, they contravened the city's road system, or they were located in areas of the city destined for industrial uses.[33] The city's road system and zoning followed the guidelines of an idealized master plan that was the urban planner's great aspiration but remained incomplete during the 1940s and 1950s.[34] Planning discourse justified the creation of an increasingly baroque bureaucracy, producing a situation in which it was not clear who was in charge of approving what.[35] The confusion reached such an extreme that in 1947 the Master Plan Office took on the task of drawing up a master plan that indicated, in different colors, the projects approved by the DOP, the City Growth Regulatory Commission, the Planning Commission, and the unapproved projects.[36]

All these commissions and offices contributed to delimiting the political field of urban informality. On the one hand, the DOP sought to control the city's growth through a master plan and the urban planning regulations derived from it. On the other hand, subdividers and settlers pursued the formalization of their neighborhoods with the support of political leaders, ranging from city regents to federal representatives to local political brokers. The support of these leaders represented an obstacle for urban planners, as expressed by the architect Luis Ángeles in a session of the City Growth Regulatory Commission: "We have found a number of *colonias* that have recently emerged and that are building where they want and that ask the [regent] for water and sanitation services without taking into consideration the difficulties involved and ask us to do the planning quickly."[37]

As such observations attest, urban regulation created the conditions for a "clientelist" political pact by which urban settlers offered political support in exchange for their "integration" into the city in the form of public services, official plans, and property titles—all of which ensured permanence in the city.[38] This integration into the city was achieved through clientelistic politics, but it was also consistent with the social constitutionalism of the postrevolutionary era, the effort by lawyers and policymakers to use laws and policies to achieve a progressive social transformation.[39] This contrasts with other clientelist pacts, such as the Brazilian one, where politicians were more likely to grant tolerance and favors rather than juridical rights to the city.[40]

We distinguish two key periods in this era of urban informality: an integrating and "formalizing" period in the 1940s, followed by a moment of "informalization" during the 1950s. During the integrationist moment of the 1940s, the DDF resolved the tension between planning imperatives and settlers' demands for political integration through the establishment of *colonias proletarias* (proletarian neighborhoods). *Colonias proletarias* constituted a political, legal, and administrative experiment to distribute land and public services to settlers organized in "improvement" associations sanctioned by the government.[41] The category of the *colonia proletaria* included myriad political and legal relationships between the settlers and the government. To name a few typical cases, the category included *colonias* built on land expropriated or purchased by the government (e.g., Ramos Millán; fig. 1.1); *colonias* divided by property disputes, expropriated by the government to resolve these conflicts (e.g., Escuadrón 201); *colonias* without property conflicts but lacking public services, whose inhabitants negotiated official recognition as *colonias proletarias* to facilitate water distribution.[42] Despite these differences, *colonias proletarias* were administered sui generis: the obligations of the private developer were "transferred" to the authorities, who negotiated the payment of public services with the residents.[43] Although there was enormous variety in the three hundred or so *colonias proletarias* registered in 1950—in their history, location, and social conditions—all of them were, by definition, included in a government registry and subject to a set of rules and administrative practices that integrated them into the urban order. In this sense,

FIGURE 1.1. **Colonia Gabriel Ramos Millán, 1950–1951.** Source: AGN, Fondo Hermanos Mayo. Cronológica: HMA/CR1/04785.2.

despite the fact that their formation entailed one or another violation of urban planning norms, these irregularities did not bring with them the inhabitants' stigmatization, thanks to the way they were politically processed. In fact, in bureaucratic practice, the verb *to plan* was often used to describe the set of adjustments and corrections that the technicians of the DDF made to the layout of the neighborhoods already in the process of formation, as part of its recognition as *colonias proletarias*.[44]

Colonias proletarias experienced their peak in the 1940s, when hundreds were formed and recognized by the DDF.[45] During these years, they were visualized, by the government and by their settlers, as the building blocks— political and territorial—of a corporatist city. In the state discourse of the time, the term *colonia proletaria* implied a neighborhood inhabited by the working classes. In a decade characterized by revolutionary and corporatist language in Mexico and around the world, this expression had a positive connotation, implying that such neighborhoods represented the newly legitimated interests of a significant organ in the national body politic. The expropriation decrees that gave rise to dozens of *colonias proletarias*, for example, argued that their formation was a matter of public utility. "When expropriating . . . a piece of land to found an urban colonia, it cannot be said that only private individuals will benefit, but also the State and the Municipality to which the colonia to be founded belongs, a circumstance for which the concept of public utility has been established."[46]

The policy of founding and recognizing *colonias proletarias* reached its limits around 1950. In 1951, the Supreme Court declared the expropriations to create *colonias proletarias* unconstitutional (when justified by the concept of public utility).[47] In the early 1950s, the National Congress and the DDF discussed a series of laws to definitively institutionalize the administrative regime of the *colonias proletarias*, making them a permanent policy in the city and at the federal level.[48] These initiatives did not prosper, and in 1953, the city's new leader, the "iron regent" Ernesto P. Uruchurtu, hindered the recognition of new *colonias proletarias*. During Uruchurtu's administration (1953–1966, the longest in the city's history), the process of gaining recognition as a *colonia proletaria* became much more difficult and these colonias—which a decade earlier would have enjoyed recognition as proletarian—suffered instead the price of illegality and stigmatization.

Uruchurtu used urban laws and regulations to try to contain the growth of the city, prohibit the construction and recognition of new *colonias proletarias*, and ensure that urban services (especially water) were provided once residents complied with planning regulations and paid a series of fees.[49] Upon his arrival to the government, Uruchurtu suspended subdivisions that did not comply with urban legislation: the lots on these lands could not be sold, receive a series of licenses (*alineamientos*), and be connected to the drinking water network until their situation was regularized.[50] To regularize the suspended subdivisions, the DDF required compliance with a series of provisions of the Regulations and the Planning Law of 1953, including donations of land for public spaces, payment of water fees, and so on. The provision of water remained—as it had been half a century before—the main cause of disputes between the government, the subdivision owners, and the settlers. In those years, the Dirección de Aguas y Saneamiento became the main obstacle to the signing of the plans for many *colonias*.[51]

There is a belief that Uruchurtu's restrictive policies prevented the creation of *colonias* for low-income sectors in the periphery of Mexico City,[52] but this would imply undue efficacy: the truth is that his government was incapable of achieving his objectives. Both through the urbanization of the ejidos, analyzed in the following section, and through the proliferation of unauthorized subdivisions, the process of informal urbanization continued during the 1950s and 1960s, though no longer with the support of the political and administrative apparatus that had functioned until 1952.

The informalization of the *colonias proletarias* was allowed by, and was a result of, the stigmatization and marginalization (to use a term of the period) that they suffered in the 1950s. The word *proletarian* referred, during the 1940s, to workers and had a positive connotation. However, during the 1950s, *colonias proletarias* became practically synonymous with colonies created through land invasions. A representative article described them as formed by "squatters . . . who after taking possession of a piece of land, built their shacks with tin, mud. . . . Lack of urban services, promiscuity and lack of hygiene were their personal attributes. Simultaneously, along with the birth of the *colonias proletarias*, another problem surfaced: a group of immoral leaders made their appearance as a correlate of illegal land possession."[53] If in the 1940s the *colonias proletarias* were a sort of public urbanization policy for the poor (if a policy of uncertain scope and ambiguous legal sense), by the 1950s they had been reinterpreted as *the* housing problem of Mexico City. This problem was defined in urbanistic, architectural, and (sometimes) juridical terms, as evidenced by the mentions of "squatters." But the political existence of the *colonias proletarias*, as the object of public policies and the result of political mobilizations, was ignored during this period. This act of ignoring is highly significant because the informalization of the *colonias proletarias* was the result of their loss of political legitimacy. This shift was part of a larger historical change, which consisted of the adoption of policies to promote private capital in the postwar context and the correlative abandonment of the revolutionary discourse and policies that had been forged in the 1930s. In other words, the vision of a revolutionary, corporatist city for the poor—a vision that materialized in the *colonias proletarias*—would be ephemeral and would begin to disappear in the 1950s. On the other hand, the postrevolutionary agrarian project—materialized in the ejidal regime that we will now describe—would remain in force, with ironic and undesirable consequences for the city.

Agrarian Informality

In the 1950s, as the *colonias proletarias* ceased to be a predominant form of habitat for Mexico City's urban poor, a new type of informality appeared, made possible by the existence of properties granted to the former *pueblos* and to groups of landless peasants as part of the agrarian reform on the outskirts of the city. This type of informality is distinguished from the others because the way the situation of the inhabitants of these neighborhoods is defined is a (paradoxical) urban application of regulations developed within a property system originally conceived for the peasant world.

To place agrarian informality in a broader context, it is worth asking how it was possible that, between the 1950s and the 1970s, an important part of the city's growth consisted of *colonias* created outside the law, when the government had stopped supporting the creation of proletarian *colonias* on the margins of the city. The answer is that the settlement of the periphery by low-income sectors adopted two new modalities over which the city government exercised no responsibility. The first was the emergence of neighborhoods in the State of Mexico, that is, outside the limits of the capital—Ciudad Nezahualcóyotl was the most important such settlement of those years.[54] The second was the formation of neighborhoods on ejido and agrarian community lands that, according to a convenient interpretation for the city government, were under the jurisdiction of the federal authorities responsible for agrarian reform.

Many of the rural populations of Mexico City's hinterland, which today are called *pueblos originarios*,[55] received land from the 1920s forward as part of the postrevolutionary agrarian reform. As we have said, a remarkable aspect of this agrarian reform was that the old *pueblos* lost their political authority and ended up simply as collective subjects who owned collective land. On the one hand, this process created a new way of framing them within the nation: the former *pueblos* would become agrarian nuclei; thus, in official language, the Indians became peasants. On the other hand, the law recognized two types of collective subjects: communities, when rural communities were recognized as having historical property, and ejidos, when groups of peasants were granted land simply because they lacked it. Both types of subjects had the character of corporations in a double sense: in a juridical sense, because the law granted the community personality as a "moral person" owning the land; and in a political sense because landowning communities were the form of social organization par excellence of the corporate order that implied a subordinate inclusion of the peasant masses.

Very soon, part of the lands distributed or recognized as belonging to the *pueblos* in the agrarian reform would be used to satisfy Mexico City's infrastructure and equipment needs; to cite one example, the Ciudad Universitaria, an enormous campus and an emblem of Mexican modernist urbanism, was built on expropriated ejido lands in the early 1950s.[56] But from those years onward, communal lands also began to house poor neighborhoods. By the 1960s, almost 70 percent of the city's expansion took place on them.[57] Between 1950 and 1960, thirteen colonias appeared in the Federal District in the *pueblos* and their surrounding ejidos, and in the following decade, another forty-four appeared. If in 1950 only 89,495 people lived on the lands of agrarian nuclei in the Federal District, in 1960 there were 180,164, and by 1970 there were already 506,082.[58] Thus, in only two decades, the population living on this type of land grew almost sixfold. This does not mean that new *colonias* had ceased to appear on privately owned land or that the form of the *colonia proletaria* was suddenly abandoned.[59] But what is certain is that this new modality was particularly successful in allowing "lower-income social sectors access to urban land."[60]

Agrarian informality, in contrast to the types of informality that dominated during the first half of the century, has a paradoxical character. Both sanitary and urban informality position the inhabitant "out of place" because their habitat does not correspond to the norms of the idealized modern city, that is, the "correct" way of living in the urban context. Here, what places the inhabitant outside the law are norms originally designed for the rural world, which inspired agrarian law. To understand this paradox, it is first necessary to remember that the fundamental legal feature of the agrarian regime in postrevolutionary Mexico is inalienability. The two types of agrarian nuclei—ejidos and communities—owned their land but could not sell or alienate it. Until the neoliberal reforms of the 1990s, ejido and communal land was inalienable, and any sale and purchase transaction involving it was "nonexistent" in the eyes of the law.[61]

Naturally, the issue of inalienability gave rise to endless discussions about what it meant for the peasants who benefited from agrarian reform. But the truth is that very few people noticed the fact that, in the urban peripheries, starting in the 1950s, the land that only a few decades earlier had been given (or recognized as belonging) to the peasants was being informally designated to house poor families—that is, the same sectors that in previous decades had found a place in the *colonias proletarias*.

Despite the prohibition established by law, members of ejidos and communities, but especially their leaders, began to sell lots to poor settlers. The procedures they used to give the sales a legal appearance are described later, but for now, it is sufficient to point out that those who bought a lot to live on in these neighborhoods became part of a new type of informality, which was not the responsibility of urban planning or health officials, but rather of the agrarian authorities. These authorities had been created to manage the peasants' access to the land recognized as theirs or granted to them by the agrarian reform. Now they had to face a new problem: that agrarian land was leaving the rural world as a result of the proliferation of what would later be called "irregular" settlements.

For settlers who purchased land in ejidos, this form of access to land did not, as a general rule, represent an experience of insecurity. Although they did not have titles to prove property rights, the fact is that their possession was almost always recognized by the agrarian nuclei (especially when they did not take long to build their homes on the lots they acquired), and authorities only rarely threatened them with eviction. What has prevailed, from the 1950s to date, has been a broad tolerance on the part of authorities (agrarian and otherwise) of the extralegal property transactions of the agrarian nuclei, which contrasts sharply with the treatment given to private landowners, who were sometimes treated as responsible for the crime of fraud and, in some cases, subjected to legal proceedings.[62] The explanation for this tolerance would require a deeper analysis of the symbolic place of the peasantry in postrevolutionary Mexico.[63] Suffice it to say that one of the most prominent specialists of the rural world described the *ejidatarios* (ejido members) as "the favorite children of the regime."[64] The contrast is striking precisely because, in the context of the ideology of the Mexican Revolution, it goes unnoticed. While the individual landowner who sells lots outside the law is labeled a "speculator" and is sometimes legally prosecuted, when the *ejidatario* or *comunero* does the same, they come to be seen as victims of the urbanization process.[65] The legality and legitimacy of the exercise of property rights follow different paths.

Over time, the urbanization of the ejidos became more visible, especially because of the market price that some of them commanded due to their locations.[66] Thus, little by little, the issue came to be construed as a public problem, the object of policies developed by government agencies created specifically to deal with the problem of "irregularity." Since the early 1970s, agrarian informality has been the object of one of the farthest-reaching regularization policies in the world: that conducted by the Commission for the Regularization of Land Tenure (CORETT, by its Spanish initials), created in 1974. The sales that had given rise to the settlements were considered "nonexistent" by law, and that legal fiction had practical effects: the only way to regularize land tenure was through expropriation. CORETT charged the settlers a fee, usually affordable, with which it paid the compensation it owed to the agrarian nucleus for the expropriation of their land. This was how the property passed from the latter to the former. It is true that this system put settlers in a situation that would seem unfair, because after a long wait in conditions of "irregularity," they still had to pay again for land they had bought years before. But it is also true that, in general terms, this system was much less cruel for the urban poor than other forms of access to land in Latin America, and even in Mexico. Although all urban planning rules were violated, governmental tolerance made possible the creation of ample areas where settlers gradually built urban spaces that ensured them a place in the city. Both for its dimensions and for the type of tolerance that made it possible, this type of irregularity is unique in Latin America.

What urban planners came to see as the perverse cycle from irregularity to regularization was not born overnight.[67] In the 1950s, the ejidos were used for a variety of purposes for which they had not been intended, from infrastructure to high-income neighborhoods such as Pedregal de San Ángel, the most exclusive of that era.[68] To justify these uses, a variety of legal forms were used, such as expropriation and land swaps. But the scandals that this produced led private investors to stop buying ejido and communal land because of the risk it represented, and (as we have said) the government made it difficult to authorize new subdivisions, so investors took their capital to the neighboring State of Mexico. Thus, since the end of the 1950s, the ejidal lands have housed mainly poor families and—in some cases—housing developments promoted by the state.

For a long time, agrarian informality had a semblance of legality, thanks to the use of what the agrarian law called the *ejido urbanization zone* (ZUE, by its Spanish initials). Since the 1930s, it had been recognized that peasants needed not only land for cultivation but also a space where they could form their settlement and where each ejidatario would receive an urban plot of land to establish his or her home—"over there," in the rural world, it is understood. But it was also accepted that people who were not *ejidatarios* but who were engaged in a trade "useful to the community" could live in the settlement; these were called *avecindados*. Thanks to the pioneering work of Ann Varley, we know that when the city began to reach the ejido lands in the middle of the century, the ZUE provided "an ideal opportunity for the ejidatarios to engage in the massive sale of their lands to the low-income population."[69]

It is true that this was a fraudulent use of a legal form that had been designed for the rural world. A regulation was even issued in 1954 to try to prevent its "misuse." But the fact is that, until the advent of massive regularization policies two decades later, "most of the irregular settlements on ejido land were developed within or around an urban [ejido] zone," as if all this were occurring in a rural space disconnected from the city.[70] And the truth is that this had a benign effect on those who acquired a lot in this system of simulation: everyone had a piece of paper proving they had bought from the ejido and, with it, at least the reasonable expectation that they would not be treated as squatters.

This does not mean that the urbanization of ejidos and communities has been free of conflict. In the south of the city there were at least two highly contentious processes that also involved large extensions of land. One was that which arose in the area known as Padierna, belonging to the ejidos of San Nicolás Totolapan and Padierna, from the end of the 1960s, where sales were contested and land invasions were also denounced.[71] The other was the occupation of the *pedregales* of Coyoacán, to the east of the University City, where after the settlement began by means of invasions at the end of the 1940s, multiple owners appeared who disputed the power to sell the remaining land, among which there were also *pueblos* that claimed communal property.[72]

In this context, it is also important to add that the urbanization of the ejidos did not completely replace the formation of *colonias* on privately owned land, which resulted in continuing conflicts between *colonia* residents (who faced the label "parachutists" and continued to seek recognition as *colonias proletarias* until the end of the 1960s) and subdivision developers, who did not fail to take advantage of the fragility of purchasers even as they themselves were sometimes legally prosecuted.[73]

In any case, although agrarian irregularity was not the only mechanism for the formation of low-income neighborhoods, it did become the most important one: by 1970 it housed more than half a million inhabitants in the Federal District, not even counting those who settled in the metropolitan municipalities of the State of Mexico. The only group who has systematically complained about the urbanization of the ejidos is urban planners, because it is a process beyond their control and one whose political benefits have been capitalized by the agrarian bureaucracy (as well as by the Institutional Revolutionary Party, or PRI, that governed Mexico until 2000). As early as the 1930s, the most influential urban planner of the time, Carlos Contreras, warned that "ejidos have been distributed to the so-called towns of Nativitas, etc., in what we could call full future urban residential zone."[74] In the 1950s, the noted urban planner Mario Pani remarked that peasants who had received ejido land near the city were the beneficiaries of the increase in capital gains in this zone, becoming "small multimillionaire capitalists."[75] For Pani, the city's ejido zones should have been off the market and in the hands of urban planners, giving them the power to decide how to integrate them into the city. The complaints had become more bitter at the end of the 1960s, as seen in the master plans coordinated by Enrique Cervantes for more than ten cities, commissioned by the federal government. In one of them, Cervantes singled out the Department of Agrarian Affairs because it "limit[ed] itself to making an orthogonal geometric drawing in which blocks, lots and streets are indicated, which do not obey any foreseen orientation. The street width specifications are almost always excessive, and the lot type does not seem to follow a defined criterion either, since they range from 1,200 square meters to 275 square meters."[76] In short, planners identified the urbanized ejidos as a problem and as a threat to their own authority over the city. However, planners were not strong enough to stand up to the legitimacy of peasant communities and settlers.

With the appearance of land tenure regularization in the 1970s, agrarian informality acquired two distinctive features: the informal market of ejido lands was institutionalized and, at the same time—paradoxically—the new urban spaces it created came to be characterized as a problem related to the lack of property titles. That is, on the one hand, although the irregular nature of ejido land sales was never denied, tolerance of them, together with the existence of a regularization program, created stable expectations among the actors (*ejidatarios* and settlers) that such land sales would never be challenged, which allowed the land market to flourish. On the other hand, the very existence of a bureaucracy in charge of dealing with the "irregularity" of those operations through the issuing of property titles for settlers, contributed to the definition of those neighborhoods as a public problem. It was very convenient that the problem was the lack of property titles and not the lack of services or the material condition of housing. Thus, this specific form of urban informality, which we call agrarian informality, was constructed as a public problem only to the extent that it could be "solved" by a state agency by issuing property titles. And this was made possible, to a large extent, both by the legal rules of the ejido and by the symbolic place of *ejidatarios* in postrevolutionary Mexico.

Up to this point we have tried to illustrate the specificity and, above all, the paradoxical nature of the informality that characterized the formation of poor neighborhoods on ejido lands between 1950 and 1970. Agrarian informality did not impose itself overnight, nor did it completely supplant the earlier *urban informality*, but it did become a system of access to land that both allowed the urban poor to find a place in the urban periphery without entering into conflicts with the original owners of the land. At the same time, agrarian informality allowed the government to conceal the failure of its efforts to stop urban growth, especially that led by the urban poor. This was possible because agrarian informality operated under two assumptions that dominate the legal imagination of Mexican agrarianism: one, that ejidos and communities belong to a world outside the world of the market and urbanization; and two, that state responsibility for what happens on their lands corresponds exclusively to federal agrarian authorities, which provided local authorities, and in particular the teams in charge of urban planning, with the perfect excuse for not taking charge of it.

Environmental Informality

In the mid-1980s, a fourth type of informalization of poor people's urban space appeared, this time inspired by environmental concerns and expressed in the delimitation of conservation land as part of urban planning. What we now know as environmental criteria had already been inspiring government policies for a long time. Conservationists such as Miguel Ángel de Quevedo had left their mark on public discourse about natural resources since the first half of the century.[77] What was new was that the environmental argument was used to place low-income colonies outside the law. While agrarian informality continued to be the predominant form of habitat for the poor in the municipalities of the State of Mexico surrounding it, within Mexico City what defines new settlements as informal is the fact that they occupy areas defined as environmentally fragile. This produces a stigma that is more difficult to overcome than the previous ones.

By the end of the twentieth century, the other three types of informalization we have described had become marginal. Not that they had completely disappeared; there were still neighborhoods with different types of vulnerability and deficits in public services. But since the 1980s, when we speak of "irregular settlements," we are almost always talking about neighborhoods on conservation land—that is, on the more than eighty thousand hectares that make up 58 percent of Mexico City's territory.[78] Both in public opinion and in governmental discourse, the regularization of these settlements appears to be unacceptable—although sometimes it does happen. And it is no exaggeration to say that the use of force to evict those who settle on that land enjoys broad legitimacy.

Before the 1980s, the environmental argument as a source of a specific type of informality had hardly any force in the public space. Apart from a few isolated voices of environmentalists, most formers of public opinion, academics, and urban planners were not concerned about the environmental effects of today's so-called irregular settlements. Beginning in the late 1960s, invasions in the Padierna ejido, in the middle Ajusco area, generated significant tensions between settlers and *ejidatarios*. This is documented in the archives of the Ministry of the Interior, which generated numerous political reports on the situation.[79] However, the reports indicate only conflicts over property ownership and demands for services, with no one appearing to have made an environmental argument to stop urbanization. As late as 1974, there was talk of creating a city that would house a hundred thousand inhabitants in the "recently expropriated" ejido of Padierna.[80] Both journalism and academic production in the 1970s overlooked the environmental impacts of the poor *colonias*.[81]

The first glimpses of the "environmental turn" in Mexican urban planning appeared in 1976 with the Human Settlements General Act, which included explicit environmental objectives as part of urban policies,[82] which should not surprise us, because it was then that the modern environmental movement had its first boom in both the United States and Europe.[83] That piece of legislation gave rise not only to a new generation of plans but also to a new generation of planners. However, the truth is that environmental irregularity did not appear immediately in urban planning documents; in fact, the city's first master plan (*plan director*), which was prepared and published the same year of 1976 under the new legislation, registered only air pollution as an environmental problem. What defined the low-income neighborhoods in the south of the city was still the lack of services: "In the last two decades and due to demographic pressure and migratory flows, spaces that are not suitable have been occupied . . . such as the ravine areas of Álvaro Obregón, the lowlands of Lake Texcoco, neighboring areas or on some hills, rocky areas of Coyoacán, and others, which makes it difficult to provide adequate services to the population that resides there, both due to the high costs of urbanization and to frequent land tenure problems."[84]

The formulation of the problem was very different in a new version of the master plan published in 1980: "The growth of Mexico City's urban area is the result of an uncontrolled process of incorporation of agricultural land, ecological conservation zones, ravines and hills unsuitable for urban use, phenomena that are predominantly determined by market mechanisms. It has been estimated that, of the total number of irregular human settlements, which total approximately 500 neighborhoods with 700,000 properties, 60% are located on communal land, 30% occupy ejido zones and the remaining 10% are privately owned properties. This Plan establishes the southern, southeastern and extreme northern portion of the Federal District as a non-urbanized area subject to a strict conservation policy."[85]

That was the first time that the "conservation zone" that would define environmental irregularity was created, but it was not until the mid-1980s that the incipient "ecological" movement burst into the public space and began to point out the urbanization of certain areas on the periphery of the capital as an environmental problem. The Pacto de Grupos Ecologistas, created in 1985, was the most emblematic organization of those years and it is notable that one of its "sections" was dedicated precisely to the conservation of the previously mentioned Ajusco area.[86]

That same year, the city government announced its intention to apply a new planning scheme: the Urban Reorganization and Ecological Protection Program (PRUPE in Spanish), which aimed, among other things, to stop the expansion of the "urban sprawl" through the unusual proposal to expropriate more than seventy thousand hectares to create conservation land.[87] The communities that owned these lands, which today identify themselves as "native peoples," or *pueblos originarios*, expressed their rejection so forcefully that the proposal was withdrawn a few months later. The issue was put on the back burner by the earthquake of September 19, 1985, but shortly thereafter, the government began to take direct action to prevent the proliferation of human settlements on conservation land. One of them was the signing of "zero growth agreements" with representatives of the settlers. These agreements have a notable component of legal creativity, since in them "the settlement," as if it had legal personality, is obliged to avoid its own growth. To date, such agreements are part of the policy of the environmental authorities.[88] Undoubtedly the most drastic action of those years took place in 1988: the eviction, by force, of Lomas de Seminario, a neighborhood that was forming in the middle of Ajusco.[89] It was the first time that state force was exercised on the basis of the environmental argument.[90]

Thus, within a few years, the urbanization of conservation land had come to occupy in the environmental agenda a place almost as important as that of atmospheric pollution, which at that time had given Mexico City worldwide fame. There was a proliferation of "planning instruments" that repeatedly decreed what had already been clear since the 1980 master plan: the existence of conservation land protected from the creation of irregular settlements. Thus, a sort of palimpsest was formed; on it, cartographies and legal categories were superimposed to proclaim environmental informality in all the bureaucratic languages imaginable.[91] In 2001, the Environmental and Land Management Attorney's Office (PAOT, in Spanish) was created, which has since taken legal action against settlements arising in conservation land, and in the same year the General Ecological Land Management Program was issued, which overlaps with urban development plans and reinforces this territory's designation for agriculture and livestock. Among many other cases, we can cite the eviction of the settlement known as Los Zorros in May 2013, which was proudly announced by the environmental authorities and quickly celebrated by environmental organizations.[92]

Thus, since the 1980s, environmental informality has placed those who live in the conservation land in a very different situation from that of the inhabitants of the *colonias* that arose before environmental policies, because regularization does not appear as an option. If agrarian informality had a solution through regularization and was even a source of political capital for the government, then environmental informality appears, in principle, to be unacceptable.[93]

In fact, there are still procedures to modify the boundaries of rural settlements on conservation land or to "reclassify" *colonias* in order to introduce some public services in them.[94] However, these are exceptional cases, far removed from the active regularization policies carried out by CORETT and other entities in past decades—or from those operating in other jurisdictions.

In Mexico City, horizontal expansion is no longer an option for housing the poor.[95] As we have explained, the political justification for this land distribution was the Mexican Revolution. The strength of the environmentalist discourse coincided with the erosion of revolutionary principles and the weakness of the low-income sectors vis-à-vis the city government.

Conclusion

Several histories intersect in the history of informality in Mexico City: the history of the Mexican Revolution, of the Mexican state, of scientific and legal knowledge, and of one of the first megalopolises of the "Global South," whose growth was often interpreted as a sign of crisis. Unlike colonial informality, identified by Priscilla Connolly and other authors, in the four types of informality we identified, different urban spaces and their inhabitants were constructed as public problems, that is, as problems requiring a state response because they concerned society as a whole. However, the resulting political relations between the state and "informalized" social groups were of a very different nature; therefore, we do not write of informality as a singular phenomenon. Rather, we see different informalization processes carried out by social actors (governmental and nongovernmental) at specific historical conjunctures.

For the Mexican state, what was at stake in the governance of informality was the place that the poor would occupy in the urban order. Sanitary informality produced the same kind of stigmatization experienced by the urban poor since the nineteenth century in other parts of the world. It is a typically modern phenomenon that, among other things, was associated with the emergence of the so-called social question and the shaping of the hygienic idea of the citizen.[96] The same sanitary conditions that had prevailed for centuries became unacceptable and the aim was to eradicate them.

In contrast, the urban informality that gave rise to the proletarian neighborhoods resulted not in the eradication of these spaces, but in their regulation and integration into the city. During the 1930s and 1940s, the proletarian neighborhoods were integrated into the city through various mechanisms, always under the social justice discourse of the Mexican Revolution. There were two forms of intervention by the city government in the dynamics of these neighborhoods: the recognition of the inhabitants' organizations as legitimate interlocutors to process their demands and the correction of some of the problems of layout and structure of the neighborhoods, through what, significantly, was called "planning" in bureaucratic language. Certainly, the formation of these neighborhoods was never free of conflicts, and the political subordination of the poor was the cost they had to pay to obtain state recognition. But the proletarian neighborhoods offered their inhabitants integration into a city that did not cease to offer opportunities to its migrants to "reinvent their lives in the cities" in the context of the Mexican economic miracle.[97]

For its part, in agrarian informality, the presence and magnitude of ejidos in the processes of popular urbanization stands out. Despite the fact that ejido members had sold their lands to the urban poor, the ejido organization did not cease to be present, sometimes for several decades, because of the inalienable condition of the property, a situation that continued even after the 1992 legal reforms eliminated that condition. The fact that neighborhoods formed on ejido lands have developed with relatively little conflict, compared to other Latin American countries, is a result of the privileged political-legal status of the peasant corporations created by the postrevolutionary state. From the perspective of government and a large part of the public opinion, such status implied that peasants were not seen as individuals subdividing land for profit who could be legally prosecuted. Therefore, the government intervention in the case of agrarian informality has essentially consisted on granting property titles to the residents of the neighborhoods built on ejidal lands. Although the merits of regularization were magnified by the government agencies in charge of carrying it out, the truth is that for decades, this purpose was largely fulfilled.

Finally, environmental informality was and is presented by the government as a public problem that cannot be solved through political negotiation, regularization, and definitive integration into the city. It is still too early to know what the future of informal settlements on conservation land will be, but the Mexican government has been much harsher with the poor in these places, whose inhabitants no longer enjoy (or enjoy to a lesser degree) the political and discursive resources of the Mexican Revolution.

The revolution is now history, and its conclusion helps us understand the extent to which it endowed Mexican informality with distinctive features. It is true that sanitary and environmental informality occurred in a very similar way to what happened in other parts of the world; both are the result of transnational movements with profound legal reverberations. However, urban and agrarian informality derived from more original informalization processes that are the result of revolutionary laws, languages, and political forms. The Mexican Revolution introduced a language of social justice that advocated the extension of rights to the popular classes. But beyond language and laws, the revolution made possible the mobilization of millions of people in the city. The Mexican government used the law—sanitary, urban, agrarian, and

environmental—to channel this mobilization, define its limits, and negotiate the space that the poor would have in the city. This is one of the classic
themes of Mexican history and political science; in this text, we simply analyze what legal devices demarcated the relationship between the government
and the urban poor. Our conclusion is that the Mexican poor could not be
marginalized like those in the other cities explored in this volume.

From Insalubrious Housing to Unauthorized Neighborhoods: The Conceptualization of Urban Informality in Italy, 1880s–1960s

FRANCESCO BARTOLINI

This chapter traces changing understandings of informal city building in Italy from the late nineteenth to the mid-twentieth centuries. At the beginning of this period, the idea that there was such a thing as improper habitation arose mostly from observations regarding the inadequate quality of the urban housing stock. The city was understood as a unitary organism, and its irregularities received their share of attention, especially in relation to vital internal networks of communications and transportation that were hindered by the "buildings' flawed arrangement."[1] But after Italian unification (1861), legislation mainly dealt with the construction of a hygienic model of domestic living, formalized in the 1880s, which prescribed a specific articulation of living quarters and specified their proper use in daily life. At least until the 1930s, the problem of improper habitation in Italy remained limited mostly to the question of unsanitary housing in the consolidated city's most derelict buildings—the so-called *tugurio* (hovel)—without considering the effects of the development of an unplanned periphery.

The issue of inadequate habitation in Italy took on a properly urban, metropolitan dimension—linked to the development of unauthorized agglomerations or settlements, especially on the fringes of large cities—only after World War II, in connection with accelerated urbanization. Within this transformation, which we can summarize as a transition from worry about the "unsanitary" home to concern with the "illicit" neighborhood, it is also possible to see the evolution of the very concept of habitability from a strictly domestic and hygienic focus toward a community and urban planning model. This implied a shift from compliance with a regulatory code based on building standards to a form of regulation guided by the creation of an integrated urban system.

To understand this evolution, some peculiarities of the Italian context deserve attention. First, there is the persistence of a high urbanization rate of ancient origin, which marked the development of social life in the peninsula more than in other European regions, especially during the Middle Ages and the early modern era.[2] Presumably, when this rate of urbanization began to decline during the seventeenth and eighteenth centuries, opportunities increased for poor migrants to access a built patrimony—however degraded—consolidated within city walls.[3] It is thus no coincidence that, even at the end of the nineteenth century, urban administrations' greatest concern was excessive crowding in the old central districts rather than the haphazard expansion of precarious buildings in more peripheral areas.

In addition, Italy began to feel the domestic effects of mass rural-to-urban migration stimulated by industrial development only in the early twentieth century. During the last decades of the nineteenth century, employees, professionals, artisans, and intellectuals moved to the capital or to the most productive urban centers while peasants mostly emigrated abroad. It was only after the upheavals of World War I that a mass migration began within Italy, mainly affecting large cities and triggering the country's first serious crisis caused by the lack of public housing.[4]

The Italian case stands out for some specific features that caused informality to develop in ways that differed partially from the Latin American experience or other European ones. It is no coincidence that in late nineteenth-century Italy, albeit within a common context of hygienic alarm and a pressing need to rationalize urban space, the unplanned growth of precarious housing in areas outside the city limits was not a specific topic for public reflection and debate. In the main Italian cities—unlike, for example, in Madrid—unauthorized agglomerations of precarious housing were a little-recognized presence, not perceived as a specific threat to the built environment or social cohesion.[5] Informal suburban sprawl began to significantly shape views of urban development only in the 1930s and especially after World War II. Its conceptualization, however, was still initially linked to questions of housing—the structural adequacy of homes and the proper use of their interior spaces—rather than to the effects of a marginalized population's irregular presence on the urban outskirts. Given this, it is not surprising that the very perception of the *quartiere abusivo* (illicit settlement) as an urban phenomenon to be deciphered in its full economic and cultural complexity emerged much later and more uncertainly than it had in Rio de Janeiro, where the "favela" had begun to consolidate as a category in the early 1900s and was as important as the traditional sanitarist paradigm by the 1930s.[6]

Finally, to decipher the Italian context, it is appropriate to note two other factors. The first relates to a weak urban planning culture that struggled initially to shake off its original association with the fascist regime and establish itself in public discourse.[7] The second and more relevant factor concerns the development of *abusivismo* (illicit construction), defined as any alteration of extant dwellings or construction of new housing undertaken in violation of building codes or urban planning regulations. *Abusivismo* was widely tolerated in the second half of the twentieth century as a tool for creating political consensus and diffusing property ownership at a competitive cost, becoming a cross-class strategy that was not always associated with poverty and marginality and was therefore difficult to interpret solely through the lens of economic and social inequality.[8] These two factors help in understanding why informality in Italy has long been regarded more as a housing issue than as an urban problem—that is, as a phenomenon destined to transform the very idea of the city.

The Unhealthy Home

Between the 1880s and the 1920s, the sanitarist ethos predominated: a body of knowledge, institutions, and practices that, as elsewhere in Europe and Latin America, had the aim of "sanitizing" the city, albeit at different times and using different methods.[9] Often, the notion of excessive density or agglomeration legitimized desires for normative, moralizing interventions in urban space. In Italy during this period, the major concerns for public authorities were overcrowding and the internal subdivision of residential space. As the Council of State had underlined in 1869, "with the imposition of rules on how houses must be built and how those built defectively *ab antiquo* must be adapted, the entire urban population is assured salubriousness, comfort and light in their dwellings."[10]

In 1881 the general population census highlighted housing conditions in "basements" and "attics," which accounted, respectively, for 5.4 and 11.1 per thousand dwellings in Italy's urban centers.[11] The basements caused special concern among public authorities because they were on average smaller lodgings where, "for the most part, entire families live in a single damp and poorly-lit cave": "Underground dwellings are found most frequently in city centers, and are also comparatively more numerous in the Abruzzi, Basilicata, Puglia and the Roman countryside, where many families maintain wretched living quarters in caves specially dug in volcanic tuff or in stone quarries. In the rest of the Kingdom this type of housing is almost unknown."[12]

Another phenomenon is interesting for the purposes of our discussion, although it was not given particular prominence in the census: families who

lived in "mines, quarries, huts and sheds." This category is not easy to decipher. It was seemingly mostly reserved for sectors of the extraurban population, or those who were temporarily homeless, but that did not preclude the
existence of urban or periurban groups who lived permanently in precarious
housing. It is significant that this classification was conceived as a tool for in-
vestigating cohabitations that did not correspond to "proper families," rather
than as a source of information about housing conditions. The final count
showed that more than 8,000 families and 50,000 individuals lived in these
dwellings; among these, the statistical district of Rome clearly predominated,
with 3,105 families and 21,118 people.[13]

Still, the idea of improper habitation was mainly linked to the existence of
tuguri (hovels) in city centers. Thus the special law for Naples of 1885, which
became the archetype for remedial interventions in Italian cities, aimed
mainly to eliminate the *tugurio*.[14] After a cholera epidemic in September
1884 claimed over seven thousand victims, the government presented a bill
identifying the source of the evil "in the deplorable conditions of the sewers
and subsoil, where thousands of wells and springs of bad water, the natural
vehicle of infection, collapse and teem; in the agglomeration of the poorest
classes of the people in *tuguri* and filthy basements; in the general insalubrity of housing in various sections of Naples."[15] In addition to laying the
groundwork for planning a new modern city, restructuring the central area,
and constructing popular neighborhoods on Naples's eastern outskirts, the
law formalized a repressive mechanism against housing deemed "insalubrious," granting the mayor broad powers to condemn or renovate. The public
health law of 1888 would generalize and further detail these powers, listing a
series of defects that defined housing as unhealthy—damp walls, a lack of air
or light, inefficient waste disposal, the absence of latrines, washbasins, and
drinking water—and leaving the mayor to identify "other obvious causes of
insalubrity."[16] This latter definition of habitability was more strictly regulated
in 1896 through a series of "ministerial instructions on the hygiene of soil and
habitats," developed to translate the 1888 requisites into minimum standards
and concrete measures.[17]

At the beginning of the twentieth century, then, the supporting structure
for regulating sanitarist urbanism was almost complete. As far as cities were
concerned, regulation was thought of primarily as a tool to modernize the
oldest centers. In public discourse, there was still no urge to thwart the development of the self-built city that had grown up around residential areas.
But was there still, in this period, something identifiable as urban informality,
composed of precarious and haphazard buildings? And if so, what characteristics did it have?

Judging by the results of surveys by national and local authorities on urban "hygiene and sanitary conditions," urban informality was not yet clearly perceived or conceptualized. An 1886 inquiry organized by the Directorate General for Statistics noted the conditions of roads, the functioning of sanitation services, and the lack of sewers and latrines, but the crux of the "housing question" remained the proliferation of accommodations in basements and attics.[18] In an 1899 investigation promoted by the Ministry of the Interior, provincial doctors insisted on the need to improve housing, demolish unsanitary buildings, and gut unhealthy neighborhoods, but they rarely denounced hovels, *baracche* (shacks), or precarious housing as elements of urban disorder.[19] The main concern was always the basements, which epitomized inadequate housing.

Even in the various housing surveys promoted by municipal administrations in the first decade of the twentieth century, *baracche*, precarious housing, or unregulated self-built dwellings were almost never raised as an issue. Alarm increased about worsening housing conditions resulting from the first industrially driven migratory movements. Higher levels of agglomeration were often recorded in the most peripheral popular neighborhoods. Occasionally, the most extreme examples of housing distress occurred in suburban areas, although unhealthiness there aroused less concern "due to low territorial density, which decreases the danger of the spread of infectious diseases, and because of the beneficial modifying effects of air, light and space."[20] But the idea of a form of disorder linked to the expansion of precarious settlements did not emerge.

Of course, there was no lack of *baracche* in Italian cities. In the last two decades of the nineteenth century, there were significant agglomerations around Rome and some other large cities. In some respects, the general population census of 1901 testified to this when it tallied those who lived in "wagons, *baracche*, sheds, quarries, and outdoor places," a category modified from the 1882 census to distinguish such arrangements from the "dormitories of workers and farm laborers." Over 24,000 people were registered under this new heading, which nonetheless remained difficult to interpret. Among municipalities with over 100,000 inhabitants, Rome still stood out, with 4,204 people in that category.[21]

A decade later, the data in the 1911 general population census confirmed that a significant informal periphery was emerging in the capital. This tally, as compiled by the municipality's statistical offices, highlighted the existence of 7,760 "abnormal" and 2,055 "very abnormal" dwellings.[22] The former were located in basements, ground floors, shops, and attics, while the latter were identified as *baracche*, huts, and stables. What is striking here is the use of generic and evaluative categories instead of objective and legally prescriptive descriptions to map different forms of housing—as if in reality the only aspect of interest was the infringement of a standard of "normalcy," from which both improper housing or self-built shacks diverged, albeit to different degrees.

A significant geography of informality emerged from the distribution of "abnormal" housing in Rome, which also sometimes revealed the coexistence of makeshift housing and luxury homes. Evidently, the *baracche* and huts abounded where open land prevailed, regardless of the status of the groups that predominated in any given neighborhood. The Nomentano and Parioli districts, where there were villas and small houses, had a substantial number of *baracche*, while there were only a few in the eminently working-class Tiburtino district, which was almost saturated with buildings.[23]

The Specter of the *Baracca*

During the 1920s and 1930s, *baracche* proliferated in many Italian cities. As in other geographical contexts, this expansion was one of the effects of increasing rural-to-urban migration.[24] The cities in the northwest and in the center of the peninsula attracted the most migrants: between 1921 and 1936 the number of people in Rome rose from 660,091 to 1,150,338; in Milan, from 818,000 to 1,115,768; in Turin, from 499,823 to 629,115; in Genoa, from 541,562 to 634,646; and in Bologna, from 212,754 to 281,162.[25] The intense influx of new arrivals sustained this growth, which natives sometimes perceived as a siege. For example, in the newspaper *Corriere della Sera*, Senator Luigi Einaudi, one of the most authoritative Italian economists, commented on "the spectacle of sprawling cities, which have grown by absorbing inhabitants from the countryside and distant regions":

> Are these real cities? No. There is the ancient city in the center, where true citizens live, those who feel an attachment to their place of birth, who want it to be beautiful and great, who are willing to sacrifice for the benefit of future generations. Around that, there is the camp. Living in the camp are those who came in search of fortune, those who abandoned land and ancestors to look for a new life. These are men worthy of all state protection; [yet] I can hardly believe in their fitness for choosing the ruling political class. They are the new barbarians, those who aspire to the beautiful things of the earth; eager for enjoyment and impatient with the sacrifices necessary to that end.[26]

A substantial number of these new urbanites struggled to find adequate housing; they flocked to the hovels in the most dilapidated neighborhoods and built precarious houses in peripheral urban areas. The *baracca* gradually became a visible presence in the urban landscape. For public authorities, they also became an emergency to be resolved.

It is not surprising that, from the beginning, the fascist regime chose *baracche* demolition as a prominent rhetorical theme, using it as a metaphor for social rehabilitation and overcoming the anarchy of the liberal age. Thus, by the mid-1920s, some cities initiated *sbaraccamento* (slum clearance) programs. Examples included Messina, hit by an earthquake in 1908, where a disordered expansion of *baracche* had sprung up alongside provisional housing built by the Genio Civile (a public corps of civil engineers),[27] and especially Rome, where demands for police control over a mobile population dovetailed with the urban decorum requirements necessary to transform the capital into the celebratory stage of fascism. Here, the governorate constantly monitored the *baraccati* population, carrying out repeated censuses. From the mid-1920s to the end of the 1930s there were at least five, the most complete of which was conducted in 1933. They noted family composition, residents' origins and professions, and the number of rooms and building materials used in each structure. In 1933, 4,405 families living in the *baracche* were meticulously registered, for a total of 19,218 people.[28]

Significantly, almost none of this information was publicized. Only a few articles appeared sporadically in the governorate's official magazine *Capitolium*, citing scant census data and mainly showing fascist authorities' commitment to definitively eradicating a phenomenon that was deemed on its way out.[29] In reality, internal communications within the administration show that the *baracche* continued to proliferate and that authorities struggled to regulate their inhabitants. But obviously, doubts about the results of the *sbaraccamento* campaigns were not allowed to leak outside the municipal offices.

In this way, during the 1930s, the *baracca* disappeared from public discourse—the term became almost absent. In one of the cultural summaries of fascist Italy, the Giovanni Treccani Institute's *Italian Encyclopedia of Sciences, Letters, and Arts*, the entry *baracca* (written by Gaetano Minnucci, one of the era's most famous architects) makes no reference to auto-construction from scrap materials.[30] It is as if there were no precarious shelters used as homes.

This tendency toward concealment became even more evident, in some respects, in a special housing survey carried out in 1931 to coincide with the general population census. For the first time, a specific housing questionnaire was distributed along with the household survey with the aim of extending the quantity and quality of information about residences in Italy's 422 municipalities. Presented as "the first Italian Census of housing understood in the broadest sense," the survey collected detailed information about rooms, urban services, the degree of crowding, the inhabitants' social condition, and their forms of cohabitation.[31] It was obviously impossible to deny the presence of basements, caves, and *baracche*, but in the general report, the positivist sociologist Alfredo Niceforo (a member of the Superior Council of Statistics and the Technical Committee of the Central Institute of Statistics) scaled the question down to a waning problem. While admitting the difficulty of making a precise comparison with past data, he in fact opined that the numbers had "considerably decreased despite the strong population increase."[32] In support of this, Niceforo presented a table showing a minimal percentage of precarious housing: in the entire country, there were only 18,830 lodgings located in "*baracche*, boats, etc."; 3,564 in "shops, inhabited warehouses, etc."; and 404 in "caves and the like."[33] Once again, however, Rome's primacy stands out, with 3,414 lodgings concentrated in "*baracche*, boats, etc.," compared with 386 in Milan, 261 in Genoa, and 51 in Turin—a surprising difference that confirmed the capital's emergency situation.[34]

During the 1920s and 1930s, the struggle against unhealthy housing did not spur a rethinking of urban sanitary regulation. Until the end of the 1930s, what stands out is the ideologization and increased political exploitation of sanitary norms, often used by police with authoritarian arbitrariness.[35] This authoritarian tightening harmonized with the regime's totalitarian ambitions, but in various forms, it was also detectable in other countries, where security needs assumed increasing importance in the face of increasingly mobile populations.[36] It is true that the 1934 Health Act introduced an obligatory habitability permit, formalizing a preventive inspection power that had previously appeared only in municipal regulations.[37] However, this new order did not transform the concept of habitability, which remained substantially linked to the sanitarist tradition. It was not until a 1939 law (which curbed the expansion of large cities) and a 1942 urban planning law (which formalized a de-urbanization policy that in reality had already stimulated many fascist choices, starting with the design of the Roman *borgate*) that we glimpse a new idea of habitability, which would only mature in the late 1940s with the new political and cultural context of the Republic.[38]

Outside Modernity

The effects of World War II and mass migration refocused attention on the phenomenon of informality, which began to be observed through new eyes. This was partly because the housing question increased in ideological-political significance as an instrument of modernization and social stabilization but also because authorities, influenced by urban planning discourse, established a new concept of habitability.[39] Significant in this regard was the definition of the "essential requisites of housing" that emerged from the first three articles of a "housing code" drawn up by a commission of politicians, entrepreneurs, urban planners, architects, and senior public administration officials appointed by the Ministry of Public Works in March 1948:

1. The essential requisites of housing are met within the home only insofar as it is integral to a larger and more varied built environment that constitutes the residential habitat.

2. In order for a group of houses to constitute a residential habitat, it must have the resources to satisfy the needs of inhabitants' individual, family and collective lives in relation to the following factors:

   spiritual;
   commercial;
   cultural-educational;
   hygienic-sanitary;
   recreational.

3. In order for a group of dwellings to be established, it is necessary to ensure in advance that they are linked to the inhabitants' customary workplaces, so that the time required to go and return is in fair proportion to the duration of the work itself.[40]

Two aspects are striking in these directions: the transcendence of sanitarist positivism (understood as a mere quantification of minimum requirements) and the complexity of the concept of *abitato* (habitat), which would lead paradoxically to an expansion of what the city considered "inadequate." It was no longer enough for hygienic housing to comply with specific spatial dimensions, standards, and guidelines; it was essential that it be connected with the rest of the city, allowing effective participation in community life.

Furthermore, the category of *altri alloggi* (other housing) appeared for the first time in the 1951 general population census, aiming to systematically quantify those who lived in places "not functionally intended for housing."[41] Over 870,000 Italians resided in makeshift accommodations that included "caves, *baracche*, cellars, warehouses, shops, offices, schools and barracks, lodgings in refugee camps, arches in ancient walls and bridges, and mobile caravans."[42] This estimate did not even count those living in dilapidated and overcrowded dwellings such as the Neapolitan *bassi*, the *catoi* in Palermo, or the dwellings in the Roman *borgate*, which, while considered "functionally" suitable premises in statistical surveys, actually accounted for the bulk of

FIGURE 2.1. **Caves of Naples.** Photo archived by United Nations Relief and Rehabilitation Administration (UNRRA), 1948. Source: United Nations Archives, S-0800-0003-0004-00005.

housing distress in Italian cities. Awareness was thus growing of the need for state intervention to assist those without a home or those living in what were generically called *tuguri* (hovels).

In 1952, two special laws were approved, one for Naples and the other for Matera. The first, in which the state allocated 6 billion lire for the construction of *fabbricati a carattere popolarissimo* (popular housing), stemmed from the pressing need to assist displaced families who lived in caves, shacks, *baracche*, schools, and abandoned public buildings.[43] The more than three hundred individuals who lived in caves—the so-called cave dwellers—struck a particular emotional chord, having already captured press attention internationally as well as locally in the immediate postwar period (figs. 2.1 and 2.2).[44] Overall, as underlined in the law's explanatory memorandum by Minister of Public Works Salvatore Aldisio, over twelve thousand Neapolitan people were forced into an "unbearable and inhuman existence."[45] For this reason, in Aldisio's opinion, conditions in Naples were serious enough to justify an exceptional measure, which would also have the advantage of promoting social discipline among the most marginalized populations. For Aldisio, intervention was urgent because "the population grows and renews itself in a state of degradation, which breeds abnormal and illicit unions and fosters the most brutal criminal instincts."[46]

It was in Matera, however, that improper habitation took on real iconic significance as the city's *Sassi*, ancient lodgings dug into volcanic tuff, became the example par excellence of a way of life incompatible with modernity.[47] In the explanatory memorandum for the bill providing state redevelopment assistance, Aldisio again highlighted the situation's dramatic nature, specifying that "the situation of the 'Matera *Sassi*' cannot be seriously compared

FIGURE 2.2. **Dwellers in the caves of Naples.** Photo archived by United Nations Relief and Rehabilitation Administration (UNRRA), 1948. Source: United Nations Archives, S-0800-0003-0004-00017.

with painful situations existing elsewhere, since it is it is rare to find such an agglomeration of people, comprising approximately two-thirds of the entire city's inhabitants, camped at best in blocs that do not allow them to enjoy the good air that is usually accessible even to the poor."[48] In the two *Sassi* districts there were, in fact, 1,641 "troglodyte dwellings," "devoid of air and light and impregnated with moisture in the walls, ceilings and floors," of which more than 70 percent were classified as uninhabitable.[49]

The situation had also made an impression on Prime Minister Alcide De Gasperi, who visited Matera in July 1950.[50] Back in Rome, De Gasperi had vowed to promote government intervention. Thus, a few months after the approval of state money for Naples, parliament was called on to approve another special law providing for a loan of 4.7 billion lire for the renovation of the *Sassi* and the construction of new housing and infrastructure.[51] It is relevant, for the purposes of our discussion, that this provision became, in many respects, an opportunity to experiment with a new paradigm of habitability. In fact, significant debates developed around whether to eliminate these centuries-old dwellings completely or partially, around the criteria for situating new houses according to their inhabitants' social profiles, and around how to build new settlements while preserving some aspects of an urban tradition that derived from unregulated living.[52]

Shortly afterward, in 1953, the Parliamentary Commission of Inquiry into Poverty in Italy and How to Combat It helped raise the alarm over the deplorable state of the "improper housing" that lodged thousands of families.[53] A statistical analysis was carried out using data obtained from a sample survey of more than 58,000 families: when "overcrowded" housing (in which about 2.5 million families lived) was added to that considered "improper" (about another 324,000), more than 24 percent of Italian families were classified as living in inadequate dwellings. Specifically in regard to "improper habitation," which was notoriously difficult to identify rigorously, 0.8 percent of families lived in "caves and *baracche*," while 2 percent resided in "cellars, attics, warehouses, etc."[54] In this analysis, the category of "improper" tended to be incorporated into a broader concept of uninhabitability, a dysfunctionality brought about not only by a lack of adherence to the space's intended use but also by excessive overcrowding.

This focus on the phenomenon of the improper habitation stands out especially in the reports of parliamentary delegations visiting the so-called suburbs of great cities, namely Naples, Rome, and Milan. Although precarious housing flourished in all the country's "depressed areas," especially in the south, the most accurate investigations into the world of the *baraccati* were sited in working-class neighborhoods and on the outskirts of what were considered the three most emblematic Italian metropolises, taken to represent different urban living conditions in the south, center. and north. The commissioners endeavored to compile detailed counts of *tuguri* and "improper" dwellings to show the drama of urban destitution: in Naples, over 19,000 people resided in caves and *baracche*; in Rome, more than 93,000 lived in "improper" habitations; in Milan, about 2,500 lived in irregular *baracche* and 2,100 in municipally approved shacks.[55] The commissioners described these people's everyday living spaces in great detail, aiming to arouse both solidarity and sometimes appreciation for informal communities' efforts at self-organization. They described, for example, a *baraccopoli* (shantytown) built in Naples in the courtyards of a former school building:

> This community lives somewhat autonomously. There is a postman, there is a shop selling summer watermelons, a bar, a greengrocer, etc. All of this at very honest prices, prices meant for poor customers who have little money to spend. . . .
>
> However, the feeling of solidarity is alive among these poor people, at least so it seems. There is a kind of brotherhood among this population, needy beyond belief, so much so that the members of the Delegation were invited by those present to visit other people who were in far worse conditions, always perhaps in the hope of finally finding someone capable of making influential referrals.[56]

Furthermore, the commissioners were careful to point out variations among apparently identical phenomena in each city. In Milan, for example, living in *baracche* would be distinct from Naples and Rome because, in their opinion, it often represented "only an initial stage in Milanese life": "In fact, it is proven that these [people] become integrated in the productive life of the city at a remarkable pace, so much so that this phenomenon can be considered, within certain limits, less an index of individual misery than a symptom of potential for economic advancement, and therefore ultimately of liberation from need (this is limited, of course, to talented and enterprising people who do not lack a spirit of sacrifice). The less gifted, however—and they are the majority—remain to swell the ranks of the local poor."[57]

Nonetheless, there were also the usual warnings about the need to prevent "moral degradation," portrayed as a citywide emergency. This was particularly true in Rome, where the number of people living in improper housing was so large as to constitute a threat to social order: "For these groups the lack of homes worthy of the name contributes to physical and above all moral decadence; for these individuals, the possession of a home is a precondition for their rehabilitation as human beings, in hopes that they might contribute to the community, however modestly, with their labor. If things continue as they have proceeded thus far, society will have to shoulder a large part of the burden of maintaining these people and will have itself to blame for most of that situation's harmful moral and material consequences."[58]

The mobilization of political parties also demonstrated the public salience of the "improper housing" problem. Both the Christian Democrats and the communists presented bills providing significant resources for new housing construction, reserved exclusively for members of marginalized classes who lived in precarious lodgings. These initiatives also highlighted the limits of previous public housing policies that had in different ways effectively favored blue-collar workers and the white-collar middle classes, marginalizing social groups whose unstable employment prevented them from regularly paying even subsidized rents. For the Christian Democrats, it was necessary to intervene to preserve the physical and moral health of the *baraccati* by dispelling that "shadow of backwardness and disorder that is projected throughout the country and that, in addition to debasing the lives of numerous families, also devalues the admirable efforts at progress that have been made thus far."[59] For the communists, who shared this moralizing focus, it was also necessary to insist on the community's recovery of productive energies, lost as a result of "the appalling living conditions in which most of the laboring classes are forced to live and die."[60]

Thus in the summer of 1954 a law was approved—promoted by the social democratic minister Giuseppe Romita—that outlined for the first time a national plan of multiyear financing (a total of 168 billion lire) for the construction of housing to "accommodate families lodged in caves, *baracche*, basements, public buildings, unhealthy premises, and the like."[61] These new accommodations, which varied in size and features according to the different residential models of Italy's regions, were allotted by a prefectural commission, with no need for the beneficiaries to submit applications.[62] The Genio Civile was charged with eliminating unhealthy homes or obstructing their entries; anyone who tampered with the closures was excluded from housing allocation. This last provision aimed to hinder the widespread strategy of occupying a *tugurio* to obtain low-rent housing.

Most relevant for the codification of a new paradigm of habitability was the Ministry of Public Works' authority to dispose of 0.30 percent of the allocated funds for the construction of "buildings of a social nature such as schools, nurseries, churches, recreation centers, etc." in the new *borgate*, as well as the power to provide "ancillary public works essential to ensuring the habitability of housing in municipalities deemed unable to support the related expenditure."[63] The law thus formalized the ways in which connection, socialization, and participation in community life were unavoidable requisites of habitability, right alongside compliance with the usual sanitary requirements. But it also inevitably stimulated attempts by local governments and authorities to expand the category of "improper" housing in order to qualify for state funding.

A significant case in this regard involved the Sicilian section of UNRRA-CASAS, which, following the 1954 Romita law, launched an investigation into "unhealthy" housing on the island with the aim of "locally ascertaining the social and environmental aspects of the housing problem in order to provide the relevant state agencies with the necessary elements to formulate effective and adequate interventions."[64] From a methodological point of view, it is striking how the concept of "unhealthy habitation" was modified according to the object and objective pursued:

> Improper habitations, namely caves, *baracche* and basements and single-room dwellings are considered 'unhealthy' and, therefore, subject to legislative measures enacted to eliminate unhealthy housing.
>
> In this regard, law no. 640 expressly contemplates the plight of families settled in "unhealthy premises"; there can be no doubt that most of the single-room dwellings in Sicily should be considered "unhealthy premises."[65]

The investigation's report placed considerable emphasis on the terrible living conditions in the "single-room dwellings" found in ancient buildings in urban centers, precisely to eliminate any doubt about including these *tuguri* among the cases covered by the Romita law:

> These buildings can sometimes be centuries old, such as the houses in the Arab quarter of Mazara, the "catoi" of Catania and Palermo, [or] the peasant dwellings of agricultural communities in the interior. . . .
>
> Toilets and the most rudimentary domestic appliances are almost always lacking.
>
> There is hardly any plumbing and water is drawn from public fountains, sometimes distant from the homes. The streets in front [of the houses] often serve as sewers.
>
> About 30% of these houses lack electric light, an absence generally explained by the destitution in which the occupant families find themselves.
>
> In the final analysis, these are veritable hovels, for the great majority of which the definition of "improper housing" can be considered completely justified.[66]

Overall, an extremely complex panorama emerged, where it was evident that the phenomenon of improper habitation had to be examined in different local contexts: there was no doubt that "the problem of the Messina *baraccati*" was substantially different, for example, from that of "the phenomenon of the 'cave-dwellers' of Modica and Scicli," just as the "needs and problems of the families housed in the Palermo 'catoi' were different from those of the fishermen occupying the basements of Porto Empedocle."[67] In addition, the report emphasized the need to avoid overly rigid categories of analysis, because housing deprivation could reveal itself in unexpected forms, to the point that sometimes "caves and *baracche* could be considered better homes than the average single-room accommodation."[68]

Outside the Rules

Between the end of the 1950s and the beginning of the 1960s, new inquiries began to read urban informality primarily as rule violation, or as *abusivismo*. In 1957, in a census of "precarious housing" carried out by the Municipality of Rome, the criterion of illegality prevailed over that of uninhabitability. The concept of precariousness was in fact equated with provisional, meaning a temporary condition destined to disappear when respect for the law was restored. In this sense, "precarious" housing did not necessarily correspond to "improper" housing. Unlike the latter, precarious housing could be functional and possess all the requirements of a "proper" home. What distinguished it was a lack of respect for the rights of third parties and noncompliance with current building codes:

> Precarious housing cannot always be considered the opposite of a "proper home." In other words, it cannot be defined as something other than a true home or, according to the imprecise current expression, as an "improper habitation."
>
> A true and proper home is in fact defined as a room or set of rooms intended to function as a dwelling, built or subsequently adapted as a home for a family or for several families living together.
>
> This means that to establish whether a home is true and proper, one only has to observe whether the structure is appropriate for habitation; it does not matter if it is provisional, nor whether it has been built, installed or adapted illegally, or whether the rights of third parties and the current laws and regulations have been respected. The definition of precarious housing, on the other hand, takes these last requirements into consideration and therefore observes housing from a completely different point of view.
>
> There is thus no shortage of precarious lodgings with all the characteristics of "true and proper homes." They must, however, be considered "precarious" because they are installed or built illegally.[69]

In this survey, moreover, there are obvious attempts to categorize irregular housing complexes, defined as "ecological units inserted as abnormal settlements in the body and on the edges of regular urban agglomerations."

This reveals growing attention to analyzing informal sprawl from an urban planning perspective.[70] Hence emerged a different classification of "settlement forms," categorized as "scattered dwellings," "nuclei," "agglomerations," and *borghetti* (hamlets). The latter were the most stable agglomerations, constituting the backbone of the *città abusiva* (illegal city): "The *borghetti* should be considered stabilized settlements in the sense that, in general, they are not subject to further expansion. The available spaces are all occupied. Over time—since these settlements were formed early—the families living there, or their predecessors, have provided for gradual housing improvement through successive upgrades."[71]

This awareness of the expansion of a *città abusiva* (illegal city) within and on the margins of the official one took on different meanings in social surveys that sought to decipher the character and behavior of the "subaltern classes." Here, *abusivismo* is interpreted as a practice of survival, an inevitable consequence of public policies and housing market dynamics, which also appeared likely to become grounds for political mobilization by irregular inhabitants. In 1960, two communist intellectuals, Giovanni Berlinguer and Piero Della Seta, published a study on Rome's *borgate*, presented as the "first history of the Roman periphery," in which they emphasized the dialectic between the "neighborhoods" of the "ruling classes" and the "periphery" of the *abusivi*, who were long considered irregular because fascist legislation had denied them residence permits, so they ended up living in the "spontaneous *borgate*."[72] This last category is described as the "bulk of the phenomenon" of so-called urban marginality, understood as the expansion of a "periphery" consisting of "clusters of poverty-stricken homes, arising spontaneously (or created as 'official' public housing) in distant areas, devoid of the most elementary public services, according to standards that conflict with the dictates of contemporary urban planning," which develop "on the edge of the 'city,' guided by speculation, as far as possible from the 'official city.'"[73] Even given substantial differences among them, Berlinguer and Della Seta choose to lump such places together under the term *borgate*: "The *borgate* are, above and before all, 'peripheries.' They are peripheries even when—as is the case with the *borghetti*—they have spread into the city's more central areas, even when they are now sometimes joined to regular settlements. They are peripheries because they are far away, because they lack amenities and connections, but mainly because they are detached from the rest of the urban organism, because they are distinct bodies, because they fail to fit into the 'city' despite being used and dominated by it."[74]

That same year in Milan, two other Marxist intellectuals, Franco Alasia and Danilo Montaldi, published research on the *coree*, residential clusters auto-constructed by migrants in the rural hinterland. This was in many ways a distinctive form of informal expansion, constituted not by clusters of *baracche* or precarious buildings built in the city's interstices or at its peripheries, but by complexes of respectable masonry buildings, often even built with permits, developed without urban planning in areas administered by the province of Milan's small municipalities. Living in *corea* was a popular choice among migrants from the southern countryside because it often allowed them to become homeowners: new arrivals could buy an affordable lot, build a house in their time off from their jobs—almost always in Milan—and gather their families.

Alasia and Montaldi interpreted this peripheral world not only as separate from the official city but also as a representation of wider changes in Italian society in the early 1960s, especially the spread of a new individualism:

> The topographical arrangement of the first *Coree* reveals a deeper intent to detach, a greater sense of the private. If the first house is arranged facing forward, the second is deliberately built with another orientation, so that windows and doors do not face each other. Within this refusal to socialize lies a backlash against previous experience: it is better not to relate to others; we don't wish to recognize ourselves in their situation; the problem is personal, it is that of the family, the house, the continuous work of arranging a new home. One house across the street, one oriented sideways, one isolated, *Corea* are born—distant, disorganized, disadvantaged, a segment of the country that has no official name, no roads, no services. When the gaps have been filled, a tangle of alleys will spring up; alleys before streets.[75]

The *coree* is an apparently disordered space, which grows according to precise logics, mostly inspired by mimetic practices: "*Corea* remain a city created by exclusion. Everyone tends to isolate themselves; in the *Corea* new stratifications recreate themselves; having no economic raison d'être, these persist as personal or family stances, vindictive attitudes and behaviors that tend to imitate customs in the 'real' society of the metropolis. The world *below* tries to organize itself like the one *above*."[76]

Another almost contemporaneous study, this time coordinated by the sociologist Leone Diena, reached similar conclusions and did not hesitate to perceive in *coree* morphology the possibility of new forms of urban organization: "A completely shapeless and inorganic settlement presupposed that the buildings arose without any order or logical criterion. The data seemed to prove this hypothesis. However, the fact that an urban sort of neighborhood had arisen rather than a settlement of scattered houses, and that some common services such as electricity, gas, water, had been arranged, suggested that there was a conscious will among the population to build an urban area. In other words, it can be assumed that inhabitants had an awareness of urban planning, not simply a desire to have a home anyhow and anywhere."[77]

The surveys by Alasia and Montaldi and by Diena, based on statistical data but also making wide use of testimonials and interviews, enhanced recognition of the needs of those who lived in an irregular city that did not always coincide with the unsanitary city. An awareness of urban informality emerged that was no longer legible through the usual socioeconomic categories, but rather required an understanding of new ideological-cultural codes with respect to habitation.

However, it is also evident in the 1960s that public discourse on the phenomenon of *abusivismo* (unregulated building activity) began to conflate the category of illegality with that of uninhabitability. In this regard, two events appear particularly significant. The first occurred as part of the process of preparing Rome's new Urban Master Plan, approved in 1962, involving the legalization of forty-four irregular settlements that had mainly arisen near the official *borgate* built during the fascist period.[78] This choice was motivated by the desire to integrate into the city a substantial part of the Roman periphery that had developed between the 1930s and 1950s outside the master plan and was inhabited by some 200,000 people. Here, for the first time, the state formally recognized the state of necessity that prevailed among the *abusivi*, authorizing the legalization of their buildings and making an official commitment to oversee the construction of infrastructure and services that would integrate the irregular and regular cities. This decisive step did not, however, distinguish between different reasons for illegality—between need and speculation—and thus constituted a fundamental precedent for subsequent amnesties.[79] From that point forward, in fact, the legalization of illegal constructions began to seem legitimate and became, especially in Rome and the southern cities, an indispensable resource for public authorities and political parties in building electoral consensus and managing urban emergencies. In other words, the building amnesty was transformed into a tool for governing relations between institutions and informal inhabitants, constituting a negotiation practice that was vital for the functioning of local government but based on a clientelistic logic that inevitably favored individual interests over public ones.[80]

The other relevant event in the conceptualization and representation of *abusivismo* was a public debate that developed during the summer and autumn of 1966 following a huge landslide in Agrigento that caused four buildings to collapse, damaged dozens more, and displaced over 7,500 inhabitants.[81] Building speculators were accused of encouraging the proliferation of illegal construction. A technical commission appointed by the Ministry of Public Works to investigate the city's urban planning and construction situation denounced a veritable "explosion of *abusivismo* and illegality" fueled by the "synergy between municipal action and builders' activities," going so far as to estimate that more than 8,500 of the 20,000 rooms built between 1955 and 1965 violated building regulations.

> In Agrigento, real estate companies and largescale builders did not take part in the action: the latter—limited in any case to two or three examples—preferred to operate in other sectors. Instead, construction activity was carried out by numerous small builders, who were often just improvising. And yet there was still building speculation in the "city of temples," even if it manifested itself in atypical forms. . . . It was a widespread phenomenon—a mass speculation, so to speak—basically fueled by easy credit, the lure of greater profits, and the desire to obtain, with municipal complicity, more than was allowable and to exploit the land's construction capacity beyond what was licit.
>
> Speculation by these improvised developers proved in a sense even more pernicious than the well-known speculation of large real estate and construction companies, partly because their lack of sensitivity, tradition, technical capacity or professional experience meant that their activity manifested itself in crude, shabby, and absurd forms.[82]

In the mid-1960s, therefore, the phenomenon of *abusivismo* in Italy emerged in all its complexity. On the one hand, there was the periphery of the marginalized, with its precarious buildings and its uninhabitable *baracche* built with scrap materials; on the other hand, there was the periphery of speculators, with its unlicensed buildings that were subsequently legalized and its neighborhoods that arose without order or public spaces. In the middle was a periphery that was auto-constructed by migrants, composed of permanent and mostly decent homes but lacking public services or efficient connections with the official city. These off-the-books spaces constituted a substantial part of the urban expansion that accompanied Italian modernization in the 1960s, a gigantic informal periphery that bore little resemblance to the "improper" city of previous decades.

Conclusion

In conclusion, it is possible to understand the formalization of the idea of habitability as an important parameter for the definition of urban "modernity" between the 1880s and the 1960s. Essentially, this process unfolded as a transition from a sanitarist conception, linked to the elimination of structural defects in homes and buildings, to a communitarian conception, more connected to the construction of an integrated urban space. This transformation was accompanied by increasing public regulation, which inevitably redefined the nature and boundaries of the irregular city. This last process was strongly conditioned by the need to adapt national legislation to diverse local contexts, where municipal and provincial authorities tended to interpret and classify housing distress according to the criteria for assigning state funds for urban renewal.

Until World War I, improper habitation was mainly identified with the most dilapidated homes in central urban neighborhoods, especially with *tuguri* located in the basements of old buildings. But from the 1930s onward, with the intensification of rural-to-urban migration and accelerated metropolitan expansion, the idea of urban impropriety began to be associated with the multiplication of *baracche* and unauthorized settlements on the peripheries of regular residential areas. The fascist regime tried to counter this disorder—characterized by mobility, precariousness, and marginality—with police measures and social discipline policies.

After World War II, there was a new wave of urban migration and an expansion of the informal periphery. In addition to dismay about the persistent of unsanitary housing in older neighborhoods, there was also alarm about the incessant proliferation of irregular settlements in the peripheral areas of large cities. These, however, took on features that could not be reconciled with the view that urban informality implied insalubrity and social marginalization. Furthermore, technical and administrative authorities identified this out-of-control construction as the main impediment to the development of the functionally integrated city paradigm that urban planning culture had brought to the center of political debate.

It is no coincidence that the issue of illegality began to prevail over that of uninhabitability, reinforcing a conceptualization of informality as a violation of building and urban planning regulations, or *abusivismo*. This *abusivismo*, however, manifested with a dual nature: that of the needy, excluded from economic and social dynamics, and that of speculators and opportunists able to exploit both inefficiencies in public administration and the structural contradictions of the market. Despite its semantic ambiguity, the concept of *abusivismo* assumed a key role in debates about the problems of the city and continues to play an essential role in analysis of the dynamics of urbanization in contemporary Italy.[83]

A Century of Governing with Informal Urbanization in Madrid, 1860s–1960s

CHARLOTTE VORMS

In Spain, as in the rest of southern Europe, so-called shantytowns epitomized the urban misery of the 1950s–1970s, a period of unprecedented urban growth fueled by a mass rural exodus. While the words used to refer to these spaces vary from one city to the next, they were known in Madrid as *chabolas* (shacks). The *chabolas* developed in the aftermath of Spain's Civil War (1936–1939) under Franco's dictatorship and are associated in Spanish historical memory with the penury and repression that characterized that period.[1] In 1960, there were a reported forty thousand *chabolas* in Madrid, accommodating approximately two hundred thousand inhabitants (around 10 percent of the population).[2] These *chabolas* housed many Andalusian families who had come to the capital in search of a better life. Unlike the *bidonvilles* of metropolitan France, which were mainly inhabited by foreigners and colonial populations,[3] Madrid's informal settlements (like those in Italy and Latin America) were populated by rural nationals from the country's poorest provinces who had the same legal status as the rest of Madrid's inhabitants. As a European city situated outside the colonial context with an exclusively national population, the case of Madrid shows that urban informality was not confined to the so-called cities of the South and invites us to complexify a narrative that associates urban informality mainly with societies shaped by structural inequalities derived from phenomena such as colonialism or slavery.

This *chabola* period is in fact just one chapter in a long history of the segmentation of Madrid's real estate market into two sectors, one official and another situated on the margins of the urban regulatory framework. Madrid exemplifies more clearly than any other European city that the informal urbanization of the mid-twentieth century was actually just a continuation, albeit in a new legal and political context and on an unprecedented scale, of a form of popular peripheral expansion that had existed since the mid-nineteenth century. Like the mid-twentieth-century *chabolas*, the peripheries of 1860s Madrid were also situated on the margins of urban regulation, having emerged on the fringes of the vast area that public authorities had earmarked for the bold new, modern city whose construction was underway. The *ensanche de población*—a national framework for urban expansion and modernization in nineteenth-century Spain—had the immediate effect in Madrid of dividing peripheral land into two spheres, which were being constructed in parallel, each according to completely different modalities.[4] Over more than a century, the successive incarnations of the *ensanche*, which evolved into a flagship tool of Spanish urban planning, also served to craft Madrid's informal peripheries, which were shaped by the fact that they were defined as spaces external to Madrid's zones of planned urbanization.

The case of Madrid highlights very precisely how self-built, self-regulated urbanization—only minimally supervised by the public authorities—both predated and survived the advent of large-scale urban planning. It showcases planning's role (and that of the law more generally) in dividing urban spaces and real estate markets into official and unofficial segments, the latter of which was defined as any urban space that had grown outside of the zone of urban planning. Self-built urbanization was relegated to the second segment by the invention of the first. This division made it possible to create affordable space for people of modest means even while inscribing Madrid in the transnational circuits of urban modernity. The specific characteristics of Spain's Restoration regime (1874–1923), which was based on institutionalized clientelism, perpetuated this segmentation and thus the division of the urban population into citizens with unequal rights. As such, Madrid's spatial division was also a mode of governance. The city of Madrid is thus a particularly illuminating laboratory for studying the mechanisms of the emergence of an informal sector and its perpetuation over time.

This phenomenon continued after the Civil War (1936–1939), but in this new context, it was viewed differently. An analysis of this post–Civil War period reveals how a long-standing reality was reformulated into a new type of problem, warranting a resignification of the term *chabola* to refer to it and the creation of new ad hoc policies to deal with it. The word *chabola*, originally of rural and Basque origin, had already been used to refer to urban dwellings in Madrid before the war, but it was rare. In the 1950s, it became the blanket term—at once administrative, scholarly, and everyday—for precarious housing among Spanish speakers across the region. By extending our analysis of Madrid's self-built urbanity from its nineteenth-century iterations to the twentieth century, when it was formulated as a problem and policies were implemented to respond to it, we can see how four different political regimes made varying uses of informal urbanization, gaining insight into both the inner workings of each regime and the ways in which informal urbanization can operate as a mode of governance.

A Century of Self-Built Urban Production

Madrid presents an interesting example of clear continuity in modes of self-built urban expansion. However, peripheral settlements have been named and represented differently over time, and they have also been targeted by discrete policies; because of this, the various phases of peripheral development have been constituted as distinct realities. In the nineteenth century, these spaces were known first as the *arrabales extramuros*. Following the adoption of the *ensanche de población* in 1860, they became known as the *arrabales del extrarradio*. Finally, under Francoism, they became known as *suburbios* or *barrios de chabolas*. As the nomenclature changed, so did the representations and policies related to these spaces and their populations. The two most pivotal moments—1860 and the decades from 1940 to 1960—correspond to two different stages in Spanish urban planning history and two periods of transformation in the urbanization regulatory framework.

In adopting these conceptualizations, scholars have approached the *arrabales del extrarradio* of the 1860s–1930s and the *chabola* settlements of the 1950s–1960s as two separate objects of study. However, if we set aside the ways in which public authorities governed peripheral settlements, the form of their buildings, their real estate dynamics, and the intrinsic mechanisms through which they were produced, clearly show they are part of the same phenomenon. For over 150 years, low-yielding agricultural land was subdivided by landowners and sold to workers (mainly men who had come from the countryside), who then auto-constructed modest family homes. Madrid's industrial economy centered on smaller-scale production until the second half of the twentieth century, and the construction sector was the main provider of jobs categorized as "industrial" before that period. Many of Madrid's manual workers were thus skilled builders.[5] Materially, the housing they produced changed little over time. Although plot sizes tended to decrease, as did home sizes (from around forty square meters to fifteen square meters or even less), the buildings were still mostly small one-story brick houses with tile and sometimes tin or even canvas roofs (fig. 3.1).

Cases of occupation without land rights—or invasions, as they were some-

FIGURE 3.1. Jaime el Conquistador *chabola* settlement, July 13, 1956 (photographed by Juan Miguel Pando Barrero). Source: Instituto del Patrimonio Cultural de España, MCD, PAN-072909.

times called in Latin America—were rare in Madrid. The small pockets of precarious housing built on land occupied without property rights were concentrated in specific places—Civil War ruins, sloped embankments, quarries abandoned by tile factories or brickworks, or riverbanks—and they sometimes took the form of caves. However, most of the large *chabola* settlements—and the ones that remained the most emblematic in people's memories, such as Pozo del Tío Raimundo and Orcasitas—developed from the subdivision of previously agricultural land, which was sold directly to workers by landowners. While these land sales were usually notarized and were not illegal according to Spanish property statutes, the lands' subdivision into building plots was illegal, as were the land-use changes and housing construction that followed the sales.

This same kind of informal urbanization can be observed in most of the countries examined in this volume. While "invasions" or "takeovers" (*tomas*) in countries such as Chile, Venezuela, Peru, and Brazil have attracted a lot of attention, these cases are far from representing the essence of informal urbanization. In Latin America and the French colonial Maghreb, subdivisions resembling that which occurred in Madrid are widespread not only in former agricultural areas but also on land where legal landownership is in question, on land where the supposed owner has in fact appropriated public property, and on land that cannot be sold because it is environmentally protected or collectively held (Mexican *ejido* land is a case in point).[6] These three kinds of subdivision are often rendered invisible by local terminologies that distinguish working-class peripheries from places that are labeled "shantytowns," such as Brazil's *favelas* and Argentina's *villas miseria*, but the practice of irregular subdivision modulates property relations in a wide variety of temporal and geographical settings.

In the Beginning There Was the *Arrabal*

Urban growth was very slow in Madrid until the last third of the nineteenth century. The city's population increased from 200,000 at the beginning of the century to only 280,000 in 1857, just before the *ensanche de población* was introduced. It then doubled over the next four decades to 575,000 in 1900 and only really accelerated with a period of economic growth that began during World War I, reaching 1 million in 1930. Spain's true urban transition, however, came in the 1950s and 1960s. Madrid's population rose from 1.3 million in 1940 to over 3 million in 1970, by which time the city's suburban municipalities had also begun to expand.[7]

As in other cities, these uneven waves of demographic growth led to the densification of Madrid's old center and to the spatial expansion of the built environment. Between the building of the last city wall in 1762 and the adoption of the *ensanche de población* plan in 1860, urban expansion was driven solely by a succession of individual decisions, taken by private actors. The houses they constructed outside the city wall—which were located mainly to the north of the city in the first half of the nineteenth century, forming the *arrabal* of Chamberí—were Madrid's first modern examples of self-built, working-class urbanization.[8] They developed as an extension of the built-up area. Landowners would parcel out their land and sometimes construct houses themselves, and business owners—primarily in the building materials sector (tile factories and brickworks)—would also sometimes construct housing for their workers. Thus, the neighborhood gradually came into being. The local roads, which were sometimes summarily laid out by the landowner, remained in private ownership until the introduction of the *ensanche de población*, which encompassed Chamberí.

The Creation of a Modern New City and
Its *Extrarradio* Peripheries

This situation completely changed in 1860, when Madrid adopted the *ensanche de población* plan, designed by the engineer Carlos María de Castro. A 1,500-hectare ring around the old city, delimited by the fiscal wall, was declared "urban." There, the municipal authority expropriated the space necessary to construct the streets, which were to be laid out in a grid pattern. After that, they leveled the ground and installed the infrastructure for urban services. All construction in the square blocks delimited by that grid pattern had to meet strict architectural standards. The *ensanche de población* was Spain's attempt to bring order to nineteenth-century urban growth and the problems it posed. The *ensanches* (understood here as expansion zones) were conceived not as peripheries but as new urban centers. Just like Paris's Haussmannian boulevards or Vienna's Ring, the *ensanches* aimed to create residential districts for the urban bourgeoisie, prestigious addresses for business, and spaces for theaters, restaurants, department stores, and other symbols of nineteenth-century modernity. In this vein, even cities with slow urban growth sought to create *ensanches*.[9] The *ensanches de población* were, in short, the Spanish expression of the modernizing impulse.

Because the municipality of Madrid extended over a very large area, the new *ensanche* zone did not extend to the communal perimeter, leaving a third ring, measuring some four thousand hectares that was intended for agricultural use. Within the *ensanche* zone, the development of self-built *arrabales* like Chamberí came to an abrupt halt because they did not conform to the type of urbanization that planners foresaw. The actors who had driven Madrid's self-built urbanization did not have the financial capacity to build new dwellings to the plan's high specifications. In addition, the price of land in the area shot up along with the promise of its bright future as a modern, well-built, well-equipped district. The *ensanche* plan thus had an immediate effect on the real estate market. The *ensanche*'s perimeter was clear on maps of property values long before it became visible in the landscape. Land within the *ensanche* could fetch prices between ten and three hundred times higher than land in the agricultural outer ring, which would come to be called the *extrarradio*.[10]

Simultaneously, the kinds of people who had settled in Chamberí were becoming ever more numerous as Madrid's demographic growth accelerated as a result of migration from the countryside. They could not afford to pay rents high enough to make it profitable to construct apartment blocks to the standards required by the *ensanche*. As a consequence, the growth of popular neighborhoods spilled out into new peripheries, this time located beyond the *ensanche* zone, which remained empty as it awaited development. These new settlements were the product of an even cheaper form of urbanization, located much further away from the existing city than the previous generation of *arrabales* and aimed at a less heterogeneous clientele, comprising mainly low-income working people. The relegation of working-class urbanization to lands beyond the official frontier of urbanization also contributed to longer-term degradation because everything built there was isolated from major urban service networks.

The first building plots in this third zone, which was in theory reserved for agricultural use, were sold a year after the introduction of the *ensanche* plan. With the exception of land adjacent to the small number of watercourses running through this territory, the area's dry lands had a very low agricultural yield. Hence, with no plans in place to formally approve the land for urbanization, the landowners resolved that, on balance, the best way of making a profit on the land was to subdivide it for a working-class clientele. No attempt was made to develop or service either the streets or the small plots (three hundred square meters for a typical plot in the Prosperidad neighborhood), which were sold to working-class families who would build themselves small homes in their spare time. This was the origin of the *extrarradio arrabales*, which developed in line with Madrid's demographic growth, particularly between the 1890s and the 1920s, before the Great Depression slowed down expansion and the Spanish Civil War brought it to a complete stop. In 1930, 145,000 people lived in the *extrarradio*, or 15 percent of Madrid's population. Built in the middle of fields, with no water supply or sewage system, no amenities, and a configuration that was a hodgepodge of individual ad hoc decisions, these peripheries quickly constituted a major problem for public health and urban planning.

Informality as a System of Urban Government during the Restoration

The *ensanche* plan and its regulations cut through the heart of Madrid's municipal territory. They divided the city and its real estate market into two discrete segments. These two spaces became a permanent feature of Madrid's morphology, and the two segments of the real estate market began to undergo divergent evolution in terms of both price and the nature of their transactions. The resulting peripheral city did not correspond to Madrid's extant urbanization or housing standards, and from the 1900s onward, its obvious material shortcomings led to long-term stigmatization. Thus, Madrid's first informal sector was born; it was the result of a legal vacuum that was consolidated rather than filled, bequeathing to future generations a problem that only grew with time.

The peripheral neighborhoods that emerged in these years were not technically illegal. The *ensanche* plan provided that "any future buildings constructed outside [the *ensanche*] should follow a plan previously approved by the Government."[11] However, no such plan was ever drawn up. In addition, the subdivision and sale of land was not subject to any specific regulations or authorization requests. There was simply no provision for any transactions in this territory outside of the agricultural land market, which was sluggish because of the area's low agricultural yield. Lot sales were therefore treated strictly as private law transactions, carried out before a notary like any other land sale.

In 1892, the municipality adopted new ordinances, which included provisions for private streets. Such streets now had to meet minimum standards and required authorization. The landowner also had to pave the roads and install and maintain the sidewalks, lighting, water, and sewage systems. The transfer of private streets to the public domain was conditional on the prior installation of all utilities by the landowner. Thus, in theory, all landowners were now required to design street systems complete with urban services and submit their plans for municipal authorization. However, in practice, these ordinances, which had undoubtedly been conceived with the *ensanche* zone in mind, were never applied to the *extrarradio*. Until the 1930s, Madrid's *extrarradio arrabales* were therefore subdivided without authorization, much less adherence to planning regulations.

Although the subdivision of rural property into building plots was not regulated, all construction carried out on municipal territory required a building permit. In the early 1860s, the first building permit applications from the *extrarradio* were submitted to the Ensanche Commission, which was responsible for the official and unofficial expansion of the city. The committee's director, Carlos María de Castro—who was also the author of the *ensanche* plan—greeted them with indifference. Because the land was located "at a great distance from the boundary" and posed no danger to the city under construction, he saw no reason not to approve them.[12] The municipal authority's and Castro's initial approach highlights the *ensanche*'s function as a status symbol. The aim was not so much to control the city's expansion or respond to housing shortages in an age of urban growth as to build a residential area that conformed to international standards of urban modernity and could thus serve as a representative space. The *extrarradio* neighborhoods were thus tolerated as long as they did not compromise the modern city under construction—because, after all, working-class families had to settle somewhere.

In the early days, district authorities would verbally authorize construction on the *extrarradio* plots, thus exempting the plot owners from having to apply for an official permit. However, the municipal authorities clarified this situation in 1872, reminding owners that they needed to have a formally approved building permit for all new construction, even in the *extrarradio*, and inviting anyone who did not have one to regularize their situation. When this circular was published, plot owners in the Prosperidad neighborhood responded with a collective petition.[13] It was the first of many. The signatories, twenty-five in total, demanded a lower building permit fee and an exemption from the obligation to present a plan approved by an architect. To justify these two demands, they deployed an argument based on the principle of equity. They asked to pay a reduced building permit fee because they did not benefit from any of the municipality's public urban amenities. And they did not need an architect because they built only very humble homes using low-grade materials. The tax on the building permit was thus understood as a charge for the use of urban amenities and services. These plot and home-owners were not asking for access to the urban modernity enjoyed by the "people of Madrid," but for a fee that was, like their urbanization, second class. They were not challenging the sociospatial hierarchy; they recognized their status as a social group that was subordinate to those inhabiting the city center. They were just asking that their obligations be made consistent with their rights. The municipal authorities accepted the validity of the petitioners' argument. These people received less, so it was fair that they pay less. They therefore decided to apply the tax rate normally paid for extension and renovation projects to new construction and generalized this practice to the whole of the *extrarradio*. This pragmatic decision paved the way for the creation of a precarious class of building permits.

The municipal architect who dealt with this petition suggested that a clause be included in the permit releasing the municipal authority from any responsibilities that could be incumbent upon it in the future. This amounted to depriving these second-class permit holders of the benefits of public protection. The new building permits issued for the *extrarradio* contained two noteworthy stipulations: First, "The city does not commit to providing paving, sewerage, lighting, or any other public services in the locality in question."[14] Second, "The interested party must understand that this concession does not give them any rights in the event that the city's development projects render it necessary to survey the alignments and gradients in this zone."[15]

The latter clause raised concerns among the plot owners in Prosperidad, who were attentive to the law and mindful of equity. The twenty-five signatories of the original petition wrote again to request that the second clause be removed and expose how unjust it was:

> We have no right to claim any services nor compensation of any kind in the locality in question. We were greatly surprised when we read the words underlined above. We analyzed them carefully numerous times and always came to the same conclusion: that they meant we had no right to compensation for any wrongs or damages that the municipal authority might inflict upon us. That is, it can, without compensating us, destroy our properties and strip us of our possessions, whether it be to widen an avenue, to create a rural road, to carry out works on area streets, or for any other unforeseen reason. Although we are firmly convinced that this cannot actually be the municipal authority's decision, because it is unjust and despicable, it is quite logical to interpret these underlined words in the way that we have, meaning that our right of ownership would be reduced to a myth with no value whatsoever in any transactions. . . .
>
> Since we contribute proportionate to the benefits we receive, our property must have the same guarantees and rights as those of other inhabitants complying with municipal regulations and ordinances.[16]

This time, however, they lost their battle. The municipal authority claimed that they had misunderstood the clause's meaning and refused to remove it. The state would endorse this decision twenty-two years later with the Royal Order of September 4, 1902. This confirmed the legitimacy of the clause, which could therefore be entered in the Land Registry.[17] The municipality had thus created a precarious building permit that did not guarantee ownership of the buildings in question. At the end of the 1910s, a municipal engineer denounced the provisions as contrary to property law.[18] The permit was in fact just a certificate of provisional tolerance, a precarious authorization of use rights. As long as the buildings did not interfere with municipal projects, they were not prohibited. This permit was the most obvious expression of the public authorities' paradoxical attitude in managing the urbanization of the *extrarradio*. It was tolerated, and in practice they controlled it, but it was not officially recognized, and tolerance was not accompanied by the preventive resolution of foreseeable and anticipated conflicts. The few elements of regulation applied to the *extrarradio* projects thus aimed not to formalize them but to condemn them to precariousness.

This policy of tolerating a situation in practice while at the same time condemning it to legal precariousness and depriving it of any rights is at the heart of the mechanism of informal urbanization. Indeed, it can be found in most of the case studies presented in this book.[19] It develops when a public authority puts in place urban regulations that cannot be applied to all the spaces inhabited by a population because they are too stringent. The aim in Madrid was to produce a modern city, the *ensanche*. The urbanization standards required to achieve this effectively excluded a large part of the population from the legal city. The popular city was therefore consigned to a vital margin, tolerated so long as it did not get in the way but bereft of rights and relegated to a well-defined state of precarity. Because this periphery was needed to accommodate the humble households that were arriving in the city in increasing numbers, tolerating it without granting it any rights was in fact the most economical solution. New housing could be constructed below the standard required for urban modernity—and therefore cheaply—but it was not officially recognized.

The consequence of this mode of urban government was that part of the population was deprived of the benefits of public protection, namely ownership and occupation rights. They were similarly deprived of urban services and networks provided at public expense, precisely at a time when these were undergoing modernization. In fact, while the clause that seemed most unjust to the Prosperidad petitioners was that the owner of a building whose construction had been duly authorized had no guarantee of their right of ownership over it, the fact that the permit did not confer a right to urban facilities was also extremely significant. This clause clearly stated what was at stake when authorities chose to tolerate this impoverished urbanization without officially recognizing it. In the last third of the century, Madrid was undergoing a radical overhaul of its public lighting, pavement, water and gas supply, transport, and sewage and wastewater disposal systems, entailing new public costs. Madrid's informal regions emerged precisely at this moment, and that made it all the more urgent to delimit the perimeter of the city with rights. In the same way that political rights forced states to define the contours of nationality and social rights obliged them to control migration and establish which foreigners were entitled to benefits, so the renewal and expansion of urban facilities meant that the official city's legal and administrative boundary—which in Madrid was also a spatial boundary—had to be mapped out.[20] Madrid's modernization was possible because it did not include the whole population. Finally, the authority's decision to tolerate informal urbanization without clarifying its administrative and regulatory situation also led to the development and consolidation of a situation that would, over the long term, prove both inextricable and costly.

Planning and the Penalization of Vernacular
Urbanization under Francoism

The second pivotal moment in Madrid's history of informal urbanization came with a 1944 law that established the principle of regional planning, inaugurating the era of zoning master plans for large cities. The accompanying package of measures, which were redrafted a decade later in the 1956 Land Law, definitively relegated the popular peripheral urbanization that had been happening in Madrid for almost eighty years to a precisely defined state of illegality.

Before looking at these reforms, it is essential to understand the context in which they were introduced. The country was on its knees after the Civil War. Madrid had been wrecked by bombing and was exhausted and starving after more than two years of siege. The Spanish Republic had been proclaimed in Madrid. Along with Barcelona, Madrid had been one of the most powerful Republican bastions during the war. Nonetheless, the architects of the Franco dictatorship chose to retain Madrid as the capital of the new regime after the war. The regime therefore established itself in a hostile city that it abhorred and set out to control the population and subject it to a new public order. Citizens were closely monitored by the police, the Falange (the dictatorship's sole legal party), and tax authorities.[21] A state of war remained in force until 1948, almost ten years after the Republic had capitulated, and the city's government was militarized for a long time. In this context, the popular peripheral neighborhoods, which had been the cradle of socialism and a refuge for anarchist networks, became the object of particular attention.[22] The new regime launched a "redemption of the *suburbio*" program, which consisted of urban redevelopment and the social supervision of the peripheral population by the Catholic Church, which redesigned its parish network and developed its educational, health, and social enterprises in these spaces. The regime's treatment of the *chabolas* and their inhabitants can be properly understood only when this context is taken into account.

The 1944 law that laid the foundation for the planning of Madrid established that "any subdivision of land not considered agricultural" required authorization and that "no buildings may be constructed without the prior installation of utility and drainage services in the area."[23] No construction would be allowed without a building permit, which would be issued only if the project complied with Madrid's master plan. Finally, subdivision and building permits were both subject to the prescriptions set out in the city's urban planning documents (i.e., the master plan and the local implementation plans). Although the subdivision process was referenced and regulated, the control procedures and sanctions defined by the implementation decree of October 17, 1947, concerned only construction.[24] Sanctions could range from a simple fine to complete demolition. A building inspection service was created to control peripheral territory. By 1957, this had expanded into a full-fledged police force for the periphery, whose main task was to control and repress informal urbanization.

Given the misery that reigned in Madrid in the 1940s, as well as the destruction wrought by wartime bombings and the resurging of migration in the mid-1940s, the proliferation of precarious housing was a necessary solution. By introducing urban planning regulations that it did not have the means or perhaps even the will to enforce, the Spanish state cemented the exclusion of an increasingly large number of urban working-class households from the legal housing market and put them at the mercy of its repressive measures. In addition, a 1946 urban lease law consolidated rent control legislation that Spain had introduced in 1920, in step with the adoption of a range of similar rent control measures in other Western European countries. This further reinforced the exclusion of new working-class households from the legal market. By making leases hereditary, the law essentially froze the rental market in perpetuity, making it extremely difficult for newcomers to gain a foothold. This conundrum was the subject of a 1959 comedy, *El Pisito* (*The Little Apartment*), which tells the story of a young man who resolves to marry the sick old woman that he lodges with in the hope of inheriting her leasehold rights and thus being able to marry the girl he loves.[25]

A new land law, adopted on May 12, 1956, further reinforced the illegality of unauthorized urbanization and gave the town planning authority the power and means to repress it.[26] This law, which remains the basis of Spanish town planning law to this day, enshrined the principle of public involvement in urban development and placed planning at the heart of urbanistic activity.[27] Landowners therefore lost their central role in the production of the city to the developers.[28] In practice, public authorities and large developers shared the planning role, and major developers' projects would generally be approved regardless of whether or not they complied with the master plan. Developers thus become the dominant actors in Madrid's urbanization.[29]

The new land law reiterated the provisions of the 1944 law, and it also prohibited subdivision in areas without a local implementation plan. The notaries and employees of Spain's Land Registry served as guarantors of the legality of all transactions, as they could register a land subdivision only if presented with a valid subdivision permit. This law prohibited construction on any plot of land resulting from a subdivision that did not comply with these

rules. Finally, it also gave the local town planning authority the power to suspend any subdivisions, service installations, or construction that did not ad-
here to these rules or to the plan for which the permit was granted. The local
planning authority was authorized to either demolish or regularize any such
constructions. In the case of unauthorized subdivision, Article 171 allowed
the authority to expropriate the land without the need to present a project
for its use. The 1956 Land Law thus definitively discredited the self-built, vernacular mode of production that had prevailed in Madrid's peripheries since
the nineteenth century and that had enabled successive generations of rural
migrants to settle in Madrid.

From this point on, no space could change use without its developer requesting authorization from the competent regulatory body and complying
with the provisions of relevant urban planning documents. Furthermore,
changes in land use were possible only in areas earmarked for urbanization.
The limitation of property rights that naturally accompanied the development
of the urban planning law went hand in hand with the emergence of a new
professional group in Franco's Spain: real estate developers.[30] Often emerging
from the construction industry, some of these individuals were favored by the
Franco regime because of their engagement in the self-designated "national"
camp during the Civil War.[31] The decisions taken by the town planning board
show that it did not hesitate to revise its urban planning documents to meet
these entrepreneurs' demands. Taking advantage of public construction
subsidies, these developers built huge housing complexes (e.g., Banús constructed twenty thousand dwellings over three phases in the Pilar district of
Madrid) and accumulated vast fortunes.

Just like their *extrarradio* predecessors eighty years earlier, the landowners with properties that the master plan did not zone for urban construction reacted to the sudden devaluation of their land by subdividing it for a
working-class clientele to try to extract at least some profit. Again, like their
counterparts in the *extrarradio*, they sold off small building plots to manual
workers arriving from the impoverished countryside. However, this time,
their sales were completely illegal. The landowners would subdivide their
land, and buyers would build on it without making any attempt to apply for
a permit, because they knew it would never be approved. The administration
soon began to use the word *clandestine* to describe these activities.

This illegal urbanization came under increasing pressure from public authorities as it continued to expand during the 1950s with the acceleration in
migratory flows and the revival of construction, which was encouraged by
the state. In 1957, a decree and several articles of the law establishing a Social
Emergency Plan for Madrid specified how it would be impeded. The decree

of August 23, 1957, enacted "rules to avoid clandestine settlements in Madrid." Its objective was to limit migration, which it linked to the "systematic con- struction of *chabolas*, caves, and similar structures on the city's periphery." The decree required anyone wishing to settle in Madrid to present a docu- ment to the mayor of their commune of residence certifying that they had "adequate housing" in place. Employers were mobilized to enforce this mi- gration control. They had to "refrain from hiring workers who cannot prove that they had previously fixed their administrative residence in Madrid." The town planning authority was permitted "to demolish without delay . . . caves, *chabolas*, *barracas*, and similar constructions built without a permit on Ma- drid's periphery and to initiate the process of expropriating the land thus oc- cupied," extending those actions if necessary to any "surrounding unfenced areas presenting the risk of an illegal occupation." The inhabitants of the de- molished structures had to be transferred to their former domiciles (it was assumed the inhabitants came from outside the city). Finally, the decree pro- vided for the creation of a surveillance service for Madrid's periphery, which was in practice ultimately entrusted to a corps of the Civil Guard deployed specially for this purpose.[32]

The text of the Social Emergency Plan (PUS in its Spanish acronym), which was adopted a few months later, included and clarified these provi- sions. It listed the offenses that constituted "gross misconduct" and desig- nated those who were responsible for them. Every stage in the process of unauthorized peripheral urbanization was condemned, from the subdivision of land and construction without a permit to the sale, rental, and occupation of buildings. Anyone associated with these activities was held liable, and all the relevant actors were listed, including the landowner, the builder, and the inhabitant. Sanctions consisted of the voiding of transactions, the seizure and demolition of buildings without compensation, the issuing of fines, and the transfer of inhabitants to their former commune of residence. The voiding of transactions pertaining to land and buildings was accompanied by expropria- tion or outright confiscation, depending on the owner's degree of liability.

This extremely repressive legislation, which regulated both urbanization and internal migration in a single policy, was probably inspired by the mea- sures implemented in Rome by the fascist regime, which served as a model for Francoism in many areas. Fascism regulated migration to the Italian capi- tal and purported to "repatriate" the inhabitants of the demolished shanties to their home provinces.[33] This kind of policy was common across the globe. For example, Casablanca's "floating populations" were expelled to their re- gions of origin in the interwar period, and a similar project was envisaged for Recife and Rio in the 1930s.[34] These policies were based on the idea, common

to many societies, notably in Latin America, that the informal city was populated by economically superfluous people who were attracted by the illusion
of an easy life and therefore destined to swell the ranks of the marginalized
and destitute, weighing on the urban economy.[35]

The two complementary regulations led to the construction of informal
urbanization as a specific category in Madrid, distinct from other infringe-
ments of urban planning law. Their targets were impoverished self-built
housing developments that lacked urban amenities and had been typical of
the peripheral expansion of Madrid since the previous century.

All the same, the definition of this new legal category of informal urbanization in Madrid was still very imprecise. It even varied between the two
texts. The decree targeted "the caves, *chabolas*, *barracas*, and similar constructions built without a permit on Madrid's periphery," while the PUS referred to "buildings of all kinds, built clandestinely to serve as housing." The
decree combined a legal criterion (the existence of a permit) and a criterion
of material precariousness implicitly expressed by the words *cuevas*, *chabolas*,
and *barracas*, while the PUS retained only the legal criterion. Finally, these
texts constituted a highly repressive framework that gave the urban planning
authorities in charge of Madrid extensive powers to expeditiously clear the
targeted areas and expel their inhabitants.

To enforce these regulations, the Civil Guard was placed at the disposal of
urban planning authorities to monitor the city's periphery and impede illegal
urbanization. Their instructions encouraged the corps to maximize the ways
it might apply pressure. It was to "prohibit any type of improvement to existing buildings and more importantly any extensions or subdivisions thereof."[36]
The corps thus had to endeavor to make life difficult for the inhabitants by
preventing them from carrying out necessary repairs, such as patching up
their roofs. To prevent construction, it sought to starve the site in question of
necessary resources, principally by reducing the supply of water and building
materials. The corps was also urged to obstruct the activity of building materials companies known to supply illegal building projects by blocking road
access to their sites or using administrative tools to harass them: "You shall
endeavor, by inspecting building permits and industrial permits, checking
that tax payments are up to date, etc. etc., to shut them down."

Because the police kept a register of infringers, repeat offenders could be
quickly identified. The instructions stipulated that the corps was to detain
these individuals "for as long as possible" and "seek a pretext from the provincial labor committee to withdraw or suspend their work permit."[37] The
authorities were thus applying pressure simultaneously to the two essential
components of survival, namely housing and work. This is a constant in the

modern history of migration control. Work and housing are interlinked, and residence permits are conditional on access to the legal segments of these two markets. The exchanges between the inhabitants and the administration (in the form of summonses, correspondence, and official reports on face-to-face meetings) reveal that the inhabitants were now living in fear of being thrown out onto the street.[38] *La Piqueta*, a typical postwar social realist novel published in 1959, tells the story of a family from Jaén (Andalusia) in the fifteen days between the announcement of their *chabola*'s imminent demolition and its execution, which led also to the family's dispersal. The novel expresses the powerlessness of these rural emigrants in the face of a reality that they could only endure and documents a power relationship wherein they were completely dominated.[39]

A Century of Building outside the Plan

If we think about the mechanisms of urban production that have shaped Madrid, we can thus observe a perennial mode of expansion based on the simple subdivision of agricultural land and auto-construction by workers. The social function of this mode of urbanization had been evident since the beginning of the nineteenth century: it provided shelter for working-class families, particularly those from the countryside who did not yet have a home in the city. Subsequently, when authorities sought to promote a second, more modern mode of urbanization through regulations and public policies, they differentiated it from that older form. As a result, the first, perennial mode was misidentified as a new and problematic phenomenon and quickly stigmatized. In other words, the invention of the *ensanche* zone—the more modern mode—actually created the *extrarradio arrabales*, which epitomized the wrong kind of urbanization for eighty years, until the next stage came along.[40] At that point, Francoist urban laws introduced modern urban planning to Spain, inventing new urbanization zones and providing a solution to the problem of the *extrarradio* by filling the legal vacuum that had allowed the informal *arrabales* to flourish. The new urbanization zones were generally built by one or more large developers and gave rise to vast urban complexes, mainly composed of apartment blocks with identical architecture throughout. These modern neighborhoods have been widely criticized for their insufficiencies, lack of basic amenities, and poor workmanship. They were nevertheless markers of modernity in Spain from the 1950s to the 1970s, just like the large housing estates constructed in the French suburbs, across Eastern Europe, and in various Latin American cities during that same period.[41] As with the *ensanche* a century earlier, these new districts were the product of real estate transactions that yielded large profits and drove economic growth. However, the counterpart to this new official urbanization was the emergence of another wave of informal urbanization. Now referred to as *chabolas*, this sector was identified as a new problem and became the target of increasingly repressive public policies.

Over the whole century examined here, Madrid's informal urbanization was defined as that which was built outside of the plan—this defined the infraction. The prominence of the urban plan as a zoning instrument in Spanish planning from the mid-nineteenth century on thus actually explains the prevalence of this type of informality. The main tool that produced Spain's model urban spaces, epitomized in the *ensanche* zones, also produced the cities' informal districts.

From a Regime of Exception to a Regime of Extensive, Discretionary Repressive Power

While the phenomenon we are interested in—self-built, popular urbanization—remained the same throughout the period, it was shaped into distinct avatars as urban planning's regulatory frameworks evolved over time. However, there was one major difference between the two phases—*extrarradio* and *chabolas*—described here. The future of the two spaces, and therefore of their populations, diverged. While the *extrarradio* neighborhoods were gradually supplied with urban amenities and ultimately integrated into the urban fabric, the *chabola* settlements were mostly demolished. In both cases, the existence of this segment, its maintenance in a precarious legal situation, and the modalities of its administration were a way of governing poverty that was based on an organization of powers specific to each period. We now turn to this last point.

Between 1860 and the 1920s, municipal public authorities tolerated the development of the *extrarradio* neighborhoods and were keen to mark their presence within them. The first church in Prosperidad was built through a public subscription, and when it was consecrated, the district head and a number of other municipal dignitaries took the opportunity to visit the neighborhood for the first time. Municipal authorities would also always send representatives to festivals held in the neighborhood. They were responding to invitations from the inhabitants, who sought to gain official protection in that way. The visits also allowed officials to mark their presence (and therefore their authority) in the territory. Municipal authorities aimed to know and control peripheral urbanization, which is why they would also remind the inhabitants of the requirement to apply for authorization for any building projects.

Although they had been told they would not be entitled to public services, plot owners and inhabitants of the *extrarradio* soon began to demand them, notably a public water fountain and pavement and lighting for some streets. Until municipal administration was reorganized under the dictatorship of Primo de Rivera (1923–1930), the *extrarradio* remained an area officially reserved for rural use. There was no budget or procedure in place for its urban development. Nevertheless, in the 1890s, municipal authorities gradually paved and lit some peripheral streets. In accordance with the *extrarradio* peripheries' place in the urban hierarchy, it became common practice to carry out these projects with materials (e.g., cobblestones, lampposts) that had been reclaimed from the older streets of the modernizing urban center. Similarly, when public fountains were installed in the *extrarradio* in Madrid's northeast, they were supplied not by the city's drinking water network—the connection would have been very costly—but by the irrigation canal in the city's east, which did not provide clean drinking water. These works were carried out piecemeal, without an overarching framework or specific policy or program in place, and in violation of extant regulations.

During the Restoration regime (1874–1923), characterized by caciquism, a form of clientelism institutionalized on a national scale, the inhabitants' demands for infrastructure were satisfied with one-off projects, such as the installation of lighting or paving on a particular street.[42] These works were carried out on ad hoc budget lines and outside the normal administrative mechanisms, because none had been designed for these areas. Generally speaking, funding for such works resulted from lobbying by a well-connected landowner or a benefactor with a foot in the door of municipal administration. Yet the streets thus improved remained under private ownership, leading to increasingly intricate legal situations, which made the possibility of regularization ever more difficult. This mode of government, which could be described as informal because it was based on exceptional measures and did not comply with the rules in force, allowed individuals at all levels to consolidate their position. The local councilor who interceded on behalf of small plot-holder acquaintances thus secured their votes as his protégés.[43] The prominent figure who owned several rental properties or a particularly important business in the area would use his connections with the municipal authorities to establish himself as a benefactor among his neighbors. This system of government through a regime of exception, while it ran counter to the public interest, served a multitude of individual objectives, and the accumulation of these made the transition to another system difficult and costly.

This balance came under threat in the 1920s with the acceleration of Spain's rural exodus, which caused a new wave of expansion in the *extrar-*

radio and gave rise to a new generation of inhabitants. The result was an internal segmentation of the *extrarradio* population. On the one hand, there were the descendants of the first inhabitants, who lived in the oldest streets, which were equipped with at least some urban amenities and now constituted the heart of the district. On the other hand, there were the newcomers, who settled on recently allotted land that was still under construction and not yet supplied with any amenities. In this context, urban demands became politicized. The early petitions were replaced by demands that did more to go on the offensive, which were soon channeled through the Partido Socialista Obrero Español (PSOE, or Spanish Socialist Workers' Party) and incorporated into its discourse. This division of the social unity of the *extrarradio* neighborhoods contributed to a crisis in the system of urban governance that had existed since the 1860s. It was one of the factors in the crisis of the Restoration regime and one cause for the rise in social conflict that characterized the 1910s, leading to the establishment of the Primo de Rivera dictatorship in 1923 and the Second Republic in 1931.

The first Republican municipal government, dominated by the socialist group (1931–1933), sought to pursue a social urban policy that rebalanced the distribution of urban resources in favor of the peripheries. During a period that is too short to properly assess, it was torn between providing instant satisfaction to the demands of peripheral inhabitants by installing services on a mass scale or regularizing the settlement's status and thus preventing the problem from recurring. To this end, it envisaged the municipalization of all peripheral land, but it never ultimately managed to implement that plan. The question of the informal peripheries was still not resolved when the Civil War broke out, although urban amenities were nevertheless slowly installed.

Today, this generation of peripheries is integrated into Madrid's urban space.[44] Ownership of the buildings—which, as we have seen, was not theoretically guaranteed by building permits—was never challenged. Successive generations have been able to reap the benefits of the first small, working-class properties built in these neighborhoods from the 1860s onward by setting up workshops in them or using them as rentals. In short, they have inherited part of the added value produced by changes in urban land use. The *extrarradio* neighborhoods have thus, for some of the working-class families who settled there in the nineteenth century, been a vector of social advancement.

The situation was very different, however, for the rural families who first arrived in Madrid in the 1950s and settled in the *chabolas*. In terms of function and its intrinsic logic, there was clear continuity from one period to the next in this informal sector, but over time the Francoist administration came to govern the *chabolas* very different from how the Restoration regime had governed the *extrarradio*. Although the law consigned these peripheries to a reinforced and well-defined illegality in the mid-1940s, public authorities initially seemed to accommodate their presence. Informal urbanization even had some defenders in high places, who saw it as a necessary solution to the housing shortage.[45] In the mid-1950s, however, the policy changed, and lawmakers constructed a legal arsenal to extinguish the *chabolas*. The archives of the planning authorities show that this arsenal was indeed used. Why this change? Why did Francoism not continue to govern the illegal peripheries in the same way that the Restoration had governed the *extrarradio* neighborhoods? Part of the answer, of course, lies in the evolution of urban planning and housing standards and in the scale of urban growth. Moreover, it is not surprising that a government as repressive as the Francoist regime would pursue a policy targeting poor families living in shanties. But it is worth deepening these explanations.

Illegal urbanization was identified as a major problem and became the target of public action beginning in the first third of the 1950s. In the context of Spain's negotiations to join the Western Bloc of the Cold War, which began in 1951–1952, the desire to project a positive image of Spain and its capital put the *chabolas* in prominent relief. In addition, the extensive informal occupation of the land around the city proved a hindrance to the state's plans when it launched the initial phases of its policy to stimulate the construction industry, notably in 1954 through the introduction of an affordable housing law and a national housing plan. The government's aim was to recover the land, which was sometimes relatively well situated, for the construction of this new housing. Madrid's Social Emergency Plan, launched in 1957, therefore designated the *chabolas* as its main target at the same time as it set up a support system for private construction. This is the context in which the term *chabola* came to gradually replace others.

This stage marked the end of the integration of Madrid's self-built, popular urban spaces. From the mid-1950s onward, they were earmarked for demolition, although this sometimes did not happen until decades later. The implementation of a plan to demolish and reconstruct an impoverished area rather than gradually integrate it into the city required either a strong commitment to social policy—which was obviously not the case here—or the belief that it would be economically profitable and politically possible. Profitability was assured thanks to Madrid's strong real estate growth from the mid-1950s onward, which was supported by public authorities and orchestrated by a construction sector newly structured around a few large developers. As to the political challenge of forcibly dislodging and displacing large contingents of people, the Francoist regime's repressive character spoke for itself. At the time of the removals, the *chabola* neighborhoods were more essential to the city than ever; in 1960, they housed around 10 percent of Madrid's population. Nevertheless, public authorities would evacuate and raze the zones earmarked for development. These resettlement operations offered rehousing only to families deemed meritorious (around 45 percent of the families were excluded from rehousing in the 1954–1955 removals).[46] Some rehousing was a clear improvement vis-à-vis the conditions that the families had known in the *chabolas*, but some was more akin to temporary shelter. The division of the inhabitants into families deserving of public housing and families that would be evicted without further compensation was an opportunity for public authorities to exercise their discretionary power and to display their paternalistic benevolence toward the deserving poor.[47]

In the areas not immediately affected by Franco's development project, existing informal settlements remained and fulfilled their social function of accommodating poor households. However, whenever the police discovered a construction site or an unauthorized new house in the area, they would report the offender for violating the law. Theoretically, in accordance with the 1957 legislation, the police report would be followed by the eviction of the family and the demolition of their home without compensation or any other form of due process. The demolition registers for the years 1961 to 1965 show that there were indeed a large number of demolitions during this period, but only between 26 percent and 45 percent (depending on the year) of the buildings whose construction had been the subject of an official police report seem to have been actually demolished.[48] More generally, these repressive demolitions also served to remind the *chabolas'* inhabitants that they were in the wrong and therefore at the constant mercy of the authorities. Their permanence in the spaces was tolerated only very temporarily and as an act of goodwill.

As in the previous period, this type of housing fulfilled a social function, and the public authorities were aware of its usefulness. However, unlike the previous period, the regulations were clear, and the illegality of the *chabolas* was unambiguous. Informality was no longer a system of governance in the sense that it had been in the previous period, when a gray zone had been cautiously elaborated and maintained. Yet it remained a system of governance in the sense that sanctions were applied differently depending on the specific case and actors at all levels of the administration made extensive use of their discretionary power. The archives show that some demolitions were canceled, and some constructions or renovations were tolerated, either to avoid the inhabitants' mobilization or as a gesture of "humanity." There are also numerous references in the archives and in oral testimonies suggesting that a number of actors would take money in return for their leniency. The *chabolas'* vague definition—highlighted earlier—allowed authorities to apply the law according to their own criteria, using informal urbanization as a justification for their power to dispose however they wished of peripheral land and the families who had settled there.

Conclusion

The Madrid case shows how urban planning legislation—and especially the urbanization plan, which was such an important tool in the Spanish tradition—created the city's informal urbanization zones by relegating working-class urban expansion first to a gray zone and then to illegality. Constantly, for more than a century, the same urban planning formulations that drove the construction of the modern showcase city also led to the construction of built spaces that fell far below prevailing urban standards. The new modern neighborhoods could not exist without the informal neighborhoods, which fulfilled the function of providing a roof over the heads of working-class families, especially those new to the city. The population of this impoverished periphery, which was tolerated but not recognized, was condemned to precarity and to a form of second-class urban citizenship in which they were excluded from access to urban amenities and their ownership and tenure rights were not protected.

In the *extrarradio* in the 1870s, municipal authorities conceived a policy of precarious tolerance, which would theoretically have allowed them to one day demolish self-built homes without compensating the owners or occupants. It is likely that they quickly abandoned the idea of using such power (if it had indeed ever envisaged doing so) because it ran counter to the institution of private property and was economically and politically untenable. The meaning of the clause about building permits was mainly that it confined the *extrarradio* to a gray zone of regulatory vacuum, an administrative nonplace, which consigned the governance of these peripheries to informal practices and fomented clientelistic relationships.

During the Francoist period, the law unambiguously condemned popular peripheral urbanization and created a repressive arsenal to counter it. This arsenal gave urban planning authorities the means to do whatever they liked with peripheral land. Public authorities were certainly not going to attempt to improve the inhabitants' living conditions, at least not directly. The *chabolas'* governance was no longer characterized by a regime of general exception but rather by the discretionary use of extensive power at all levels of the administration. The *chabolas'* inhabitants were all considered illegal, and therefore they all lived under the permanent threat of sanctions, especially eviction. Only clemency could grant them a temporary reprieve, so they were forced to seek the authorities' benevolence.

This evolution was accompanied by a shift in power from landowners (which characterized the first period) to developers and can be understood only in the context of an extremely repressive dictatorship. From the 1950s onward, the inhabitants of the informal neighborhoods lost any room for maneuver that they might have previously had and had less access still to urban integration and the urban amenities and services that came with it. The only way they could access these now was through rehousing, which was dependent on the administration's goodwill and reserved for families deemed deserving. The *extrarradio* urbanization system was based on a relationship, for better or for worse, between the inhabitants and the landowners, who enjoyed free use of their property and who still held political power in the municipality. During the Francoist period, the state partly subjugated the interests of these landowners to those of a new class of actors, the real estate developers, thus severely limiting the range of urban possibilities open to the protagonists of informal urbanization.

PART II

Urban Informality and Political Struggle

4

"The Order Came from Above":
The Political and Ideological Foundations of Fascism's
Struggle against the *Baracche* in Rome

LUCIANO VILLANI

Under fascism, the uprooting of Rome's *baracche* (shacks) assumed the frenzy of a crusade. During the liberal era, the *baracche* had become a problematic issue that concerned authorities because of their possible harmful effects on public health.[1] But the shacks had not yet acquired the political significance and extensive administrative intervention they would attract during the fascist *ventennio*. Indeed, in the mid-1910s, after having ordered a series of demolitions and evictions, municipal administrators were convinced that the issue had been resolved.[2] With fascism in power, however, the struggle against the *baracche* not only resumed but also became relentless. Despite lackluster results, authorities attacked the *baracche* with unprecedented determination and frenzy, consuming far more energy and resources than in the past and engaging institutions at all levels.

This chapter reconstructs the political-ideological assumptions within which fascism's hostile attitude toward Rome's *baracche* unfolded and traces the many reasons for its persistence. If we consider the extent of fascism's ideological and emotional investment in the Roman myth and the peremptory way in which the new government claimed credit "for having morally and politically endowed the nation with a capital,"[3] it is easy to grasp how the question of the *baracche* was affected by the great symbolic importance that fascism conferred on the city's image.[4] Mussolini's directives inspired the establishment of a new monumental structure in the central part of the city. Highlighting ancient vestiges in a modern public space—traversed by wide thoroughfares cut into the fabric of the old city—Mussolini's planners visually represented the ideal and spiritual connection between *romanità* (Romanism) and fascism, casting the latter as the legitimate heir to the Roman tradition and the renovator of its civilization's primacy.[5] But fascism's projects for the capital were not limited to excavating the memory of past greatness through a series of archaeological enhancements: its ambition was to try and realize a modern "fully fascist" Rome, capable of defying the centuries by continuously projecting its civilizing will upon the world.[6] This new Rome was first concretized in the Foro Mussolini (today's Foro Italico complex), then in the Universal Exposition of 1942. These grandiose urban renewal projects paid special attention to the capital, giving it a preeminent urban planning function, higher than that of any other Italian city. Only by adapting its structure to the standards of a modern capital could Rome exercise its historical mission and rise again as a city of universal values. Rome had to possess "all the requisites of a great modern city," argued Giuseppe Bottai, the main interpreter of the modernist variation of the Roman myth, "so that it can fulfill its domestic function as a modern capital and can later fulfill the function that we all aspire to, of being the capital of the modern world."[7]

These programs and statements frame the general context in which fascism's obsession with the *baracche* matured: that of a city urged to assume the face of a modern capital because it represented the global primacy of the totalitarian regime's values. Rome was thus subjected to an exceptionally political conception of architecture and urban planning, tasked with consecrating those same values in stone and space to render them eternal. In this sense, the case of the *baracche* in Rome under fascism is emblematic of an urban informality that contrasted strikingly not only with certain ideas of the city and modernity but also with the aspirations and myths cultivated by a dictatorial regime in the "powerful" context of its capital, designated to become the reference point of Western civilization. The fascist regime, identifying the *baracche* as an obstacle to the completion of its designs, was the first in Europe that sought to erase shacks from the urban landscape, thus playing a pioneering role.[8]

With respect to the themes raised in this book's introduction, this chapter also responds to the need to understand the question of urban informality within the study of wider historical, political, and social phenomena and to deepen the links between the development of these phenomena and the construction of categories that time and again define the informal city and its inhabitants. Under fascism, the authorities' attitude toward the *baracche* was far from uniform; it also experienced turning points, expressing itself through ever-heightened intolerance. There was a shift from a broader and mostly understanding vision of residents' problems to an aggressive stigmatization, conveyed through openly damning journalistic campaigns, leading ultimately to the adoption of repressive measures, including the transfer and isolation of the *baraccati* (slum dwellers) in special *borgate* (townships) scattered throughout the distant suburbs, created by the governorate to carry out dubious and demeaning social correction programs.[9]

An examination of the reasons for this radicalization requires historical contextualization that places the regime's actions against the *baracche* within the framework of its politics and ideology. Antipathy toward the *baracche*, rooted mostly in issues of image and political standing, became imbued with more marked political and ideological significance, intertwining with other rallying cries espoused by the regime. Propaganda against the social threat represented by the *baracche* and the social danger identified in their inhabitants—who were accused of exerting a disruptive influence on the customs and moral values of the national community, thus endangering the spirit of militaristic cohesion—was exacerbated by the circulation and exaltation of myths and slogans that occupied a central role in the ideological universe and conception of fascist politics.[10] Beyond Rome's exalted role as the center of national rebirth and the new regime's idealized reference point, the political-ideological coordinates for the *baracche*'s elimination were defined, above all, in the context of an antiurbanization campaign. They thus intertwined first with the question of migration and the need to control internal mobility and then with housing policy. In the 1930s, with the deepening urgency of the totalitarian project for Italians' physical and moral regeneration, the perceived need for surveillance and social reeducation became more explicit.

In this way, hostility against the *baracche* became a wedge that helped consolidate other policies, such as antiurbanism and the rural repatriation of unemployed migrants. At the same time, in a mutually instrumental manner, the speeches that fed those policies always provided a legitimizing cover for the regime's choices in its battle against the *baraccamento*. Also, it is important to clarify, the press's orchestrated denigration campaign and the ideologization of the *baracche* were entirely instrumental to the realization of a single concrete goal: to clear them from the capital. Given the categorical tone of so many statements on the subject, fascism bet on *sbaraccamento* (demolition of urban slums), a not-insignificant piece of its reputation as an imperious and decisive regime that acted in stark contrast to the reviled "formalism" that had characterized Italy's old politics. But there were limited resources available to achieve this goal. The solutions implemented thus suffered from the limited room for maneuver imposed by the capital's budget. Ideologizing the question of the *baracche* therefore served to create discriminatory premises that, though nourished by mythical thinking, ultimately aimed not to decree a true regime of social exclusion, sanctioned by appropriate norms, but to legitimize fast and cheap means—repressive when necessary—to completely eradicate the *baraccamento* phenomenon.

Taking into account the regime's political phases, its rhetoric, and the measures it adopted, it is possible to identify three successive and distinct phases in the battle against the proliferation of the *baracche*, a first from 1922–1926, a second from 1927–1929, and another from 1930–1939. These phases, described below, were characterized by significant changes of emphasis and motivation. Those changes, in turn, were reflected in the administrative procedures employed in the *baraccamento*'s control and repression.

Public discourse, however, took a different course. After an initial period in which the press did not cover the administration's frequent interventions in the *baracche*, there seem to have been two crucial junctures. Beginning in the second half of 1927, there was a decisive increase in social alarm, evidenced in an extraordinary sequence of newspaper articles dedicated to the necessary work of "reclaiming" the city from the *baracche*. Then, from 1930 on, we see (not coincidentally) the opposite trend, namely the sudden disappearance of the issue from city news and official pronouncements, corresponding to the construction of the first *borgate* sponsored by the governorate.

The *Baracche* and the Control of Urban Expansion, 1922–1926

The question of housing topped the political agenda set by Filippo Cremonesi, elected as Rome's mayor in June 1922, made a royal commissioner in March 1923, and appointed Rome's first governor in October 1925.[11] Housing was regarded as a "vexing problem," common to many Italian cities, but it took on "painfully stark" forms and proportions in the capital.[12] In the months following Cremonesi's election as mayor, the municipal administration paid increased attention to the development of "illegal constructions" (constructions "in masonry but also in wood, such as *baracche*, sheds, and the like"), as evidenced by the convening of the first meetings on that subject among officials of the Public Works Division.[13] Concern was not limited to the sanitary problems and risks to "public health" that had been attributed to the *baracche* during the liberal era; it also extended to "serious damage to the city's aesthetics and decorum."[14]

Such phraseology would become frequent in the capital's bureaucratic correspondence, but in this case, it preceded the fascist March on Rome of October 28, 1922, demonstrating that local government already felt the need to protect the capital's iconic image—a need that, of course, emerged strengthened after Mussolini became prime minister. In the wake of a "conversion" that originated with Mussolini's wartime adoption of interventionism, fascism had committed itself to fully recovering the myth of *romanità*, understood as an activist cult, a "mobilizer of energy" that drew from the past both universal values and a "model of strength and discipline" that could be projected onto the present and future of fascist Italy.[15] Once in power, fascism was determined to make the cult of *romanità* the "most pervasive mytho-logical belief" of its entire symbolic universe.[16] Shortly thereafter, Mussolini himself gave precise directives on plans for the capital's transformation. In a few years, Rome would emerge as "a city worthy of its glory" and "a marvel to all the world's peoples: vast, ordered, powerful," as it had been "in the days of Augustus's first empire."[17] The spectacle of misery offered by the *baracche*—which arose, it was said, to the "disgrace of Rome's good name"—did not fit with this image of grandeur.[18]

However, a closer and more comprehensive analysis of some of the mea-sures taken or proposed by the capital's administration suggests that the de-sire to enhance "the city's beauty" and make the sight of the capital "superb" was only the most eye-catching motive for initiatives undertaken during those years to organize and rationalize Rome's territory. On August 22, 1924, Cremonesi issued a notice, publicized through posters, aimed at putting a stop to the spread of buildings considered *disordinate e abusive* (disorderly and illicit), the character of which represented a "grave danger to public hygiene and the city's decorum."[19] What worried the administration more, however, was how the illicit building activities prevented the municipal body from "channeling and directing building activity," disrupting its plans to de-velop remedial projects in the suburbs, particularly the implementation of Legislative Decree 2318 (November 30, 1919), which had identified some areas within and beyond Rome's master plan, most already occupied by *abusivi*, upon which to launch low-cost social housing construction.[20]

This is a crucial point. In this phase, the fight against the *baracche*, while invoking hygiene and decorum, appears in reality to have been spurred by the administration's desire to take control of the processes of urban expansion. As the aforementioned notice suggests, Cremonesi's action was sweeping, meant to combat the phenomenon of "illicit constructions" in general rather than the *baracche* in particular. We can understand in the same vein a November 1926 attempt—thwarted by the government's own decisions—to stem the ille-gal subdivision of agricultural land and guarantee greater resources for public housing construction, thus relaunching public housing policy on different bases and in alliance with the Istituto Case Popolari (ICP, or Public Housing Institute).[21]

Consistent with this approach, a program of housing construction for the *baraccati* had been initiated in 1924, entrusted to the ICP and financed by the Roman governorate. With this, the government revived, with significant im-provements, a model of assisted demolitions experimented with in 1911–1912 during Ernesto Nathan's mayoral term. Describing the first group of houses for the *baraccati* built in Garbatella, inaugurated by Mussolini on October 28, 1925, the gubernatorial magazine *Capitolium* noted that the Cremonesi's measures, in addition to being prompted by humanitarian sentiments, served to "give the suburban neighborhoods a decorous layout."[22] Significantly, the same article went on to highlight the positive influence that the new houses, cheaply built but dry and clean, would exert on the modest population from the *baracche*. Residents would be induced to change their habits: workers would turn away from taverns, women would find intimate spaces of affection and care, children would abandon the streets. The home, in this way, would confirm its role as an indispensable bastion of social prophylaxis, fostering "family structure" and the "serenity of life."[23]

Thus fascism's struggle against the *baracche*, though animated by the imperative to lend luster to Rome's splendor and prestige, actually took shape at this stage as part of a more comprehensive strategy aimed at securing greater governmental control over the otherwise chaotic course of urban development. It was, in this sense, in continuity with the initiatives, ideas, and stereotypes inherited from sanitarist culture.[24]

During the first half of the 1920s, the question of the *baracche* rarely appeared in the press, except to announce inaugurations heralding the construction of homes for the *baraccati* or sometimes to assert the urgency of particular slum clearances. In early 1923, *Il Messaggero* dealt with the question more assiduously in a series of articles that provided a fairly clear picture of ideas circulating about the *baraccati* and their lifeways. The articles' caustic judgments and nasty epithets betrayed sentiments of rejection, mistrust, and even outright revulsion toward the *baraccati*. They were defined as "wretches," "troglodytes," "strangers to modern civilization," "cut off from our way of life," and "destitute debris left adrift." Their presence was considered a "filth visible to all," a "disgusting spectacle" and "shameful for the capital"; it was an "immoral mixture," a "hotbed of germs dangerous to morality and hygiene" capable of arousing "nausea and horror." These prejudices, however, were accompanied by other more substantive appraisals that mitigated the articles' incontrovertible sense of social condemnation, defusing its discriminatory potential. These claimed first that the *baraccati* were forced to live in dismal conditions by poverty and the lack of housing, implying that their encampments in the *baracche* were not the result of a natural and immutable tendency.[25] They also recognized the difficulty of demanding "respect for morality" in light of unenviable environmental conditions and insufficient space.[26] It followed that the *baraccati* were no more than "human beings" like anyone else, the only difference being that they were "denied the sacrosanct right to housing" that should be enjoyed by every citizen.[27] Finally, the articles raised the issue of political responsibility and that of the social impassivity that permitted such acute suffering, with respect to which no one could claim innocence or feign ignorance:

> The existence of these modern "troglodytes," these pariahs of society, is ignored by the highest public authorities, who prefer to turn their faces away so as not to be forced to blush, and so as not to feel obliged to take urgent action and eliminate our city's greatest shame. . . . What does society do for these wretches? Nothing. It forgets them, tries to ignore them, turns away from them and repudiates them. Ashamed of allowing such a state of affairs, it pretends to itself that it does not know and rests negligently and guiltily in its own apathy. And with this it believes it is escaping the obligations it has towards itself and towards the wretches it has disowned![28]

Another aspect deserves mention. To depict the housing conditions of the *baraccati*, this series of articles used curious cartoons rather than photographs, almost as if there were a kind of shame in relying on the apparently more realistic medium of photography. Perhaps this was out of respect for the less fortunate; perhaps such hesitation was dictated by the need to preserve at all costs the honor of the government and its capital.[29] On the whole, beyond the offensive and morally disapproving tone, it seems that contemporaries had not yet formed an openly discriminatory judgment against the *baraccati* that could herald more concrete forms of intolerance and marginalization. Their promiscuity was feared and their morality considered dubious, but no one advanced the ideas that they should be excluded from human society or that they constituted a danger to national cohesion as actual internal enemies. In 1924, for example, *La Tribuna* denounced the presence of a group of "hovels" near Porta Maggiore as "testimony of poverty, of neglect, of incivility," but also of "hardness of heart towards the poorest citizens that does not do us honor. It is a disgrace that Rome will perhaps never know how to shed."[30] This air of resignation would soon give way to prose with decidedly more triumphalist and offensive intonations.

The Antiurban Campaign and the Social Danger of the *Baracche* and Their Inhabitants, 1927–1929

If we had to establish the moment and circumstance in which fascism's attitude toward the *baracche* evolved in the direction of ferocious social stigmatization, we could pinpoint 1927—more precisely, Mussolini's Ascension Day speech, given on May 26 in the Chamber of Deputies, to which observers usually trace the beginnings of an antiurban campaign meant to encourage demographic growth and ruralize Italy.

It was a dictator's miracle to affect such a radical conceptual turnaround by means of a single speech, however persuasive. Until then, diametrically opposed perspectives had prevailed in debates on the future of cities, favoring an increase in the number and size of large centers, which were encouraged to compete with one another to attain various urban "primacies."[31] The enthusiasm aroused by this race among Italian cities, launched in pursuit of finish lines already crossed by other Western metropolises (particularly but not only in Milan) had to recede quickly when faced with Mussolini's volte-face.

In his Ascension Day speech, after focusing on the physical health of the Italian people, Mussolini expressed the need for an increase in demographic strength that would move the country away from the prospect of decline in the competition among nations: "For Italy to count for something, it must appear on the threshold of the second half of this century with a population of no less than 60 million inhabitants. . . . If you shrink, gentlemen, you don't create an Empire, you become a colony!"

A certain type of urbanism—specifically, Mussolini stipulated, the industrial form—was "destructive" for the nation's future because it led "to populational sterility."[32] Hence the need to stem urbanization processes in the cities, where the pursuit of hedonistic pleasure corrupted the spirit and weakened the body, as well as to return and retain the rural population, support agriculture, and encourage Italy's ruralization.

The topoi of the "tentacular city"—an incubator of passions and "new needs" and a receptacle of vice and delinquency—had recurred in Italy since the beginning of the twentieth century in a vast literature, including that of a progressive bent.[33] Such tropes reflected a perception of the rapid changes imposed by economic transformation and the spread of values and propensities that prefigured the emergence of a modern mass society. Such processes unfolded most fully in the metropolises, which thus ended up embodying the very essence of modernity. The city seemed to debilitate rather than advance those who came into contact with it, and doctors, physiologists, and social scientists of the time shared the belief that it reproduced pathological environmental conditions.[34]

In Oswald Spengler's *The Decline of the West*, the correlation between degenerate urban life and the falling fertility rate was an incontrovertible symptom of a crisis affecting the very survival of European civilization.[35] This inexorable decline, inscribed in the natural life cycle of every society that reached the stage of "civilization," was accelerated by the behavior of the men of the "cosmopolises," among whom, contrary to the historical attitude of the peasantry, all concern for the perpetuation of the lineage seemed to have vanished.[36] Spengler's theory had many intersections with Mussolini's thought, confirming some of his beliefs and exercising upon Il Duce a certain fascination.[37]

The antiurban policy that favored demographic expansion and ruralization proved on balance to be a failure on all fronts.[38] It is no coincidence that, to explain this, analysts often emphasize the policy's ideological and propagandistic significance; it is interpreted, for example, either as a "sentimental and utopian outlet" for the working masses' discontent with an increasingly intense production cycle that was excluded from union negotiations or as a "nativist economic stance" or "mental horizon."[39]

The polemic against "industrial" urbanism, as well as ruralist aspirations and various other avowals, seem above all to evoke Mussolini's image of the socioeconomic equilibrium upon which Italy should be founded—"a nation with a mixed economy, strong agriculture, healthy small and medium-sized industries, a bank averse to speculation, [and] agile and rational commerce."[40]

This vision, however, remained on paper. In reality, antiurban legislation and propaganda advocating a return to the land sought to achieve more practical and contingent political ends: to balance, for example, the negative effects of lira appreciation policies by ensuring that unemployment stopped bearing down on the cities and was instead diverted to the countryside. Consistent with transformations in the local administrative order, there was also a proposal to "stabilize" Italian society and control population movements partly according to the needs of industry, which ended up being protected (and with a law of November 3, 1927, which regulated the installation of industrial plants, even concentrated) rather than limited.[41] And it was precisely on the terrain of regulating migration, and thus also fulfilling a public order imperative, that antiurban policy met and exacerbated the struggle against the *baracche*.

From the Ascension Day speech forward, the rationale in support of *sbaraccamenti* (slum clearance) expanded: it was no longer merely a question of hygiene and decorum, let alone of regulating construction by bringing it within the scope of legal requirements. The repression of the *baraccamento* became an integral part of antimigration policy—or rather, the policy against indiscriminate migration, which was deemed to be a purveyor of delinquency and social maladies. The brake on mobility applied not to industrial labor, but to undesirables, vagabonds, and beggars, or at least this was the prevailing interpretation given to the antiurban regulations.[42]

The first press campaign against the *baracche*, which began a few weeks after the Ascension Day speech, was led by *Il Popolo di Roma*.[43] Initially, it

focused on some owners and landlords of *baracche*, one of whom was impris-
oned for illegal speculation.[44] The unfortunates who lived in the "dens" were
once again represented innocuously, perhaps precisely because they were
subject to extortion; indeed, the newspaper appealed directly to the governor
of Rome, inviting him to visit the *baracche* in Via Alba: "They are not savages,
Excellency! . . . They are people who need help, before they break."[45]

Soon, however, the newspaper shifted to vicious denigration of the *baraccati*, calling for their de facto banishment. The same paper's editor was quick
to clarify a few days later: "Not all who are part of the Abyssinian villages are
elements worth keeping in Rome and some, rather than a workers' cottage,
could find lodgings in forced confinement!"[46] Over the following days, an
offensive was unleashed. The *baracche*, it was said, now represented a "social danger" that should have "seriously worried political and administrative
authorities." They were inhabited by "a confused mass of men, women and
children from all regions of the peninsula," such that "born vagabonds" and
the "homeless" lived alongside unemployed workers and eviction victims:

> This contact creates the sad consequences known to the criminalist, the mag-
> istrate, the jailer and the merchant of human flesh (a rotten apple spoils the
> barrel). The Abyssinian *baraccamenti* crush in good souls all sentiments of
> dignity, moral modesty and human solidarity. They bestialize the man and
> destroy the woman so that a streetwalker can live within her. The child's heart
> is relentlessly brutalized by a way of life that has nothing human about it. . . .
> We . . . immediately sensed and denounced the dangers that flow from this
> savage way of life to society as a whole. Children who sleep in sodden wooden
> *baracche*, covered with tin scraps and rotting carrion skins, mingled amid re-
> pulsive promiscuity, are easy prey to tuberculosis. And if by some good for-
> tune they escape that terrible evil, they will not subsequently elude idleness,
> theft, and crime. Will girls born and raised in Abyssinian *baraccamenti* ever
> be brides and housewives?[47]

The rhetoric surrounding the *baraccati* thus began to echo the same discriminatory tones reserved for those reluctant to integrate into the totalitarian community educated under fascist values. The *baracche* killed "feelings of
attachment to family, society and the Fatherland"; instead, "class hatred and
the worst instincts of delinquency" took root.[48] It followed that, for "reasons
of national dignity and patriotic propaganda," they should be suppressed.[49]
Although these observations echoed discriminatory stylistic motifs that had
been in circulation from the end of the nineteenth century with regard to
inhabitants of Italy's first working-class neighborhoods, this time such discourse had practical repercussions: no one had previously dreamed that the
description of certain inclinations and bad habits—for example, the alcohol-

ism, immorality, and thuggery attributed to the inhabitants of San Lorenzo or Testaccio—should lead to the elimination of residential clusters and the forced removal of their residents.

Liberating Rome from the *baracche* was thus about national dignity, an affirmation of patriotism against antinational spirits. This nexus was irrefutably validated by the observation that the *baracche's* existence could be ascribed to the wickedness of liberal democratic and socialist doctrines, guilty of endorsing dissolute and savage forms of social life; the task of erasing that ignominy once and for all could belong only to a regime operating in clear discontinuity with that tragic past.[50] The construction of a discursive system to delegitimize the *baraccato* was complete: it was identified as a malevolent agent from whose nefarious influence society had to be protected.

At this juncture, Mussolini began to take a personal interest in the question of the *baracche*. The first occasion came as part of initiatives planned to celebrate the fifth annual March on Rome (October 28, 1927); he closely followed preparations for the mass *sbaraccamento* of Portonaccio, in all likelihood prompted unscrupulously by *Il Popolo di Roma*; inhabitants were transferred to accommodation arranged by the ICP.[51] Once briefed, Mussolini wanted a sober but effective ceremony to "emphasize the occasion." But he also aimed to build consensus: "It is the only way to get these people to contemplate fascism," he wrote to ICP's president Alberto Calza Bini.[52] In this way, Mussolini stood as benefactor to the *baraccati* while simultaneously calling resolutely for their rural repatriation. On November 25, 1928, Mussolini himself ordered an "exact census" of the *baraccati* to select both candidates for outright deportation and the *ruralizzabili* (those eligible to receive horticultural plots in the countryside).[53]

In the days preceding this order, *Il Popolo d'Italia* published an article by Mussolini called "Figures and Inferences: Evacuate the Cities." In it, arguments in favor of deurbanization—hitherto framed in opposition to industrial urbanism and in favor of demographic growth—were closely linked with the housing question, which Il Duce considered "[an] insoluble problem until we adopt the following formula: prevent rural-to-urban migration and ruthlessly evacuate the cities. . . . The more houses are built and the more people are urbanized—even through the preliminary hell of the *baracche*— the more housing is needed. Thus it goes to infinity—that is, to monstrous cities; . . . the operative concept is this: facilitate exodus from urban centers by any means—including, if necessary, coercion; hinder by any means— including coercion—the abandonment of the countryside; and oppose by any means mass migration to the cities."

From this point of view, displacement from urban centers would help alleviate an impending housing crisis generated by a liberalization of rent control set to begin on June 30, 1930: "[If we] clear the cities and prevent hundreds of thousands of individuals from migrating to them between now and 30 June 1930 . . . , the date set for lifting all constraints will pass without concern."[54]

Within a month, the first antiurbanism law was passed, granting prefects the power to issue ordinances "to limit excessive increase in the city's resident population."[55] The determination with which Mussolini's regime opposed migration, interpreted as the main cause of the housing crisis and unemployment, gave the fight against the "Abyssinian villages" a role in solving much broader problems. The intention was to carry out operations to control the population in the *baracche*, identifying the "imported component" and encouraging return to its places of origin. The censuses and demolitions of the *baracche* would become, at least in theory, a means for carrying out large-scale repatriations. In this way, antimigrant policies and slum supervision converged on a repressive terrain that would become a model for other European countries.[56]

Indeed, in January 1929, while conducting the census Mussolini had ordered, the governor's social welfare office carried out additional investigations to distinguish indigent and undesirable migrants (who were to be brought to the attention of the area commissariats and "for the most part" sent back to their places of origin) from *baraccati* suitable for the regime's institutional housing or welfare solutions (e.g., hostels, public shelters, collective hotels, social housing).[57] This was a "ponderous" task, the office recognized, but one to be conducted carefully, given the "great interest" shown by the head of government in operations that would lead "undoubtedly to the removal from Rome of many undesirable people."[58]

Propaganda against the *baracche* underwent a further qualitative leap when inserted into a framework of urban displacement officially enacted to counter dangers threatening "the physical and moral health of the race" but also deemed effective in solving the housing problem. First of all, consistent with Mussolini's logic, *Il Popolo di Roma* could boast of having engaged through its journalistic campaign against the "Abyssinian villages" in the first avant la lettre battle against urbanization, since the expansion of the *baracche* originated in that phenomenon.[59] Adept at incorporating government speeches' every tonal variation, the Roman newspaper consequentially demanded prompt implementation of the "coercive means" cited by Il Duce, namely the intensification of checks and expulsions. Things were said to be happening in the *baracche* that could not "even be reported. Episodes of exceptional gravity, intolerable to the Fascist Regime." Referring to a specific group of *baracche*, it added: "The population of these *baracche* is 'undesirable' in Rome. Not only because it is not Roman, but because it is comprised— with rare exceptions—of morally dangerous people. . . . In short, this is not a problem of housing construction, etc., but rather a problem for the police, one that should have already been settled and that must be resolved as soon as possible. . . . Not, of course, for our own satisfaction, but in the supreme interest of Rome and in obedience to Fascism's the social policies."[60]

The paper had thus shifted from advocating for police measures against speculators to stigmatization of the *baraccati* and demands for police action against them. Antiurban and rural repopulation policies were reduced to the enactment of social cleansing measures that, far from rebalancing urban and rural development, ended up being applied exclusively in the sphere of public order.

Meanwhile, the building program developed by Mayor Cremonesi in the early 1920s, seen as a stimulus for the *baracche*, had been repudiated by the administration and hastily discontinued. But the more general intention to combat illicit urbanization was shelved right along with it. As the aforementioned article made clear, the question of the *baracche* was no longer considered a "simple" problem of housing construction.

The condemnation of the wooden *baracche* contrasted with substantial benevolence toward small dwellings and brick *baracche* built on legally owned plots, provided that there was an explicit will to transform them into affordable working-class housing; that is, the regime showed tolerant condescension toward the illicit construction practices of small landowners, shopkeepers, professionals, white-collar employees, and workers, often of peasant origin.[61] As part of its journalistic campaign against the *baracche*, the fascist press claimed that the constraints of Rome's master plan should not be confused with "many little things that have nothing to do with it." The message was clear: the *lottisti* (subdividers of peripheral land) must be free to build their little houses in areas that lay outside the master plan; indeed, to correct the "old bureaucratic routine," Rome's governors had to prove themselves "fascistically industrious" in issuing building permits and meeting these groups' demands, thus favoring the rapid development of suburban subdivisions.[62]

The articles that appeared in *Il Popolo di Roma* at this juncture revealed a controversy over whether to distinguish between wooden *baracche* and brick huts, which would be tolerated so long as they were being renovated.[63] This reflected the fluctuating character of discourse concerning the informal city's problematic characteristics, which involved increasingly discretionary elements and criteria, such as those relating to the morality of the inhabitants or the external appearance and material composition of the *baracche*.[64]

In contrast, the encouragement and relative institutional tolerance of illicit construction in the Roman countryside depended on two factors. First, auto-construction of houses in places far from the consolidated city eased pressure on the housing market, especially during building crises such as that of 1926–1927. Second, fascism didn't intend to alienate the economic and social actors involved in *abusivismo*, ranging from large landowners to agricultural cooperatives to small-time purchasers. This permissive attitude would have considerable repercussions in subsequent years.

The *Minorati della Casa* and the Process of Building the New Man, 1930–1939

The solution to the housing emergency caused by rent liberalization was neither mass displacement nor the halt in mass rural-to-urban migration that Mussolini had hoped for. It came instead through the construction of the *borgate ufficiali*, a quick and economical system that allowed for ongoing *baracche* clearances and demolitions while also absorbing many of the residents displaced by the eviction surge.[65] After decelerating in the early 1930s, due in part to the failure of initiatives such as one that advocated for suburban hostels, the dismantling of the *baraccopoli* resumed with some vigor thanks to the *borgate*.[66]

Often, the demolitions were dictated by motives that might be considered routine. Many *sbaraccamenti* occurred as a result of pressing urban development imperatives. Clearance operations and *baracche* demolition preceded the construction of many roads and more than a few great public structures during the 1930s: the Ministry of Aeronautics in 1930; the University City in 1935; the Hospital del Littorio, in 1935; and the Universal Exposition of 1942, from 1937. In other cases, it was a question of ensuring the capital's aesthetics and urban decorum on special occasions, such as Princess Marie-José of Belgium's marriage to Umberto di Savoia in January 1930 or Hitler's visit to Rome in May 1938.[67] These occasions revealed the ambiguity and arbitrariness of clearance criterion: in the days preceding Hitler's arrival, 420 *baracche* were demolished, but a summary of the operation shows that another 131 *baracche* were left standing after being "cleaned up" (figs. 4.1 and 4.2).[68] Other interventions occurred due to pressing hygiene and sanitary imperatives (as in the Lido di Ostia in 1935, one of the largest *sbaraccamenti* of the decade).

Ideological, moral, and pedagogical motivations also deepened in such a way that the *baracche*'s inhabitants seemed less and less salvageable in view of ongoing efforts to build the fascist "New Man." Alberto Calza Bini, president of the ICP, did not miss an opportunity to emphasize that public housing rep-

FIGURE 4.1. **Photographic census of** *baracche* **taken a few days before Hitler's arrival in Rome, May 1938.** Among the precarious buildings in the Ponte Lungo zone there are also more solid brick houses. Source: Archivio Storico Capitolino (Archivio Fotografico, n. 1006).

FIGURE 4.2. **Photographic census of** *baracche***, May 1938.** Source: Archivio Storico Capitolino (Archivio Fotografico, n. 1043).

resented "an instrument of education, sanitary and moral rehabilitation, and of integration into the fascist order."[69] The institution's housing assignments were meant to reward good citizens, industrious men, the nation's deserving.[70] Conversely, those who had no home and did not even seem to want one were deemed social wreckage. The regime, Calza Bini argued, was already doing its best to ensure "sanitary and affordable homes for the people":

> But without fabulous means, one cannot reach the lowest strata; one cannot give a house worthy of the name to those who do not want it or who want it for free. Here one enters an infinite field of assistance, in which some cases have only partial solutions. Clear out the nuclei located in central areas touched by urban development, avoid the organic formation of other groups, and provide at most for local regulation and the most elementary norms of life. As for the rest, one can only ignore, as in essence one does ignore, the teeming mass of shelters for a stray and lowly population that, as the other foreign metropolises teach us, not even a higher general standard of living or more intense purging can eliminate.[71]

Calza Bini's position of opposition to the "totalitarian" *sbaraccamento* and to assigning houses to the *baraccati* had to do with rent defaults: former shack dwellers assigned to public housing were less inclined than other social categories to pay rent or to pay it on time. Here, however, it is especially interesting to note the change in views that had occurred compared with the early 1920s regarding the type of human being represented by the *baraccato*, who had gone from a person in need of help and understanding to an irredeemable nonentity who should be ignored: "He who does not have a fixed place to rest, where he can feel the 'master' of something, where he can dream of a better life . . . is a human wreck. . . . A man who does not have a home is a 'nothing' lost in a great chaos of misery and social injustice."[72]

The *baraccato* personified this "inhuman" specimen. The *baracca* was said to exercise a "sinister power." By lowering man to the level of a beast, it rendered him unable to perform any social function: head of the family, husband, brother, citizen, soldier, or worker.[73]

This list of social roles can be speculatively and partially superimposed on another given in a text by the Roman fascist leader Giuseppe Bottai in which he philosophically defined a number of the fascist New Man's salient characteristics, in accordance with the regime's totalitarian conception of politics: "Man, according to Fascism, becomes whole in the family, in the professional group, in the economic corporation, in the nation, in the State. . . . The Fascist man is oriented entirely toward the totality, he ascends from his own particularity to the unity of the State; in this ascent he may leave behind scraps

FIGURE 4.3. **Borgata Gordiani.** Source: Archivio Storico Capitolino (Segreteria Generale, *carteggio* 1923–48, b. 686, cl. 20 s.cl. 2, 1940).

of freedom along the way, but he acquires awareness of himself, of his own character."[74]

The inhabitants of the *baracche*, anthropologically antithetical to the fascist conception of the New Man, found themselves counted among the enemies of Blackshirt Italy.[75] This despite the fact that there was certainly no shortage of *baraccati* who, for one reason or another and with different degrees of conviction, also were professed fascists.[76]

What, then, were the *borgate ufficiali*, the public settlements created from 1930 to 1935 by the governor's office to relocate evicted *baraccati*? Without going into excessive detail, suffice it to say that they consisted of eight encampments built in Rome's extreme periphery, made up of *casette rustiche* (rustic houses) with two rooms and a toilet as well as, in the last three projects, annexes divided into one-room shelters ("brick *baracche*" according to the ICP definition) without kitchens or bathrooms and sharing common toilets (fig. 4.3).[77] The areas selected were deemed suitable both for their low cost and because the lay of the land lent itself to "sufficiently concealing the encampments."[78] In the governatorial *borgate*, the inhabitants sank into such acute hardship that they longed for the living conditions they had endured in the *baraccamenti*. For our purposes, however, it is most important to understand how the institutions that created the *borgate* discussed them and what image they projected of the settlements both officially and in private.

According to Francesco Boncompagni Ludovisi, the governor who established the *borgate*, they were "full of air and light," and the poor people who moved there would be elevated "to a new life."[79] Raffaello Ricci, the delegate for welfare services and the system's creator, said that what was being accomplished through the *borgate* was "true hygienic and spiritual regeneration."[80] For his part, Calza Bini, president of the ICP (the body that, after a period of inactivity, took over the management of the *borgate* from the governor's office in 1935), referred to the ex-*baraccati* dwellers in the *borgate* using the expression *minorati della casa* (housing impaired). For them, the institute promoted a form of reeducation that began with compliance with the "principle of economic discipline," that is, the punctual payment of rent.[81] Tenants, who lacked a standard lease, were punished in the event of nonpayment by the "padlock practice," which consisted of locking their front doors; recidivists were automatically transferred to public dormitories. It was common wisdom, after all, that this population needed to be straightened out and its habits corrected, as it was prey to the "germs of an antisocial education" that deprived it of a sense of home and family.[82]

In the period following the accomplishment of the first rudimentary projects, idyllic descriptions appeared here and there of a lush life shining with "spiritual light" that had reemerged in the *borgate*.[83] Thereafter, one of the clearest effects of the *borgate*'s inauguration seemed to be ever-rarer press coverage of both the *baraccati* and the settlements that replaced them, almost to the point of total disappearance. In this way, the age-old problem was considered resolved, included among the successes attributable to the resoluteness of fascism. Of course, neither the *baracche* nor the alarms and concerns raised about them by bourgeois defenders of order had disappeared.

Among police authorities and political figures, as well as representatives of high society, there was no lack of those who considered it inadvisable to spatially concentrate social malaise and made their concerns known to the relevant institutions. Their records are significant for two reasons. On the one hand, they demonstrate continuity in the stigmatizing rhetoric that had previously circulated publicly in the fascist press and was now expressed privately by members of the ruling class with equally prejudicial harshness. On the other hand, they clarify the most tangible repercussions of the social reeducation program that the *borgate* were intended to implement.

The tendency toward rhetorical continuity was exemplified in a report of the carabinieri on the *borgata* Gordiani, where "a multitude of families from southern Italy" were "amassed," among whom "prejudicial elements" abounded: "This state of affairs is not well regarded, and one wishes it would not occur in the capital, not least because these motley population clusters constitute an incentive to immorality."[84]

The response given by Riccardo Moretti (Ricci's successor at the social welfare office) to the prime minister's undersecretary, who was alarmed by news about the plight experienced by inhabitants of the *borgata* Tor Marancia, is particularly indicative of the second tendency: "It is necessary to provide a bare minimum of help to these unfortunates, for the most part persona non grata at Police Headquarters. But it would be extremely dangerous, from a social perspective, to ameliorate their present living conditions even slightly, given that these masses, with rare and precarious exceptions, are made up of people who are unemployed due to profligacy or incapacity; any small enticement provided to individuals prone to idleness would only serve to accentuate their negligence and to activate the migration of undesirables, against which Public Security is tested in its daily activities."[85]

Reeducation thus took on clearer contours. The *borgatari* were knowingly deprived of basic services both to fight their apathy and to discourage the capital-bound migration of other "dead weight," to coin another expression that Moretti used to describe the *baraccati*.[86]

The prevalence of social prejudice over hygienic considerations forced a change in the administrative procedures surrounding slum clearance. When consulted on the matter, the governor's legal office expressed strong doubts about whether Article 153 of the Consolidation of Municipal and Provincial Law, which granted the mayor the power to carry out urgent public hygiene and safety measures, could be applied in every case.[87] Given the aesthetic and moral objectives of many measures against the *baracche*, public action involving illicit brick structures could be carried out only through the ordinary contravention procedure (a very slow and uncertain process), and wooden *baracche* that provided no grounds for hygienic alarm could be cleared only through the executive intervention of police headquarters.[88]

The ideologization of the fight against the *baracche*, in short, involved a shift from concerns related to sanitary protection and building regulation—addressed in the mid-1920s through specific policies involving housing and territorial control—to imperatives concerning the city's cleanliness and public image, which were soon entwined with propaganda calling for indigent people's removal from the city. That case was framed on grounds of social, moral, and national defense and fought for from then on with police measures as a problem of public order. When these failed, a project of segregation and isolation emerged that concentrated the *baraccati* in special public settlements devoid of public works and subject to strict disciplinary control and close surveillance by fascist and police authorities.[89]

Yet one essential aspect should be clarified. The *baraccati*'s social isolation resulted, above all, from fascism's fierce desire to achieve the complete elimination of the *baracche* from the city (a desire that later proved completely in vain), along with the belief that this result could be obtained with only the small initial expenditure required to install temporary settlements (an assertion that would prove false when maintenance turned out to be costly). The fascist project did not count among its ultimate goals the segregation of the *baraccati* as a form of apartheid planned and enshrined once and for all.[90] Otherwise, it would be inexplicable that when more resources became available in the second half of the 1930s, the *baraccati* were once again included in the ICP's public building programs, which involved the construction of second-generation *borgate*.

Conclusion

During the fascist period, the inhabitants of the *baracche* were the target of increasingly aggressive discriminatory propaganda that regarded them as dangerous individuals, carriers of disease, immorality, and delinquency; as social parasites closer to beasts than to men, incapable of working and serving the country; and as good-for-nothings irredeemable from the perspective of constructing the fascist New Man who should be isolated when not actually persecuted. This was a gradual progression, at first mostly geared toward resolving definitively and cheaply the old question of the *baracche*, which had jumped to the top of the Roman administration's concerns and was a central preoccupation for Mussolini from 1927 forward. The call to remove the *baracche* intersected with some of the most seductive mythologies that fascism used to spur political action and mobilize the masses: the myth of *romanità*, the myth of ruralism and of peasant Italy as foundational elements of an antiurban ideology, the myth of creating the fascist New Man.

Propaganda against the *baracche*, despite supposed backing from the scientific findings of doctors, criminalists, sociologists, and epidemiologists, was often based on questionable convictions and beliefs. The hygienic conditions in the *baracche*, though certainly not exemplary, were not all that much worse than in other housing situations. In 1939, Governor Giangiacomo Borghese sent a report on social housing to the General Directorate of Public Health at the Interior Ministry that focused on surveys carried out by various organizations and agencies.[91] The report noted how existing houses in the Roman governorate, "not excluding those recently built according to rational hygiene guidelines," recorded rates of overcrowding "detrimental to public health to a greater extent than occurs in isolated *baracche*."[92] ICP investigations carried out in the late 1930s into the demographic and social dynamics of its tenants, including those sheltered in the provisional *borgate*, showed that the incidence of mortality from infectious and parasitic diseases such as tuberculosis was lower than the city average (0.88 per thousand habitants in ICP homes, 1.95 in Rome). Even more remarkable was the data on the infant mortality rate, which was also below the city average, differentiated as follows among the various categories of ICP lodging: 8.1 per thousand in social housing, 7.3 in affordable housing, and 7.14 in shelters and governatorial *borgate* (acquired by ICP in 1935).[93] In summary, infant mortality was lower in the settlements to which the *baraccati* had been transferred than in housing for working-class and petty bourgeois groups.

Examination of the *baraccati*'s occupational situation, surveyed in 1929 as part of the Social Welfare Office census, showed that 60 percent of household heads worked as either common or skilled workers and 12 percent as public or private employees.[94] It was also not true that the *baraccati* were all migrants. Data from the 1933 census leaves no room for doubt: of the 4,416 families surveyed, 1,447 (a third) were of Roman origin, while among migrants, those who had lived in Rome for more than five years constituted the absolute majority (2,303 out of 2,969 households, or 77.5 percent).[95] Unsurprisingly, following this survey and further investigations by police authorities, police headquarters designated just thirty-six *baraccati* families for repatriation, for a total of 140 people.

In this sense, urban deportation projects, beyond being based on erroneous assumptions, proved completely impracticable, even when limited to "undesirables."[96] Above all, the larger effort to eradicate once and for all the scourge of the *baraccamento* in Rome was a failure: in spite of the regime's intense activity, which resulted in the construction of shelters and *borgate ufficiali*, in 1939 there were 5,163 *baracche* housing 22,592 inhabitants, double the number registered in 1924.[97]

Both the antiurban legislative framework (embodied in a 1939 law that was not repealed until 1961) and the prejudices against the *baraccati* and the *borgate* inhabitants persisted in the years after World War II, one of the many political-cultural flaws bequeathed to Republican Italy by the fascist period.[98] The *baracche* continued to mark the capital's urban landscape until at least the 1980s. But it was in the development of *l'edilizia abusiva* (illicit construction), beyond the policy of the *borgate ufficiali*, that we can trace the most profound impact of fascism's choices on the city's peripheral structure.

While part of the building expansion that took place after World War II can be traced back to the *borgate ufficiali,* as they foreshadowed connections between Rome's peripheral neighborhoods and its suburbs, the change in attitude toward illicit subdivisions that occurred in the second half of the 1920s decisively conditioned the city's development and the nature of its growth, giving an unmistakable imprint to the landscape of the Roman periphery. That expanse has become immense over time, composed mainly of hundreds of informal settlements that arose beyond the scope of urban planning and that have acted as a driving force in Rome's metropolitanization.[99]

The permissiveness that characterized the processes of subdivision and auto-construction—fueled by strong social pressure and by the speculative interests of land developers, but also, as we have seen, aggressively demanded by press organs—detonated a phenomenon that had previously been limited to a few clusters in the city's east and northwest. The formal establishment of "building nuclei" in 1935 (comprised of nineteen partially subdivided areas not included in Rome's 1931 master plan, where construction was legitimized through building permits) effectively ratified the practice of land subdivision outside Rome's regulatory plan.[100] This later continued on a massive scale, rendering almost irreversible the assault on and disintegration of the Roman countryside. From this point of view, the fascist legacy is easily identifiable; a simple inspection of the place-names and locations of the illegal settlements that were consolidated and absorbed into the regulatory plan by subsequent measures (approved in 1962 and 1978) shows that many of them represent nothing more than the densification of the urban "building nuclei" first mentioned in the 1935 resolution.

Carioca Favelas and the Catholic Church after World War II: The Case of the Fundação Leão XIII's Interventions in Praia do Pinto

RAFAEL SOARES GONÇALVES

This chapter analyzes the role of the Catholic Church in Rio de Janeiro's postwar favelas, focusing especially on a community called Praia do Pinto, located on the edge of the Leblon neighborhood on the Rodrigo de Freitas Lagoon in Rio's South Zone. The South Zone, one of Rio's most aristocratic regions, is wedged between the Tijuca massif—home to the Tijuca National Park and the well-known Christ the Redeemer monument—and the Atlantic coast. The mid-twentieth century witnessed the symbolic consolidation of this part of the city, which was marked by a dramatic real estate boom, especially in the famous neighborhood of Copacabana. During the postwar period, the seaside neighborhood of Leblon emerged as one of the most expensive South Zone neighborhoods.

South Zone districts located further from the beaches, such as Jardim Botânico, Gávea, and those bordering the Rodrigo de Freitas Lagoon, still retained their working-class character. The Praia do Pinto favela was one of many around the lagoon that were destroyed during the 1960s and 1970s during a broader clearance campaign carried out by the military dictatorship.[1] Most of these favelas' inhabitants had been initially attracted by nearby factories; later, they continued to be drawn by expanding employment opportunities fueled by the coastal real estate boom. From the 1950s onward, the real estate market extended to inland South Zone neighborhoods, where the presence of the favelas raised tensions over the region's occupation.

With time, a broader public reflection on the phenomenon of favela expansion gradually consolidated, framing the communities as the city's greatest public problem. Debate over these spaces permeated newspapers, legislative discourse, the construction of public policies, and even the census. Politicians, political parties, and private organizations inserted themselves into the daily lives of these places. Among these organizations, the Catholic

Church, in particular, made the favelas an important space for pastoral action, with strong political repercussions.

This chapter's principal aim is to analyze the role played by a Catholic institution that was crucial to the favelas' history in Rio, the Fundação Leão XIII (FLXIII).[2] Under the influence of Rio's then archbishop Dom Jaime Câmara, this foundation was established by Presidential Decree 22.498 of January 22, 1947; its mission was to "provide ample social assistance to the residents of the hills, favelas, and similar places in Rio de Janeiro."[3]

In addition to periodicals and public archival collections, this chapter develops its analysis based mainly on data from the FLXIII's records of social service family visitations in the Praia do Pinto. Based on previous works that have used these records, we offer a more detailed reflection on their content.[4] The records in question refer mainly to Praia do Pinto residents who were transferred to the Bairro São Sebastião, a housing project built in cooperation with the government by another important Catholic institution, the Cruzada São Sebastião.[5] The Bairro São Sebastião was located near Praia do Pinto and began to accept residents in the second half of the 1950s.[6] Each individual file contains statistical data about the residents as well as reports from social workers. This material constitutes an intriguing source for bolstering our understanding of social service work in Rio's favelas, as well as the ways different private and state institutions acted in these spaces. It also opens opportunities to reconstruct residents' daily lives.

In her 1953 social work thesis about the FLXIII's work clearing Neimeyer, another South Zone favela, Maria José Valença explained that initial family visits were carried out by *visitadoras*, who then presented their cases to a social worker for resolution.[7] Each family received a registration number, and each visit was recorded on cards that together evolved into an archive of the consultations and even provided data for a statistical survey: "[This] permits an evaluation of each favela's various problems and thus the establishment of a plan of action that will serve as a basis for favela eradication."[8]

In the case of Praia do Pinto, the files indicate that residents were not allowed to house family members or friends in their homes without the FLXIII's consent; such people would be considered clandestine and asked to leave the favela. The FLXIII's social service thus manifested its control over everyday family life. Religion's strong influence was evident in the fact that residents were asked to regularize their marital status and baptize their children. The files also expose elements of residents' daily lives, identifying issues of gender, family violence, and race relations. Similarly, these files partially describe Praia do Pinto's everyday realities—the houses, the streets, the businesses, as well as relations among neighbors—opening a window on favela life from the late 1940s to the early 1960s.

The Praia do Pinto favela traces its existence to the beginning of the twentieth century. The 1906 Census of Rio de Janeiro states that there were 37 buildings and 208 inhabitants in the area.[9] By the time of Rio's 1948 Favela Census, Praia do Pinto had 1,232 residences, 25 commercial establishments, and 24 mixed-use constructions; the 1950 national census identified 7,142 residents.[10] Praia do Pinto's living conditions were probably quite precarious; Alberto Passos Guimarães described the challenge of carrying out the 1950 census, which required aerial photographs because of the "disorder and the dispersion with which the houses were erected, without any planned streets."[11]

Public authorities' precarious tolerance of the favelas during this period served to maintain the communities' fragile and provisional qualities, especially when they were centrally located.[12] As we reiterate throughout this chapter, Praia do Pinto's precariousness was a political project. Even though its residents were relatively well integrated into surrounding labor markets, the favela still suffered dubious housing conditions because authorities exercised rigid control over any improvements in the houses or their locale.[13] This chapter discusses the role of the Catholic Church, and particularly the FLXIII, in the governance of the informal city and the maintenance of its precarity. Using data from the FLXIII's files, we describe social workers' practices and detail *favelados'* daily life and mobilization strategies.

Rio's Postwar Favelas and the Establishment of the FLXIII

After World War II, as Brazil democratized following the demise of Brazil's dictatorial Estado Novo (1937–1945),[14] the Brazilian Communist Party (PCB in Portuguese) was briefly legalized (1945–1947), garnering strong political visibility. Through democratization and in the wake of a proposed Popular Front alliance with those who resisted Nazi fascism, the PCB decided to enter institutional politics. It received almost 10 percent of the votes in the 1945 presidential elections and made large inroads in urban centers, notably in Rio de Janeiro (27.5 percent).

After the promulgation of the new constitution in September 1946, communists launched campaigns for state offices and constitutional conventions; elections were held in January 1947. Communists obtained excellent local results, electing a large number (36 percent) of representatives to Rio's city council.[15] Communist councilors' tenure was short, however, as Brazilian authorities canceled the PCB's legal registration in May 1947 and annulled the mandates of its elected representatives in January 1948.

Although brief, the communist councilors' actions were intense, especially in the favelas.[16] The growing number of favela residents, the stigmatization imposed upon them, the absence of public services, and police repression all contributed to the expansion of communist ideology in the favelas.[17] The communists demonstrated great agility in organizing dozens of Popular and Democratic Committees (CPDs in Portuguese), which were involved in various neighborhood problems and debated issues such as housing, access to public services, the cost of basic necessities, education and public health, leisure, and so on.[18] Even if many of these organs were not openly linked to the Communist Party, they were largely influenced by party militants, serving as legal structures for Communist political activism.[19]

The materialization of the PCB's ideological commitment to strengthening the education of the masses can be seen in several forms of proletarian organization beyond the CPDs, such as the Uniões Femininas (Women's Unions) or the Peace Committees formed in the early 1950s as part of a PCB-led campaign against sending Brazilian soldiers to the Korean War.[20] Like the CPDs, such institutions permeated daily neighborhood life, and while they did not openly proclaim themselves communist, they were under the influence of the PCB. Although they were not closed down, political police records held at the Public Archive of the State of Rio de Janeiro (APERJ in Portuguese) indicate that they were under strict police surveillance.

The postwar expansion of Rio's real estate market also turned toward favela land. Frequent evictions were an important factor in the articulation of social struggles.[21] Many favelas would not have survived the numerous evictions of the 1940s and 1950s without the organization and assistance of the communists.[22] They were one of the few political groups that advocated openly for favela residents' land rights and directly questioned urban regulatory legislation, calling for upgrades in Rio's hills.[23]

Besides resisting evictions, these institutions fought for other community improvements such as schools, waterspouts, electricity grids, and policing, organizing discussions and debates among candidates, activists, and local residents. Communists did not describe the favelas as temporary or precarious spaces but instead conceived of them as spaces in transformation, which could achieve more livable conditions through political mobilization and public action. Debate did not revolve around developing housing policies that would require favela clearance; it focused instead on their gradual improvement. This discussion embedded favelas in larger urban dynamics and acknowledged that, beyond housing, the *favelados* were seeking a place in the city.

Rio de Janeiro's favela residents were partly responsible for the Communist Party's success in both the 1945 and 1947 elections.[24] After the PCB was outlawed, the party maintained its favela presence. Many of the CPDs gradually transformed themselves into neighborhood associations to evade police repression.[25]

During this period, direct government intervention in the favelas was limited. On September 6, 1946, the federal government set up an interministerial commission to study the causes of favela expansion; its recommendations only reinforced repressive provisions against favelas set out in Rio's 1937 Building Code (Decree No. 6000). In 1946, the government of President Eurico Gaspar Dutra created the Fundação da Casa Popular, aiming to increase the availability of new housing beyond that being produced by Brazil's Retirement and Pension Institutes (IAPs in Portuguese). At the same time, government authorities instituted several commissions to analyze the housing problem and formulate public policies. Mayor Mendes de Morais established a local favela clearance commission on November 28, 1947, to launch the definitive eradication of such spaces.[26] Although the commission produced nothing concrete, it did organize Rio's first favela census in 1948.[27]

Other initiatives were instituted on a federal scale, such as the national plan for favela extinction announced by the National Commission of Social Welfare (CNBS in Portuguese). Created under the Ministry of Labor, the CNBS set up the Subcommission on Housing and Favelas, raising hopes that the government would consolidate public resources to create a national popular housing policy.[28] But the mentioned subcommission had a negligible role studying the issue. At the municipal level, Ordinance No. 66 of January 28, 1952, created the Favela Commission to study the favela problem and plan an ambitious project.[29] The Favela Commission functioned as a council and brought together all city departments working on the issue.[30] It determined that no favela should be removed without arrangements for its residents to be resettled elsewhere and that greater control should be established through a police force empowered to immediately demolish any new construction erected on these sites.[31]

Regarding the PCB's influence in the favelas, the state and the Catholic Church coordinated a movement to neutralize communist activities. The church, guided especially by the social encyclicals, spared no effort to win over the popular neighborhoods targeted by the communists. This close relationship between church and state dated to the Estado Novo, concretized through an alliance between the cardinal of Rio de Janeiro, Dom Sebastião Leme, and head of state Getúlio Vargas. Under the leadership of Cardinal Leme, the church pursued a strategy of infiltrating state structures to impose its worldview from within and guarantee expanded social presence in an effort to Christianize society.[32]

Cardinal Leme, under the influence of Catholic intellectuals Stela Faro and Alceu Amoroso Lima, founded the Institute of Social and Family Education in 1937. The organization trained qualified professionals (social workers and family educators) who began working in the city's various welfare agencies, especially those focused on the *favelados*.[33] The institute's purpose was "to form among the women, not of one class, but of all social classes, a Christian community consciousness that will replace selfish liberal individualism without falling into inhuman state socialization. To this end, [it will] shape social workers, family educators, and housewives who will be true agents of personal and Catholic renewal in the environment in which they live and work, in the institutes in which they teach, or in the social environments in which they operate."[34]

This institute would become part of PUC-Rio (Rio's Catholic University) in 1946, imprinting the mark of the lay apostolate on the origins of social work in Rio de Janeiro.[35] In this context, the church's slogan regarding the favelas in the postwar period was "We need to climb the hill before the Communists come down."[36] In partnership with Dom Leme's successor, Cardinal Dom Jaime de Barros Câmara, Mayor Hildebrando de Goes created a commission to build favela cultural and recreational centers. The first was inaugurated in October 1946 in the North Zone's Barreira do Vasco and another that same month in the centrally located Morro da São Carlos.[37] Finally, in January 1947, the FLXIII was founded, headed by a board comprising one representative from the archdiocese, one from the municipality, and one from the Abrigo Cristo Redentor.[38] The auxiliary bishop Dom José Távora was the main patron of the institution and its director between 1949 and 1955.[39]

The FLXIII's actions focused largely on the creation and promotion of social action centers. These were important spaces for the church's political and social activities inside *carioca* favelas.[40] In 1953, six social action centers had already been inaugurated (Barreira do Vasco, São Carlos, Jacarezinho, Telégrafos, Salgueiro, and Rocinha) along with two provisional social agencies (Praia do Pinto and Cantagalo), designated as such because city hall had decided to eliminate those favelas.[41]

Grounded in the triad of education, health, and housing, the FLXIII also worked toward sanitation and urbanization, installing basic services such as water, sewage, electricity, and road networks; because of that, it was virulently criticized for contributing to favela consolidation.[42] Cezar Honorato explains that the Catholic influence on the FLXIII was only relative; the institution was supported by the church and private donations, but it was subordinate to governmental authority and especially that of the Federal District.[43] The FLXIII

was one of the main arms of municipal favela policy and was eventually incorporated into the favela's direct administration through the Coordenadoria
de Serviço Social do Estado da Guanabara in 1962.[44]

Public interventions in favelas during this period walked the fine line of
precarious tolerance, which maintained the tenuous and provisional character of the favelas. It is already possible to see the idea of selective urbanization
in the FLXIII's 1949 report: "There are favelas that must be extinguished and
their residents, presently housed in *vilas populares*, [should be relocated] to
other areas. There are favelas that must be transformed, little by little, into
popular neighborhoods, through the construction of houses built in accordance with urbanization plans."[45] Interestingly, these latter favelas were not
located in the South Zone: as Maria José Valença noted, "The aim is the total
extinction of the South Zone favelas and their residents' transfer to other locales, which should first be developed and equipped with well-built houses."[46]
This corroborates Samuel Oliveira's understanding of the FLXIII's selective actions in building and managing a workers' villa in Barreira do Vasco, a favela
located in the then-industrial North Zone neighborhood of São Cristóvão.[47]

With the goal of enabling "upwardly mobile populations" to become "less
subject to exploitation by unscrupulous politicians and extremist agitators,"
the FLXIII also exerted a strong influence on local associational life, promoting the formation of residents' associations and the so-called light committees, responsible for electricity distribution in some favelas.[48] It is also important to emphasize the disciplinary character of its initiatives, expressed
through educational services and recreational and leisure activities. The
Sports Olympics, an annual event of utmost importance for the institution,
attracted around ten thousand people in 1953.[49]

As the historian Sidney Chalhoub has argued for Belle Époque Rio, practices of social control tended to focus on the daily experiences of the working
class. This meant disciplining different spheres of life, from the strict control
of time and space in the workplace to the regulation of workers' personal or
family relationships, passing also, as the author argues, through the continuous surveillance of the bar and the street, everyday spaces of popular leisure.[50]

Much of the social control of the *favelados* took place through the FLXIII's
Social Service Department, which had as its "main objective the education
of people residing in the favelas through initiatives aimed at benefiting the
family."[51] The Social Service Department exercised strong control over favela
residents' daily lives, even making decisions about possible improvements or
new construction in communities where it operated. Maria José Valença explained how they exercised this control in concrete terms: "Each favela where

there is an agency has two or three guards from the City Hall of the Federal District, whose main purpose is to prevent when possible the settlement of new families and demolish any unoccupied or abandoned shacks."[52]

As mentioned earlier, provisional social agencies were also built in favelas marked for clearance. For example, the FLXIII built the Ana Néri agency on a site ceded by the Federal District near Leblon's Parque Proletário, next to the Praia do Pinto favela.[53] At this agency, two social workers and four *visitadoras* provided religious, legal, and educational services, in addition to offering recreation to the residents of Praia do Pinto.[54]

In later years, the Special Service for the Recovery of Favelas and Unsanitary Housing (SERFHA in Portuguese), founded in 1956 under Negrão de Lima's municipal administration, and the Cruzada São Sebastião, founded in 1955, gradually took over part of the FLXIII's favela operations. Nonetheless, the foundation still maintained authority and its presence in key favelas until 1962, when it became part of the state of Guanabara and an important arm in the dramatic favela clearance operations that began in that era.[55]

Marginalized or Workers?

Theoretical constructions of marginality in the 1950s and 1960s understood favelas as separate and isolated from the wider society, as "enclaves within the city."[56] They reduced favelas to spaces of degradation and radicalism, equating residents to rural migrants unprepared for modern industrial life and unable to take advantage of possible material improvements in the places they lived.[57]

In this sense, concepts of marginality became the theoretical justification for many social welfare programs that in fact merely reproduced the status quo in the name of "helping the poor."[58] In this context, the emerging Social Service Department was framed as an effort to prepare *favelados* for life in society. Its discourse was geared toward classifying and denigrating popular forms of housing, always to prove their inadequacy.[59] It was necessary to eradicate them to finally integrate their inhabitants into a modern way of life.

It is possible to identify such understanding in numerous works about Rio's favelas from this same period, such as the research reports from the Market Research Institute (IPEME), *Favelas e favelados do Distrito Federal* (1957) and *A vida mental dos favelados do Distrito Federal* (1958). These reports are replete with prejudices about the favelas and their residents. IPEME had clear interests in the real estate market and attempted to establish that South Zone favelas, dubbed parasitic, should be cleared, whereas more peripheral favelas, dubbed useful, could be urbanized.[60] Maria José Valença's social work thesis also reproduced these negative representations, underlining that "the favelas of the Federal District grow alarmingly, stripping the city of its aesthetic qualities and threatening to make Brazil's capital the city with the most maladjusted people."[61] The social worker Maria Luiza Moniz Aragão's description of the favelas reinforced a similar understanding: "The [preceding] picture of moral misery becomes complete with that of large-scale material misery. Favela, a picturesque expression with a certain literary flavor, which has inspired many prize-winning Carnival ditties, actually signifies filth, hunger, promiscuity, disease, and prostitution."[62]

Perceptions of favelas as marginal spaces were also permeated with racial connotations. The racist propositions of the Federal District's 1948 favela census, which stated that black and brown people were "hereditarily backward, lacking in ambition and ill-adjusted to modern social demands," are already well known.[63] It even lamented that authorities did not take into consideration eugenicist measures "capable of improving the human race."[64] Maria José Valença concurred with this racist understanding, stating that in the favelas:

People "of color" predominate, from the *preto retinto* [those with the darkest skin] to the *pardo disfarçado* [brown-skinned people who passed as white]. Such predominance is not surprising in a country where the importation of Africans manpower occurred for so long. The *negro* brings with him a very heavy inheritance: slavery, which reduced him excessively to a "thing" and that, once abolished, could not offer him a bright future because it left him, as it found him, ignorant, without a profession, long incapable of directing his own destiny. After the *senzala*, the favela . . . Some of these people spend their days gambling, or indolently sleeping, without a glimmer of energy to lift them from this state. Blacks are, in general, more distrustful due to heredity.[65]

One can identify this same racist attitude in the FLXIII's family visitation forms in the Praia do Pinto favela. The *visitadoras* always made particular note of interracial relationships, as well as possible Afro-Brazilian religious practices. A family from Praia do Pinto file 23 is a case in point. During a visit on July 20, 1961 to verify the family's eligibility for transfer to the Cruzada São Sebastião's housing project, the FLXIII *visitadora* noticed a picture of São Jorge on the living room wall, with two glasses with water and leaves as well as a lit candle, all important elements of Afro-Brazilian spiritual practices.[66] On August 10 the family went in to explain that they did not like spiritism or macumba and that they always complained about noise from one of the favela's macumbas.[67] Family members returned that same day to the FLXIII office to understand why they were not allowed to pick up the keys for an apartment in the Bairro São Sebastião. The *visitadora* in charge recounted the meeting as follows: "The head of the service said that there are no apartments for those who practice macumba, Mr. Américo denied it, saying he is not a spiritist and doesn't practice macumba." Ultimately, FLXIII arranged for a "counterinquiry" to investigate; according to notes from August 14, a neighbor stated that the family did not practice macumba and that they had nothing against them.[68]

Analyses of the files' observations should take into account that they were made by the *visitadoras*. All the same, it is possible to identify forms of agency among the *favelados*, who used what strategies they could to take advantage of the complex context of social control in which they lived. In file #23, the family had no interest in acknowledging their religious practices, especially in the face of the enormous prejudice against Afro-Brazilian religions and the risk of losing the right to access the apartment in the Bairro São Sebastião. The following comment by Maria José Valença underscores the FLXIII's position and the forms of control it exercised over such religious practices:

> A person who calls himself Catholic and divides his time between macumba and spiritism reveals a complete lack of common sense. Their bizarre rituals are not rare in the favelas, because macumba often finds in their bosom a favorable environment for its development because our people are excessively superstitious and ignorant, giving themselves without reservation to these practices. Macumba is a religious practice of Bantu origin, syncretized with Catholicism and spiritualism, tending mostly toward low spiritism. They gather at the homes of *macumbeiros* at least three times a week and spend them indulging in those vulgar beliefs, which only bring evil to both body and soul.[69]

In this period, especially from the 1950s on, the 1948 favela census's racist pronouncements were no longer commonplace in official documents. The ideology of "racial democracy," dominant among the Brazilian cultural and political elites of the time, aimed to transform Brazil into a "racial laboratory," providing the empirical backing necessary for UNESCO's scientific critique of Nazi horror and the legal systems of racial discrimination in countries like South Africa and the United States. Thus, official statements avoided racializing public debate. But racial tensions were obviously present in everyday practices, and they permeated social relations. The social workers' racist statements probably did not represent the FLXIII's official position, but they did indicate the inherent prejudices of this social group, composed largely of well-off white women.

It is important to emphasize that racial silence, in the field of urban policy as elsewhere, was understood as an ideal and not as an omission, constituting an essential element in the ideological construction of Brazilian racial democracy. This process helped to sweep racist practices under the rug and disguised racialized urban development processes, discouraging the creation of specific tools to combat such inequalities.[70]

Despite this tendency toward racial silence in urban policies and even in urban studies, Luiz de Aguiar Costa Pinto did focus on Rio de Janeiro's racial picture in 1953, analyzing the deep social disparities between white and Afro-descendant people. Attentive to stereotypes associated with black people, he noted, for example, the strong prejudice against interracial marriages, also identifiable in the social workers' reports. His work called into question the ideology of racial democracy.[71] For Costa Pinto, the social changes brought about by urbanization also provoked reactionary attitudes among dominant sectors threatened with losing privileges on the basis of racial prejudice. Despite the importance of pro-miscegenation rhetoric in ideologies of racial democracy, Costa Pinto claimed that modernity elicited racialization, not its cancellation.[72] Racial segregation in Rio de Janeiro was evident in the fact that "favelas present themselves as segregated nuclei of the poor and colored population in exactly those neighborhoods where whites constitute the majority."[73]

Finally, the FLXIII represented a way of simultaneously helping families and controlling their daily practices. The pedagogic character of the FLXIII's work presupposed its insertion within workers' leisure space in order to occupy their free time. This constituted a critique of popular recreational practices—themselves racialized—that was similar to the FLXIII's censure of popular religious practices.[74] Maria José Valença, once again, reproduced this view in relation to Carnival: "People from the favelas deprive themselves of what's essential in favor of the superfluous, with no ambition for a higher standard of living. Some spend what they can't afford in *gafieiras* [dances] and for Carnival they flaunt rich costumes that cost them tons of money. Both women and men worry too much about toiletries. The men usually wear blue, yellow and even pink Panama shirts. They spend without scruples, and live on the verge of indigence."[75]

Especially in the world of samba, the Carnival organizations already exercised a central role in the favelas year-round, often with a political cast. In the postwar period, the PCB also tried to insert itself in popular spaces through the samba schools.[76] The pejorative comments about Carnival and its alleged exotic character are obviously strange. The consolidation of Rio's official Carnival parades in the 1930s involved the direct participation of Pedro Ernesto's City Hall, as part of his attempt to insert itself in Rio's favelas and popular spaces and as part of an economic strategy that bet on Carnival as a major tourist attraction.[77] Anthony and Elizabeth Leeds emphasized this in the 1970s when they stated that Carnival involved numerous actors, including public authorities, textile and beer companies, newspaper, radio, and television networks, nightclubs, and the "bankers" at the head of the *jogo do bicho*.[78]

Other kinds of recreational associations were also set up the favelas. José Alípio Goulart described, for example, the importance of local soccer clubs: "Rare is the favela that does not have its own soccer club, with headquarters where members gather for dancing and commemorative celebrations. The clubs' headquarters, besides the specific purpose, also host other kinds of meetings, including political ones."[79] This was the case of Praia do Pinto's Club Expressinho, which attracted so many people that the resident from file 16 requested during a home visit on November 14, 1949, that a fence be built to isolate his shack from the club's many regulars.

In addition to criticizing popular daily practices, the portrayal of favelas as marginal spaces identified them as a stage within a supposed linear process that would lead to rural migrants' integration in the city. It was thus necessary to eradicate such spaces in order to limit the reproduction of marginality and finally integrate the *favelados* fully into modern society.

However, Anthony and Elizabeth Leeds identified situations in which favela occupation took place in a different way; that is, migrants first occupied formal areas and only later settled in the favelas as homeowners.[80] The case of the resident from file 23 exemplifies this observation. Doing odd jobs as a floor finisher, he had worked at the Jockey Club but was laid off along with other workers. He then worked as a doorman in the "Rio" apartment building, where he lived before coming to Praia do Pinto.[81] The fact that he lived in the favela did not mean that he was excluded from formal work, as he remained there even after he got a job with the electric company (Light) in July 1949.[82] Leeds and Leeds noted that the movement of people into the favelas was not the same as movement down the social scale. While the favela could be just an urban stage in the lives of migrants, for many it was a more permanent living space. The authors even stated, "Finally, as has been said, some people like living in the favelas."[83]

Likewise, it is possible to affirm that the favelas and their residents played an important role in shaping Rio de Janeiro's world of work. Maria Lais Pereira da Silva writes that the policy of producing workers' housing was inefficient and that beginning already in the late 1930s, the "workers' favela" developed, replacing the workers' villa.[84] Still, according to Silva and based on data from the 1948 favela census, 50.27 percent of workers in the favelas were employed in industry; of these, 42 percent were construction workers, followed by

24.21 percent in services and 10.35 percent in commerce.[85] Samuel Oliveira, analyzing data from the 1948, 1950, and 1960 favela censuses, found that despite representations of the *favelados* as rural, the percentage of workers in rural activities was less than 1 percent. The majority of favela workers took part in urban labor dynamics, which were concentrated in activities in manufacturing, commerce, service provision, or transportation.[86]

The FLXIII files show that many Praia do Pinto residents worked in local factories and even contributed to the Instituto de Aposentadoria e Pensão dos Industriários (IAPI). According to file 8b, the daughter of the registered head of household, Teresa, and her fiancé were working at a factory.[87] Of the 1,307 working people surveyed in the analyzed files, 294 of 593 female workers worked in household labor, while 178 of 707 male workers labored in construction.[88] This is the case, for example, of the couple in file 19: "Inquiries with neighbors. We had the best possible account of the family. Sr. João continues to work in construction (bricklayer). Salary 20,000. Wilma works as a domestic earning 3,500."[89]

The predominance of these activities also appears in the conclusions of the 1957 IPEME report, which, while recognizing that the *favelados* were workers, harshly criticized the favelas' expansion, arguing that it could be explained by two things: "First, the high percentage in the South Zone's residential areas of domestic servants who live in favelas. This regrettable phenomenon is due, evidently, to the proliferation of apartments without maid's rooms in Copacabana." A second issue was the lack of housing on construction sites, which required workers to seek housing in the city's favelas.[90]

Marilda Iamamoto and Raul Carvalho have argued that such residents, in view of their extremely irregular connections with the labor market, were not under any company's socialization and control and were thus considered marginal, "delinquents without crimes."[91] But it is important to add complexity to this debate. The FLXIII files indicate that residents related to the labor market in various ways, sometimes through stable public employment, others through an array of odd jobs, and others through extremely precarious activities. Most intriguingly, these realities were sometimes mutable; the same workers could move through different working conditions at different moments. Such strategies can be explained by the contingencies of the labor market itself, as well as by the personal strategies of families that could in some contexts engage in odd jobs or operate small shops in the favela itself. In many cases, the favela's privileged location in the city was the most stable element in residents' daily lives.

Leeds and Leeds identified various instances in which *favelados* circulated among different formal and informal activities; such was the case of Sócrates, a migrant from the northeastern state of Ceará, who served in the army and worked as a typographer at the *Jornal do Brasil* but then decided to quit his job to set up a grocery in the favela because he could earn more money.[92] There is also the case of Osmar, a worker from Praia do Pinto who used severance pay from his job at a movie theater to buy and run a *lotação* (a vehicle that transported passengers or goods).[93] Other residents of Praia do Pinto worked in *biroscas* (small grocery stores) or did general odd jobs. Many work activities were even directly related to the favela's local conditions. Some Praia do Pinto residents, for example, performed the extremely precarious and poorly paid work as water carriers. According to file #1403, "Constantino, despite being 'psycico' [he probably suffered from some mental illness], works fetching water for his neighbors."[94] The son of the resident profiled in file 42, in turn, earned a living through odd jobs as a bricklayer, "but at the moment he fetches water for his neighbors."[95] Not to mention the work of the washerwomen, like the resident in file 8b who, abandoned by her partner, "washes clothes, but intends to find work as a cook. Her daughters are employed as seamstresses and help with household expenses."[96]

A closer look at statistical data and documentary sources such as the FLXIII family visitation forms shows how *favelados* were integrated into Rio de Janeiro's world of work. Despite negative representations associating favelas with marginality in the 1940s and 1950s, some observers from that same era already questioned these views, including José Alípio Goulart, who stated that "the great majority of those who inhabit the 'favelas' are useful and productive people who are constantly active in various branches of honest work."[97]

In addition to the notion that *favelados* were not integrated into the labor market, there was a very recurrent perception that they were politically passive or easily manipulated by various political interests, especially the communists. The IPEME report emphasized as much: "The favelas are a veritable breeding ground for social agitators. The *favelados*' passivity has, until now, prevented them from achieving obvious success. But their persistent propagandizing, based on realities of which those concerned are gradually becoming aware, suggests that the apparent calm of the moment cannot be expected to last much longer."[98]

The understanding of *favelados*' insertion into the world of work was widely explored in the postwar period. Besides the strong presence of the Communist Party, through the communist-inspired entities mentioned previously, it is also important to note the creation of the Union of Favela Workers (UTF) in 1954. The UTF formed under the leadership of lawyer Antoine de Magarinos Torres after he was contacted by the residents of the North

Zone's Morro do Borel to defend them from eviction. From Borel, UTF centers spread to other favelas and sought to represent *favelados* before public authorities, sometimes assuming the role of neighborhood association. Importantly, the UTF recognized *favelados* as "workers," which promptly drew elite attention, provoking fears of possible political manipulation.[99]

The FLXIII files suggest that the residents were not necessarily politically passive, as shown by the example of Francisco from Praia do Pinto, registered in file 18. When told during a family visitation on November 9, 1949, that he had to leave his house because the Leblon Company wanted the land for construction, he said that he hoped "Getúlio" (Brazil's leader from 1930 to 1945) would be president again, also noting that he would prefer that the city find him a place to live in Rocinha, because "the country has an obligation to give *favelados* housing." The resident further stated that "Getúlio is not Gaspar Dutra [the Brazilian president at the time], who only wants politics."[100] A few years later, the *visitadora* wrote, on June 13, 1960, that they had "the impression that Francisco is one of those agitator types. He talks about his acquaintance with important people and hints that he could use this influence at any time."[101]

As we will see, despite FLXIII's strict control over any kind of home renovation or upgrading, the residents' petitions to the FLXIII for targeted improvements, emergency renovations, and even home expansion revealed numerous conflicts. The home—and in its way, the favela—itself represented an indispensable urban resource for these families' integration into the city, including in the labor market.[102] Much of the era's political mobilization was constituted through the struggle for permanence, which manifested itself in the improvement of the locality and in the consolidation of local homes. The alleged urban informality of the favelas did not necessarily imply informality in the labor market. The FLXIII files reveal families with stable jobs and even some who contributed to their respective Retirement and Social Security Institutions. Some of these families owned lots in peripheral areas, but, as we will see, they mobilized to stay in Praia do Pinto.

Residents' Daily Life and the Struggle for Permanence

Despite numerous lawsuits filed by landowners or land-grabbers to evict *favelados* in the postwar period, no significant number of evictions took place until the 1960s. However, favela residents always faced the specter of removal. Maria José Valença's work described how the FLXIII supported the clearance of the Niemeyer favela, near Praia do Pinto. Valença affirmed that unexpected family relocations to areas far from their jobs created problems because the "great majority worked in the South Zone, in Leblon itself."[103] Yet most of the families (177 out of 218 removed) were transferred to the distant Coelho Neto neighborhood; the remaining families "were transferred to other locations, including only one to Praia do Pinto, three to Rocinha, two to Barra da Tijuca, and the rest to land owned or donated by sympathetic people."[104]

Maria José Valença stressed that, despite the FLXIII's efforts, the transfer was problematic, especially for women, because "most of them are domestics; almost all of them work in Copacabana, the older ones as laundresses and the younger ones as factory workers in Gávea."[105] Again, contrary to theories that depicted favelas as spaces where marginality was reproduced, they in fact served to integrate workers into the city. Despite many studies that established the importance of the favelas' location, the proposed solution was always the favelas' destruction and their residents' transfer.

Housing policies relied on the work of the Social Service to instill in residents a desire for the fundamentals of modern life, including access to private property, ideally in the city's periphery. However, the records of the FLXIII visitations indicate a desire among Praia do Pinto's residents to stay in the area. When *visitadoras* and social workers encouraged the residents to buy lots in the suburbs, *favelados* always invoked the favelas' existing social networks—as well as their privileged access to public services and the job market—as a justification to stay in place; residents did not aspire to move to a peripheral lot. When questioned during a visit on May 13, 1949, about the importance of buying plots of land outside the favela, the resident from file 1356 answered the *visitadora* "grumpily, because he is not willing to leave the favela with his *birosca* [small shop]." The next day he went to the FLXIII office to resolve the *birosca* issue because he had been ordered to close it: "He told us that he lives from the *birosca*, because he had an accident and was left disabled."[106]

Many residents, however, did buy peripheral plots as a safeguard against the risk of eviction. For example, on May 27, 1952, the resident from file 10 reported paying for a peripheral plot of land in distant Mesquita. During a visit on June 11, 1954, the aforementioned resident of file 16—who had used his severance pay from a movie theater to buy a *lotação*—also said that he had bought a piece of land in the distant district of Campo Grande.[107] We can also cite the *visitadora*'s notes in file 6, which verified that the family it documented owned a piece of land in the also-distant neighborhood of Realengo, "but the [female] partner doesn't want the man to build a shack. He is paying $858.60 a month for the land; if possible, he asks the Foundation to provide materials for him to build a room so he can move with his family."[108] Upon learning that another resident was building a house in the peripheral municipality of Caxias, another *visitadora* reported, "We made him see the evils that exist in the favela, that it is not a family environment."[109] However, despite having purchased those lots, those families remained in Praia do Pinto and were later transferred to the Cruzada São Sebastião's housing project.

The *visitadoras'* stimulus of peripheral land purchases also emerged in their criticism of residents who purchased other kinds of expensive goods, as reported in file 8b, when a family visit on October 2, 1951, gave the *visitadora* "a great surprise. We saw in Paulínia's home a huge *radio-vitrola*. We told her that when we advised her to buy land, she said she couldn't, so how could she buy a piece of furniture like that?" The *visitadora* completes her account by stating that she advised the family "to buy land, which was more essential than the *radio-vitrola.*"[110]

In addition to the labor market, living in Praia do Pinto provided access to leisure and better public services such as schools and health care. According to an October 5, 1948, *visitadora* report, a man named Sr. Rodrigues owned a *birosca* and had no intention of leaving the favela. A few months later, on February 8, 1949, he reiterated this position to the *visitadora* and said that he didn't want to leave the favela because he had children being treated at the nearby Hospital Miguel Couto.[111]

In addition to encouraging residents to leave the favela, the FLXIII exercised strong control over local construction. Any and every renovation had to be approved by the Social Service Department, which often denied all requests. Emergency renovations, such as leaks or collapses, were usually authorized after inspection by the surveillance police, but we did not find any approved requests for additions or for replacing fragile construction materials with masonry. Residents had to initiate construction within a month after obtaining a permit.[112]

The FLXIII also exercised control by closely monitoring construction work. The *visitadora* for file 18 reported on March 1, 1950, that she had received a complaint that a shack under construction near a well-known road had been expanded. Arriving at the site, the *visitadora* checked the measurements and found that the structure was half a meter larger than initially proposed. The local residents were furious at having to make their shack smaller, and complained loudly about the FLXIII assistants, accusing them of taking bribes. The next day, Sr. Batista, the shack's owner, went to the FLXIII office and asked the *visitadora* to go to the site and mark which part of the shack needed to be removed so that they could continue the work.

While the FLXIII monitored construction, it relied on other agencies to grant licenses and crack down on unauthorized work. The Favela Commission, along with the surveillance police, participated in this oversight, as an excerpt from March 27, 1955, tells us: "We went to Dona Luiza's house to bring her the repair permit. We needed to reach an understanding with her, because she wanted to build a first floor [above the ground floor], claiming that the shack in front and the one next door had 1st floors that blocked the sun in her house. We showed in every possible way that this was impossible because of the Favela Commission members' presence in the favela. Finally Dona Luiza agreed with us."[113]

The *visitadoras* followed up to see if renovations conformed with what residents had requested, and officials frequently destroyed additions made without the required permit. The Social Service Department monitored construction; a *visitadora* reported in file 10 on September 14, 1949, that "while passing by the area, we saw that Sr. José was repairing his roof, but he didn't have the necessary permission, he claimed he didn't know and offered to come and get it." The resident in file 8b, in turn, came to ask on May 2, 1951, to add another floor to her shack. The *visitadora* explained that this "depends on Sr. Serafim, we can say almost certainly that he will not consent, but we noted the request and [said she should] come back another day for the answer."[114]

On February 2, 1951, the resident of file 985 asked for permission to build another room in her shack, claiming that her son was going to get married and live in the shack as well. The *visitadora* promised to note the request in the ledger where Mr. Serafim signed the permits. However, the *visitadora* visited the construction site on May 11, 1951, and ordered the dismantling of a fence that had been built without Mr. Serafim's permission.

Construction permit requests were indeed a tense issue in the relationship between residents and the FLXIII. The *visitadora* in file 1281 informed residents that they could not build a new shack because of the "contents of Code 6,000."[115] The homeowner's son would not accept the answer and told his father "not to attend to these women from the F., and that he should do whatever he wanted because we had nothing to do with that." The *visitadora* told him to shut up and told the person in charge of the shack to accompany them to the FLXIII office to pick up a "repair permit."[116]

There are even reports in the files of attempts to bribe the *visitadoras* in exchange for improvement authorizations.[117] The *visitadora* in file #5 reported on January 9, 1952, that the resident secretly asked her for "a permit to raise the shack [higher] to accommodate her daughter, whose husband does not sleep in the shack for lack of space. He promised me money if we would secretly allow him to augment the shack and he would not say anything to anyone." The *visitadora* explained that the surveillance department would not consent to any expansion, and if he broke the law, the guards would destroy the shack. She even reported that she communicated the matter to the "guards so that they would be on the lookout."[118]

Here, we identify how the urbanistic freezing of the favelas was concretized through the effort to control any improvements, such that the material aspects associated with informality were preserved with the direct participation of public authorities and in partnership with various actors.[119] The Catholic Church, through FLXIII, was one of these actors that played a strong role in the management and reproduction of informality. It controlled the favelas' growth and ensured the houses' precarity; it also disseminated and reinforced prejudices associated with these places and their inhabitants and encouraged residents to buy plots in peripheral areas. The files even contain reports on the FLXIII's participation in the removal of a small favela called Areinha (located next to Praia do Pinto), where it brokered the interests of a Leblon real estate company. The FLXIII later removed some of the favela's residents to Praia do Pinto.

If marginality theories depicted such spaces as apart from the city, José Alípio Goulart had already noted to the contrary, "There are favelas in which the paths have names as if they were streets; and the shacks have numbers just like the houses in urbanized centers." In this way, Goulart affirmed that, far from being exclusive to these areas, favela lifeways were in dialogue with those of the rest of the city.[120] The fight for favela consolidation was evident in the struggle for local improvements, especially in the effort to install collective services such as water and electricity. However, the policy of precarious tolerance allowed favela dwellers only limited access to certain collective services, thus preserving the favelas' precarious and supposedly temporary character; as such, tolerance could not give rise to a de facto recognition.[121] This precarious access relied directly or indirectly on the actions of public authorities and was often mediated by politicians or institutions active in the favelas, such as FLXIII.

Water supply was thus extremely precarious, mainly provided through the *bicas d'água* (waterspouts). As Goulart emphasized: "Water, like electricity, is one of the *favelados'* greatest demands; where there is no *bica* (rare is the favela that doesn't have one), the installation of one is the first request that the residents make to the authorities and the first promise they receive from candidates for elective office."[122] This was the case, for example, of Sr. Adalberto, from file 3, who stated on October 4, 1948, that he had talked to then councilman Breno da Silveira and that he would not move from the favela unless it was to the new houses that were being built in Gávea.[123] He also said that the councilman promised to install a water spout.[124]

Goulart also reported that in each favela, municipal spouts were meant to provide water for all local residents, but they "do not always supply those who seek them with water, the precariousness of which is accentuated in those environments." The author stated that the *bicas* were usually installed "on a small cement base, like an island, in the center of the mire that spreads around it; it is commonly placed as close as possible to the urbanized street that passes closest to the favela." Goulart continued his description, stating that everyone—men, women, old men, children—carried water to their residences: "The liquid is carried in lard, kerosene, or gasoline cans, through the mouth of which they thread a piece of wood—usually a broom handle—to facilitate transportation. But the cans are often carried on the head, and a good part of the contents are lost on the ground or spill on the carrier as he walks."[125]

Fernanda Barcellos also described water's centrality: "Water is the most precious element in the favelas . . . Everyone carries water."[126] She went on to state that at "4 o'clock in the morning there are already people at the *bica*."[127] According to Goulart, "The water does not flow all day and there are specific times to collect it, especially at night when there is greater pressure in the pipes, which increases the agglomeration of people, especially women, around the *bicas*."[128] Maria José Valença also stressed this issue, underlining the constant lack of water that "is distributed at night in many favelas, depriving these people, already so long-suffering, of even the right to sleep, because they must spend the night collecting water for the next day."[129] She explained that for water collection, residents set up long queues of water cans; depending on their can's distance from the spout, people would even go back to their homes, returning later to collect their water.

The search for water was obviously a source of great hardship in residents' daily lives. On May 28, 1956, on the verge of the first residents' transfers to the Bairro São Sebastião housing project, the *visitadora* reported that a resident came to the Social Service Department to say that his wife lived in the favela (one of the requirements for transfer to the apartments), but that she spent fifteen days in the favela and fifteen days at her mother's house in Mesquita because she was very ill and could not carry water.[130]

The residents struggled similarly for electricity. As noted earlier, the FLXIII actively participated in the organization of local electric grids. The National Department of Gas and Lighting, through Ordinance No. 1 (April 6, 1948), established the FLXIII as the entity responsible for organizing the existing electric networks or approving their installation in other favelas, even those where the foundation did not operate directly.[131] The ordinance established, first of all, that it was essential that the FLXIII or some other legal entity authorize the installation of electricity networks in the favelas. Danielle Bittencourt affirms that twenty-four "light societies" had already been formed in 1949, involving about eight thousand members.[132]

As early as 1951, however, the FLXIII stopped intervening directly in electric supply, acting more as an advisory body. The foundation ended its electric service in 1952, and requests for installation or maintenance started to be negotiated directly between the favela residents and the government.[133] By then, the favelas were already largely served by electric networks. José Alípio Goulart described the favelas at night: "The hills of Rio de Janeiro, with a few exceptions, are dotted with luminous hubs, showing not only the extent of electricity in the favelas but also the settlements' reach."[134]

Despite negative descriptions of favela spaces, it is important to understand that their alleged precariousness was in a way perpetuated by strict limitations on possible upgrading. The FLXIII exercised such control in Praia do Pinto and its files demonstrate that the *visitadoras* and social workers always advocated for the residents' removal and the favela's eradication. For the residents, Praia do Pinto's privileged location was an important resource, which sparked a strong movement for permanence; for them, Praia do Pinto was not a provisional reality.

Conclusion

In the late 1950s, the Cruzada São Sebastião partly absorbed the FLXIII's favela activities. These two initiatives expressed divisions within the Diocese of Rio de Janeiro over pastoral projects: the FLXIII represented a more conservative wing, associated with Archbishop Jaime de Barros Câmara, whereas the Cruzada São Sebastião expressed an early renewal of the Catholic Church's social action, headed by the then auxiliary bishop of Rio de Janeiro Dom Helder Câmara.[135]

Even if the practices of the Cruzada São Sebastião were not yet progressive, they indicate a gradual change in the Catholic Church's pastoral work, which began to express greater concern for marginalized sectors. Especially from the 1960s on, the axis of Brazilian pastoral action—following the direction of the church internationally—revolved around social advocacy, leaving questions of doctrinal orthodoxy in the background.[136]

With regard to the Praia do Pinto *favelados*, the Social Service Department of the FLXIII was very active in choosing the residents who were transferred to the Cruzada São Sebastião housing project. The candidates from Praia do Pinto had to meet the criteria established by the Cruzada, namely, having lived at least four years in the favela; being relatively poor; having a legally constituted family, or at least one that "respected natural morals"; having children; and finally, having no "delinquents" in the family.[137]

The Cruzada São Sebastião's criteria for accepting new residents in the housing project still associated the favelas with marginality and showed the Social Service Department's attempts to use the residents' transfer to new housing as a way of solving that problem. The apartment was, thus, a counterpoint to favela shack. Although the files did show some residents' fears about moving to the new apartments—because of the high monthly payments and the risk of being expelled for default or due to the Cruzada Social Service's strict supervision—the files do not reveal any sign of strong resident mobilization against the transfer.[138]

The church's seal of approval, the quality of the buildings, and the fact that the housing complex was only a few meters away from their previous homes were elements that ensured a certain adherence to the project among residents. Those who were transferred to the apartments continued interacting with Praia do Pinto for a few years; it was only totally eradicated during the military dictatorship after an infamous 1969 fire. At that later point, the transfer process looked quite different, both because it was done amid the urgency of the disaster and because they were sent to distant locales—all in the context of the great wave of favela clearances that occurred in the 1960s and 1970s, expelling tens of thousands of workers from Rio's central areas and removing all traces of the favelas around the Rodrigo de Freitas Lagoon.

All in all, contrary to the claims of marginality theory, this chapter has shown that favela residents were integrated into the city through their use of local services and especially through their integration into the labor market. The favelas were not necessarily transitional spaces for urban migrants; in the postwar period, many families had already lived in these places for decades. Despite *favelado* mobilization in favor of upgrading their homes and the favela itself, there was an effort, led by FLXIII in the case of Praia do Pinto, to maintain their precarious and provisional features.

In a context of political effervescence, with the end of the Estado Novo dictatorship in 1945 and the beginnings of the Cold War, a new understanding emerged of how to deal with Rio's favelas, one that resulted in "negotiated control" rather than definitive solutions.[139] In this context, Catholic Church institutions participated in the dispute for electoral power and ideological influence over workers through various favela initiatives. This was exemplified in the FLXIII, which was present in favelas across the city, providing assistance to families but also exercising strong control over their daily lives.

Democratizing the Republic by Instituting the Informal: *Barrio* Irregularity in Caracas and Venezuelan Democratization, 1941–1964

SERGE OLLIVIER

In 1987, Venezuela's legislative body called for the country's informal urban areas—the so-called *barrios*—to be integrated into the urban fabric within the framework of the Ley Orgánica de Ordenación Urbanística (Organic Law for Urban Development).[1] This new law assigned local urban planning authorities the task of identifying "areas of uncontrolled growth" with the aim of "incorporating them into the urban structure."[2] It marked the first step toward the regularization of urban planning and land markets in these neighborhoods, which were already home to almost half of the country's urban population.[3] By that point, the *barrios* were not just a major feature of urban space but also a major focus of attention for public authorities and elected representatives. The 1987 law was not the first time that authorities had recognized the *barrios'* existence. But it was novel in extending official recognition to the domain of civil law, marking the beginning of a transformation of the legal and institutional environment in which the *barrios* had developed, which was described by the jurists Rogelio Pérez Perdomo and Pedro Nikken in 1979 as an "official informal order."[4]

This apparently paradoxical order was characterized on the one hand by the illegality of *barrio* housing and on the other by the recognition that such housing gained through the actions of local executive authorities. Until the end of the twentieth century, the *barrios'* irregularity was multifaceted. Most of their housing was built following "urban land invasions" (irregular land occupations), which meant there was no legal guarantee of ownership for the occupier builders.[5] In addition, their housing was often illegal because it did not comply with building regulations, which made it unregistrable and rendered its rental unlawful. However, municipal authorities, public legal aid services, and public urban planning authorities would often operate outside the dictates of civil law and the legal market to provide support for *barrio* housing through urban service provision and efforts to prevent or resolve land conflicts.

For observers in the late 1970s such as Rogelio Pérez Perdomo and Pedro Nikken, this *contra legem* support for the *barrios* from official bodies and their various representatives was characteristic of the electoral and institutional system of the Fourth Republic of Venezuela (1958–1999).[6] Before democratization in 1958, various administrations had pursued—albeit ineffectively—a policy of *barrio* regularization. These attempts had taken two forms. One, notably implemented by the social democratic governments of 1945–1948 (the so-called Trieno Adeco), focused on installing utilities and urban amenities and officially registering the *barrios* that were located on land deemed suitable for construction. The other, implemented by the military junta of 1948–1958, aimed at expulsion and demolition. These two diametrically opposed policies were followed from 1958 onward by another, completely different approach.

This chapter aims to show that the democratization of the Venezuelan political system in the early years of the Fourth Republic led public authorities to abandon de facto the policy of legally regularizing Caracas's informal neighborhoods. This evolution becomes visible from two perspectives. Systemically, it emerged through the development of a sui generis and eminently politicized way of constructing the popular city—the *barrios*—which were at once legally irregular and an enduring feature of their social and political environment. Historically, especially in Caracas, the policy evolution resulted from social and political tensions that made the association of the *barrios* with the nascent democratic regime an obstacle to political stabilization for the new elites in power.

From 1958 onward, the Venezuelan capital saw a simultaneous shift toward a political regime of representative democracy and an "official informal" regime that governed the production of the popular city. This twofold shift was largely a consequence of the city's meteoric economic and demographic growth. The Venezuelan economy had been revolutionized by the oil industry in the 1920s, and Caracas had captured oil revenues and the profits derived from their investment. The tensions created by this process came to a head under the dictatorship of Marcos Pérez Jiménez (1952–1958), who sought to take advantage of the oil boom to transform Caracas into a beacon of modernity.

Pérez Jiménez's fall on January 23, 1958, marked the invention of mass politics in Venezuela's political landscape. Transitional leaders replaced the policy of eradicating the *barrios* with support for land invasions during the first months of 1958. Official support was improvised, organized, and structured in conjunction with the deployment of the democratic parties' networks among the popular sectors. Communist and social democratic municipal councilors had already pursued this policy a decade earlier under the social democratic government of Acción Democrática (AD) from 1945 to 1948. Following a chronology that was itself political, the policy was reconstituted and consolidated in two stages. In a context of great political uncertainty marked by the Cold War, it was reshaped first in 1958 for the benefit of Marxist militants and then from 1960 to 1964 for the benefit of a resurgent AD.

By 1963, the "official informal order" that characterized the *barrios* had become entrenched. Official speeches and documents justified and euphemized it through the lexical field of "community development," a fitting credo for a new republic that was being constructed in partnership with the United States and the United Nations.

However, this "official informal order" was, in practice, anything but orderly. It was a form of day-to-day politics comprised of ad hoc official protection and urban improvements, implemented through partisan cronyism or in response to resident mobilization. Its erratic nature was accentuated throughout this period by an administrative jumble that involved three levels of public jurisdiction in the management of informal urbanization in the Metropolitan District of Caracas: first the two municipal councils (the Departamento Libertador to the west and the Distrito Sucre to the east); then, from the 1950s forward, the two federated states (the Federal District in the west and the state of Miranda in the east); and finally the Metropolitan Area of Caracas, a third jurisdiction that emerged in response to the growth of the urban area beyond the borders of the Federal District and the federal state.

This chapter examines the historical process through which the informal construction of Caracas's *barrios* became officialized, drawing on an archival corpus that allows a comparative study of official discourses and local practices. An examination of the local press, oral sources, the archives of communist activists, and early social science research on informal districts complements the analysis of official documentation (legal texts, government reports, public speeches).

1941–1958: From the *Campaña* to the *Guerra*

In 1935, Venezuela entered a twenty-three-year phase of accelerated modernization and political conflict over an uncertain democratization. Throughout the presidencies of the military leaders López Contreras (1936–1941) and Medina Angarita (1941–1945), and in the subsequent periods of El Trieno Adeco (1945–1948) and the military regime (1948–1958), Caracas was both the center of the country's political reconfigurations and the privileged object of modernizing efforts.[7] The capital's informal urbanization gradually became a public issue during this period, owing to its massification and the fact that it did not fit with the various regimes' modernization plans. According to Juan José Martín Frechilla and Beatriz Meza, who have studied the evolution of official positions regarding the *barrios* prior to 1958, three major features characterize this period.[8] The first is the emergence, classification, and quantification of the problem of informal urbanization, which was mainly characterized (and discredited) according to building type (the traditional shanty, known as the *rancho*) and location (the *quebradas*, or ravines, and especially the *cerros*, or hills). The second is the almost immediate discrepancy between a federal government discourse that promised to eradicate the *barrios* and the Departamento Libertador's management of their expansion.[9] The third is a radical shift around 1950 from a draft federal policy drawn up in 1946 under the democratic government to regularize the *barrios* and install services to a policy of systematic eradication implemented by the military junta from 1951 to 1958.[10]

RANCHOS IN THE CAPITAL

Unlike other Latin American capitals such as Mexico City, Rio de Janeiro, and Buenos Aires, Caracas still had a provincial feel at the beginning of the twentieth century. In 1920, it had a population of only 118,000. Venezuela itself was still sparsely populated, with fewer than 2.5 million inhabitants.[11] However, the sudden onset of oil exploitation strengthened the capital's economic weight and, consequently, its growth. By 1936, the population of Caracas had more than doubled to 258,000, and by 1941, it was 354,000.[12] In the space of two decades, the city's population had grown twice as fast as that of the country.

Between 1926 and 1930, Caracas experienced its "first boom in private real estate development," or *urbanización*, when developers "with questionable property titles, ongoing disputes, and no permits" parceled out irregular, unserviced land across "the flat areas and hills of the parish of Sucre," located in the west of the Federal District.[13] Despite fraudulent sales and permanent tweaks in the regulations, the official sources do not yet record any problematic land issues.

In 1929 and 1930, health and public works officials determined the illegality of these housing developments by the topographical site they occupied (the *quebradas* or the *cerros*), which had been declared unfit for development because of the impossibility of installing a water supply or sewage system. This prohibition was determined by two administrative bodies that came under the authority of the Interior Ministry and the Ministry of Public Works and was addressed to the governor, the municipal engineering department, and the municipal council, which were jointly responsible for enforcing it.[14]

At this same point, the shortage of housing also became a social issue for the city council of the Departamento Libertador,[15] although it did not officially begin to diagnose the problem until a decade later. Municipal authorities defined the irregularity of Caracas's popular housing as a land issue for the first time following the democratic and socialist opposition's victory in the 1938 municipal elections. In 1940, the commission responsible for land registry, common land, and municipal land administration classified the terrain occupied by *barrios* into three categories: municipal land with irregular status, land with questionable property titles, and federal land.[16]

During this same period, the Ministry of Development introduced questions about residential sanitary facilities into the seventh national census. The 1941 census thus officialized the traditional *rancho* as a category of housing defined as having a straw roof, earthen floor, and an almost systematic lack of water or sewage services.[17] In a country where 65.1 percent of the population was rural, the census results showed that 60.8 percent of the housing was classified as *ranchos*, painting a "disconcerting picture of housing in Venezuela."[18] The *rancho* was associated with ruralism, backwardness, and above all, a lack of hygiene. The fact that this type of housing was so prevalent rendered it harmful.[19] The national census linked the housing problem to the *rancho* problem, especially in the big cities, where urban growth stemmed mainly from intensified rural emigration. The number of *ranchos* in Caracas rose from 5,437 in 1941 to 12,738 in 1944.[20]

By 1945, the housing problem in Caracas was thus officially associated with the *barrios*. The area covered by these informal settlements in the Federal District more than quadrupled in the space of a decade and a half (21 hectares in 1930 and 94.5 hectares in 1941).[21] Public authorities took most of those fifteen years to define why the *barrios* were considered irregular, eventually homing in on three aspects: the site (steep, dangerous, and difficult to install services on), the property's legal status, and above all, the types of structures used for housing. The *cerros* and *quebradas* as well as the *ranchos* were rejected mainly on the grounds of hygiene.

From a legal perspective, the *barrio* problem was entrenched when a new version of the 1942 Civil Code reaffirmed existing land law. Article 557 confirmed the "poder de atracción del suelo," stipulating that the landowner was also the owner of any building erected on their land, unless the value of the building greatly exceeded the value of the land (Article 558). According to Article 788 of the Civil Code, the landowner could have the building demolished if the occupant was acting in bad faith, which was technically the case for the vast majority of *barrio* occupants because they had no valid documents.[22] This land legislation, which was weighted heavily in favor of the landowners, would remain unchanged until the 1980s.

Nevertheless, it was extremely complicated for landowners to evict occupants from the *ranchos*. They had to be able to clearly identify each "invader" and present evidence of their own continued ownership in the form of property titles. The Federal District's constitutional law of October 1936 also made any eviction subject to a declaration from the governor that the land invasion constituted a disturbance of public order.[23] The land tenure system in force therefore made it impossible for occupants to legalize their *ranchos* and practically impossible for landowners to evict them. It gave the Federal District's governor and later the state of Miranda's governor the ultimate power of arbitration. Because local officials rather than the courts decided on possible evictions, arbitration was more political than judicial.

1941–1948: THE DEMOCRATIC PARTIES AND THE BEGINNINGS OF UPGRADE POLICIES

The period from 1941 to 1946 saw the formalization and politicization of the two opposing public responses to the *barrios*' irregular status (eradication and improvement). The eradication policy put the construction of new collective residential housing at the center of its urban planning program and argued that the *barrios* should remain illegal. The improvement policy, though, valorized individual housing and auto-construction and supported the legal regularization of the *barrios*.

These debates crystallized around the largest development project of the time, the El Silencio *reurbanización*, which involved the demolition in 1942 of a urban residential area and the construction of seven blocks of residential apartment buildings, completed in 1945. The project was managed by the Banco Obrero, a public fund established in 1928 to fund housing for individual workers, which ultimately evolved into a full-fledged agency for the construction of popular housing. Supported by President Medina Angarita, the modernist project was criticized by some urbanists and by the democratic opposition. The planners believed that new urbanites would fail to adapt to living in modern collective housing.[24] The elected members of the Partido Democrático Nacional—which became the AD in 1941—and the elected members of the Partido Comunista de Venezuela (PCV) rejected the project because it was too costly, not just for the public purse in the economic context of World War II but also for the city's most modest income earners, who would be unable to afford the mortgage plan.[25]

The elected representatives of AD, who formed a majority in the municipal council from 1939 to 1942, distanced themselves from the El Silencio project and instead focused on organizing an upgrade of the existing *barrios*. They
created the Caja Municipal de Crédito Popular, a municipal fund that provided public loans to individuals to finance the construction of their homes.
That same year, the council established its first Juntas Pro-Mejoras (executive
councils responsible for urban development) at the parish and *barrio* levels
as well as the Ligas de Colonos (settlers' associations). An AD (Adeco) leader
named Gonzalo Barrios also set up a humanitarian executive council called
the Junta Pro-Habitantes de Puentes y Quebradas (council for the inhabitants
of bridges and ravines).[26] During these three years of the AD-PCV majority
in the Departamento Libertador's municipal council, the elected members
established the first municipal public support agencies charged with installing services and upgrading the *barrios*. Their action focused on *barrios* situated on national land that had been purchased by the Departamento Libertador. The AD and PCV representatives advocated within the council for an
extension of the *barrios*, which they saw as a better solution to the affordable
housing crisis than the construction of collective dwellings.[27]

After the democratization of 1945, the federal government took up their
recommendations. The sudden fall of Medina Angarita on October 18, 1945,
had put an end to a democratic opening that had been controlled by military
generals, giving way to Venezuela's first social democratic government: the
Revolutionary Junta led by Rómulo Betancourt. Universal suffrage and the
secret ballot were introduced in March 1946, replacing the previous male-
only, public voting system. The first national policy addressing the housing
shortage launched with the creation of the National Housing Commission on
January 14, 1946, and a decree (no. 144) setting out the administration's objective to build forty thousand workers' homes over the following ten years.[28]
A number of AD officials with experience at the municipal level in Caracas,
such as Gonzalo Barrios, steered the administration in the direction of a program centered on servicing and improving the *barrios* of the Federal District.

In June 1946, Alejandro Oropeza Castillo, the former managing director of
the Banco Obrero and an Adeco official, submitted a general report on behalf
of the National Housing Commission on the objectives of Decree No. 144.
This report in fact constituted a road map for a national policy for installing
services in the *barrios*. It set out a "plan for the improvement of low-income
housing" for households that were unable to meet the mortgage payments
necessary to purchase a Banco Obrero apartment. This was the first time a national public body had officially acknowledged that there was a lack of public
resources to rehouse residents from the *ranchos* and recommended that the

existing *barrios* be upgraded. The plan proposed that a local council, called a Junta Pro-Vivienda Popular, would be responsible for installing services, constructing foundations, and selling building materials to future occupants in each municipality that had signed a contract with the Banco Obrero.[29] The project's two objectives were to develop serviced land for the rehousing of inhabitants from the *cerros* and to provide materials to facilitate the construction of permanent houses. Known as the "anti-*ranchos* campaign," the project aimed to put an end to the *ranchos* not by demolishing them but by improving them through auto-construction.

In August 1947, Betancourt referred in one of his speeches to an "emergency plan" to provide "building materials to poor communities . . . so that they themselves can rebuild their homes."[30] This plan was never implemented, even though it was probably only envisaged for Caracas,[31] but it was the first time a federal government had officially supported a policy to improve the self-built *barrios*.

Betancourt's Revolutionary Junta and the National Housing Commission thus legitimized the action of the social democratic and communist members in the Departamento Libertador's municipal council. The two members who were most active on this issue within the newly elected council, initiated in January 1948, were Eduardo Gallegos Mancera of the PCV and Raúl Díaz Legórburu of the Unión Republicana Democrática (URD). Gallegos Mancera proposed that municipal technical assistance should be made available free of charge to the *barrios'* occupier builders regardless of their land regularization status. Díaz Legórburu called for the Departamento Libertador to designate public land reserves and advocated for the decriminalization of *rancho* construction. Both men stressed in numerous speeches to the council that the public authorities had to recognize that the development of the *barrios* had become an irreversible phenomenon.[32]

The 1940s saw a considerable increase in emigration from the countryside to Venezuela's cities. The 1950 census results show that the country's urban population was in the majority for the first time, accounting for 53.8 percent of Venezuela's total population of 5 million. In particular, the *barrios* of Caracas had expanded as a result of the Adeco government's support for *rancho* improvements. In 1945, there were 78 *barrios* in all in Caracas, with 60 located in the Departamento Libertador and 18 in the state of Miranda in the east. In 1948, these figures had increased to 122 *barrios* overall, with 97 in Libertador and 25 in Miranda. In the Departamento Libertador alone, there were a recorded 20,953 *ranchos* in 1949, accounting for more than 20 percent of all the capital's housing.[33]

The rapid democratization during the period El Trieno Adeco thus coincided with a clear acceleration in the *barrios'* expansion, a consensus between the social democratic (AD and URD) and Communist Party leaders regarding their regularization, and the creation of the first informal institutional tools—the juntas—to organize the installation of public services.

1949–1957: LA GUERRA CONTRA LOS RANCHOS

The military coup of December 2, 1948, put an end to Venezuela's first social democratic experiment and, consequently, to any plans to regularize the *barrios*. The military government, led first by Carlos Delgado Chalbaud and then after 1950 by Marcos Pérez Jiménez, deposed Venezuela's elected officials and suspended elections. A favorable economic climate marked by an increase in international crude oil prices aided its modernization drive. Venezuela's gross national product, boosted by oil revenues, increased by 95 percent between 1950 and 1957.[34] The country had the strongest economic growth of any on the continent during this period.

This new prosperity promised to turn the regime's modernist ideology, the "new national ideal," into a concrete utopia. Pérez Jiménez dreamed of making Caracas the metropolis of the Caribbean.[35] Approximately 60 percent of national investment in public works was allocated to Caracas during his dictatorship. Obsessed with modernism, the government decided that the *ranchos* had to go. Dictatorship emancipated the government from the electoral game, and new fiscal resources gave it the means to realize its ambitions. Popular housing in the capital would either be functionalist, modern, and collective or would not exist at all. The Banco Obrero soon followed the regime's lead and, in 1949, declared "war on the *ranchos*." Its publications propagated condemnations of the *ranchos* on hygienic and moral grounds and claimed that life in the *barrios* made workers forget their "creative, active impetus."[36] Despite a 1951 report from a presidential commission of urban planners—which had been addressed to the governor of the Federal District and proposed that the government install urban services in the majority of the capital's *barrios* and allow the inhabitants to construct their own homes—military leaders and various administrative directors were persuaded that the *ranchos* should be eradicated.[37]

In 1952, Pérez Jiménez presented his "presidential plan for the elimination of the *barrios*." The eradication campaign accelerated in 1954 following the publication of a report that put the number of *ranchos* in Caracas at 53,360 and the number of inhabitants at 310,976, 38 percent of the capital's population.[38] In 1958, 750 hectares of *ranchos* were destroyed by force.[39] The regime built collective housing during this period, most notably the emblematic

2 de Diciembre complex, built between 1955 and 1957 and consisting of thirteen superblocks and fifty-two apartment blocks intended to house 180,000
people.[40] The program was not completely achieved, but between 1951 and
1957, more than 23,000 housing units were built in Caracas, accounting for
70 percent of the national total.[41]

However, by 1957, it was clear that this strategy had not lived up to the
government's rhetoric, mainly because the transformations in the capital had
accelerated demographic growth. Between 1950 and 1958, the city grew from
704,000 inhabitants to more than 1,200,000, expanding to the east through
the state of Miranda as far as the colonial town of Petare.[42] The concentration of investment in Caracas and its spectacular growth had increased its at-
tractiveness because the capital's modernity and standard of living contrasted
more sharply than ever with that of the rest of the country. However, the
high cost of the new popular housing units and the limitations of Caracas's
job market precluded rural migrants from integrating into the regular housing market.

A large proportion (521 hectares) of the *barrios* initially managed to resist
the bulldozers.[43] Many of the 2 de Diciembre apartments still lay empty, but
most of the displaced *barrios* inhabitants rebuilt their *ranchos* further south
or west, in the Federal District, or in the east, toward Petare. Hence, fifty-
three new *barrios* appeared in the Metropolitan District of Caracas during
the military regime.[44] In early 1958, some 220,000 people were living either in
the old, densified *barrios* or in the new *barrios* located outside the city center.
Overall, their housing conditions had deteriorated.

This meant that the sudden onset of a recession in the second half of
1957 had especially dramatic consequences in Caracas. Public investment fell
sharply, which led to a scaling down of activities, especially in the construction sector.[45] In January 1958, unemployment reached an all-time high in the
city, and in the *barrios*, where a large proportion of construction workers
lived, it hit 30 percent.[46] The social crisis delivered a double blow to the working classes in the form of mass unemployment and a housing crisis, which
was exacerbated by continuing evictions and by the inaccessibility of the new
collective housing.

From Mass Revolt to Voting En Masse

On January 23, 1958, an uprising of the country's principal sectors succeeded
in putting an end to the dictatorship. Throughout January 1958, there had
been successive official pronouncements against a backdrop of riots in Caracas. While street protests had played their part in the political crises of the

previous two decades, this was the first time in the country's history that a regime had been brought down by crowds mobilized on the streets of Caracas.

The "spontaneous combustion" of January 23, 1958, as Arturo Uslar Pietri and many other contemporaries called it, signified an eruption of social tensions that had been exacerbated by sudden mass unemployment in a city under construction.[47] However, the social crisis did not disappear with the dictator, and the insurrectionary climate in Caracas, fueled alternately by the crowds and by a military anxious about the transition, prevailed through all of 1958. At the center of the political arena once more, AD had to contend on the one hand with the economic and military sectors and on the other with the PCV, in a Cold War context that was far more tense than it had been in 1945–1948.

The pivotal year of 1958 marked Venezuelan national memory. The historiography has mainly framed it in terms of negotiations among elites, with a notable focus on the democratic leaders' success in forging a new political equilibrium through a carefully orchestrated political agreement among the major parties.[48] In Caracas, however, the reconfigurations were more profound. A new political openness and the first social measures proposed by the interim government's junta gave rise to a renewed wave of migration to the capital. In response to the social crisis, the junta proposed the Plan de Emergencia para los Barrios. This was the first effective, official, national public policy to install public services in the *barrios*. A transitional measure with lasting consequences, The Plan de Emergencia provided improvised official sanction to the informal *barrios* and marked the democratic transition with that hybrid stamp.

During this historic year for Venezuela, the question of the *barrios* assumed the republic's center stage. 1958 began with the fall of the dictator and ended with the reinstatement of national elections; in Caracas, it witnessed the rise of an insurgent populace and ended with the vote of the citizen masses.[49] The results of the general elections of December 7, 1958, established the *barrios* as a burning electoral issue; in stark contrast with the popular vote in the rest of the country, Caracas's working-class voters had voted for Wolfgang Larrazábal, the president of the interim government.

CARACAS IN AN INSURGENT CONTEXT

Throughout January 1958, the opposition to Pérez Jiménez spread agitation throughout the city from their base in Caracas's popular neighborhoods. The Federal District's *barrios* were closed off to the authorities; the streets were barricaded, and protesters greeted the police by banging pots and pans and throwing stones and Molotov cocktails if they tried to approach. Rioters from two popular neighborhoods close to the city center, 2 de Diciembre and San Agustín, made their way toward the city's business district on January 23.

In the parish of San Agustín, whose *barrios* bordered the city center to the south, the front lines of the conflict had been crossed several times during confrontations with the Seguridad Nacional, whose nearby headquarters were set on fire on January 23.[50] The 2 de Diciembre complex, located just west of the city center, was another epicenter of the riots. The fact that hundreds of the new flats in the superblocks were still empty caused outrage. In these areas, opponents sought to benefit from the regime's concrete legacies even as they opposed it.[51]

On the morning of January 23, when the news broke that Pérez Jiménez had fled the country, a massive crowd gathered in the city center. Many photographs captured the occupations of the capital's main squares, taken throughout a historic day of festivities during which Pérez Jiménez's was burned in effigy.[52] Many experienced the day as a liberation. But it marked not only collective mobilizations' pinnacle but also their forceful legitimation. By the evening of January 23, the street had gained a newfound political weight.

Demonstrations continued in the months that followed and soon seemed to bestow the Caracas masses with a particular political spirit. On May 13, thousands of demonstrators met the US vice president Richard Nixon with an angry response during an official visit to Caracas.[53] On July 23 and September 7, tens of thousands of demonstrators took to the streets to oppose attempted putsches against the interim government. Contemporary commentators saw this as a continuation of popular pressure for democratization.[54]

Hostile to the US government and prodemocratic, the street mobilizations also took on social content. An unemployed workers' movement had been forming in the capital since January 23, with thousands demonstrating every day in front of the presidential palace.[55] The secretary of the interim government's junta, Edgar Sanabria, would comment two decades later that the junta had been faced from the outset with "a sort of chemical binomial: either lead or silver."[56] In other words, had to choose between a repressive policy (the "lead," symbolizing bullets) and a social policy (the "silver," symbolizing income from subsidized jobs). The junta chose the social option in the form of the Plan de Emergencia para los Barrios.

THE PLAN DE EMERGENCIA PARA LOS BARRIOS

On March 13, 1958, the interior minister, Numa Quevedo, proclaimed the Plan de Emergencia para los Barrios, indicating that the problem was to be considered a matter of public order. He announced "a basic emergency plan to solve to the extent possible the problem of unemployment on a national scale. . . . This plan, which will be coordinated by the competent bodies, will include the twenty states and federal territories . . . and will be implemented by June 30, the end of the fiscal year, for a total sum of 127 million bolivares."[57] He added that the funds released should be used to respond to the major national challenges of improving roads, public hygiene, and education.

The 1953 constitution was still in force, as was its legislative calendar, with a budget vote due in June. The Plan de Emergencia, which had been drawn up in February, was therefore intended as an interim solution in anticipation of the new budget.[58] The radio, the press, and official documents referred to it as the Plan de Emergencia para los Barrios.

The plan's contents were detailed when it was approved in July as a public policy, inscribed in the budget, and placed under the direction of the Ministry of Public Works. It was then officially renamed the Plan de Obras Extraordinarias (special public works plan), although the press and ministerial reports still commonly called it the Plan de Emergencia para los Barrios.[59] The plan was placed under the direction of a young municipal engineer and AD activist named Celso Fortoul, who presented a report to the ministry in July that was at once an appraisal and proposed work plan.[60]

Fortoul immediately highlighted the plan's lack of planning. He characterized it as a "reactive and interim" response aimed at "temporarily solving the problem of unemployment in the Federal District and the state of Miranda." He detailed the projected works and added housing upgrades to the list of priorities that the interior minister had outlined in March, which had included roads, public hygiene, and education. No major infrastructure project or urban planning initiative was envisaged. Only "minor" works would be carried out, such as sidewalks, road surfacing, sewers, primary schools, and police stations, and unregulated aid for the construction of individual homes.[61] The Fortoul report thus validated and made plain what the plan had been about since March: the installation of public services in the *barrios*.

The plan was effectively an unacknowledged employment program. Its sole objective was to create jobs in Caracas's construction sector. Thirty thousand new jobs were announced in July 1958, followed by an additional twenty-eight thousand in January 1959.[62] The Banco Obrero recruitment offices hired workers for six-month periods. However, only half of the workers were actually employed on construction sites.[63] Limited by the lack of planning, the administration was instead forced to let its employees work on upgrading their own *ranchos*, using materials originally intended for other projects within the plan.

When the accounts were submitted at the end of 1960, they showed that the government had injected nearly half a billion bolivares into the *barrios* in 1958 and 1959.[64] The Departamento Libertador's *barrios* had benefited from the greatest improvement, with new services installed and homes upgraded. However "interim" the plan may have been, it represented a radical change in urban policy. For the first time, the *ranchos* had received substantial support from the state. In the streets of Caracas, Fortoul was soon dubbed the "people's engineer." For inhabitants, the urban development set out in the plan represented not just a material contribution to their *barrios* but a public recognition of their permanence.

All the same, nothing had been altered in the legal or administrative order to favor urban land occupations, either through property law or through municipal decree. The reason for this was that there was no elected parliament in place, and the municipal councilors, who had been elected in 1948, lacked legitimacy after they returned to office.

Nevertheless, the introduction of a nonlegislative measure did contribute to a significant administrative evolution. On February 24, 1958, Banco Obrero launched a campaign to reimburse the occupier builders of the *ranchos* destroyed during the dictatorship. It declared that it wanted to recognize the ranchos in legal terms as legitimate improvements—*mejoras* or *bienhechurías*—and compensate the occupier builders, provided that the individuals had acted in good faith according to Article 788 of the Civil Code. This was not a legal breach, as the Banco Obrero announced in the press that it would reimburse only those who could present a rental contract for the land the *ranchos* were built on as well as the most recent receipt for rent payment and invoices substantiating construction costs.[65]

While most inhabitants of the demolished neighborhoods were unable to present the documents, Banco Obrero's positioning was nevertheless significant on several levels. Politically, it represented a complete reversal of Pérez Jiménez's eradication policy. Legally, it contributed to a recognition of the value of the *rancho* structure, provided there was a written agreement with the landowner. Administratively, Banco Obrero abided by the municipal council's decisions for all *barrios* located on municipal land and encouraged the occupier builder to obtain the landowner's agreement in the case of private land occupations. From this point on, land "invaders" seeking to establish permanent *barrios* always had to obtain the consent of either the municipal council or the private landowner. During the early years of the new regime, this served to channel land "invasions" away from private land and toward municipal land.[66]

The end of the dictatorship and its war on the *ranchos*, combined with the introduction of the Plan de Emergencia, rapidly catalyzed colossal migratory pressure on Caracas. The growth of the *barrios* exploded beginning in February 1958. A year later, in January 1959, the Banco Obrero estimated that more than a hundred new *ranchos* were being built in Caracas every day, particularly in areas relatively far from the city center, such as the parishes of La Vega and El Valle in the southwest of the city, where the population almost doubled in one year.[67] Because no census occurred that year, it is very difficult to assess precisely how many people immigrated to the capital and settled in its *barrios*. In any case, between 1957 and 1960, the population of the Metropolitan District of Caracas gained almost 300,000 new residents, growing by more than 20 percent and reaching about 1.3 million inhabitants.[68]

By the time the plan ended in January 1960, sixty new *barrios* had been established in the Metropolitan District of Caracas, mostly in the city's east (Petare) and northwest. More new *barrios* had been created in the space of two years than in the previous ten. For contemporary commentators, the phenomenon was striking. The valley looked completely different. Many of the verdant *cerros* were suddenly pitted with stacks of wood and metal sheets. In 1959, the political rupture was also a rupture in the capital's urban history.

MAKING THE LAND "INVASIONS" PERMANENT

The dozens of new *barrios* that appeared in 1958 resulted from urban land "invasions"—that is, through the irregular occupation of municipal or private land. Although the authorities may have been caught unawares by the phenomenon's new scale, the invasions were neither spontaneous nor disorganized. Very quickly, each *barrio*—old or new—set up a neighborhood junta. These became the inhabitants' interlocutors with the municipal and urban planning authorities. The juntas were inspired by an old Ibero-American tradition, but also by the Ligas de Colonos and the first Juntas Pro-Mejoras that had been created two decades earlier by the elected AD and Communist city councilmen in the Departamento Libertador.

The return to power of these parties stimulated the creation of the new juntas, especially since the administrators of the Plan de Obras Extraordinarias encouraged them. Fortoul's report called for the creation of a communal center in every *barrio* to manage collective infrastructure and services. This was essentially dependent on the creation of the Junta Pro-Mejora (junta for upgrades). The report specified that in "*barrios* that have a Junta Pro-Mejora, this stage is very smooth" and conflated the future communal center management committees and the Juntas Pro-Mejoras.

Although these plans remained hypothetical in the initial state of emergency following the 1958 revolution, the communal centers proposed in Fortoul's report served as a tool to gain recognition for the Juntas Pro-Mejoras. The success of improvement projects carried out in the *barrios* within the framework of the plan already relied on the existence of a neighborhood junta. The installation of sewage and running water systems occurred only in "*barrios* that meet certain minimum organizational conditions." The report did not add any new conditions with respect to the plan's resource distribution. Rather, it clarified the de facto modus operandi that had been set out in March and attempted to give it a veneer of planning rationality.

These juntas had no legal status or even any official generic title. They were usually named after the inhabitants' demands, hence the Junta Pro-Mejoras. Sometimes they were called Juntas de Vecinos de Barrios (residents' associations) or, when the *barrio*'s permanence was not assured, Junta Pro-Defensa del Barrio (junta for the *barrio*'s defense). Whatever they were called, their main role was to obtain support for local requests from the municipal council and the urban planning authorities. They would apply to the communal junta of their parish or directly to the Departamento Libertador's municipal council in the Federal District or the Sucre municipal council in the case of the *barrios* located in Petare in the state of Miranda.

The municipal counselors (*concejales*) very quickly resumed their role as the neighborhood juntas' preferred interlocutors. The archives of Communist Party municipal counselor Eduardo Gallegos Mancera contain a list of the juntas' requests and his responses to them.[69] On his return to the Departamento Libertador municipal council in May (he had originally been elected in 1948), he directed his activity toward the Juntas Pro-Mejoras. He supported the requests they addressed to the municipal agencies in charge of economic matters and land registration, he approached the Instituto de Crédito Popular and the housing commissions to propose a construction program, and he followed and coordinated the dealings of one particular junta with the Fundación de la Vivienda Popular (Foundation for People's Housing), private companies, and the Plan de Emergencia.[70] He conducted all his interventions on the municipal council's letterhead.

Amid the effervescence of 1958, elected municipal officials directed *barrio* inhabitants to the appropriate public bodies and helped to legitimize their actions, even when the *ranchos* in question occupied "invaded" land. Their archives provide information both on the prevalence of the municipal council in Caracas's revitalized democracy and on the dynamism of the ever-expanding *juntas de barrio*.

FROM THE *BARRIO* JUNTAS TO THE *BARRIO* VOTE

Each junta was politicized from its inception. At least one of the local leaders in every junta was affiliated with a political party. Any petitions or letters of request from a *barrio* came from its junta. The junta's president then systematically addressed them to a municipal councilor belonging to the same party. The relations between the two entities thus fell within the domain of partisan sociabilities. These militant links dated to the creation of the first Juntas Pro-Mejoras on the initiative of the Partido Democrático Nacional members in 1938. From February 1958 onward, they were reestablished and systematized.

The politicization of the juntas became a key issue in Caracas politics on June 16, 1958, when the governor of Caracas, Colonel Vicente Marchelli, dismissed Fortoul as the plan's director. Fortoul had become a political embarrassment in conservative circles, with which Marchelli was closely associated, but he had become extremely popular with the *barrio* inhabitants because of his implementation of the plan. More importantly, he was also an open member of the Marxist wing of AD, known as the *muchachos*.

On June 17, thousands of demonstrators descended on the Plaza Bolívar to demand that Fortoul remain in his post. Larrazábal, president of the national Junta de Gobierno, concurred with their demand. Fortoul kept his post, and Governor Marchelli resigned that evening.[71] The PCV's regional committee quickly understood the significance of this show of force. The Frente Pro-Fomentista was created less than two weeks later by a group of communist activists,[72] many of whom had led the June 17 demonstration. The first postdictatorship federation of Juntas Pro-Mejoras was born, and it was communist.

In the wake of this, the Venezuelan Communist Party rationalized and structured the link between the formation of a junta and entry into the party. The coordination of *barrio* activism responded to the inhabitants' expectations. In July, for example, activists from the La Ceiba *barrio* in San Agustín drew up a plan for political and cultural activities in their neighborhood and asked their local PVC committee how they could "get in touch with the Juntas Pro-Fomento to find out how they are organized and how our comrades can join."[73] The local Juntas Pro-Fomento emerged during July and August under the aegis of Olga Luzardo, a journalist and poet in charge of the local PVC committee.[74] In August, with an eye on the general elections of December 7, the local PCV committee set to work on expanding the party. It adapted the party's organizational structure to the urban fabric of the rapidly expanding *barrios*. Each PCV cell was to be given a map of the "precise zoning" of its local area so that it could be regularly redivided as new *barrios* were created or broke off from the old ones.[75] An "organization week" at the end of October concluded the restructuring of *pecevista* activism in the capital and launched the last phase of the electoral campaign. All activists living in the *barrios* were required to contribute to what was described as "peripheral work," participating in the operation of their neighborhood junta and trying to integrate it into a larger network of Juntas Pro-Fomento.[76] Communist activism, from that point forward, involved participation in the *juntas de barrio*.

In Caracas's popular neighborhoods, partisan networks had emerged emaciated from the dictatorship and the clandestinity imposed in 1948 on the AD and the PCV and then in 1952 on the URD. The Christian Democratic Party, COPEI, which had remained legal during the dictatorship, was still a party of the wealthy classes in the capital.[77] The PCV was the quickest to rebuild its networks in the *barrios*. The sources give no information on the total number of communist activists in Caracas in 1958, but it is possible to estimate them at a few thousand, perhaps 4,000 at most, because 4,490 were registered with the regional committee in July 1959.[78]

Wolfgang Larrazábal left his post as president of the national junta and returned belatedly to the campaign trail on November 14, 1958. He was the URD's official presidential candidate and had accepted the PCV's support while also declaring unequivocally that he was not a Communist. In Caracas, the campaign quickly swung in his favor. The three main reasons for this were his prestigious reputation, due to his personal charisma and his association with the Plan de Emergencia; the militant support he received in the *barrios* from the URD and the PCV; and the Caracas AD regional committee's fierce political opposition to their own party's candidate, Rómulo Betancourt.

This last, purely political reason had consequences. The AD regional committee in the Federal District had been led since January 23 by the *muchachos*, the leftist wing of the party that had taken the reins of AD when it went underground in 1948 and all its founders either disappeared or went into exile. This young generation of AD militants, led by Alberto Domingo Rangel and Simón Sáez Mérida, had honed their activism and leadership alongside the communists in the struggle against the dictatorship. They aspired to radical social change and adhered more to Marxist-Leninist ideas than to the social democracy that Betancourt wanted to build.[79] There was thus a deep chasm between them and the party caciques, who were two decades older and practically strangers to the younger militants when they walked back in and took over the party leadership in August 1958.

In Caracas, the *muchachos* led the party throughout 1958. Right up to the last day of the campaign, the AD machine never really supported the AD's presidential candidate; the *muchachos* had even supported Wolfgang Larrazábal. Fortoul, who had been appointed secretary-general of the Caracas AD's regional executive committee in July,[80] had pushed Larrazábal to visit the *barrios* and the plan's construction sites with him. The distribution of the plan's resources thus fell to a heterogeneous front of anti-Betancourt activists. The revolutionary youth of AD, which effectively directed the plan's implementation, made sure its largesse benefited those *barrio* juntas that shared their political leanings toward the URD and the PCV.

URD and PCV activists, for their part, conducted a fierce campaign in Caracas in support of Larrazábal, specifically targeting the *barrio* vote.[81] With two weeks to go before the election, the PCV's regional committee organized a full afternoon of Frente Pro-Fomentista plenary meetings with the members of the Juntas Pro-Fomento.[82] Between the active support of the URD and PCV activists and the discreet support of the AD, the electoral campaign in the capital's popular districts almost exclusively supported Larrazábal.[83]

The former president of the national junta had thus proved unexpectedly popular. In addition to being associated with the benefits of the Plan de Emergencia, he had, during his interim term as president, shown a great talent for communication. His "singular, trailblazing personality" came into its own during street-level engagements, and he made sure to participate in as many as possible during his short election campaign in Venezuela's big cities.[84] He ended his campaign winding his way through the *barrios* in the west of Caracas, standing or sitting on the roof of a car and wearing a type of shirt (*camisa llanera* or *camisa criolla*) that signified popular Venezuelan identity. This was the first time a major presidential candidate had openly and personally campaigned in the *barrios*.

The democratic transition was consummated on December 7 with a peaceful election and a voter turnout of 92.15 percent.[85] This democratic victory belonged first and foremost to Betancourt, who won 49.18 percent of the votes, followed by Larrazábal, with 34.61 percent.[86] In Caracas, however, Larrazábal won the vote with 69.33 percent against only 14.15 percent for Betancourt, who took third place.[87] AD as a whole in fact took fourth place in the capital's presidential and congressional elections, overtaken by COPEI, the PCV, and the URD, with a landslide victory. Never had the electoral gap between Caracas and the rest of Venezuela been so great. In the city's popular parishes, Larrazábal enjoyed a landslide victory.

For politicians on all sides, it was clear that 1958 had redefined Caracas's political and electoral landscape. In a capital that was in a state of social and political turmoil, the new government identified the reasons for Larrazábal's popularity and used them to formulate a strategy to win over the popular electorate and forge a "policy of the masses" that could stabilize the new regime. The winning formula was clear. The government had to subsidize the installation of public infrastructure and services in the *barrios* via politicized Juntas Pro-Mejoras, and elected representatives at the municipal and even the national levels had to publicly recognize the legitimacy of these juntas' demands. Through the streets and the ballot box, an officially sanctioned and eminently political order that favored the *barrios'* recognition and permanence was therefore established without a single urban planning debate or legislative action.

1959–1964: An Official Informal Order

In February 1959, Betancourt was inaugurated as head of an AD, URD, and COPEI coalition government. Yet this did nothing to calm the social and political situation in Caracas. Migration from the countryside continued to rise, *ranchos* continued to be built, and the *barrios* continued to expand. In 1961, Caracas had 1,336,464 inhabitants, 5 percent more than at the end of 1959. In the eyes of contemporaries, the population of the *barrios* had seemingly doubled in those same two years: a parliamentary commission reported in 1969 that the number of people living in *barrios* had risen from 20 percent to 40 percent of Caracas's total population between 1959 and 1961.[88]

In addition, dual economic and political constraints had prompted the government not to reverse the policy of supporting the Juntas Pro-Mejoras. As the economic slump continued, the business community sought to revive activity. It blocked any urban and land reforms and therefore any regularization of the *barrios*, even though the inhabitants could not afford the mortgage payments for regular housing due to mass unemployment. Politically, the country was entering a new Cold War phase marked by the Cuban Revolution. The Marxist left, which had won the *barrio* vote in December 1958, took an insurrectionary stance against the government in 1960, soon mounting armed opposition. For Betancourt and AD, it was essential for the stability of the regime to prevent the *barrios* from becoming red bastions. They therefore decided not to abandon the Juntas Pro-Mejoras policy that had made Larrazábal so popular in the *barrios*, resolving instead to build on it and turn it to their advantage.

REASSURING THE BUSINESS COMMUNITY AND OUSTING THE MARXISTS FROM THE *BARRIOS*

After Betancourt's inauguration, Venezuela experienced a liquidity crisis and a period of sluggish growth. Between 1959 and 1961, GDP growth slowed to

1.5 percent per year. The construction industry was on its knees, and almost half of the workers in the sector, many of whom were *barrio* inhabitants, remained unemployed.[89] To boost hiring and honor the 1958 agreements with employers, the government introduced a "stimulus policy for the private sector" and provided the country with the credit institutions and mortgage lenders needed to finance the private real estate market.[90]

Venezuela's land tenure system, which protected investors and allowed expropriations only in exchange for compensation at market price, therefore endured, making it prohibitively expensive to create new public land reserves in areas occupied by the *barrios*. This was the case, for example, with Banco Obrero's attempted 1961 expropriation of the five-hundred-hectare La Urbina hacienda in Petare, where a dozen new *barrios* had recently been established. The compensation requested by the owners, deemed legal, was far too costly, and the expropriation was canceled.[91]

The 1960 law on the sale of subdivided lots further alienated the *ranchos* from the legal regime. While it protected apartment and house purchasers from developers, the law accentuated the illegality of *barrio* housing. Whether they had "invaded" or bought their plot of land, very few *barrio* residents had received the "documento de urbanización y de loteamiento" (urbanization and subdivision document) that the law required. The document was supposed to detail the land's property titles for the twenty years prior to its purchase by the current owner and also list urban public services in compliance with municipal decrees. Both were impossible to provide for the *barrios*.[92] Despite these measures, the business community was still wary of AD, whose Marxist origins they had not forgotten.[93] Betancourt tried to give them guarantees and implemented an austerity policy, which was rejected by the left.

The other major source of confrontation between the government and the Marxist left was the Cuban Revolution. The movement was very popular in Venezuela, where Fidel Castro had made his first official visit as head of state on January 23, 1959, barely two weeks after he marked the revolution's victory with a triumphant entrance to Havana. Castro's revolution greatly affected the PCV and was a formative influence on the new Movimiento de Izquierda Revolucionaria Revolutionary (MIR), founded in July 1960 by former *muchachos*, who had definitively severed their connections with Betancourt. In 1960, the confrontation between the two Marxist parties and the government pushed the country to the brink of civil war. Following the breakdown in diplomatic relations between the Betancourt government and Havana on November 11, the PCV and the MIR called a general strike. This evolved into an armed insurrection, particularly in the 2 de Diciembre district, which had been renamed 23 de Enero (January 23) in honor of the 1958 triumph against

Pérez Jiménez.[94] The PCV and the MIR then opted for an armed struggle, which drove them underground in May 1962.

The Marxist left's entry into guerrilla warfare distanced it from the activism of the *barrios* and the life of the juntas. However, the PCV was able to draw on its Juntas Pro-Fomento to lay the groundwork for the uprisings of November 1960.[95] From 1960 to 1962, the insurrectionary climate prevailed, and the *barrios* were at the heart of governmental concerns. For AD, the rallying of the Juntas Pro-Mejoras was a key element in the struggle against Marxist subversion.

THE *BARRIO* TRANSFIGURED INTO A *COMUNIDAD*

Between 1958 and 1960, newly founded *barrios*' inhabitants adapted with agility to the new competition between the democratic parties by forming pluralistic *juntas*. To maximize opportunities for public support, the few families leading a neighborhood junta would usually present at least one junta committee member for each party represented in the municipal council.[96] The government then gradually phased out the Plan de Obras Extraordinarias between August 1959 and March 1960. Deprived of the plan's resources, the *pecevista*, *urredista*, and *mirista* juntas faced an effective "embargo" from the Ministry of Public Works.[97] In November 1959, the PCV's regional committee noted "a certain decline in the Pro-fomento movement . . . in response to the government's decision to wind down the Plan de Obras Extraordinarias."[98] When the PCV went underground in 1962, it had already lost control of most of the juntas previously affiliated with the Pro-Fomento movement. Disillusioned by the armed struggle and the impossibility of service installation in their *barrios*, many neighborhood leaders distanced themselves from the party.

The government's main aim was to link the Juntas Pro-Mejoras to the regime (including both the Betancourt administration and the AD). The project was led by Alejandro Oropeza Castillo, appointed by the president as governor of the Federal District in 1960. Oropeza Castillo was a longstanding AD official, a member of the party's hard core for three decades, and a loyal Betancourt supporter. His career had also made him a housing specialist. As director of the Banco Obrero during El Trieno Adeco, he had authored the 1946 report supporting aid for auto-construction in the *barrios*. During his subsequent exile under the military dictatorship, he had worked as an international civil servant, heading up the UN's technical assistance office for Latin America. All the tools and personnel required for an informal, permanent, and politicized administration of the *barrios* were set up under his leadership from 1962 to 1964.

Oropeza Castillo intended to administer not the *barrios* as such, but their "community" of inhabitants, because the Juntas Pro-Mejoras were officially aligned not with urban planning or urban policy per se, but with the transnational credo of community development. *Desarrollo de la comunidad* emerged as an objective in the 1960 four-year national economic and social development plan and was described, broken down, and defended in publications and conferences by senior civil servants who were integrated into the networks of the United Nations and its Economic Commission for Latin America (ECLA).[99] Community development was characteristic of the new regime's developmentalism and quickly permeated official public discourse. The AD deployed its political and administrative apparatus in the *barrios* under the community development banner and effectively mobilized its discursive elements.

In January 1962, the government created a financial and technical lever for its community development policy called FUNDACOMUN, which was financed by the US Agency for International Development as part of President Kennedy's Alliance for Progress. FUNDACOMUN was a semiautonomous funding agency that supported municipal councils in small-scale projects. Its president was appointed by Venezuela's president. Alejandro Oropeza Castillo took over as its head in 1964, shortly before his death in a plane crash that same year.

In the spring of 1962, as governor of the Federal District, Oropeza Castillo created the Movimiento Pro-Desarrollo de la Comunidad to coordinate the services of the Public Works Ministry, the Departamento Libertador's municipal council, and FUNDACOMUN. It was common knowledge that the Movimiento was an offshoot of AD. The governor appointed an Adeco activist, Rubén "Charlita" Muñoz, its president.[100] Whether in his capacity as president of the Movimiento or as AD activist, Muñoz would always publicly defend AD and told US State Department officials that the Movimiento was dedicated to "isolating and eliminating leftist groups" in the *barrios*.[101]

At the beginning of July 1962, a Comité de Remodelación de Barrios (Committee for *Barrio* Remodeling) was created within the municipal urban planning office, again on the governor's initiative.[102] Oropeza Castillo oversaw this committee as well as the Movimiento, and both worked hand in hand. As a municipal agency, the committee applied for and obtained funds from FUNDACOMUN, which it then transferred to the Movimiento.[103] The *barrio* juntas affiliated with the Movimiento, which were often referred to as Juntas Pro-Desarrollo de la Comunidad, were also directly supported by FUNDACOMUN and the Ministry of Public Works, with whom they had signed contracts.[104] In 1964, the Movimiento expanded to the eastern district of Sucre and to the *barrios* of Petare.

By the time Betancourt handed over power in March 1964 to the newly elected president, his AD comrade Raúl Leoni, AD had become the leading electoral force in the *barrios* of Caracas. Its activists ran the majority of the Juntas Pro-Mejoras. These juntas worked with public institutions and agencies, which recognized them as representatives of their "community."

Informal status meant parallel administration. The *barrio* space was managed through the "participation" of the "community"—which involved the entry of local leaders in AD networks, formalized as the Movimiento Pro-Desarrollo de la Comunidad. The Movimiento integrated all the stakeholders, from junta members all the way up to the state governor, and defined the framework for an informal, semiprofessionalized, undeclared management of *barrio* urbanism. Operating in the spirit of community development—a programmatic tenet central not only to the Venezuelan regime but also to the UN and to Inter-American cooperation—and financed by a semiautonomous foundation (FUNDACOMUN), the Movimiento coordinated and facilitated the administration of the *barrios* and the installation of services by the municipalities and the Public Works Ministry at the margins of both the law and of municipal and federal budgets.

THE JUNTAS: INFORMAL INSTITUTIONS FOR PRODUCING THE *BARRIOS*

In 1964, although it stopped short of legalizing the *barrios*, AD pieced together all the political and administrative supports that had allowed them to develop since 1958, thus institutionalizing the "official informal order" noted by Pérez Perdomo and Nikken in 1979.

This newly institutionalized order led to an official *contra legem* recognition of the *barrios* through the links that united the Juntas Pro-Mejoras with public institutions and above all with the municipal councils. These links were based on Adeco cronyism (*compadrazgo adeco*). The informal administration of the *barrios* corresponded to a mode of management based on personalistic ties. The founding and consolidation of a *barrio*, the two critical phases in its creation, thus depended on the partnership of three classes of actors: the elected municipal official, the civil servant (generally from the Ministry of Public Works), and a resident leader of the neighborhood junta.

The Julián Blanco *barrio*, located in the former La Urbina hacienda in

Petare, is a paradigmatic example of the early stages of *barrio* urbanization and has been extensively studied by researchers.[105] It began as an urban land "invasion" led by seventeen families in August 1960. The three men who organized it and ensured its success were the founder himself, who set up his own *rancho*, a municipal police subcommander, and a municipal councilor named Julián Blanco. All three were Adecos.

The urbanization of the *barrio* did not begin until 1968. The founder had moved away in the interim, leaving a lethargic junta that was taken over in 1966 by a new resident, Edmundo Rondón. At the age of twenty-seven, he already had a great deal of knowledge about how a junta operated from his experience in the older, more central Unión *barrio*, also located in Petare, where he had grown up. As head of the junta of the newly renamed Julián Blanco *barrio*, he worked with a senior official from the Instituto Nacional de Obras Sanitarias (INOS, which was affiliated with the Public Works Ministry), a representative from the city council, the city council's attorney, and the municipal councilor Julián Blanco, who was well respected among residents. In 1968, INOS installed a piped water system, Electricidad de Caracas extended electric infrastructure, and garbage collection commenced. In 1973, the junta persuaded INOS to install sewers and construct steps on the *barrio*'s slopes. It was considered "consolidated" because it had been equipped with the basic urban services.

Both the foundation and the servicing of the *barrio* had thus resulted from an administration that was at once informal and official. It was official because the junta and therefore also the *barrio* were recognized by the municipal council, which allowed the junta to contract with INOS and other urban planning agencies. In addition, the municipal council recognized the inhabitants' attestations of residence and good conduct (*constancias*) issued by the junta's presidency. More generally, the Departamento Libertador's Juntas Comunales and Sucre's municipal council would also provide land occupation permits, certificates of residence, and good conduct references for residents and their *ranchos*.[106] In the case of the Julián Blanco *barrio*, the municipal council's support also prompted private landowners to accept the occupation.

Yet the administration was also informal because the *barrio*'s junta had no legal status. The president acted in his own name when contracting with INOS and other agencies, recruiting workers from among the inhabitants, and collecting water fees. Rondón, like many other Juntas Pro-Mejoras leaders, was a true junta entrepreneur, an unacknowledged specialist in the urbanization of his *barrio* and the management of its urban services. All inhabitants' accounts describe him as the prominent figure of the *barrio* and a renowned *adeco* who stayed true to the party all his life. Such junta entrepreneurs strongly affiliated with one ruling party dominated neighborhood life in all the *barrios* created by "invasions" from 1958 onward. In the *barrios* created by plot purchases, where the need for political patronage was limited to servicing the *barrios* and did not guarantee their legitimacy, the junta's leadership tended to be less individual and was shared between neighbors affiliated with the AD and COPEI, putting neighbors forth as president of the *junta* in accordance with the municipal council majority.

Establishing and servicing the Julián Blanco *barrio* as a permanent settlement was also an eminently politicized process. Every individual involved in the urbanization was an Adeco activist. They were all part of the Movimiento Pro-Desarrollo de la Comunidad created by Julián Blanco in the Distrito Sucre in 1964. The urbanization of the *barrio* therefore depended on intermediaries and elected representatives of the party in power. It was also subject to the electoral calendar; in the Julián Blanco *barrio*, the installation of services had been made possible by election-year cronyism in both 1968 and 1973. There, as in the rest of the capital, the servicing of the *barrios* progressed in step with the election cycle; effective junta leaders then played both the cronyism and the collective mobilization cards to obtain the installation of services, through means that ranged from soliciting support from higher-up comrades to organizing petitions and public protests. When interviewed in the early 2010s, *barrio* residents tended to remember the 1960s and early 1970s as years of collective mobilizations and recalled the junta leaders' partisanship as nonpreemptive and even instrumental to community improvement.[107]

Conclusion

In the late 1970s, the researchers Pérez Perdomo and Nikken were surprised to find no court decisions concerning landowner-occupant disputes in the *barrios* of Caracas.[108] Although the *barrios* had remained confined to an almost unchanged state of illegality since the early 1940s, they had been built to stay, albeit outside the legal and judicial systems.

Beginning in the 1940s, two major but contrasting shifts in the political and social environment had led to the *barrios'* official recognition: the legalistic and modernizing authoritarianism of the military government and the democratization of 1958. These two political shifts resulted from an attempt to respond simultaneously and in an accelerated time frame to land issues, social issues, and Cold War political tensions.

From 1941 to 1948, the social democratic and communist parties, in contrast to their conservative opponents, gradually positioned themselves in support of the development of the *barrios*. The 1948 coup d'état brought down the AD government before the National Housing Commission's legislative initiatives could be put on the agenda. The new military junta aligned itself with the interests of the real estate and landowning sectors by pursuing a resolutely legalistic policy toward the *barrios*, which were subject to eradication.

In a context of falling oil exports, the interim government of 1958 assembled, in a very short space of time marked by social crisis and electoral reconfiguration, an extralegal policy to install services in the *barrios*. While this new informal urbanization policy was a continuation of that proposed by the Adeco government of 1945–1948, it differed in two crucial respects: the unprecedented scale of informal urbanization and the political benefit that the Marxist parties derived from it at the very moment of the Cuban Revolution.

Toward the end of 1958, the Betancourt government realized it needed to recognize the *barrios* and equip them with services if it wanted to stand any chance of success in the upcoming elections against the revolutionary parties. Yet they also had to safeguard land rights to prevent economic elites from supporting a scenario similar to that of 1948. The "official informal order" was thus institutionalized. It became a form of compromise, an improvised, urbanistic third way that helped to consolidate democratization. As occurred in the *colonias proletarias* in Mexico City during the 1940s, the massive occupations that occurred in Caracas from 1958 onward were tolerated and partially supported by public authorities who considered themselves nationalists and democrats.[109] The occupations were also stimulated by the populist interim government and the Communist Party "mass struggle" strategy in the capital. Yet unlike in Chile, urban land occupations were not suppressed along with the PCV. Communist support for the irregular occupation of urban land by the new residents of the *barrios* was instead assumed by social democratic leaders and municipal counselors committed to preserving Venezuela's fragile democratization.[110]

The debate around regularization thus disappeared even as the *barrios* expanded to a mass scale. It was not until 1974, when the country was enjoying renewed prosperity thanks to a new oil boom, that Venezuelan authorities tried to revive the plan for legal management of the *barrios*, this time by putting them in order through both service installation and eventual legal regularization.[111]

The Invention of the *Toma*:
Informality and Mobilization
in Santiago de Chile, 1945–1957

EMANUEL GIANNOTTI AND

BORIS COFRÉ SCHMEISSER

On October 30, 1957, the Chilean evening papers featured prominent headlines about the occupation of a vacant lot in the south of the capital, Santiago. *Las Noticias de la Última Hora*, a newspaper close to the Socialist Party, declared, "6,000 People Took the La Feria Site by Force." A photo portrayed a group of people in an open field, with the comment: "Children, women, elderly people, and men installed themselves on these CORVI-owned lands, and with no other protection than some ragged Chilean flags they settled on sites where they plan to build their homes."[1] A similar photo occupied the front page of *La Segunda*, the evening paper of the influential Edwards family. The next morning and on the following days, national newspapers continued to cover the story.

The images portrayed a protest action known as a *toma*, which became familiar to Chileans in subsequent years. In 1957, however, it was to some extent a new and unexpected event. Occupations were not usually so massive, nor were they staged in front of the entire country, as happened with the *toma* of La Victoria, the name later given to the event that took place on October 30.

It is generally accepted that La Victoria was a milestone that inaugurated a period of intense mobilization of the *pobladores sin casa*: "the unhoused," people who lived in precarious and informal situations.[2] During the 1960s, the *pobladores* achieved prominence in debates about urban development and in national politics, resorting to a varied repertoire of mobilizations, among which the *toma* was most emblematic.[3] In Chile, as in many other

This chapter is a shortened and revised translation of Emanuel Giannotti and Boris Cofré, "La invención de la 'toma', o cómo se transformaron las ocupaciones de terrenos en Santiago de Chile entre 1945 y 1957," *Historia* 54, no. 1 (2021): 107–50. It is a product of FONDECYT Grant 11150589.

Latin American countries, housing movements acquired enough strength to be recognized as urban social movements, and land occupation took on strong political connotations.[4]

Some authors consider La Victoria the first planned *toma* in Chile and even in Latin America.[5] However, a large body of studies carried out during Salvador Allende's government (1970–1973) agreed that the occupations, supported by the Communist Party of Chile (PCCh), began in the second half of the 1940s.[6] The same thesis was reiterated in the 1980s, and some oral history accounts detail certain such events.[7] Recently, extensive research into three case studies reaffirmed that these should be considered *tomas* that foreshadowed the movement that resumed in 1957.[8]

So, did the *tomas* begin in 1957 with La Victoria, or a decade earlier? Our thesis is that the *toma* was a particular form of occupation that took on definite features in the mid-1950s. Previously, informal settlements were established through silent occupations, which blurred with other ways of accessing land. In the 1950s, though, the occupations entered public space and were configured as staged actions, aimed at demanding a solution to the housing problem from political authorities. Thus, the occupations evolved from silent, direct actions carried out to obtain a place to live into loud, collective protests, or *contentious performances,* to use Charles Tilly's category.[9]

In line with numerous studies on Latin America, which have emphasized that popular urbanization and informal settlements have not occurred autonomously or spontaneously, we believe that the transformation of Chilean land occupations can be explained by changes in the institutional environment and the political system.[10] Thus, the process that led to the "invention" of the *toma* sheds light on some broader issues: how poor people's access to land changed in tandem with urban regulation; how specific categories of urban informality emerged from a political context in which tolerance for informal settlements decreased significantly; and how those transformations impacted the ways in which the *sin casa* organized and mobilized, fueling a shift from the defense of settlements threatened with eviction to performative occupations that demanded housing rights from the government.

The period under study, from the end of World War II to the eve of the Cuban Revolution, coincides with the first years of the Cold War.[11] It was marked by a change in Chile's national political system, which had been led for more than a decade by three successive presidents from the Radical Party: Pedro Aguirre Cerda (1938–1941), Juan Antonio Ríos (1942–1946), and Gabriel González Videla (1946–1952). They governed through diverse political alliances, involving both Marxist and right-wing parties. A crisis of the radicals

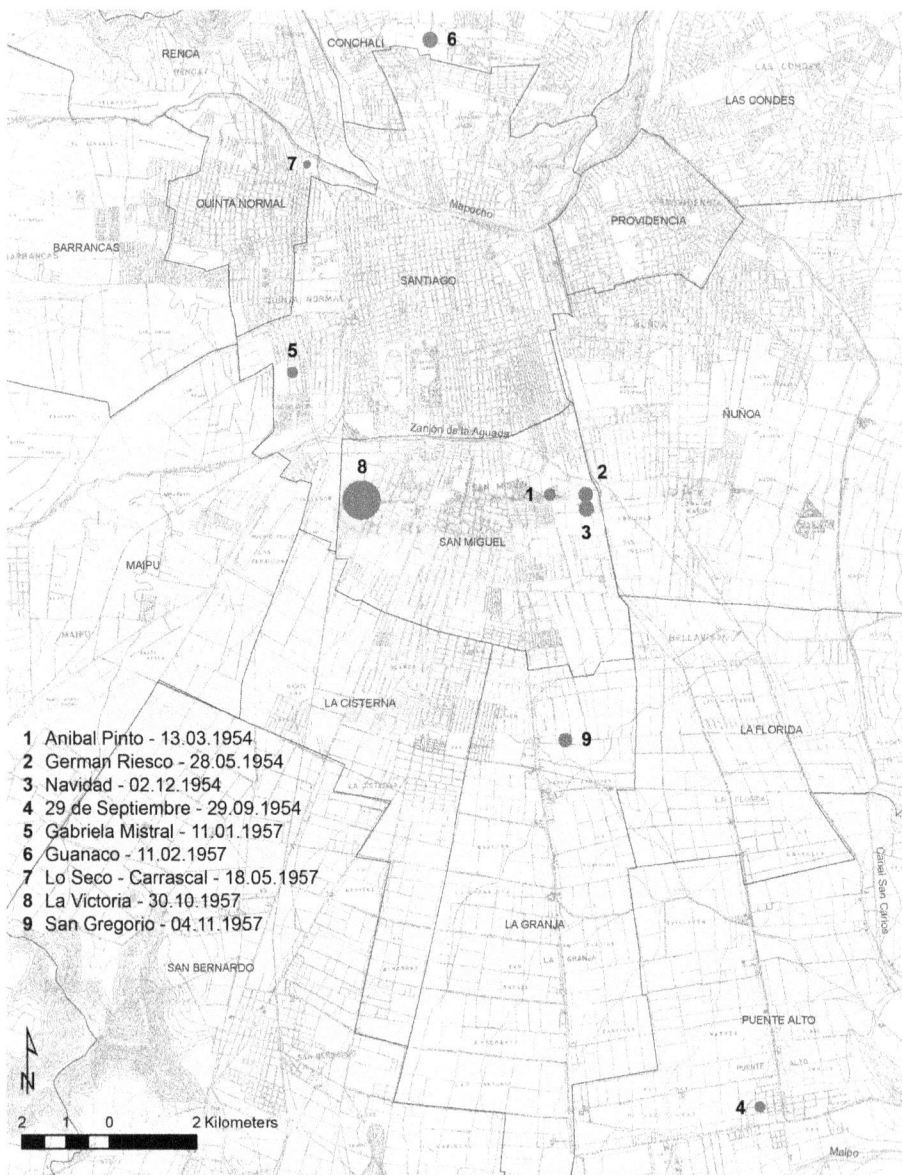

FIGURE 7.1. *Tomas* realized in Santiago between 1954 and 1957. Source: Authors' map on the *Plan Regulador Intercomunal de Santiago* (1960).

and other traditional parties opened the doors to General Carlos Ibáñez del Campo's triumph in 1952. During his six years in government, marked by a pronounced populist discourse, the parties gradually repositioned themselves to form three blocs. On the right, the Conservative Party and Liberal Party formed an alliance; on the left, the communists and socialists managed to overcome the deep divisions of the 1940s; and at the center, the Christian Democratic Party, founded in 1957, quickly gained prominence.[12]

To analyze the changing nature of occupations carried out in Santiago between the 1940s and the 1950s, we mainly used journalistic sources, which were cross-checked with archival information gathered from various public institutions. In this way, we were able to reconstruct a series of events, some more carefully than others, and place them in political and institutional context (fig. 7.1). In this chapter, after a review of the dynamics of access to popular housing between the nineteenth and twentieth centuries, we analyze two cycles of mobilizations, beginning with some conflictive cases that arose in the second half of the 1940s and ending with a series of occupations carried out in the mid-1950s, which culminated with the *toma* of La Victoria. In addition, we examine how the *sin casa* organized during these two periods. In the conclusion, we attempt to synthesize the factors that explain changes between the two cycles of mobilization.

Popular Housing and Urban Informality in Santiago

In Santiago, precarious dwellings—called *ranchos*—have existed since colonial times.[13] However, it was in the mid-nineteenth century's nascent republic that they spread in the urban periphery and became a visible phenomenon.[14] During these years, they were viewed with growing concern by the elites and the authorities and were the object of several urban reform proposals.[15]

Sometimes, the *ranchos* occupied municipal lands or vacant spaces inappropriately. More frequently, the popular classes gained housing access through the market, renting from owners or intermediaries. By 1850, the subdivision of land in order to rent small lots to the poor, where they would then build their *ranchos*, had become an excellent business.[16] A few decades later, similar mechanisms spurred the proliferation of *conventillos*, properties located in the city's central sectors and subdivided into rented rooms that ensured their owners ample profits. In the context of the growing concern over urban hygiene,[17] *conventillos* came to monopolize public debate and replaced *rancheríos* as emblems of the unhealthy and immoral conditions of popular housing.[18]

These processes developed in a context where urban regulations were weak and urban growth was driven by landed profits.[19] In addition, the 1891

Autonomous Comuna Law allowed the administrative fragmentation of Santiago and the creation of numerous peripheral municipalities, where central-
ized authority was reduced.[20] The mayors and aldermen of these *comunas*
often owned rural plots or estates and themselves promoted the highly profitable parceling and selling of land. This resulted in new residential areas,
known in Chile as *poblaciones*, which targeted different social groups depending on their location.[21] Toward the east, in the *comunas* of Providencia
and Ñuñoa, *poblaciones* were built for the middle and upper classes, although
in the latter, there were also popular settlements. In the southern, northern,
and western districts, such as San Miguel, Barrancas, and Renca, the popular
sectors predominated.[22]

As in other Latin American cities, the first decades of the twentieth century saw intense tenant mobilizations sparked by eviction threats and continuous rent increases.[23] The most critical moments were the tenants' strikes
of 1922 and 1925.[24] There were also conflicts related to the sale and lease of
peripheral land. Owners and intermediaries tended not to register the deeds
of sale or monthly payments, giving rise to various abuses. They also failed
to comply with promises to urbanize the areas through public works such as
plazas or pavement. Through evictions, they exposed tenants, called *mejoreros*, to the risk of losing the value of any improvements they had made to the
sites, including their auto-constructed homes. To defend their rights, installment buyers and *mejoreros* began to organize, eventually forming the Frente
Nacional de la Vivienda in 1933.[25]

The scarcity of urban regulations that helped these conflicts flourish gradually evolved. Particularly in the 1920s and 1930s, as part of a process of state
modernization, important laws were passed in four interrelated fields:

1. Pressured by social movements, rents were regulated by Decree Law 261
   (1925). After the 1929 crisis, which hit Chile very hard, the Commissariat
   of Supplies and Prices was created (1932), with powers to contain price increases in basic necessities, including rents. The commissariat could also
   intervene in evictions.[26]

2. In the mid-1920s, the subdivision of land for sale or lease began to be
   regulated. Decree Law No. 740 (1925) required for the first time that new
   poblaciones include urban public works such as pavement, drinking water, drainage and lighting. Decree Law No. 33 (1931) regulated the sale
   and lease of lots, requiring a public deed to identify the site and set the
   price and terms of payment. Law 5579 (1935) created a fund to facilitate
   the acquisition of land by *mejoreros* and installment buyers in irregular
   situations.[27]

3. Law 4563 (1929) and Decree Law No. 345 (1931, published in 1936) created a permanent legal body to regulate construction and urbanization processes.[28] At the same time, Chile launched its first experiment with urban planning, which led to the approval of a master plan for the *comuna* of Santiago in 1939.[29]

4. Beginning in the early twentieth century, various laws were passed to address the housing problem. The state took a more decisive role with the constitution of the Caja de la Habitación Popular in 1936 and its reform in 1943. This institution's main mission was to build housing for lower-middle-income workers. It was also empowered to build emergency housing and to regularize the situations of the *mejoreros* and installment buyers.[30]

However, measures to regulate urban development were scarcely supervised, and few housing units were built with state assistance. Land speculation and rental did not stop and continued to be the main ways for the urban poor to find a home.[31] A 1939 article estimated that there were 800,000 Chileans who lived in their own homes, 1,800,000 who lived in free housing, and 1,500,000 who rented. The latter group included tenement tenants, *mejoreros*, and buyers who paid for land in installments without deeds.[32] In Santiago, which in 1940 had reached 1 million inhabitants, the situation was worrisome. According to a 1945 study, a third of its population sheltered in *conventillos* or auto-constructed housing.[33]

These sources show us that only a minority of Chileans owned their homes in the mid-twentieth century, while the majority lived in a variety of informal situations. In spite of popular housing's very heterogeneous conditions, its common feature was precariousness, both materially and in terms of tenure, which exposed the dispossessed to the continuous threat of eviction.

Evictions and Mobilizations

According to the communist newspaper *El Siglo*, in April 1944 there were ten thousand tenants threatened with eviction in Santiago.[34] On numerous occasions, this newspaper reported on the "irritating spectacle" of household goods and furniture thrown in the street.[35] Most of the news referred to one or a few families renting rooms in central areas, but in some cases, it involved larger groups, even entire *poblaciones*.

Similar dynamics had gone on for years in the context of inflation that undermined low-income families' purchasing power. Since Pedro Aguirre Cerda's electoral victory in 1938, some measures had been taken through the

Commissariat of Subsistence and Prices. However, the commissariat's actions varied considerably according to the political conjuncture. On one side, the right wing, landowners, and business sectors exercised strong opposition. On the other, left-wing parties insisted on greater intervention.[36]

Among the many protests that arose against the "high cost of living" were struggles against rent hikes and evictions, which were supported by the Frente Nacional de la Vivienda and other organizations formed in those same years. Influenced by leftist parties, particularly the PCCh, all of them promoted the formation of tenants' committees and organized rallies and marches. There were also some direct actions promoted by the residents themselves, such as those aiming to reinstate evicted families.[37] The most prolonged and structured mobilizations took place when threats of evictions involved entire *poblaciones*. Two examples were the Población Valdés de Barros Luco and the Población Varas Mena. In both cases, over several months in 1945, the inhabitants organized themselves, staged protests, formed defense brigades against the threats of eviction, and sought support from the authorities.[38]

As was true in Brazil and across Latin America, the PCCh was the party that most recognized and supported these struggles. As part of the party's leftward turn between the end of World War II and the beginning of the Cold War, "mass struggle" emerged as a central element of its strategy.[39] Congresses held in 1945 emphasized the need to form antispeculation committees in each neighborhood, using "the most varied forms of action."[40] Communists praised successes in halting evictions, singling out the poblaciones Valdés de Barro Luco and El Pino.[41]

The Población El Pino

In June 1945, *El Siglo* reported that the *mejoreros* of the Población El Pino, located on the north bank of the Mapocho River, were under threat of eviction.[42] This was because the Caja de la Habitación was acquiring the land to build a housing project.[43]

On July 7, the El Pino committee wrote to the president of the Republic. It reported that the committee had been founded on November 15, 1942, and represented about two hundred *mejoreros*, settled on land that had remained vacant for many years. More than half of them were threatened with eviction by the landowner. The letter requested that the eviction be blocked and that the land be expropriated and sold to the *mejoreros*.[44]

Consulted about the petition, the vice president of the Caja de la Habitación Popular emphasized that the property had been "occupied by third parties, against the owner's will, surreptitiously." As such, the inhabitants did not have the protections given to *mejoreros* under current laws. He thus opposed the petition, so as not to set "the dismal precedent of giving preference to the first occupier."[45]

In November 1945, eviction once again seemed imminent. On November 5, residents "gave up going to work and flew Chilean flags throughout the entire humble encampment," preparing to resist.[46] That same afternoon, the leaders visited various newspapers. Accompanied by four hundred children, they paraded through the downtown streets in nine wagons, "publicly exposing the serious problem they were facing."[47] The eviction was suspended, and authorities offered public lands for a temporary relocation. The leaders rejected the proposal, because they wished to "stabilize their lives definitively."[48]

In December, eviction again loomed.[49] The thirteenth congress of the Communist Party, which was being held at the time, voted unanimously in support of the residents, who once again staked flags throughout the encampment on December 13, 1945.[50] That same day, communist deputies and leaders of the Frente Nacional de la Vivienda, among others, met with various ministers and succeeded in suspending the eviction.[51] Days later, they reached an agreement. The majority of the *pobladores* accepted a solution similar to the one they had rejected a month earlier: temporary transfer to a piece of land owned by the state, where they began to settle at the end of December 1945.[52]

The events described above are interesting for several reasons. In the first place, they involved novel mobilization strategies: the march through the city center with carts and children, meant to publicly expose the problem, and above all, the use of the national flag to resist eviction. This could be the origin of the later use of the Chilean flag in the *tomas*.

Second, it is interesting to note debates about how to describe the inhabitants. At first the press called them *mejoreros*, only to later use the word *pobladores* more frequently. While the left-wing newspapers supported and defended the inhabitants, the authorities of the Caja de la Habitación considered them illegitimate occupants, as did the conservative *El Diario Ilustrado*.[53] That newspaper's judgment was even more explicit in relation to another case involving a settlement built with cans and scrap material near the Zanjón de la Aguada, a waterway in south Santiago, which had been covered to build an avenue. The article stated: "The most important thing is that a very serious problem is being created: each family that builds a structure on the bed of the waterway believes it owns those improvements and, therefore, believes it acquires a right; when the avenue is built, it will no longer be possible to evict them except through the cumbersome and slow action of the judicial

process, and then only if they are not included among the beneficiaries of the
Law of *Mejoreros*; these neighborhoods are doomed to become the perennial
scourge of the city of Santiago."[54]

The Problem of the *Poblaciones Callampas*

At the end of 1946, Gabriel González Videla, the Radical Party candidate,
won the presidential elections. González Videla represented the left wing of
the radicals and had formed a coalition with the Democratic Party and the
PCCh, which helped form the government. During 1947, labor conflicts and
mobilizations intensified. These protests were supported by the PCCh, while
the other parties in the governing coalition assumed an increasingly intransi-
gent attitude. In this context, exacerbated by the beginning of the Cold War,
the communist ministers were forced out of office in April.[55] At the same time,
the PCCh began to be accused of encouraging social disturbances, including
occupations of vacant sites. There are indications that the latter were accelerating, driven by rising evictions and increasing rents. We do not have reliable
data to prove it, but what is certain is that the resulting settlements garnered a
great deal of press attention during the second half of 1947. In June, threats of
eviction were reported for the Zañartu, El Pino Bajo, and Recabarren *poblaciones*. In the first case, Mayor René Frías, a communist militant, refused to
use public force to evict the occupiers.[56] Frías had acted many times in favor
of those threatened with eviction; his actions aroused mounting criticism and
were challenged in court.[57]

In August, René Frías was replaced, giving way to a new wave of evictions
in the capital.[58] That same month, President González Videla signed a military treaty with the United States, formed a new right-leaning cabinet, and
expelled all communist governors and mayors. In September, the repression
of strikes and other mobilizations increased, and communist militants began
to be persecuted.[59] At the end of the month, the Investigative Service raided
the home of a leader of the Población Zañartu and arrested three men linked
to the PCCh.[60]

In the last months of 1947, the threat of eviction seemed imminent for
several peripheral settlements that had arisen through occupations. These
settlements began to be perceived as "a new social problem, that of the so-
called *poblaciones callampas*," or mushroom settlements, according to an *El
Diario Ilustrado* article from late October.[61] This is the first instance we found
where the adjective *callampa* appears in association with a settlement in the
news. In the following weeks, other terms were also used, such as *poblaciones
fantasmas* (phantom settlements) or *poblaciones relámpagos* (lightning settle-

ments), but *población callampa* was the one that, from that point on, referred to informal settlements in everyday speech.

The newspapers published appeals to landowners to fence off vacant sites to prevent the proliferation of *callampa* settlements. They accused "communist agitators" of encouraging the people to occupy lands.[62] Such denunciations became insistent between the end of 1947 and the beginning of 1948, when the repression of communist militants was reaching its peak. During 1948, Law 8987—known as the "damned law"—outlawed the PCCh, closed *El Siglo*, and limited the right to strike.[63]

Among the cases covered by the press during these months, those that attracted the most public attention, because they had the most acute conflicts, were the *población* Gabriela Mistral and the *población* Zañartu.

Población Gabriela Mistral or Anexa Lautaro

In August 1947, *El Siglo* reported an eviction threat against 140 families occupying a plot of land next to Población Lautaro in the Barrancas district. The residents, who stated that they had been renting the land for years, called their settlement Gabriela Mistral.[64] They accused Oscar Waiss (a Socialist Party leader) and Manuel Cortés (a socialist alderman from Barrancas) of having bought the land and requested the families' eviction.[65] For their part, Waiss and Cortés declared that they had bought the land, which they called the población Anexa Lautaro, on behalf of a group of working-class families. According to them, the property was forcibly occupied on July 14, 1946, infringing on the purchasers' legitimate rights.[66] This second version was supported by the socialist *La Opinión* and the conservative *El Diario Ilustrado*.[67] The inhabitants of Población Gabriela Mistral tried to defend themselves, but in January 1948, the eviction took effect, and the families were moved to public land.[68] This was the origin of Población Los Nogales.[69]

A more detailed account of this case can be found in the minutes of the Barrancas Municipal Council. In the 1930s, the municipality approved a plan for the land, owned by one Señora Zenobia Zamudio. This allowed the entire property to be subdivided, including the parcel that was in dispute in 1947. In 1942, Zamudio requested authorization to sell the land, leaving the installation of urban services to the purchasers. The municipality approved, but with the condition that the land would be sold only up to Santa Nora Street, a demarcation that did not include the disputed parcel.[70] In 1945, the same ruling was reiterated. Zamudio said she agreed and complained that people were settling on the property, requesting municipal intervention.[71]

The land to the west of Santa Nora Street was sold to Oscar Waiss and

Manuel Cortés in the first half of 1946.[72] In June of the same year, *El Siglo* reported that fifty low-income families were threatened with eviction in Población Gabriela Mistral. On the day of the eviction, the inhabitants planted national flags to stop the *carabineros* (military police). The authorities stayed the order.[73]

In November 1947, Mayor Carlos Balbotin accused the socialist alderman Manuel Cortés of irregularities in the purchase of the land.[74] The dispute became heated and dragged on for months. After the occupiers were moved to Los Nogales in January 1948, leaving the site vacant, the mayor refused to grant building permits to the other group of families who had purchased the land through Manuel Cortés, impeding them from moving in. On several occasions, the socialist alderman protested, pointing out that, in other *poblaciones*, buyers had been allowed to build in even more irregular situations. According to Cortés, it was clearly a form of persecution for the mayor to demand that the buyers of Anexa Lautaro comply strictly with the law, because the same had not been required in other *poblaciones*. The mayor, little by little, relented.[75] In the following months, the buyers were able to move in and build.[76]

Land occupation was thus a complex process. Conflict stemmed from recurrent dynamics in the formation of peripheral settlements, where land speculation, political agendas, and urgent housing problems intersected in a context of scarce urban regulation.

Población Zañartu

An even more intense conflict involved the Población Zañartu in the Ñuñoa district. The dispute escalated in the middle of 1947 and was resolved during the first months of 1948. In February of that year, *La Nación* reported that the Población Zañartu covered seven blocks.[77] A month later, *Vivienda Popular* reported that there were more than seven hundred occupying families organized in a central committee and block subcommittees.[78] The situation of the residents of Block 1 was regularized in February 1948.[79] The inhabitants of the other blocks began to be moved to public land. The transfer was completed in the following months, giving rise to the Población Nueva La Legua.[80]

The records related to the Población Zañartu are fragmented and provide conflicting information. The Población Zañartu probably covered a fairly extensive area, made up of state, municipal, and private lands where there had been different modes of settlement over the years. For example, according to a document from the Caja de la Habitación, a large number of *mejoreros* were already living in the Población Zañartu in 1935, and some succeeded in legally regularizing their status.[81]

In March 1946, *El Siglo* denounced that the conservative mayor intended to evict the Población's three hundred families.[82] A year later, between April and May 1947, the Municipal Council discussed the possibility of evicting two hundred families occupying municipal property.[83] In June 1947, several parties filed complaints against occupations. The main one was made by an agriculturalist who rented public land.[84] He discovered a group of thirty young men who had entered the area the previous night and were building shacks. Over the following days, the shacks multiplied and families with children appeared. The complainant emphasized the occupants' order and discipline, from which he inferred that the operation was part of a preconceived plan.[85]

That same June, *El Siglo* warned about a threat to the Población Zañartu. Compared to previous reports, there was now talk of more families: nine hundred, with a total of four to five thousand people, organized in a single committee.[86] In July, the communist newspaper reported that *carabineros* were monitoring the two hundred families of the neighboring Población Valdivieso. The police force prevented the construction of new shacks and destroyed some already built.[87] The *pobladores* mobilized, supported by the Frente de la Vivienda and the PCCh.[88]

In November 1947, *El Diario Ilustrado, La Opinión,* and *La Nación* reported again on the Población Zañartu, this time with different data. They referred to one hundred families, with a total of eight hundred people, who since May had been living on private property owned by Pablo Maske, who had obtained an order for their expulsion. According to *El Diario Ilustrado,* the families had "built temporary dwellings on lands that had been neither ceded nor sold, [but were rather] occupied overnight by perfectly organized caravans, which even carried their modest furnishings in municipal carts."[89] The president of Chile and other authorities took an interest in the problem. They offered to work out a solution, which, as we have seen, materialized in 1948.[90]

The sources reviewed thus suggest that one or more occupations were carried out in mid-1947, with a certain level of planning. It is probable that these provoked the eviction orders and the repressive actions that *carabineros* executed over those months. However, the occupations were hardly covered by the press, from which we can infer that they were not intended to be public acts. Moreover, they were part of a complex settlement process that had been going on for several years. We thus believe that they cannot be considered as *tomas,* a word that began to be used only in the 1950s.

However, the cases of Zañartu, Gabriela Mistral, and similar *poblaciones* show that tolerance toward the occupation of vacant land had ended amid the climate of repression that characterized the beginning of the Cold War in Chile. It is not accidental that a specific expression was coined to identify a phenomenon that was previously effaced within the vague category of *mejoreros*. The term *poblaciones callampas* attests that the occupations had come to be perceived as a problem that had to be eradicated. The strategy of silent occupations, which had worked during the previous years, was rendered ineffective.

From the Frente de la Vivienda to the Agrupación de Pobladores

The political tensions and restrictions on freedoms introduced with the "damned law," in addition to divisions among left-wing parties and within the Confederation of Chilean Workers, curtailed strikes and popular mobilizations after 1948.[91] This affected *poblador* organizations, particularly the Frente Nacional de la Vivienda. Since 1942, the Frente had been led by communists, including its president, Juvenal Gordillo.[92]

In June 1947, according to *El Siglo*, the Front organized fifteen thousand *pobladores* in Santiago.[93] Concurrently, it was accused of swindling the *pobladores* and instigating land occupations. The accusations came from an organization that also used the name Frente Nacional de la Vivienda but was associated with the Socialist Party and supported the government. Its president was Pedro Cáceres.[94] In this way, as of 1947, there were two parallel institutions that disputed the same name for a few years.[95]

The progovernment Front, led by Cáceres, at first concentrated on the defense of the tenants, later gaining more influence among the peripheral *poblaciones*.[96] At the same time, the Communist Front, led by Gordillo, was trying to restructure itself.[97] In 1948, it organized a congress in southern Santiago's Comuna San Miguel as well as a provincial housing congress.[98] Although there were attempts to overcome the two fronts' divergences, they remained separate.[99] The institutionalist Frente repeatedly stressed its distance from the Communists, declaring itself an apolitical institution and governmental collaborator.[100] The Communist Frente, on the other hand, was replaced by the Agrupación Provincial de Pobladores de Santiago, which was formed during a convention held on November 9–10, 1951.[101] The abandonment of the name Frente de la Vivienda in favor of Agrupación de Pobladores shows an important change in the PCCh's conceptualization of the popular housing problem. In January 1954, the Communists formed an Agrupación Nacional de Pobladores (National Settlers' Group), which succeeded in bringing together numerous grassroots committees during the following years.[102]

Returning to 1952, Carlos Ibáñez del Campo triumphed in the presidential elections with a nationalist and populist discourse, promising to sweep away corruption and solve social problems, among them that of the *poblaciones callampas*. The new government, supported by sectors of the left, attenuated the persecution of communists and was more receptive to the demands of the working classes.[103] At the end of 1952, *El Siglo* was able to resume publishing, and in February 1953, the Central Única de Trabajadores labor federation was founded. The *pobladores'* organizations, however, had no institutional representation. This, together with the new government's many unfulfilled promises, could explain why the struggles of the unhoused tended to develop outside of institutional frameworks.

A New Cycle of Occupations

A few days after the new government took office in November 1952, the minister of the interior announced a plan to eradicate the *callampas*.[104] A commission was formed at the end of November and met between December and February 1953.[105] The commission conducted a survey that counted 7,329 families living in Santiago's *callampas* and another 6,154 in the rest of Chile. As a solution, it proposed eradicating almost all of these settlements by providing residents with urbanized sites on public lands.[106] This was very similar to the solution proposed a few months earlier with Law 10.254, whose enforcement was being demanded by both the Frente de la Vivienda and the Agrupación Provincial de Pobladores.[107]

These government efforts were part of a broader plan.[108] During 1953, Chile carried out an important administrative and legal reform of the housing sector. The Ministry of Public Works (MOP in Spanish) was restructured, and the Corporación de la Vivienda (CORVI in Spanish) was created under its auspices, merging with the Caja de la Habitación Popular. The government passed a new General Law of Construction and Urbanism and formulated Chile's first National Housing Plan. By 1954, this plan called for the construction of more than thirty thousand housing units, one-third of which were earmarked for *callampa* residents, although construction levels in the following years were far below those projections.[109]

In this context, the occupations became a specific form of popular protest. Some signs of this were already visible in 1952 and 1953, but the key events occurred in 1954 in the *comuna* of San Miguel. The main protagonists were the *agregados* of Nueva La Legua, who in 1950 had formed a committee.[110] For years they had mobilized with the support of leftist deputies to ask for land, obtaining only unfulfilled promises.[111] In March 1954, they occupied half-built housing in a nearby CORVI housing project.[112] According to *El Siglo*, the action involved 120 families who occupied the housing structures on the night of Saturday, March 13. Three hours later they were evicted by *carabineros* and left on the streets of La Legua with their belongings. The following morning, several authorities and deputies visited the families and promised to mediate a solution.[113]

By Monday, there were four hundred families who had set up a "genuine improvised encampment."[114] A photograph in *El Siglo* showed a woman sheltering her five children from the sun's rays under an improvised tent, built with three poles that formed a triangle and a blanket. Other similar photographs appeared in the following days' editions. The minister of the interior, during a visit on the same Monday, promised to deliver building plots.[115] By Tuesday, the number of families had reached 618.[116]

In a few days an agreement was reached. CORVI offered land at the nearby Población Germán Riesco, with space for 440 building plots. Although insufficient, they were accepted by the *pobladores*, who decided to take in the remaining families with the promise that CORVI would find them a permanent home.[117] *El Siglo* emphasized that it was possible to achieve a housing solution through collective action.[118] By occupying the street after the eviction, claimants had found a way to publicly demand a solution and negotiate with the authorities from a stronger position. The strategy of noise—bursting into public space to demand a right—had proved effective.

With some delays, the transfer began in late March.[119] The incomplete solution, which left some families still unhoused, led to a new mobilization. On May 28, 174 families settled on nearby land; women took a leading role in setting up shelters. In this occupation, the national flag reappeared and would subsequently become a constant symbol. This is how *El Siglo* described the situation: "Every family with a national flag among their belongings flew it on the trusses that would later support their homes. An elderly woman, Señora Carmen Jara, told us: 'Other times the police forces respected the four poles that mark our houses so as not to destroy the flag when demolishing them. When they tried to destroy our houses, we showed them the flag and sang the national anthem and they let us live where we were. Now we all hope that our right to live will be respected.'"[120] Months later, the committee of the Población Germán Riesco agreed to participate in a self-help housing plan for all the families, financed thanks to an agreement with the United States.[121]

A third occupation occurred on December 2, 1954, on a neighboring plot of land, and the number of occupying families quickly reached two hundred.[122] *El Siglo* wrote of an "improvised encampment with innumerable Chilean flags" and featured a photograph of a group of *pobladores* with a flag blazing.[123] Two days later, they reiterated the image: a photograph showed a child and the national flag in the foreground, and in the background was a mother sitting on her bed in the open air.[124]

These events show a change in the dynamics of mobilization and in the movements' use of symbols. Some were already present in previous years but took on new meaning. Furniture thrown in the street had been a common image of eviction. Yet when the Nueva La Legua occupants decided to remain in the streets themselves, they transformed the image of beds in the rough into both a powerful representation of precarious housing conditions and a demand addressed to public authorities. Similarly, the flag had already been used to resist eviction threats in the poblaciones El Pino and Gabriela Mistral, but it now became the symbol of the *toma* of a plot of land on which to build a home, claimed as every Chilean's right.

Hasta la Victoria

1955 unleashed an inflationary crisis of such a magnitude that Carlos Ibáñez's government, influenced by the right, hired US experts to make a diagnosis and propose a solution. The mission, known as Klein-Saks, suggested reducing the fiscal deficit, containing salary adjustments, and eliminating price controls.[125] Trade union organizations opposed the measures while rising prices deteriorated the popular sectors' purchasing power. The housing statistics were dramatic: in 1955, only one-third of the fifteen thousand planned units were built.[126]

In this context, occupations resumed. On September 29, 1956, a brief news item on the front page of *El Siglo* reported that one hundred families from Puente Alto, who were threatened with eviction, had occupied public land. A photograph portrayed a woman building a *rancho* with her children, with a Chilean flag flying over her belongings.[127] Apart from this note, the press did not cover the event. However, the report was important because it described a land occupation using the word *toma*, which had previously been used only for the occupations of housing. Furthermore, according to an important PCCh Deputy, this event was the party's rehearsal for the future *toma* of La Victoria.[128]

Other occupations took place in the first months of 1957. On January 11, a few families occupied land adjacent to Los Nogales.[129] Two days later there were more than one hundred families, and the settlement resembled "a gypsy camp" where each site had a Chilean flag.[130] The *pobladores* remained on the land, creating a new Población Gabriela Mistral.[131] *El Siglo*, the only newspaper to cover the event, noted, "In the last four years, hundreds of *pobladores* have obtained building plots and housing from CORVI, not because the current government has offered it, but because the *pobladores* proceeded to occupy the land, otherwise they would never have obtained it."[132] In February, the inhabitants of a *población callampa* located in Cerro Blanco occupied public land in Conchalí in response to unfulfilled promises of being moved to that location.[133] They arrived in five trucks, erected shelters with blankets and sheets, and flew flags. This time *carabineros* evicted the occupants, in spite of a communist deputy's negotiation attempts.[134]

During this period, protests intensified against rising prices, led by workers and students. *Poblador* organizations participated in these protests, denouncing rises in rents and evictions, which continued to be widespread in Santiago.[135] On April 2, the accumulated social discontent turned into a popular riot, due to an increase in public transportation fares and the repression of earlier protests. The result was a social uprising controlled by the military, with a large number of wounded and about twenty dead.[136]

On May 18, forty families occupied a plot of land with flags and were violently evicted, despite the presence of a communist deputy.[137] This, along with other events since 1954, evidenced a recurrent rituality and symbolism that were acknowledged in the communist press. *El Siglo* depicted the *tomas* with images of improvised tents, cots in the rough, mothers with their children, and Chilean flags, accompanied with captions that claimed housing as a right. The rest of the press, however, paid little or no attention, at least until the massive occupation that was staged in front of the whole country on October 30, 1957. This was La Victoria, an action that paradigmatically encapsulated this new form of popular protest.

The facts are well known.[138] The inhabitants of the *población callampa* Zanjón de la Aguada, exasperated by unfulfilled promises and fires that had affected several areas, decided to take over an expanse of land called La Feria Norte. They were supported by leftist deputies and by the Hogar de Cristo, a charitable foundation founded by the Jesuit priest Alberto Hurtado. According to the Investigative Police, the "illegal occupation" began at midnight, when the occupants, organized in a commando, cut the fence surrounding the land. By morning, the occupants exceeded a thousand, monitored by the *carabineros*.[139] Cardinal José María Caro's prompt intercession with the president of the Republic prevented the eviction, legitimizing de facto the occupation, which was consolidated over the following months and years.[140]

All national newspapers covered the event, although their accounts were quite dissimilar. *Clarín* reported more on the policing aspects, while *La Nación*, a government newspaper, focused on the measures being taken by authorities to solve the problem. Conservative newspapers devoted little space to the event, focusing on the drama of the fire victims and the aid they received. The leftist press devoted much more space to the event, using epic tones. It emphasized the *pobladores'* heroic struggle to defend their "right to life and home," as *El Siglo* headlined on its October 31 front page. This news-paper spoke of a *toma* and estimated the number of families at 1,200, rising to 3,000 a few days later. It declared that the leaders "wanted to make a better Chile" and that, just as there was "the field of freedom, where O'Higgins and San Martín camped" (during the Chilean independence struggle), so there was now "the field of Victory"—an elision that linked the *toma* to the origins of the Republic.[141]

We can learn about the government's position from a debate that took place at the beginning of November among the board of directors of CORVI, the institution that owned the occupied land. The minister of public works, to whom CORVI was subject, declared that it was "an extremely serious event, for which we must find a definitive resolution, the momentousness of which is undeniable because it will determine whether or not these facts repeat them-selves."[142] The minister indicated a commitment to avoiding violence when confronting the occupants, although he also emphasized the government's intention to "prevent new clandestine land occupations with public force."[143]

In fact, in the early morning of November 4, a thousand people were evicted; "following the example of the *pobladores* of Zanjón de la Aguada," they had taken over a CORVI property.[144] The *tomas* disappeared for a few years, only to return in the early 1960s. Despite the harsh repression, the un-housed continued to carry out *tomas*, transforming them into the nascent *pobladores'* movement's most emblematic form of protest.[145]

Conclusion

In these pages, we have shown how the dynamics and representations of San-tiago's land occupations were transformed in little more than a decade. In the period under consideration, we have identified two cycles. The first took place in the second half of the 1940s, in a context in which the dispossessed were continuously exposed to forced displacements. When evictions threat-ened entire settlements, the inhabitants organized and carried out prolonged public protests, at times resorting to novel actions, such as the use of the na-tional flag. The processes of occupation through which these settlements had been formed, however, were carried out silently and incrementally, becoming confused with other opaque processes of peripheral urbanization, such as the leasing or sale of building sites. These episodes cannot thus be considered *tomas*, if by this term we mean an organized claim-making act, carried out publicly and all at once.

The occupations assumed these characteristics in the mid-1950s, during the second cycle of mobilizations. We believe that the events of 1954, which took place in the *comuna* of San Miguel, were the first to exhibit the afore-mentioned features, although it was the *toma* of La Victoria that staged this form of popular vindication in front of the whole country. The press, par-ticularly *El Siglo*, recognized the novelty of these actions and began to use the word *toma* to describe them. In this way, the occupations, previously silent and gradual, were transformed into public acts, staged as noisily as possible, to vindicate a right and put pressure on the authorities.

To explain this transformation, we believe that two groups of factors must be considered. The first group has to do with the State's changing role in rela-tion to urban growth and the housing problem. We have seen that urbaniza-tion processes were poorly regulated, especially in the periphery, although the state showed a growing desire to control them. There were various forms of urban land occupation, all grouped under the poorly defined category of *mejoreros*. The conflicts that began to emerge in the mid-1940s responded to the desire to eliminate some traditional forms of land occupation and for-malize property relations along capitalist lines. This process reached an im-portant milestone in 1947, when the term *callampas* was coined. Authorities called for vacant lots to be fenced in and pledged to eliminate unauthorized occupations, a position they maintained in subsequent years.

During this period, the state's position also changed with respect to the housing problem, shifting from a regulatory role to more active involvement in housing construction. In the 1940s, dispossessed people found housing mainly through the market, where foreclosures and swindles were frequent. The state could intervene and punish such actions, and the main popular protests demanded concrete measures such as expropriations to regularize land ownership or limits on evictions and rent increases. During the 1950s, the reforms promoted by Carlos Ibáñez committed the public sector to solv-ing the problem of the *poblaciones callampas* and to building housing for the popular sectors, although very little was achieved. The *pobladores* began to demand solutions from CORVI: the occupations that arose during these years can be interpreted as demands directed at the state so that it would fulfill its promises.

A second group of factors has to do with the social and political conjunc-ture of the period, which helped reconfigure the opportunities and risks of collective action. In the mid-1940s, the escalation of conflicts associated with the onset of the Cold War prompted the repression of strikes and popular protests, including silent occupations, which ceased to be a successful strat-egy. In the early 1950s, Carlos Ibáñez's return to power opened new oppor-tunities. In the context of a populist government and less social and political persecution, the noisy occupation proved a potentially successful strategy.

Chilean authorities embraced dialogue, but as these events recurred, their tolerance diminished. La Victoria convinced the authorities that firm and immediate repression was necessary in the face of future occupations and that it would be advisable to respond to the problem through public policies. This position was maintained during subsequent years.

Political opportunities also changed with respect to the relationship between *pobladores* and political parties. In the 1940s, *pobladores* often formed their organizations after a settlement was established to secure upgrades or resist eviction threats. The PCCh supported these organizations and their struggles, but it was not the only actor to do so. In the 1950s, the emergence of the *toma* meant a growing level of organization on the part of the occupiers. It is difficult to know the degree to which parties participated in advance planning, but various actors certainly provided postoccupation support. Among them, the PCCh played a key role in the acknowledgment and representation of these mobilizations. *El Siglo* was the only newspaper that covered the occupations during this second cycle and began to call them *tomas*. It used photographs and stories to highlight symbols that would become the *tomas'* classic representation. In addition, it endowed the events with a vindicatory discourse, which valorized the occupations as a means of struggle to demand a stable place to live, understood as every Chilean's right.[146]

If we broaden our gaze and try to compare the case of Santiago to those of other Latin American cities, we can outline some points of interest. The first has to do with informal access to land. The literature tends to differentiate between direct occupations, such as *tomas* or invasions, and occupations controlled by an identifiable property claimant, such as clandestine subdivisions or pirate developments.[147] In fact, our case studies seem to show that silent occupations tended to be mixed with other irregular practices, such as leasing or sales, in a context of nascent urban regulations that were still poorly implemented. This seems consistent with other Latin American cases, such as Rio de Janeiro, where ambiguous regulations allowed abuses and shady dealings as well as clientelistic practices, unleashing fierce land conflicts.[148]

However, in Santiago the phenomenon of silent occupations did not reach the magnitude of Latin American cities such as Rio. This is probably due to a reduced tolerance of informal settlements and stronger vigilance of property rights, which the Chilean state strengthened over the years.[149] In the period considered here, the emergence of the term *poblaciones callampas* marked a hardening of repression against the occupations. During subsequent years, this attitude persisted, and attempts were also made to limit phenomena such as irregular subdivisions. The solution that prevailed for those was on-site regularization,[150] while the main response to irregular occupations of private properties was forced expulsion to public lands. This was put into practice as early as the 1940s but was institutionalized in the following years through massive programs to deliver land equipped with minimal urban services.[151]

This combination of territorial control and regularization through housing programs created the conditions for a change in the forms of mobilization of the *sin casa* (unhoused), which points to a second comparative point. It was in this context that the occupations were transformed into public claims with the support of the PCCh. As such, the Chilean *tomas* seem rather peculiar in the Latin American context. Similar episodes occurred in Bogotá, but they were rather isolated events with little impact on public life.[152] The massive occupations that occurred in cities such as Lima, Caracas, and Mexico City were processes tolerated or directly organized by the state in contexts of populist governments and clientelistic relationships.[153]

During the 1940s, though, the dynamics of mobilizations of the urban poor in Santiago had been quite similar to the processes that took place in other Latin American cities such as Buenos Aires, Montevideo, and Belo Horizonte or Rio de Janeiro.[154] The inhabitants' struggles were mainly oriented toward the right to remain and demands for neighborhood improvements, mostly with support from communist parties.

Whatever their claims or forms of mobilization, these cases seem to show that political relations around informal neighborhoods were complex and cannot be characterized solely as clientelistic and populist.[155] Considering the marked differences between the histories of each city, there is evidence that clientelistic practices coexisted with the inhabitants' remarkable capacity to mobilize and organize themselves, as well as with the work of some leftist political entities, particularly the communists, that encouraged protest and rights-based demands.

PART III

Race and Colonial Domination

Informality, Racialized Governance, and the *Cidade Negra* in Modern Brazil

BRODWYN FISCHER

In 1978, Abdias do Nascimento—Brazil's most prominent twentieth-century Black intellectual—synthesized a lifetime of analysis and activism in *O genocí-dio do negro brasileiro*.[1] Steeped in the transnational language of Pan-African resistance but rooted also in Brazil's brutal particularities, *O genocídio* evis-cerated the vaunted myth of racial democracy, laying bare the many hypocri-sies that allowed Brazil to celebrate racial mixture while systematically deci-mating Black lives, livelihoods, and cultures.[2]

Forty pages in, after piercing explorations of slavery, sexual exploitation, whitening, and racial silencing, Nascimento turned to Brazil's modern ineq-uities.[3] Central among the "wounds" evident in "the most superficial glance at the country's social reality" were forms of race-based economic discrimina-tion that forced Black people disproportionately to the Brazilian equivalent of "ghettos": the *mocambos* (rustic huts) of the Northeast and the basements, tenements, and *favelas* (shantytowns) of São Paulo and Rio. Famously ex-posed in Carolina Maria de Jesus's published diaries, spectacularly romanti-cized in Marcel Camus's film *Orfeu Negro*, and increasingly well documented by statisticians and social scientists, the *favelas* were nearly always majority-Black spaces.[4] This, argued Nascimento, was segregation: racism, expressed through educational and economic exclusion and enforced by white rule not so different from apartheid, forced Brazil's Afro-descendant population to endure the *favelas*' "humiliation" and "degradation."

In a transnational context in which debates about urban inequality had long focused on racism and racial segregation, this was not surprising. But in 1970s Brazil, Nascimento's assertions contradicted the dogma of racial de-mocracy championed by Brazil's military dictatorship.[5] Less obviously, they also broke with a strong current of racial silence that ran through Brazil's midcentury urban sociology and policy discourse.[6] Despite scientific rac-ism's importance to early accounts of Brazil's urban problematic, despite the unspoken persistence of racist tropes, and despite the continued importance of racial dynamics in shaping urban Brazil, most students of Brazil's mid-century race relations adhered to Arthur Ramos's 1938 assessment that "the problem of the Negro is simply the problem of the underprivileged in general with a low cultural standard."[7] Donald Pierson wrote of "the *ricos* of the ridges and the *pobres* of the valleys" in the northeastern city of Salvador, but while stratification coincided with race, this was a "multiracial class society" where "spatial distribution" was "largely the consequence of economic sifting."[8] Despite his critiques of the Chicago School, the pioneering sociologist L. A. Costa Pinto still conceived Rio's racial disparities and prejudices in its language: "The ecological pattern is mainly the product of social stratification."[9] Florestan Fernandes and Roger Bastide—whose arguments radically undermined Brazilian claims of racial democracy—still argued that São Paulo's racial inequality resulted largely from the economic and psychological legacies of slavery, which left Black men ill prepared to meet the challenges of urban modernity.[10] Political and policy debates followed a similar logic; by the 1950s, activists, politicians, and planners were obsessed with mass migration and the shantytowns that had become the region's de facto housing policy, and they described poor communities in languages of developmentalism, modernization, class conflict, or social marginality that had embedded racial meanings. But with a few significant exceptions they rarely explicitly emphasized race or its causal impact on urban inequalities.[11] In that context, Nascimento's brief passage swam against the current.

A half century of Black activism, creative production, and scholarship has since unraveled many strands of Brazil's midcentury racial silencing. The myth of racial democracy has been shredded, and many urban researchers have documented the racial dynamics of political discourse, anti-Black violence, social movements, and the present-day geographies of urban injustice.[12] Urban historians have explored the racial impacts of public health and urban planning policies that were at the core of early Brazilian state building, researched the afterlives of runaway communities (*quilombos*), documented a vital Black urban public sphere, and traced some of the racialized contours of social stratification over time.[13]

Yet the *favela*—a term Nascimento and others used as a metonym for Black humiliation and degradation—is still curiously understudied as it relates to the history of racial inequality. While *favelas* and other low-income areas remain heavily racialized in Brazil's political and cultural imaginary—and while novelists, musicians, filmmakers, and community organizations have emerged ever more forcefully to tell their own stories—Brazil's mainstream social scientific scholarship on informality has until recently still mostly side-stepped the question of race, and a generation of historians working to histor-icize *favelas* and *mocambos* are only beginning to document their racial dy-namics.[14] Reciprocally, scholars of Brazilian race relations have engaged too rarely in critical analysis of informality's many historical complexities, mostly either invoking the *favela* as the idealized heir of multisecular tradition of Black resistance or denouncing it as a symptom of racism and an emblem of Black marginalization. While the *favela* and periphery loom large as symbols and forms, informality remains underexamined as a historical and racialized modality of power and governance. In the absence of clearly delineated poli-cies that channeled Black people to informal spaces—no redlining, no racial covenants, no outright bans on Black property ownership—few have ex-plored precisely how and why Black urbanity came to be disproportionately relegated to the informal sphere or what impact informality's prevalence has had on Brazil's racial dynamics.[15] We likewise lack a rigorous understanding of how Brazilian informality was shaped by race.

This chapter broaches these questions by exploring Brazilian informal ur-banism's earliest history. It focuses especially on Rio de Janeiro and Recife—two of Brazil's three largest cities in the early twentieth century, one an ascen-dant national capital, one the regional hub of the impoverished Northeast, both notable as places where informality emerged most forcefully a public issue between the 1890s and the 1940s.

These cities' histories demonstrate how Brazilian informality was created by law in the shadow of slavery, in ways that would frame both race and in-formality throughout the twentieth century.[16] Buttressed by racist and pater-nalistic beliefs incubated during bondage, Brazil's elite implemented a slew of regulations that made legal urbanity unaffordable for the poor and dis-proportionately Black residents whose labor sustained Brazilian cities. This did not eliminate self-built urbanity, but it did force poor and disproportion-ately Black people to forge their urban lives largely outside law's bounds, in spaces with limited rights to public goods or protections. Residents defended these spaces fiercely, eventually constituting some of Brazil's most powerful social movements. Yet while such struggle preserved access to urban space and created dynamic cultures and communities, it mostly operated within the codes of racial silence and relational power, thus reinforcing the sys-tems of informal governance that sustained racial inequality. Black people suffered uncommonly from the precarious sanitary conditions of the shacks and shantytowns, and racial prejudice found cover and sustenance in myths about *favela* crime and filth. Urban informality also—from its very inception as a distinct legal and social problem, and through its practice as a system of governance—perpetuated precarious citizenship, deprivation of public goods, and private exploitation. The informal urbanism that residents heroically defended thus constituted not only a space of refuge and release but also slavery's vital afterlife.[17]

Brazilian Informality: A Brief Genesis

Facets of what we now call informal urbanism—auto-construction, tenuous property rights, lack of entitlement to public resources, sociocultural marginalization, but also creative and vital vernacular urbanities—have always been a naturalized feature of Brazil's cityscapes. People—poor and rich, white and Black, Brazilian and foreign—have long built homes and neighborhoods without regard for formal law and without recourse to institutionalized authority.[18] Poor Afro-descendant people, in particular, have often built lives and communities on land they had no legal claim to and without entitlement to public services and resources, sometimes as part of a deliberate escape from slavery.[19] In travelers' accounts, representative art, newspapers, police logs, and appeals to authorities great and small, one can find improvised dwellings in *fundos* (backyards), self-constructed suburban huts with wattle-and-daub walls and thatched roofs, precarious shacks located on hills or swamps of uncertain ownership, and rooms or makeshift subdivisions added like honeycomb cells to Rio and São Paulo's ubiquitous *cortiços* ("beehives" or tenements).

Yet as elsewhere, one of informality's most defining characteristics— the legal, regulatory, and imaginary othering of vernacular city building— crystallized only when global nineteenth-century developments converged to denaturalize popular iterations of urbanity, converting poor people's housing into a distinctive "problem" in need of legal and administrative solution. The Industrial Revolution transformed both the concept and the materiality of urban life; radical political ideologies held public authorities responsible for unhealthy and exploitative living conditions; new understandings of public health redefined domestic design and hygiene; novel technologies expanded the scope and value of public services such as drainage, water, gas, electricity, and transportation; accelerating global trade and communication diffused the innovations around the world, spurring not only material transformation but also radical shifts in global notions of urbanity itself.[20] These were entwined with increasingly rigid racial and colonial doctrines, which often explicitly elided civilization, urbanity, and whiteness at the apex of human progress.[21] After slavery's final abolition in 1888, Brazil experienced both a quickening of migration-fueled urbanization and increasing pressure to demonstrate through its cities, laws, and institutions a national capacity for civilization and progress.[22]

This translated into familiar legal and conceptual shifts. Between 1900 and 1930, in the name of public health, rational urban administration, and moral uplift—but also in the service of real estate speculation, profit, Europeanization, and whitening—Brazilian authorities legislated a novel and exclusionary vision of the legally sanctioned city. Beginning in central, densely inhabited districts and expanding unevenly but relentlessly, statutes in cities as varied as Rio, São Paulo, Belo Horizonte, São Luis, and Recife outlawed or prohibitively taxed improvised tenements and shacks, imposed ambitious sanitary and building codes, and implemented imported urban masterplans.[23] Showcase reforms transformed select cityscapes, creating soaring fortunes for landowners. At the same time, as urban land values climbed, those with the financial and political means scrambled to formalize previously ambiguous property arrangements and evict undocumented inhabitants, in what might be best understood as a form of urban enclosure. Authorities justified these measures with racialized paeans to science and progress, tying Brazil's membership in the community of civilized nations (and their commercial circuits) to its ability to construct in law the cities they could not make universally concrete.[24]

The predictable result was an acute housing crisis, which—ironically—led to a steep increase in the concentration and visibility of informalized self-built neighborhoods. Beginning with a few well-known communities—including Rio's Morro da Favela, from which the term *favela* evolved—groupings of shacks small and large concentrated in every available urban interstice or periphery. While successive generations of politicians gave lip service to affordable housing, their words came to naught, as did attempts to close the gap between the law's dictates and poor people's material and bureaucratic capabilities.[25] In the 1930s, as Brazil's political and legal system transitioned from oligarchic republicanism to corporatist authoritarianism, large-scale eradication attempts similarly failed, as did hybrid Catholic-governmental campaigns that conceived housing reform as moral regeneration.[26] Resources were always scarce, and community leaders—often in heterodox alliance with communists, Catholics, politicians, and land-grabbers—preserved their informal residences through means that ranged from political protest to clientelism, bribery, and backroom negotiation. Unlike elsewhere—especially Mexico—these strategies rarely led to regulatory incorporation or rights to the city. Instead, grace and strategic tolerance emerged as critical political currency in an age of popular politics.[27]

By the 1940s, when Brazil began an unprecedented two decades of populist democracy, the phenomena that would later be dubbed informality was
firmly entrenched as a mode of urbanization, providing shelter for 20 percent
to 30 percent of Rio's population and generating the majority of homes in
cities such as Recife and Salvador.[28] Informality was integrated within larger
patterns of governance, economy, and spatial stratification, eventually acquiring a kind of capillary power; it allowed everyone from poor squatters to
large-scale land-grabbers to survive and profit from property they did not
legally own, it allowed speculators to derive rents as they waited for the land
they owned to be encompassed by the web of municipal investment, it allowed employers to pay lower wages, it permitted municipal authorities to
reshape poor districts at will and allocate public investment selectively, and
it enabled politicians to convert their ability to protect informal settlements
into a political good.[29] Just as importantly, the informalization of Brazilian
urban poverty—defined not so much by the fact of poor, self-built, underser-
viced housing as by its legal stigmatization—promoted the fiction that Brazil's low-income self-built cities were an incidental externality: an unwanted
atavism of the colonial and slavocratic past, a temporary side effect of underdevelopment, a distortion or aberration on the teleological path toward
urban modernity and racial democracy. This perception helped disguise informality's integral role in the genesis of Brazil's twentieth-century urbanity
and delayed critical analysis of how informality influenced enduring patterns
of socioracial inequality.

Race, Slavery, and the Origins of Informality

It is not easy to untangle either racialization's role in this early history of Brazilian urban informality or the role that informality has played in the history
of Brazilian racialization.

Quantitative data, such as they are, certainly affirm that the residents of
poor, extralegal, self-constructed urban housing have historically been disproportionately Black and Brown.[30] Qualitatively, even informal settlements
with significant numbers of white residents are often perceived as Black in
the public imagination.[31] Yet the link between Blackness and informality cannot be explained by its mere existence. To understand the racialization of
informality—and its significance for the development of racial and urban
inequality—we must stretch far into the nineteenth century, both to the urban forms that preceded twentieth-century *favelas* and *mocambos* and to the
power relationships that shaped the place of poor, Afro-descendant people in
Brazilian urban space.

Long before anyone counted Brazil's urban shacks, they were understood as Black. Rustic huts acquired a strong association not only with Afro-descendant people, but also with the processes through which they sought and attained precarious freedom. In the Northeast, the very word *mocambo*—a hut but also a *quilombo* (maroon)—derived from the Kimbundu language of western Africa.[32] In 1816, a French cotton merchant observed "cabins made of leaves in which free blacks and *mulatos* live" in the Recife suburb of Afogados.[33] Around the same time, a visiting Frankfurt-born naturalist wrote that for most enslaved people, permission to construct their own "cabin" was the closest attainable thing to freedom.[34] More than a century later, the novelist Lima Barreto wrote of how, for "people of color," shacks served as "a kind of protest through possession against slavery's dependency," and the sociologist Gilberto Freyre described the nineteenth-century *mocambo* as the material iteration of freedom because it had its own "window and door."[35] According to the historian Mary Karasch, mud huts with palm-thatched roofs were the typical residences of nineteenth-century Rio Afro-descendants who had attained some independence—as freeborn Brazilians, as freed persons, as enslaved individuals allowed to live on their own account, or as runaways living in the city's hills, swamps, and peripheries.[36] In 1835, Johann Moritz Rugendas's *Viagem pitoresca através do Brasil* included a lithograph titled *Habitation de nègres* that depicted a thatch-roofed hut in the shadow of a big house; a white woman watches inertly from a balcony as the hut's Black inhabitants go about the stuff of life—smoking, weaving straw, sleeping, caring for children, entirely involved in their own world making (fig. 8.1).

It is easy to imagine the continuum between those rustic huts and the twentieth-century *favela*. But the tenements that housed Brazil's poor urban workers in the mid-nineteenth century—variously denominated *cortiços*, *casas de cômodo*, or *estalagens*—were equally important to the racialized origins of modern informality.[37] Just as clusters of shacks emerged within the boundaries of a formally constituted city, so tenements comprised ever-expanding improvised spaces within the shells of formalized structures.[38] Most nineteenth-century urban huts were built with the permission of self-styled authorities, who claimed the right to regulate the territory they owned or controlled with dubious legal backing; so, too, the interiors of tenements were developed as private spaces where public law had no business.[39] Just as shantytowns harbored all manner of informal and illegal economies, so tenement economic life often occurred outside or against the law (though often with the collusion of state agents). And just as improvisation, extralegal property relations, personalism, and informal economies blurred the boundaries between early shantytowns and *quilombos*, so the category of the *cortiço*

FIGURE 8.1. **Johann Rugendas, "Habitation de nègres."** Source: Wikimedia Commons, https://com
mons.wikimedia.org/wiki/File:Habitation_de_négres,_da_Coleção_Brasiliana_Iconográfica.jpg.

shaded easily into that of the *zungu* or *casa de quilombo*—a type of tenement
that was also a haven for Afro-descendent culture, a refuge from and challenge to the slave regime and the domestic heart of the *cidade negra* (Black
city).[40] Brazil's nineteenth-century tenement residents ran the gamut from
enslaved to free, indigenous to African to European to Brazil born. But especially in slavery's last gasp, as the free Afro-descendant population grew and
the proportion of enslaved people working on their own account increased,
Blackness infused the tenement's Brazilian imaginary.[41] Emblematically,
Aluísio de Azevedo's *O cortiço*—the best-known of Brazil's nineteenth-
century social realist novels—centers in part on a hulking, good-natured Portuguese immigrant for whom the multiethnic *cortiço* incubates a racialized
version of Brazilianness centered on samba, sensuality, and violence.

Huts and tenements were specific forms of residential informality, the
ancestors of twentieth-century *favelas* and peripheries. Yet informality is as
much a relationship between space and power as a static form. And in Brazil's
nineteenth century—as in the twentieth and the twenty-first—many urban
informalities were not structures at all but arrangements of deliberate im-

permanence, developed in negation of the right to rooted space. A highly racialized ethos of itinerancy infused notions of what constituted adequate shelter for Brazil's nineteenth-century urban poor. Among elites it was taken for granted that they occupied the city only conditionally, at the sufferance of others, making no actionable claim in the public sphere. This bounded itinerancy influenced the development of tenements and shacks, and it also defined the version of the city experienced by enslaved domestics, servants, apprentices, and dependents, who might sleep on straw mats in corridors or dank basements, or behind makeshift curtains in stuffy attic, or on hammocks strung wherever their master allowed.[42] Such spaces, rarely denominated *informal*, nonetheless incarnated informality's liminal place between house and street, private and public. Poor workers could occupy these itinerant spaces, but they could claim them neither as a "house" that granted them autonomous control over a private space or as a "street" that subjected and entitled them to the laws and customs of the public sphere.[43] Laborers across the color spectrum lived in these ways, but the images they evoked were mostly of Black bodies, or of whites whose servile dependence recalled slavery.[44] Itinerant, liminal urbanity—like service and labor more generally—implied Blackness even when lived by phenotypically white people.

Yet Afro-descendants themselves also constructed a strikingly different relationship between space and power, equally integral to informality's deep history. The *cidade negra*, conceived by Sidney Chalhoub for nineteenth-century Rio, was not a specific form or geography.[45] It was, rather, a capillary web of city making that fomented Black identity, freedom, and autonomy, relentlessly eroding the interlocked networks of public and private power that sustained slavery.[46] The *cidade negra* was constructed and reconstructed daily through interactions as simple as mutual recognition and as complex as quilombos and mass revolts. It was built by the sound of the Kimbundu language or the smell of *dendê* (palm oil), or through the spaces of intimacy created among washerwomen as they worked. It existed in the pervasive echo of *sambas* or *batuques* or *maracatus* on weekends and saints' days, or in the *terreiros* of Candomblé or Xangô (Afro-Brazilian religions) that provoked white complaints in every nineteenth-century city. The *cidade negra* forged the chains of connection that led fugitives to the trappings of living free—clothes, shoes, employment, space in the rooming houses and *quilombos* that city newspapers often termed *coitos de escravos* (slave hideouts).[47] Those trappings, in their turn, could—cumulatively and over time—actualize freedom, even by law.[48] At its most defiant, the *cidade negra* could lead an African illegally imported as a slave to the lawyer who might help them to claim freedom; it could reconnect enslaved wet nurses to the biological children torn from them at birth; it might give an abused slave girl the poison she sought to kill her mistress; it might facilitate the planning of a mass uprising.[49] And the persistent existence of the *cidade negra* could and did undermine slavery itself, creating a *cidade esconderijo*, a "hideout city," where "the distinctions between poor free and slaves gradually disintegrated" and where private abuses were converted through the public sphere to issues of moral outrage.[50]

Anchored in both form and itinerancy, semiautonomous from both the house and the street, the *cidade negra* was simultaneously ubiquitous and invisible, mostly experienced as practice. In the backyards, domestic crannies, interstices, and peripheries of every Brazilian city, poor and working people created urbanity and freedom, hidden in plain sight. If one iteration of Brazil's urban geography bound Blackness to material precarity, temporal and geographical ephemerality, and legal ambiguity, the *cidade negra* made of all these things its lifeblood, forging an urban space that thrived on its own liminality.[51]

Race was integral to the material imaginary of nineteenth-century urban poverty; the very mention of Brazil's *mocambos*, *quilombos*, *cortiços*, and *zungus* evoked signs and sounds of Blackness. But the racialization of informality was most deeply rooted not in material forms, but in urban relationships in which legal precarity, itineracy, and Black world making functioned as a tangled and interdependent whole.

Blackness and Legal Exclusion in the Brazilian Belle Époque

From the late nineteenth century through the 1930s, Brazilian planners and authorities gradually pushed poor people's vernacular urbanity outside law's boundaries. Legislators began by taxing, restricting, and prohibiting *cortiços*, *casebres*, *mocambos*, and *favelas*—first in Brazil's central cities and eventually from all but the most peripheral or marginal urban geographies.[52] Authorities knew that the measures were not enforceable. But regulations served both as blueprints for an idealized form of urbanity and as tools to mold space and amplify informal governance.

While policies surrounding informality were only sometimes debated in explicitly racial terms, they were always nested in broader patterns of racialization, by turns vulgar and subtle, which were constitutive of informality's emergence as a system of governance. By imagining huts and shantytowns as Black spaces, even though many residents were white, authorities evoked ideas about urban space and power that had been forged under slavery, thus naturalizing legal exclusion, material deprivation, heightened suspicion, and enforced liminality.

The public health and urban planning legislation that eventually rendered poor people's housing "informal" coincided with Brazil's long and contested abolition process (running from the 1860s to 1888) and the global diffusion of positivism and scientific racism.[53] The end of the Atlantic slave trade after 1850, along with changing flows of capital and labor, upended Brazil's racial geographies as well as the informal and relational logics that slave owners had expertly deployed for centuries. Enslaved people eroded slavery from the inside and their abolitionist allies pummeled it from without; by official abolition, the vast majority of Brazil's enslaved people had already achieved some degree of freedom.[54] After 1888, in stark contrast to the United States, Brazil never legally restricted Black citizenship. Yet the upending of social hierarchies constructed around slavery hardened racial discrimination, as whiter Brazilians sought to preserve their slavocratic privilege by problematizing Black freedom.[55] Heightened scientific racism, along with the arrival of legions of southern Europeans recruited to replace enslaved laborers, intensified this racist uptick.[56]

Racial hardening was especially notable in cities, where urban whitewashing went far beyond lime and water. Aiming to eliminate diseases that discouraged European immigration and to create "postcards" of civilization and progress, but also imbued with racist ideologies that associated urban disease and disorder with Blackness, city authorities used every legal and regulatory tool within their power to transform their central districts. New building and sanitary codes set the broad outlines by banning shacks and holding all dwellings to standards beyond most residents' means; incremental decrees banning repairs on shacks and forcing the removal of specific settlements provoked periodic panic. At the same time, officials steeped in both racist criminology and inbred suspicion of the *cidade negra* intensified the policing of Afro-descendant work, leisure, and culture.

These processes depended heavily on the racialized problematization of poor homes and neighborhoods. *Cortiços*, *cabeças de porco*, and *porões*— subject to legal prohibitions and all-out eradication campaigns between the 1870s and the early 1900s—were generally racially mixed spaces, but journalists and politicians emphasized their Blackness.[57] Even in immigrant São Paulo, where the Afro-descendant population was less than 15 percent in the early twentieth century, Blackness continued to be associated with *cortiços* and *porões*, and city authorities repeatedly targeted Black spaces and cultural practices.[58] Everardo Backheuser—the highest-profile analyst of Rio's Belle

Époque housing crisis—emblematically elided race and urban misery in his classic description of a Rio de Janeiro *casa de comodos*: along with "vagrant Italians" and "dirty naked children," these "nauseating places" were home to "women whose 'natty' hair was replete with oil, singing tuneless *modinhas* while washing clothes right in their windowless alcoves" and "women of low extraction, generally *pretas*, in ignoble attire" were jumbled in the same "hive" with "poor but respectable maidens" whose whiteness could be presumed and whose neat cubicles constituted "islands of cleanliness in those oceans of filth."[59] As was true before abolition, racialized notions of promiscuity, poor hygiene, neglectful parenting, and social danger rationalized reams of legislation prohibiting the improvised tenements and basements that had constituted much of the vernacular city before the twentieth century.

Racialization was clearer still when it came to shacks and shantytowns. The very words *mocambo* and *favela*—which problematized long-standing urban forms and created new categories of legal estrangement—emerged at the juncture of scientific racism and Belle Époque urbanism. *Mocambo* crystallized in the shadow of slavery as a metonym for the rustic structures that housed the majority of Recife's families, recalling both African lineage and the supposed danger of unbridled Black freedom.[60] In Rio, *favela* was first used in the late 1890s to draw connections between a self-built community in central Rio and Brazil's Canudos War—a conflict that had been visually and literarily imprinted in the public imagination as a contest between the ferocious, atavistic messianism of the mixed-race defenders of an improvised city of mud huts in the Brazilian northeast and the brutal civilizing force of Brazil's coastal cities.[61] A similar usage developed simultaneously in the planned city of Belo Horizonte.[62] In each case, the words' echo in the elite public sphere evoked racialized notions of atavism, primitivism, and civilizational danger.

Journalistic and visual representations cemented those bonds, linking the self-built city to filth, disease, crime, disorder, immorality, and backwardness.[63] In Rio, this manifested most clearly in the sensational crime reports that titillated Belle Époque readers. Often set in *favelas* and *mocambos*, these grotesque dramas relished in affixing racial labels.[64] In 1902, a crime notice detailed the fearsome aggression of the "Baianinho da Favella"; a 1907 story described a bloody attempted murder carried out by a Black man against his lover, Rosalina, "de cor acablocada," in the aftermath of a *samba*, described as a "fearsome *pancadaria*" practiced by "those people."[65] The breathless headline, in an array of bold font, read: "Othelo na favela. Final de un samba. Amante enciumado. Tentativa de assassinato."

A similarly explicit and estranging racial descriptiveness infused journalistic chronicles of shantytown life. A 1903 description of Rio's Morro da

Favela—possibly the earliest by noted chronicler João do Rio—detailed "ragged *negras*," naked Black boys, and "suspect types" among the "strange people" that inhabited the hill's "indescribable" "pigsties" and "dumps."[66] In the hill's most dangerous region, *pardas* (brown women) lived in sin and old "black women" served as midwives, while fearsome thieves and well-known rowdies and *capoeiras* plotted sinister violence, sometimes under police instructions.[67] In 1905 João do Rio detailed with grotesque racism his visit to a Rio women's prison, noting that the majority of the Black prisoners—filthy-haired alcoholics and crazies with "libidinous monkey eyes"; "stupid," "toothless" smiles; and abundant tattoos—lived on the Morro da Favela or other nearby streets.[68]

Between the 1900s and the 1920s, *favela* cartoons printed in popular journals also regularly associated Blackness with destitution, servility, promiscuity, crime, and rurality.[69] One from 1907 set the tone: the extremely racist captions lament that the city's newfound civilization, an "apotheosis of light," is constantly interrupted by "destitute people" who "descend the Santo Antônio Hill" in search of water (fig. 8.2). The images depict a "picaresque procession" of "Blacks [whose backs are] curved by the weight of kerosene cans," "yet another Black woman in a low-cut dress," "a thick-lipped little black girl," and "a naughty *moleque*"—"in sum, a rosary of calamities, which could easily stop exhibiting itself if there were one simple thing in today's Civilized Capital: WATER."[70]

In Belo Horizonte, Afro-descendant cultural practices similarly defined the emerging categories of *morro* and *favela*.[71] In Recife, especially in the decades surrounding abolition, outsiders frequently identified *mocambo* residents as *pretos* or *pardos*.[72] Journalists regularly linked *mocambos* to *batuques* and other activities associated with Blackness, which were often the backdrop for sensationalist descriptions of crime and illicit commerce.[73] Later politicians and commentators often followed the lead of journalist Aníbal Fernandes, who praised an early workers' housing project in 1921 because it was the "seed" of policies that might eventually eliminate "the sordid *mocambo*, expression of African barbarity."[74] Two years later a column advocating a citywide anti-*mocambo* campaign lamented in vulgar terms the legacies of "negrophile" colonizers who had despoiled the Dutch planned city of Recife with the "turbid inheritance" embodied by *mocambos*.[75] Much to the ire of urban reformers, foreigners often saw things differently: their fascination with the *mocambos'* perceived Africanism created demand for a series of postcards that often featured Black residents next to their rustic homes, with captions like *negerhutten, negreries, negroes-houses*, and *choupanas dos negros* (fig. 8.3).[76]

FIGURE 8.2. **Cartoon from** *O Malho*, **July 27, 1907.** Source: *O Malho*, July 27, 1907, Biblioteca Nacional, Brazil.

FIGURE 8.3. **"Choupanas dos negros."** Source: Undated postcard, Josebias Bandeira Collection, Fundação Joaquim Nabuco, Recife.

Race and Silence

The early twentieth-century racialization of shacks and shantytowns was not always so transparent.[77] In Recife, some journalists recalled slavery's language of paternalism and Catholic charity but made no overt reference to race. *Mocambeiros* were *populares* (members of the popular classes), *pobres propri-etários* (poor property owners), humble workers, needy mothers, innocent victims of greedy landlords or natural disasters, in need of Catholic charity and public solidarity.[78] Recife's labor activists took a different tack, portraying urban informality as a rallying point for working-class solidarity in which racial distinction had no place.[79] An 1920 article in the anarcho-socialist *Hora Social* pictured a *mocambo* in ruins and argued that it was "evident witness to the current capitalist regime's iniquity and inequality." It concluded: "Come, workers, abandon and burn these wretched hovels where you who are the strength of the world are forced to live."[80]

Perhaps reacting to such appeals, or perhaps adhering to older patterns of strategic racial silence, Recife's political authorities sometimes followed suit.[81] In 1905, the public health pioneer Octavio Freitas described *mocambos* simply as the "main domicile of the poorer classes."[82] In 1908, the jurist Arthur

Orlando pointedly criticized the racialization of endemic disease as a form of colonial harm inflicted by Europe.[83] In 1920, the noted doctor and future federal congressman Antônio Austregésilo did not contain his satisfaction about "the progressive disappearance of negros" from his native city, but he problematized *mocambos* solely on public health grounds, describing residents simply as "the poor, the humble, the artisans who have been abandoned by fortune."[84]

In Rio, racially neutral discourse emerged especially forcefully in the wake of eviction threats and disasters.[85] In 1907, during a doomed effort to clear the Morro da Favella, the typographer Alfredo Innocêncio wrote an interesting editorial. Conceding that the hill's shacks "made the capital ugly," he nonetheless described the inhabitants as "unfortunate people" and "poor workers" whose abrupt removal would be "inhuman."[86] Subsequently, investigative reporters from the *Jornal do Brasil* portrayed the *favela* as a "citadel of pauperism." But its people were worthy workers, veterans, parents and children of all colors who contributed to crucial industries and maintained clean homes. While Black people dominated his photographs, the reporter pointedly omitted racial descriptors as he listed dozens of families who had lost their homes because of the decree.[87] Similarly, when an eviction decree and mysterious fire razed central Rio's Santo Antônio shantytown in 1916, some coverage oozed with disdain for the destroyed "Babylon of garbage," but journalists almost universally emphasized residents' victimization and dignity—they were "mostly workers and washerwomen," "proletarians," "poor unhappy people," "ill favored," "abandoned by fortune."[88] Photos again depicted residents across the racial spectrum.[89] An article describing one nun's relief efforts following the fire fused racial silence and paternalism, describing a "profusion of skeletal hands" that "were raised in supplication . . . they were old and young, men, women and children who surrounded that angel of goodness who was incarnate in the nun's habit."[90]

Rio's policymakers and politicians followed suit under a variety of ideological influences. The positivist engineer Everardo Backheuser noted that the Morro da Favella was home not only to the "troublemakers" of legend but also to "the poorest," "the neediest," "laborious workers that are driven by the scarcity and expense of living quarters to these high places where they enjoy relative affordability and a gentle and continuous wind that sweetens the dwelling's coarseness."[91] Sought out by a commission of "residents with family" formed to combat the 1907 eradication attempt on the Morro da Favella, the politicians Manoel da Motta Monteiro Lopes (later Brazil's first Black congressman) and José Lopes da Silva Trovão described the settlement's population as "orderly, honest, and laborious," people who owned their homes and even paid property taxes.[92] In the wake of the 1916 Santo Antônio eviction campaign and fire, Rio's prefect expressed disgust for the destroyed "zincópolis," but he also visited the hill and tacitly condoned the resettlement of its "extremely poor people" in the outlying district of Mangueira.[93]

In some cases, racial silence functioned as a precursor of emancipatory strategies that would blossom after 1930, as will be discussed later. Yet it would be a mistake to confuse the absence of racial speech with advocacy for racial equality, especially when context and allusion indicated the speaker's adherence to a powerful ethos of inequality. Unlike the blunt racism prevalent in South Africa or the US South, Brazilian discrimination has long operated sinuously and obliquely. Journalists, politicians, and Catholic "angels of mercy" did not speak in a vacuum; their utterances appeared adjacent to racist cartoons and increasingly sensational crime columns in which the connection between Blackness and informality was taken for granted, and the people who read their words already associated tenements and *favelas* with the sounds and sights of Brazil's slavocratic past. In Recife, this was almost comically clear in the city's mapping process: while official survey maps rendered the city's *mocambos* entirely invisible, engineers charged with carrying out projects in actual urban space added handwritten notes indicating the location of the "Black people's huts."[94] When a Rio journalist wrote about Santo Antônio's "junk heap of soapbox and zinc houses, with their display of drying laundry" that "does not befit the opulence of the Avenida Central," aristocratic readers would have instinctively assumed that the people who washed the offending laundry were mostly Afro-descendant, just as the people who promenaded on the elegant streets wearing those painstakingly cleaned clothes were their mostly white peers.[95] Five years later, a certain "VC" argued that the real victims of the Santo Antônio fire were not the "creatures who were left homeless . . . poor little things!" But rather "we, the others, here below, who are now obliged not only to put a roof over their heads, but also to give them clothes, bread, and all the rest—we, who are obliged to give help to those people who never did anything good, who live their lives there, separate, without ever asking about our miseries and our struggles, only seeking to profit and profit from them." It took little imagination to comprehend that the author's hardworking, taxpaying "we" was mostly white and the freeloading "miserable" population was mostly Black.[96] In a context where racial inequalities had been naturalized by centuries of sedimentary associations, public discourse regularly evoked race without speaking its name.

Such racialized understandings shaped debates about housing and public resources. Elite observers did not slur self-built settlements indiscriminately. They characterized poor residents in specific, patterned ways that reinforced

slave-era associations among Blackness, contamination, backwardness, itineracy, and rurality. Whether or not they used racial language, outsiders jour-
neyed to self-built cityscapes as if they were on safari, noting their strange
and picaresque character and highlighting sanitary and security dangers
that flowed, one way, from self-built settlements to the elite districts. Elites
also routinely denied fixity to vernacular urbanity: instruments of urban
governmentality reinforced the ethos of itineracy by systematically ignoring or undercounting informal settlements in censuses and rendering their
territory as blank space on municipal maps.[97] Even sympathetic observers
naturalized the notion that *favelas* and *mocambos* were part of the private,
relational sphere, conflict resolution that privileged negotiated tolerance over
rights.[98] Lettered discussions also consistently distanced informal urbanity
from modernity, framing shacks and shantytowns as primitive impediments
to progress. Many, finally, bridged postabolition panic about rural labor with
subsequent sociological arguments about displacement and marginality, arguing that primitive shantytown inhabitants ought not to be in the city at
all because their natural habitat was the countryside, where they would and
should have remained in abolition's wake.[99]

Such thinking had practical consequences. If shanty dwellers did not belong in the city—if their labor was worthless and their contributions nil—
then paternalistic or pious tolerance was the natural limit of human sympathy. Charity might lead Recife patrons to help a "poor Black washerwoman"
construct a *mocambo* when hers burnt down; sympathy might sometimes
condemn deliberate arson in Santo Antônio or heartless expulsion on the
Morro da Favela.[100] Corporatist paternalism might lead city officials to believe that *mocambo* dwellers "deserved favors" from public authorities, who
might tolerate *mocambos* and *favelas* in areas where land values were low or
construction difficult, much as slavocratic paternalism had opened spaces for
enslaved people to sleep in backyards or domestic interstices.[101] But the notion that poor and disproportionately Black people had a right to the city—a
right to own it, to benefit from it, and to shape it—was hardly conceivable. It
was thus seamless common sense to gradually write the Black, self-built city
out of the legalized urban fabric—by taxing shacks, by prohibiting shanty repairs, by passing health and construction codes that the poor could not afford
to meet, and finally by banning tenements and shantytowns from a steadily
expanding sphere of urban territory. Lawmakers knew full well that such
regulations would not eliminate Brazil's shantytowns. But they were effective
at relegating informal inhabitants to a zone of tolerance, subcitizenship, and
exclusion from public resources that was entirely consistent with nineteenth-
century ideologies about Blackness and city space.

Silence and the *Cidade Negra*

In this postemancipation framework, residents of Brazil's *favelas*, *mocambos*, and peripheries actively grappled with informalization's racial logic, just as they had navigated that of the slave city. But they did so in radically heterogeneous ways that reflected both the power of Brazil's informal governance practices and the deceptive silence that often enveloped Brazilian racism. Over the course of the twentieth century, residents sustained and nurtured a *cidade negra* in the territories of informal urbanism. But—perhaps in recognition of the overwhelming ethos of racial inequality that infused Brazilian society and politics—they created space for Black urban autonomy and freedom in ways that mirrored the sinuousness that increasingly characterized Brazilian racism itself. Contesting racialized understandings of the *favela* was vital to the settlements' survival, and in that context, residents exhibited the same fluid agility that characterized all of their politics of permanence. Just as residents defended vernacular urbanity by entwining resistance and complicity, so they contested racialization not so much by confronting it head on as by challenging the associations that sustained it while respecting the boundaries of racial silence.

This strategy emerged in part because some communities' survival depended on relational networks that linked them to people who had entirely naturalized Brazil's racial order. Many *favela* narratives privilege resistance, but most *favelas* and *mocambos* arose not only from residents' determined ingenuity, but also through some combination of official permission, landowner rent seeking, illegal petty entrepreneurship, and patriarchal charity. When their settlements came under threat, informal residents resisted expulsion by calling on connection and grace, often from the same people who denounced *favelas* or profited from their exploitation. *Favelados* and *mocambeiros* often had no choice but to join forces with corrupt landlords; they sent letters begging for exemptions to the same officials who regularly derided their homes, they appealed to journals that habitually decried their settlements, they played the roles of passive and subordinate victims while claiming Catholic charity, and they regularly acceded to subordinating political partnerships.[102]

In all these contexts, it would have done little good for residents to directly challenge their patrons' power or denounce their racist assumptions. Rather, in those specific circumstances, residents often operated in the bounds of normative honor codes that had long structured Brazil's unequal power dynamics—asserting virtue without contesting hierarchy, crossing the borders of the sphere of privilege without eliminating it. Women presented themselves as good wives, widows, and mothers; men, as honest fathers and providers. They sought not rights but mercies, and their claims were founded not on racial injustice but on corporate solidarity. In a slave society where Black resistance had been diffused over centuries by a thousand petty graces that allowed mobility with the goal of entrenching bondage, this logic was a devil's bargain steeped with racial history and meaning.[103] At the same time, given the ubiquity of racism, the strength of personalistic power relations and the vitality of the matters at stake, this kind of complicity was often the only pragmatic option.

Yet supplication was but one strand in the knot of engagement and counterdiscourse that sustained the informalized city. Elsewhere residents contradicted racialized logics by systematically undermining their sustaining assumptions. If outsiders normalized informalization by characterizing residents as Black and Blacks as filthy, disorderly, lazy, and criminal, residents responded by clipping each association at its root. Their homes were clean despite their exclusion from public services. They might lack policing, but they were honest and pacific people who created safety and public order on their own terms; as a Morro da Favella resident and warehouse guard wrote indignantly to the *Gazeta de Notícias* in 1902, "Not all residents have a bad reputation."[104] Perhaps to guarantee just this integrity, the Morro da Favella—foreshadowing a century of informal order making—divided its territory into quadrants, each with its own authority whose task it was to maintain public order (although one resident emphasized that men's homes were still their own paternalistic domain).[105] As *mocambo* and *favela* evictions accelerated after 1910, residents often turned the tables on criminal stereotypes, presenting themselves as honest parents and proletarians and calling on authorities to protect them from violent gangsters and corrupt land claimants who often colluded with rogue police.[106]

If we read official sources against the grain, we also find residents who understood their vernacular city as a firm negation of the ethos of itinerary so essential to Black marginalization. The warehouse guard emphasized—typically—his status as a longtime resident and taxpayer. In 1903, Morro da Favella, residents astounded the flaneur who "discovered" them with their "arrogant" pride of place: "These creatures . . . think they are superior . . . everyone we spoke with answered, pointing to their fetid hovels, 'here we have our house!' "[107] A 1917 article about the Morro da São Carlos in central Rio anticipated Gilberto Freyre's observations about *mocambos* and freedom in Recife: the reporter observed in wonder that the "unhappy workers" lacked "everything that is indispensable for life and hygiene, including water and sewage lines, but even so they are happy because they are 'in what is their

FIGURE 8.4. **Residents of the Morro da Babilônia.** Source: Arquivo Geral da Cidade do Rio de Janeiro.

own,' without fear of landlord persecution or horrible nights sleeping in the rough."[108] This sentiment can even be perceived in visual sources, where residents commonly project solidarity and strength. In a 1914 photo taken by noted municipal photographer Augusto Malta, a family stands in front of their tin-scrap home on Rio's Morro da Babilônia (fig. 8.4). We cannot be sure how much choice they had in the photo's composition, but in what they could control, the residents exude dignity and determination: one man's arms are crossed, as if to defy any attempt to uproot them, and another holds what might be a prized rooster; the women's clothing is elegant and clean; a boy on the far left is proudly dressed in the style of northeast.

Residents also ingeniously negated the idea that *favelas* and *mocambos* were antithetical to urban modernity. Like anyone else, informal urbanites adopted as they could the latest technologies and consumption habits, a fact that never failed to amaze exoticizing flaneurs. A curious example appeared in a 1936 article about the "crystal radios"—homemade, with no need for external electricity—that briefly flourished among Recife's *mocambos*. In a visit to downtown Recife, a reporter observed with wonder the precarious antennas that emerged from one settlement's improvised dwellings. He called on one "Dona Mocinha," who conversed with him while she took a sponge bath "shower" inside her *mocambo*. Mocinha, in mockingly rendered argot, gushed about her favorite radio stars and explained the marvels of the radios, ingeniously fabricated by a local carpenter who housed them in repurposed furniture consoles and amplified the sound with speakers made from old telephone receivers. The reporter never saw her, and she refused to be photographed. But his patronizing amazement at her modernity was palpable: "D. Mocinha, the woman seen by no one, may not have money, but she already has a radio and a long bath."[109]

Residents frequently used music to publicly contest racialized arguments about backwardness and social danger. From the very beginning, samba— like Afro-Brazilian religious and cultural forms across Brazil—had created spaces in which poor, mostly Black Cariocas and powerful outsiders came together in a partnership that would eventually earn a unique place in Brazil's nationalist imagination.[110] Samba forged one of the few areas of the Brazilian public sphere where Blackness and Brownness were openly discussed and celebrated in ways that went beyond primitivist stereotypes or the niceties of racial democracy. As the *favelas* grew, sambas (composed by insiders and outsiders alike) became the *favelas'* sonic avatar, projecting a counternarrative of daily life and effacing racialized tropes that infused Rio's public sphere.[111]

Samba did its racial work in multivalent and often contradictory ways. In the hands of white performers and studios, it could often be read as upholding racial democracy's harmonious myths or even rendering Black culture as nationalist caricature. Yet in both its lyrics and its performance, samba also contested—sometimes subtly, sometimes acidly—the racist assumptions that marginalized Black people and their communities. It is probably no accident that the first commercially successful recorded samba—created by a mostly Black collective with close ties to Rio's *cortiços*, *zungus*, and early *favelas*—was "Pelo telefone," a playful invocation of a "modern" contraption that few Black people had access to. Composers frequently contested racist stereotypes of Black attitudes toward work and family, often by using the roguish archetype of the *malandro* to highlight the absurdity of dominant codes of conduct in the context of most people's everyday realities.[112] In 1928, for example, a samba called "Vagabundo" deftly highlighted the hypocrisy of expectations that dead-end jobs and meaningless formalisms would lead to a better future: "I am not a friend to work / I only want to live in orgy / work doesn't lead to a future / it takes away strength and joy." It praised the "vida do malandro" and concluded, "If work is honor/the ass is the most honorable."[113] But samba could also contest marginalization by underscoring Black and Brown virtue within dominant codes: as both public funding and censorship increased in the 1930s, sambas increasingly portrayed *favela* residents as patriotic, family oriented, and hardworking.[114] Throughout, sambas continued to construct with unusual directness an alternate moral universe in which the joy and communitarian spirit of a *favela* explicitly racialized as Black or Brown contrasted sharply with the avarice and hypocrisy of the "asphalt" (formal city).[115]

A samba called *Recenseamento* (1940) united these heterodox strategies. Influenced by Getúlio Vargas's authoritarian, corporatist nationalism, the samba detailed the humiliation of a woman experiencing the first census of her *favela* home.[116] It began with stigmatizing tropes; the agent assumed she was an unmarried mother mired in poverty and that the children's (Black) father was a dissolute partier. The samba's cleverness is in the woman's retort: turning the tables, she explains that her man is part of the Brazilian navy, that their poverty is honorable, and that the fact that they samba is an indication of their authentic Brazilianness.[117]

In pointedly contesting racialized tropes that justified informalization, residents also contested the assumptions and practices that excluded poor, Black spaces from the political sphere. Flatly rejecting the notion that their communities embodied political backwardness or disorder, residents and local leaders adhered energetically to the logics of modern governance even when the institutional forms excluded them. Long anticipating Boaventura de Sousa Santos's 1970s arguments about hybrid legal practices, *favela* and *mocambo* associations created vernacular versions of the very formalities that marginalized them; they organized plots along rustic streets, recorded their property in registers that paralleled formal notaries, collected taxes to sustain residents' commissions that created schools and regulated garbage disposal.[118] Some of these arrangements were exceptionally democratic; Recife's São Miguel association, discussed further later, held neighborhood meetings and its statutes required transparency and accountability.[119] But even authoritarian leaders seem to have felt the need for "modern" forms of governance; in 1935 Recife's communist paper railed against the controlling "ruler" of an eponymous settlement called Mustardinha, yet it also reported that Mustardinha printed a *caderneta* that served as a contract and "constitution" to regulate that territory.[120] Regardless of who benefited, the act of imposing order in forms that adhered to the logic of Brazil's governing frameworks powerfully negated allegations of political incapacity and illegitimacy.

The politics of permanence also played out in the streets and public spheres. Building on nineteenth-century traditions and anticipating active postwar political participation, residents frequently lobbied prominent politicians in ways that showed a full engagement with the political process and belied racialized notions of *favela* passivity and helplessness. As early as 1907, residents formed commissions that wrote letters to the press and petitioned authorities for public services, schools, and eviction stays.[121] Many allied with left-wing movements, referring to themselves as proletarians and workers, alluding to the need for basic social and economic guarantees, and even implying consequences should their views be ignored. Others claimed higher authority: in 1924 Recife, for example, "various residents" sent a letter protesting the destruction of their "tin city." Complaining of undercompensation and eviction techniques that included marking houses with a large X, the missive denounced the "folly" of the supposed property owners vis-à-vis people pointedly referred to as "poor families"; should the eviction proceed, residents argued, vengeance would come from the "high designs of providence."[122] Samba was again a direct player. In Rio, as the French urbanist Alfred Agache prepared a master plan in 1927–1928, rumors spread about *favela* eradication; in response, the *sambista* Sinhô composed a carnival hit about the Morro da Favela that brought the informal city's counternarrative straight to the streets, painting the shack as a site of love and nostalgia, the formal city as dominated by pitiless avarice, and the community as distinct and irreplaceable.[123]

By the late 1920s, residents had become adept at marshaling these techniques in a multivalent, sustained campaign for permanence and inclusion that relentlessly chipped away at the racialized myths of disorder, immorality, laziness, itineracy, and helplessness that undergirded marginalization. When the phoenix-like community of Santo Antônio faced new threats in the 1930s, nearly seventy heads of household petitioned Getúlio Vargas, denouncing cruel threats to long-occupied affordable homes and intimating that their willingness to remain "mute" in this "century of social demands" depended on his "benevolence." A condescending memo from the public health service convinced Vargas to take no action, but a multivalent strategy—eventually achieving direct representation on the city council and inspiring a samba reminiscent of "A favela vai abaixo"—kept the settlement intact until the entire enormous hill was dismantled in the 1950s.[124] In the nearby community of Salgueiro, which endures to this day, the community samba school became an early residents' association that mobilized a stunning array of legal, political, and cultural strategies to preserve long-occupied lands.[125] In July 1933, their commission sent a telegram to Getúlio Vargas that encapsulated their eclectic strategy, at once embracing the paternalistic logic of personal power, making moral claims to long-occupied homes where they had raised their families, referencing the law of adverse possession (*usucapião*), and implying violence should negotiation fail:

[We the] undersigned live [on] Salgueiro hill . . . [with] many years' residence, having grown children born there. Now a gentleman has appeared who invites their evacuation in name [of] false rights never claimed. Cannot obey this order because have the *usocapião* [*sic*] of these lands cultivated and improved by undersigned, disposed to defend domain to last breath. Are poor people living life of suffering and ask of Yr. Exc. government protection, even to avoid disagreeable incidents as there are families wanting heated action that signatories have tried to contain. Will send memorandum explaining but ask Yr. Exc. for immediate orders to police in order to avoid violence.[126]

A final example from Recife exemplifies the heterodox approach through which residents defended Black rights to the city while operating within the ethos of racial silence. The Villa São Miguel, which had begun as an ill-fated attempt to build workers' housing in the populous district of Afogados, was by the late 1920s a *mocambo* community enmeshed in an ugly property dispute involving private claims to the public marine land where poor residents had built their homes.[127] In the face of an eviction threat, and in collaboration with working-class militants in the throes of a popular-front moment, residents deployed a creative range of strategies. Lawyers argued the case in strictly statutory terms. A letter to the head of Recife's Seventh Military Region appealed to paternalism: citing their long tenure and status as "heads of large families," along with his "farsightedness and social spirit," residents urged him to personally intervene. Nearly simultaneously, residents worked the other end of the political spectrum, corresponding in 1931 with the União Geral dos Trabalhadores de Pernambuco, whose leaders encouraged them in their "very important initiative to join forces in order to fight exploitation against all workers." In 1931–1932, residents, aided by a notary descended from a nineteenth-century provincial president, legally constituted themselves as the Liga Mixta dos Proprietarios Pobres da Villa São Miguel, democratically uniting "all of the poor property owners of the villa" under "a single flag, without distinctions of color, nationality, or political or religious creed," to defend their rights and regulate the community. The Liga was particularly concerned with controlling public messaging about the dispute and was zealous in conforming with public security laws. But it also organized a school and mobilized residents against the supposed property owner's violent tactics (arson, political denunciation, and illegal imprisonments). In 1934, residents reportedly blocked city engineers from completing a cadastral map.[128] In 1935, "residents of the Villa São Miguel" wrote to a short-lived communist newspaper to protest the "unpatriotic" expulsion of four residents and the community's victimization by "petty persecutions . . . by false property owners."[129]

After a crackdown on communist militants in 1935 and a powerful *mocambo* eradication campaign during the Estado Novo, the association seems to have retreated to a more accommodationist stance. But it would remain active, and both the community and the Liga still stand in a neighborhood long central to the history of Afro-Recife.

Despite local differences, political advocacy in Rio and Recife's informal settlements hewed a common path with an unlikely array of tools. Residents maintained keen awareness of the personal power and informal governance that enmeshed every *favela*, and *mocambo*, and they mobilized relational instruments honed during centuries of slavocratic rule accordingly. At the same time, recalling the nineteenth-century *cidade negra*, residents used the liminal spaces they had forged—as well as a gradual and halting expansion of popular politics and urban citizenship rights—to foment more emancipatory and autonomous spaces for Afro-descendant culture, education, and the right to rights.

Amid these eclectic strategies, it is significant that residents rarely explicitly denounced the racism that legitimized their communities' marginalization. This did not reflect blindness to the racial discrimination that pervaded Brazilian cities and normalized informalization. Nor should it lead us to think that residents negated their own racial identity and heritage. *Favela* and *mocambo* space incubated and sustained Afro-Brazilian religion, language, music, and cultural practices; many residents harbored powerful memories of slavery and its depredations; and the imaginative universe of samba affirmed a moral world in which Afro-descendent people embodied all that was virtuous and authentically Brazilian. Rather, from their earliest forays into the public sphere, residents seemed to understand sinuous silence as a strategic tool key to navigating Brazil's increasingly oblique racial dynamics.[130] They highlighted and shamed the crudeness of explicit racism by refocusing debates about their homes and neighborhoods on substantial issues of worthiness, virtue, and citizenship, and they refused through political engagement and action to be reduced to the status of helpless dependents undeserving of a place in the urban political sphere. Racial silence has often undermined Brazilian struggles for racial equality, but in these postabolition decades, it could also be marshaled as an antiracist tool that served preserve Black space in the city and forge the possibilities of fuller citizenship.

Conclusion

By bending dominant moral, political, and racial logics in their favor, early twentieth-century favela*dos* and *mocambeiros* forged space for a postemancipation iteration of the *cidade negra* that would, in all its contradictions, become central to every aspect of Brazil's urban world. In the years after the mid-1930s, industrialization, populist politics, grander state welfare initiatives, and rapid demographic growth upended Brazil's early processes of informalization. Migrants streamed into Brazil's cities, informality became increasingly concentrated in ever-larger settlements, and rhetorical frames once shaped by discourses of sanitarism, scientific racism, and civilization were overshadowed (though not erased) by the logics of racial democracy, modernization, development, and Cold War politics. Artists and intellectuals, most of them outsiders, imagined *favelas* and *mocambos* as idealized, antimodern spaces of Blackness and harmony; communists and socialists helped construct well-networked social movements, hoping to find in informal communities the political consciousness that they often struggled to build elsewhere. New forms of urban planning, culminating in the utopian project of Brasília, expanded the regulatory tools so key to informalization, and new institutional actors ranging from Brazil's welfare state to the progressive Catholic Church to the Alliance for Progress assumed an active role in Brazil's urban arena. Outsiders and Brazilians repeatedly reinvented Latin American informality as the symptom of a litany of transnational crises. The *favelas*—like their counterparts elsewhere in Latin America and Latin Europe—became living laboratories for theories about rural and cultural displacement, racial and economic assimilation, cultures of poverty, sociospatial mobility, political mobilization, and economic ascension.[131] From the 1970s forward, as Brazil's military government gave way to one of the world's most ambitious constitutional regimes, new and contradictory dynamics involving democratization, identity politics, deindustrialization, economic crisis, illegal economies, and increasingly uncontrolled police violence further transformed Brazil's informal urbanism.

Yet amid all this change, some of the sedimentary patterns developed during those first postabolition decades endured. Outsiders continued to play a double game, at once creating informality through law, condemning the self-built communities thus engendered, and reaping enormous economic and political profit from their existence. Residents continued to create vitality, mobility, and permanence from their own liminality, mobilizing an eclectic range of strategies ranging from personal appeals and clientelist integration to demands for rights to the city and outright defiance. From the 1930s forward, these struggles were sometimes overshadowed by high-profile defeats; Recife's anti-*mocambo* campaign of the 1930s, Rio's arsonous destruction of large lakeside *favelas* in the 1940s, massive and violent removal campaigns under military rule in the 1960s and 1970s, revived expulsions during the

convergence of the new left and neoliberal profiteering in the first decades of
the twenty-first century. Yet the larger story was one of bittersweet permanence that echoed the experiences of that first generation. Brazilian urban
informality has sometimes ebbed but mostly flowed, always remaining integral to urban economies, politics, and cultures. Residents and their allies
have successfully employed increasingly heterodox strategies to preserve informality, but formal rights to the city remained elusive, to the point that they
have often ceased even to constitute a normative ideal.[132]

The racial sediment also remains. Throughout Brazil, the percentage of
Black and Brown people living in situations of urban informality has remained heavily disproportionate and Blackness is still correlated heavily with
poverty, violence, and scarce access to the urban public goods and services.
Among outsiders, these patterns are still perpetuated and normalized by
old ideas—often evoked visually or obliquely—about itineracy, dependency,
backwardness, laziness, and degeneracy, which remain powerfully associated
not only with Black people but also with their vernacular forms of urbanity.
Images of anti-Black violence stream with horrifying regularity, wordlessly
reiterating links among Blackness, *favelas*, and criminality. Apparently well-
meaning depictions—ranging from the backward-looking *favela* paintings of
Portinari and do Amaral to Camus's *Orfeu Negro* and Meirelles's *Cidade de
Deus*—have further entrenched racialized conceptions by portraying communities as holdovers from a folkloric past or victims overwhelmed by spec-
tacularized violence.[133]

At the same time, racial silence and dissimulation have retained sway in
the urban studies and policy spheres. Despite the rise of Brazil's Black movement and an outpouring of social science documenting race-based disparities, the silence that emerged at midcentury still marks the worlds of architecture, urban planning, and even urban studies. Studies of cities that aren't
explicitly about race rarely give it much importance, and the field of informality studies largely maintains stubborn silence. Although Brazil's urban
legislation is an envy of the global planning world, as late as 2016, only two of
Brazil's capital cities took race into account in their federally mandated master plans, and debates about the equality effects of a major federal housing
program (Minha Casa, Minha Vida) generally did not analyze racial dynamics. As a result, public debate has generally obscured how entrenched racism
and exclusive legal orders have coevolved to make of informality a powerful
tool of racial exclusion.

What has changed, powerfully, are residents' own willingness to articulate
the racial dimensions of urban dispossession and the centrality of the *favela*
issue to Black politics. Throughout much of the twentieth century, neither

Brazil's best-known Black movements nor Brazil's Black press explored the *favela* question as a racial issue; *favelas*, when they appeared, emerged as culturally Black spaces, but the politics that led Black people to them remained mostly unexplored.[134] Even in Abdias do Nascimento's *Quilombo*—a landmark of Brazil's Black press—a rare article about the *favelas* in the journal's feminine column followed the cues of musical and visual culture in depicting the settlements—women carrying enormous cans of water on their heads have faces of "Black velvet," and the "great enormous strength" of the *favelados* was their innocent endurance, solidarity, and musical joy: "Poverty, destitution, and disease can't break them in their core. Young or old or child, they all enter in the samba ring, each shack is a home where a family suffers and dreams. One of the most moving aspects of the morro is the fraternity and friendships that bonds those muddy-footed beings with swing in their hips and melody in their heart."[135]

By the 1960s, however, activists began to examine race and informalization with a more critical eye. Influenced by transnational anticolonial and antiracist discourses, community leaders—many of whom were able to continue their local activism in alliance with the Catholic left even as Brazil's military government strangled most other social movements—began to ponder what it meant to be Black leaders of Black spaces in a discredited racial democracy.[136] An increasingly dense social science literature undergirded growing acknowledgment that Brazil's urban question was also a racial question. With democratization, across Brazil, Black people worked to build public and academic understanding of *favelas* both as spaces of liberation and fugitivity (latter-day *quilombos*) and as spaces of constrained political choices, racialized violence, and marginalization.[137] From the 1990s, cultural figures such as Paulo Lins and the musicians Racionais MCs and MV Bill put the *favela* at the center of an increasingly powerful Black agenda (and vice versa), and neighborhood organizations from Rio to Salvador to Recife claimed their own historical memory and articulated struggles for land and permanence as struggles for racial dignity and equality. By the time that *favela* native, police violence expert, and city councilwoman Marielle Franco was assassinated in 2018, the racialization of Brazil's informal cities had long since been converted into a racial politics.

Yet significant work remains to bring these insights to the center of debates about informality and the policies that both create and contest it—and part of that work demands deeper historicization of the relationship between race and informality. Writing about the *quilombo*'s place in the canon of Black liberationist thought in the early 1980s, the historian and activist Beatriz Nascimento sounded a warning. Despite the *quilombo*'s conceptual and symbolic importance, there were consequential historiographical "lapses": "This lapse in our knowledge of the history of Blacks in Brazil and the history of Brazil itself creates a rupture between Black people and their past, aggravating ignorance about their situation today."[138] In the 2020s, the same could still be said of the metonymic *favela*. To construct from archives and memory a racial history of the city equivalent to what scholars such as Nathan Connolly, Keeanga-Yamahtta Taylor, and Tom Sugrue have uncovered for the United States—a relentless and actionable analysis of the historical processes that defined racialized urban landscapes and disproportionately dispossessed Black urban people—historians must continue to mend the rupture by breaking open the silences that have surrounded race and informality in Brazil's modern urban historiography.[139]

By focusing on the first decades following slavery, when vernacular housing was informalized even as Afro-Brazilians claimed urban freedom, this article has broached that task. In those early postemancipation decades, informality functioned simultaneously as a Black space and a blackened space, an extension of the *cidade negra* and an extension of the *cidade escrava*, a space of emancipation and a space of exploitation, a foothold in urban citizenship and a guarantee of perpetual exclusion. Informalized spaces served different aims for different people and it was precisely that simultaneity—and residents' agility in manipulating it—that allowed informality to develop as an integral part of Brazilian city building and governance. The *favela*, like the *quilombo*, embodied an emancipatory space where Black people "took over the city, re-creating the ways of the original *quilombolas*."[140] Yet informality is also an afterlife of slavery. This is true not only because *favelas* and *mocambos* have been constructed as Black spaces, not only because their residents were disproportionately the descendants of slaves, and not only because it has exacerbated many of the material inequalities imposed by slavery. Informality was an afterlife because it has reinforced an urban order in which racial silence was the price of survival, where law begot lawlessness and where emancipatory futures were built with the same relational tools that prolonged a slavocratic past.

Bidonvilles in France:
A New Term for an Old Phenomenon?

FRANÇOISE DE BARROS

The term *bidonville* has been part of everyday language in France for decades, and its meaning is generally well understood. It always refers to a shanty-town—a cluster of dwellings that are inhabited by populations considered "marginal" and distinguishable by the precarity of both their building materials and their legal status. However, this reality existed in France before the term appeared in the mid-twentieth century. One notable example from the early 1900s was an expanse of shantytowns called the "Zone," which was the object of urbanization policy from 1919 onward. This Zone corresponded to a belt of land around the capital that had been military territory since the mid-nineteenth century. Although construction was strictly prohibited on the land, it had gradually filled with all manner of self-built dwellings.[1] In her thesis on the subject, Anne Granier saw the Zone as equivalent to the *bidonvilles* that developed after World War II, mainly in the Paris suburbs but also in the large provincial cities of Lyon and Marseille.[2] She described both the Zone and the *bidonvilles* as "urban fringes."[3] Marie-Claude Blanc-Chaléard has also developed this analogy in her book on the *bidonvilles* of the Île-de-France region.[4]

This raises the question of how and why the term *bidonville* began to be used to refer to a long-standing phenomenon that specialists had already described with a different vocabulary and that public authorities had already identified as a "problem" that needed tackling. This chapter proposes a history of the *bidonville* as a category of public action (hence the interest in the term itself) and analyzes the meanings that public actors have given to this term when using it and legislating policies related to it. The reality designated by the word *bidonville* is not examined here, either in urban and architectural terms or in social ones, although other authors have explored how those have evolved over time.[5]

In the 1950s, *bidonvilles* formed mainly in the suburbs of Paris, although they also spread in the large provincial cities of Marseille and Lyon. They were built mainly by Algerian migrants on undeveloped private or public land (e.g., industrial wastelands, fields, vacant lots). The dwellings were initially constructed using more or less precarious salvaged materials—such as metal sheets, wooden boards, discarded wagons, and tar paper. Hence the term *bidonvilles*, which refers literally to cities made out of tin cans. More durable building materials were introduced over time.

In the early 1960s, the largest *bidonvilles* were home to several thousand people. Although the phenomenon was initially associated with Algeria and Algerian migrants, media coverage of the extensive Portuguese *bidonville* in Champigny (a Paris suburb) from 1964 onward led the public to expand that association to foreign migrants more generally.[6] Some of the large *bidonvilles* did not disappear until the 1980s. Beginning in 1970, the term referred not only to self-built housing but also to other kinds of dwellings considered unfit for human habitation that housed an increasing variety of foreign nationals. The derivative terms *micro-bidonville* (micro-shantytown) and *bidonville vertical* (vertical shantytown) were also often used in cases where the *bidonville* did not extend over a vast area of vacant land or was established in derelict apartment blocks. These settlements were no longer found only in the outskirts of Paris or the large provincial cities, but in all types of urban agglomerations.

This brief general description establishes that *bidonvilles*, like many types of settlement presented in this volume, were able to form because of the existence of undeveloped private or public land within or near highly urbanized spaces (as was also the case in Madrid, Mexico City, and Rome). They also developed because landowners and authorities tolerated illegal construction as long as they did not already have plans to develop the land. As elsewhere, in France it was primarily the presence of this phenomenon in the capital that led to its formulation as a public problem. However, unlike in Italy or Spain, France's public response was formulated nationally rather than locally in such a way that it could be adapted by each big city. This was due to the particular way in which the *bidonvilles* were constructed as a problem and the specific treatment they received as such from French public authorities.

An analysis of the history of the *bidonvilles* in France calls into question standard chronological and territorial divisions, even when we focus solely on the perspective of the public actors who sought to transform or eradicate them. The *bidonvilles* were not just places but also a category that shaped public intervention in the urban fabric, established as such by two laws passed in

1964 and 1966, and they were also included as a subcategory under the larger heading of "insalubrious housing" in a third law passed in 1970. However, public interventions targeting the *bidonvilles*—like the use of the term itself—had begun long before that, in the absence of even an ad hoc legal framework. This was the case most notably in the Paris region, where members of the Paris and especially the Seine Prefectures of Police were recruited to manage the "Français musulmans d'Algérie" in the early 1950s.[7] The first use of the term *bidonville* in metropolitan France appeared in the context of these activities and in the practices of local elected officials, as can be seen in 1953 through their exchanges with civil servants concerning the first *bidonvilles* identified in the Paris-area commune of Nanterre. Thus, a decade before the first law specifying them as a category was passed in 1964, the *bidonvilles* were already the object of intense public action in mainland France.

What's more, France was an empire at the time, and both the term and the public action associated with the *bidonvilles* had appeared even earlier, in the 1930s and 1940s, in the French colonial territories of North Africa.[8] The scale of administrative action targeted at the *bidonvilles* intensified in Algeria with the introduction of the Plan de Constantine (Constantine Plan) in 1958. Any history of state intervention in the *bidonvilles* should therefore include an imperial dimension, analyzing colonized territories and the French mainland in concert and beginning long before the "postcolonial" period when France passed its three "anti-*bidonville*" laws. The imperial dimension of the history of France's metropolitan *bidonvilles* is not only evident; it is key to understanding how this category of urban space was permanently defined by the "immigrant" status of the people who lived there. However, the urban dimension of the definition of *bidonville* as a category of public intervention underwent a significant evolution during the 1960s, when major changes to urban and housing policies assimilated the *bidonvilles* to the category of *îlots insalubres*, which had administratively defined insalubrious zones in the 1900s.[9]

Defining *Bidonvilles* by Their Inhabitants' Immigrant Status

The imperial dimension of the history of the *bidonvilles* in metropolitan France is reflected both in the practices of the municipal authorities responsible for dealing with the *bidonvilles*, who were recruited in Algeria, and in the link between the *bidonvilles* and the Algerian War of Independence's ramifications in metropolitan France. The national and local interventions that targeted at the *bidonvilles* in the decade before the legislation of the 1960s defined the *bidonvilles* as a category of public action based on the identity of their inhabitants. The colonized status of a significant proportion of *bidonville* residents from the 1950s until Algerian independence (1962) became their distinguishing feature, so much so that they were explicitly defined by parliamentarians from 1964 to 1971 as a habitat specific to "immigrants."

THE *BIDONVILLES'* IMPERIAL ORIGINS, 1930S–1950S

The term *bidonville*, the reality it referred to, the explanations given for its emergence, and the public "solutions" proposed for it all combined to make it one of the last avatars of a particular form of colonial domination that was achieved through spatialized governance. Indeed, the *bidonville* originated in the geographical and historical spaces of French colonial North Africa in the early 1930s.[10] Before World War II, the word *bidonville* had only ever been used in this context, where it referred to urban settlements built by indigenous peoples who migrated to colonial North Africa's largest European cities because of a rural employment crisis caused by colonization. Algerian public authorities only began to develop "solutions" for the *bidonvilles* in the 1940s and early 1950s.[11] At that point, they sought to design and build "Muslim housing" by identifying architectural and urban methods capable of constructing a habitat that would constitute a "fair" distribution of urban resources between Europeans and Muslims in a colonized context.[12]

The term *bidonville* and the colonial conception of urban intervention that the *bidonvilles* gave rise to seem not to have crossed the Mediterranean until the 1950s, despite a significant Algerian presence in mainland France since the 1920s.[13] Although the term *bidonville* already constituted an urban category in North Africa, the word does not yet seem to have been used to refer to the North African workers' housing in mainland France, even though such housing was already a matter of concern for metropolitan authorities.[14] The relevant studies on this subject either ignored the *bidonville* completely—focusing on other types of housing—or conceived it only as a form of indigenous housing on colonial soil.[15]

It was only between 1953 and 1955 that the term began to be used to describe what were supposedly the first Algerian spaces on the mainland; those of Nanterre, a commune in the "red belt" of the Paris suburbs that had experienced exponential demographic and urban growth since the 1920s.[16] The mayor of Nanterre used the term in a report on the national population census carried out in 1954, when commenting on the difficulty of collecting data

on "the large population of North Africans settled in Nanterre." Simultaneously, the administrative staff responsible for Nanterre's hygiene and sanitation referred to this space as a "garrison of North Africans," highlighting the
"appalling" state of the "shanties" and describing them as a "Zone."[17] From
that time forward, the term *bidonville* rapidly eclipsed the traditional terms
taudis (slums) and *garnis*,[18] which had been used since the previous century
to refer to the most run-down forms of French housing, whether occupied by
Algerian migrants or by other disadvantaged populations.

The term *bidonville*'s appearance on the French mainland did not therefore
coincide with the arrival of the Algerian migrants. It appeared instead with
the "technical advisers for Muslim affairs" (*conseillers techniques aux affaires
musulmanes*, CTAMs in French), who were recruited in Algeria beginning in
1952 to manage the Algerian migrant population in metropolitan France, and
with the "North African social advisers" (CSNAs in French), who were recruited by the Seine Prefecture after 1950.[19] Housing was the area in which the
CTAMs were most active, even before the creation of SONACOTRAL (National Construction Society for Algerian Workers) in 1956.[20] This semipublic
company, which reported to France's Interior Ministry, was set up to build
and administer hostels for Algerian workers living in mainland France.[21] Following the same approach adopted in Algiers to combat the *bidonvilles*, the
CTAMs focused on ensuring not only that the Algerian migrants had proper
housing but also that they were well distributed across urban space.[22] By the
late 1960s, the category of *bidonville* had become so generalized that it became a housing category in the national population census of 1968, which
coincided with the launch of a national slum clearance policy.

There is no clear evidence that the approximately thirty CTAMs, who
were spread throughout metropolitan France, came to their posts post with
previous experience dealing with *bidonvilles*. Their professional trajectories
in Algeria suggest that this was in fact unlikely, because the vast majority had
been posted to rural areas. While the records show that the head of the Technical Assistance Division of the Français musulmans d'Algérie, which was set
up in Nanterre in 1959, had previously held a post in the Urban Administrative Division of the Clos-Salambier *bidonville* in Algiers, this individual was
a military officer who intervened in *bidonvilles* on either side of the Mediterranean only as part of the French crackdown on independence fighters.[23]

The Algerian specificity of the *bidonvilles* did not, however, derive solely
from the colonial dimension of early public policy or its socializing effects on
specialized personnel. The *bidonville*'s connection with Algeria was both reinforced and modified by the local effects of the Algerian War of Independence.

THE *BIDONVILLES* AS A PHENOMENON SHAPED
BY THE WAR OF INDEPENDENCE

From 1954 until 1962, the state of war brought extreme physical violence to French society. This development put local elected officials in a difficult position, especially when they had previously established links with Algerian independence activists.[24] *Bidonvilles* always bordered more formalized neighborhoods, comprised first of old-fashioned bungalows and then of public housing projects, whose inhabitants tended to enjoy more civic legitimacy. Local elected officials thus had to administer towns in which the families of French conscripts lived alongside thousands of Algerians whom they suspected, rightly or wrongly, of supporting independence activists or even participating in their armed activities. The *bidonvilles* were often perceived as independence strongholds. For elected representatives with ties to activists, particularly members of the French Communist Party (PCF), the war became a topic to be avoided for fear of inciting physical violence.

In 1956, wartime violence began to have a concrete impact on local politics when national service conscripts began to be sent to Algeria. This led the French population to feel the "fear or pain of losing a child, a husband, or a brother" and complicated political support for Algerian patriots.[25] Algerian nationalists distanced themselves from the PCF and the Confédération Générale du Travail (a trade union with close ties to the PCF). In that same period, political demonstrations by conscripts eclipsed those spearheaded by Algerians.[26] The latter had been organized since the beginning of the 1950s by the Movement for the Triumph of Democratic Liberties, a proindependence party founded by Algerian nationalist leader Messali Hadj in 1946. The so-called Muslim French from Algeria (FMA) had been the target of intensive electoral organizing by the PCF in Nanterre since the 1940s, which was facilitated by the links forged in the 1930s with migrant residents who were part of Hadj's political movement. The emergence of "conscript families" into the local political arena was significant, lasting, and supported by local elected representatives—who seemed to be seeking to counterbalance the dread consequences of their previous political engagement with the Algerians.

The *bidonvilles*, which were already home to several thousand Algerians, appeared to be a factor in Nanterre's heightened tensions. This was due in part to the inconveniences that neighbors experienced because of the settlements' lack of urban services or garbage collection. But the worst exacerbating factor was the violent police repression of the Algerian inhabitants. All the same, the *bidonvilles* could also serve as a means of de-escalating violence, because conflicts related to neighborhood conditions stood in for conflicts generated by the war. In other words, war-related strife could be camouflaged as disagreement over urban conditions.[27]

In 1960, six years into the war, Raymond Barbet, who had been Nanterre's communist mayor since 1935, wrote, "It is clear that the ongoing Algerian War is creating a climate *on both sides* that is making daily life more difficult and tense" and generating a *"divide* that is growing deeper every day."[28] His words were addressed to those directly concerned by the divide, namely the sixty-four "inhabitants of Petit Nanterre"[29] who had petitioned him about the *"bidonville* Algerians." The wartime expansion of Algerian-inhabited *bidonvilles* in Nanterre thus became the focal point of a latent conflict between those who lived in them and those who lived next to them. This was exacerbated by the fact that the La Folie *bidonville*, which was situated right next to the brand-new social housing estates of Petit Nanterre, became a double battleground, both for independence activists from two rival parties who clashed in 1957and for clashes between independence activists and the Paris Prefecture of Police.[30] The latter conflict worsened from 1959 onward, when a *harka*—a member of the *harkis*, a company of Algerians fighting with the French military—set up camp just across the road.[31]

While Nanterre's local elected representatives received regular complaints about the "Algerian" *bidonvilles* between 1953 and 1966, the way they handled the complaints changed significantly over this period, seemingly conditioned by the war. During the war (1954–1962), the mayor used his responses to reframe the way the complainants described the situation, aiming to deflect the accusations being leveled at the Algerians. While complainants presented themselves as the victims of aggressive Algerians, Barbet developed long written arguments explaining why the Algerians were themselves victims. However, once independence was declared in 1962, the mayor agreed with the complainants' version of the situation, describing the Algerians' practices as unacceptable. It was as if the end of the war removed the need to mitigate complaints about the Algerians. In 1965, in fact, the municipality took part in a widely publicized mobilization, which involved a neighborhood "school strike," to protest the "Algerian" *bidonvilles*.[32]

All these elements show that the French Empire weighed heavily in the history of mainland France's *bidonvilles*, whether the question is approached through the terms used to refer to them, the living conditions of the Algerians who lived in them, the nature of public policies developed to respond to them, or their effects on local populations during the War of Independence.[33]

The *bidonvilles'* clearance progressed very unevenly across metropolitan France during the War of Independence. The *bidonvilles* of Lyon, which were also inhabited almost exclusively by Algerians, were absorbed during the war, but in the Paris region, the process came to an almost complete standstill, despite the fact the *bidonville*'s presence in the capital was considered the most problematic.[34] The first two laws adopted to accelerate their eradication in 1964 and 1966 did not have the expected effects. The second law was actually implemented only in the case of three *bidonvilles*.[35] According to Marie-Claude Blanc-Chaléard, who retraced the history of absorption policies, the process began to make significant progress only after a third initiative, the Loi Vivien, was passed in 1970. One of the main reasons state actors put forward to explain their lack of action during the 1950s and 1960s was the opposition to constructing new housing for Algerians shown by the local elected representatives from communes with available land.

The hostility toward *bidonville* residents shows that the settlements were perceived, and in practice defined, through negative images of their inhabitants. The second part of this chapter will return to the implications of the three *bidonville* laws of 1964–1970 and the decisive change brought about by the third. However, it will be useful first to identify how the *bidonvilles* were being defined in the parliamentary debates. An analysis shows that the *bidonville* appears to have been framed, in 1970 more than ever, as a type of residential space defined more by its inhabitants' characteristics than by its urban irregularity (both legal and material). After being understood for so long as a type of housing specific to Algeria's colonized populations, the *bidonvilles* continued to be seen as a type of "immigrant" housing regardless of their specific legal status, urban features, or architectural characteristics.

FOREIGNERS IN PARLIAMENTARY DEFINITIONS OF THE *BIDONVILLE*

The parliamentary debates on the three *bidonville* laws of 1964, 1966, and 1970 began with the generic definitions put forward in the laws' respective explanatory memoranda, which aimed specifically to characterize the *bidonville* as an object requiring public intervention. The definition adopted in Article 1 of the 1964 law referred exclusively to the material elements of a *bidonville*, such as the land it sat on or the type of dwelling that constituted it. A *bidonville* was simply "any land on which unhealthy premises or installations, considered unfit for human occupation in regular conditions of hygiene, safety, and health, are used for housing purposes." Yet when it came to justifying legislative interventions based on the *bidonville*'s scale, proposed interventions produced in these same debates depended on an assessment of the *bidonville* that had much less to do with specific material elements than with the *bidonville*'s resident population. In 1964, the bill's senate rapporteur presented "some figures [that] paint . . . a frighteningly cruel and tragic picture . . . excepting the Paris region, there are approximately 50,000 human beings living in some 3,700 buildings in 370 different *bidonvilles* across metropolitan France."[36] In 1966, this had increased to "140,000 people . . . living in these makeshift shelters."[37] In 1970, "the figures from the Interior Ministry's survey" indicated that "1,035,000 people are currently living in this unhealthy housing: 500,000 in lodging houses, 75,000 in *bidonvilles*, and 460,000 in unhealthy, run-down, overcrowded units in conditions similar to and sometimes worse than those of the *bidonvilles*."[38] The subsequent assessment of the 1964 law (called the Loi Debré) was couched in the same terms: "the operations thus carried out concern 6,679 families and 11,378 individuals, that is a total of almost 50,000 people."[39]

Definitions of the *bidonville* put forward as a preamble to the 1964 discussions disregarded architectural features to such a point that one parliamentarian sought to clarify that "the word '*bidonville*' has only been used during the discussion for the sake of simplification and that it does not refer only to wooden or corrugated iron shanties, but has a general meaning . . . [and] can therefore include unhealthy, run-down permanent buildings."[40] It was not clear exactly what it would mean to give the term *bidonville* this "general meaning," because "unhealthy, run-down permanent buildings" seemed to correspond to the regulatory category of "insalubrious housing" that had existed since the end of the nineteenth century.[41]

In the end, parliamentary debates rarely provided general definitions. In contrast, references to residents' foreign nationality and discussions of government immigration policies occurred frequently. In fact, there was not one speech that did not flag one or the other. For example, in 1964, "the [law's] commission . . . considered that it would be appropriate to organize the ways that immigrant workers in large urban centers are received."[42] Similarly, another congressman referred to "the existence of '*bidonvilles*' inhabited by hundreds of thousands of immigrant workers and their families" and talked about foreigners' demographic presence in the Seine and in France more generally.[43] Another explained that the "proliferation of *bidonvilles*" was due "mainly to large flows of foreign immigration from Spain, Portugal, Greece, Turkey, and especially Algeria."[44] In the senate, the rapporteur drew up precise statistics by nationality on the foreigners who inhabited the "thirty-five *bidonvilles* that form a ring around the city of Paris."[45] In short, the "*bidonville* occupants" and the "immigrant workers" were becoming progressively more conflated over time in French legislative debates.

This conflation became embedded during the discussions of the 1966 and 1970 laws. In 1966, parliamentarians from all sides agreed that "workers from certain foreign countries are constantly adding to the number of unfortunate people,"[46] that "this problem . . . underlines . . . the living conditions of tens of thousands of migrant workers on the outskirts of our large cities,"[47] and that the "insalubrious shacks . . . house foreign workers and their families."[48] Often, the figures they enumerated would drift from the number of foreigners living in the *bidonvilles* into the number of foreigners living in the entire municipality. One *député* began his speech by stating that "out of 100,000 inhabitants in Saint-Denis [in the Paris region], 10,000 are foreigners, that is 10%. . . . There are around 2,000 Spanish and Portuguese families in the Francs-Moisins *bidonville* and several thousand African migrant workers living in hotel rooms and cellars."[49] While these lists of figures underlined the fact that only a minority of the total number of foreigners in any one town lived in a *bidonville*, the conflation of foreign populations and *bidonville* inhabitants endured. Hence, the discussion of the 1970 law offered an assessment of the 1964 law that encompassed housing policy for all immigrant workers—as if no housing policy could be conceived for foreigners outside the *bidonvilles* and as if the *bidonvilles* were not also home to a number (albeit a minority) of French nationals.[50] Finally, although it may appear that parliamentarians had been challenging the government on the subject of foreign immigrants since the start of the Fifth Republic, the Loi Debré was the first to specifically refer to foreigners.

As Marie-Claude Blanc-Chaléard has repeatedly pointed out, neither the majority of Algerian wartime migrants nor the majority of foreign migrants in general lived in the *bidonvilles*; conversely, the *bidonvilles* did not exclusively house foreigners. She estimates that "the *bidonvilles* never housed more than 10% of the foreigners registered in France."[51] However, the foreign status of *bidonville* inhabitants remained a defining feature of the category, regardless of the settlements' urban or architectural characteristics, so long as they were judged "unfit for human habitation." Administratively, the personnel responsible for slum clearance after 1964 were the same as those in place during the War of Independence. While their job title was changed to remove any reference to Algeria, they continued to work within the prefectures under the authority of the Interior Ministry, which had targeted its police, military, and "social" action at the Algerians throughout the war. From 1965 onward, the department was called the Service de Liaison et de Promotion des Migrants (Migrant Liaison and Advocacy Service).

This does not mean, however, that nothing changed between 1964 and 1970 in terms of how the *bidonvilles* were defined as a category of public action. The category certainly had an urbanistic dimension, which would evolve along with France's urban intervention policies.

An Evolving Urban Definition of the *Bidonvilles*

The legal design of the 1964, 1966, and 1970 laws tells us something about the urban dimensions of the decision to define the *bidonville* as a category of public action. Each of these three laws aimed explicitly to facilitate the expropriations necessary to destroy the *bidonvilles*. The decrees that implemented them also had to set the compensation rates for expropriated owners. Additional funds were of course also necessary to build new housing for the inhabitants of the demolished *bidonvilles*. The laws of 1964 and 1966 were deemed to have been financially impotent and therefore ineffective. Following the adoption of the 1970 law, the *bidonville* absorption program accelerated and reached its target over the following decade.[52] In strictly legal terms, the 1970 law had changed nothing; the legal expropriation procedures remained the same. What it did alter—by classifying *bidonvilles* as "insalubrious housing"—was the place of slum clearance in the urban administrative tool kit. The new laws defined *bidonvilles* not by the nature of their structures or their conformity with urban regulations but by the very fact that they were earmarked for demolition, for whatever reason, and thus constituted a land reserve that could be used for new construction. The issues at stake for legislators are evident from the fact that each of the three laws enshrined the entities that were to finance and benefit from the expropriations. On the basis of this new definition, *bidonvilles*, as a category of public intervention, bore a strong resemblance to the concept of "insalubrious housing" that had been forged in the nineteenth century. The reorganization of intervention policies and of the government agencies in charge of them during the 1960s allowed the 1970 law to administratively assimilate *bidonvilles* as insalubrious housing "just like any other."

APPORTIONING *BIDONVILLE* CLEARANCE BETWEEN STATE AND LOCAL AUTHORITIES

The decisive role of local elected representatives in formulating the *bidonville* issue is clear from their contributions to parliamentary debates. Among speakers who discussed the three laws that aimed to deal with "the *bidonville* problem," local representatives were overrepresented vis-à-vis their proportion in the legislature, and they used their local responsibilities to legitimate their positions on the subject: "Anyone who has been responsible for managing a large city knows the drama of the *bidonvilles* and the difficulties that mayors face in resolving the social, legal, and financial problems posed by the existence of these deprived neighborhoods."[53] It is thus hardly surprising that the preservation of municipal funding and the defense of municipal ex-propriation prerogatives vis-à-vis the relevant *préfet* (the national state's rep-resentative in each *département*) were central to the discussions of these bills.

In 1964, speakers from across the political spectrum concurred with a point made by the communist Sénat member from Essonne: "At the Assem-blée Nationale, the rapporteur clearly specified that the *préfet* could act at the request of the mayor but that he could also take this decision ex officio, re-gardless of the municipality's passivity or even opposition . . . even when such passivity or opposition is based solely on financial constraints." He added that "it is the municipalities that must have priority in dealing with the problem of their own *bidonvilles*, and we do not want this law to be a further encroach-ment on local freedoms." The entire debate in the Sénat was about ensuring that expropriations were carried out for the benefit of the commune con-cerned. All the Sénat members' statements supported amendments to this ef-fect, which were in turn accepted without discussion by the government and duly adopted. In the Assemblée Nationale, most debates were devoted to this same issue, with the aim of "granting more powers to the mayors."[54] However, the *députés* ultimately revoked the monopoly in expropriation matters that the Sénat members had granted to local elected representatives, sharing the responsibility with the national state on the condition that it would finance not only the expropriations but also the new construction necessary for re-housing. The *députés* thus ensured that the financing for *bidonville* clearance, which involved compensating expropriated owners and building new hous-ing, would fall entirely to the national state when such clearance had been decreed by a *préfet*.

The 1966 law aimed specifically to reiterate the sharing of powers set out in the 1964 law.[55] In practice, the 1966 law restricted the "sovereignty" of lo-cal authorities. According to the bill's Sénat rapporteur: "The provisions of Article 4 will partially compensate this loss: expropriated land can only be transferred to a local authority, a social housing organization, or a semipublic company. Local authority must therefore be involved at some stage in the *bidonville* clearance operation."[56] Above all, the fight resumed in the Sénat to include the "expropriator pays" principle in the law. The rapporteur asked that "in the event that the *préfet* takes possession against the mayor's advice, the state alone must bear the financial costs of the acquisition."[57]

Because the 1970 law aimed to repeal the 1964 legislation, the parliamen-tary debate focused on the same points as it had in 1964 and 1966, with even greater emphasis on financial issues. For example, the parliamentarians con-sidered it "essential to define—as the draft bill does not—the beneficiary of any expropriation, whether it be a public authority or a public institution."[58]

They also wished to retain the article of the 1964 law stipulating that "the [national] state alone shall bear the financial burden of any acquisitions."[59] On several occasions, the bill's rapporteur argued that "it would be better not to repeal the 'Loi Debré' than to begin this adventurous attack on insalubrity with no guarantee of financial means."[60] In other words, the issue was not the amount of money that would be available—which was always considered insufficient in discussions about lack of progress in *bidonville* clearance—but whether resources would come from the national state or the local commune.

The fact that the local elected representatives were engaged in an ongoing battle from 1964 to 1970 to ensure that the expropriation procedures reserved for *bidonvilles* clearance would negatively affect neither their municipal prerogatives nor their municipal finances does not mean that nothing happened. On the contrary, this battle persisted because the types of local elected representatives affected by the clearance plans diversified. In 1964, almost all of them had represented communes in the Paris region, but from 1966 onward, the proportion representing provincial communes had gradually increased, leading to a change in the material definition of the *bidonvilles* that would be the object of the proposed laws. The 1964 law had interested only elected representatives linked to Nanterre and Champigny (the two communes with the largest *bidonvilles* in the Paris region), a few "specialists" such as Eugène Claudius-Petit, and Michel Debré, the former prime minister who had proposed the 1964 law to address the *bidonvilles* in his overseas electoral constituency of La Réunion.[61] In 1966, the Paris region was still at the heart of parliamentary exchanges because of electoral rivalry between the communist mayor of Champigny and the Gaullist housing minister who introduced the law, Roland Nungesser.[62] However, a number of elected representatives who had not been present at the 1964 debates took the floor in 1966 to include in the definition of *bidonvilles* types of housing that were specific to their own Nord *département*, a region that had been hit hard by World War II. Because they used the word *taudis* (slums),[63] a term not widely heard in 1964, they were equating the *bidonvilles* with the "many temporary buildings erected in 1946, 1947, 1948, and 1949 for the war victims" (30 percent of whom lived in the Nord-Pas-de-Calais region, which housed "between 40,000 and 42,000 people").[64]

Ultimately, Nungesser claimed that his law would tackle "not only [the] large bidonvilles in the Paris region but also [the] bidonvilles located on the outskirts of major towns and cities throughout the country," adding that "in addition to the problem of the bidonvilles themselves, there is also the question of the temporary shelters built in the aftermath of the last war and even of the 1914–1918 war . . . in our western, northern, and eastern provinces" and "in our overseas départements . . . thousands of flimsy constructions, clusters of which often look just like bidonvilles."[65] He thus responded to the requests of local elected representatives from the east, north, and west of mainland France and from certain overseas *départements* who lacked the legal and especially financial means to demolish dwellings deemed uninhabitable. The legal and financial mechanisms created for the *bidonvilles* were thus extended to other types of housing, including the temporary barracks that had been built in certain cities damaged by war (which, unlike the *bidonvilles*, existed within a legal framework) and self-built dwellings in overseas *départements*. The mechanisms were thus aimed at precisely targeted circumstances and communes.

Discussions of the 1970 law, in contrast, proposed the integration of *bidonvilles* into the preexisting category of "insalubrious housing" without providing any precise definition of the situations to which the definition would apply. Unlike the two previous laws, which were titled "expropriation of land on which *bidonvilles* are built," this one was titled "elimination of insalubrious housing." According to the law's rapporteur, that category included both *bidonvilles*, which he described as "horizontal dwellings" and other buildings that he described as "vertical dwellings."[66] Thus, in his statistical assessment of the "phenomenon" that this new law proposed to address, Minister Robert-André Vivien cited 75,000 people currently living in *bidonvilles* and "460,000 [living] in unhealthy, dilapidated, overcrowded housing in conditions similar to and sometimes worse than those experienced in the *bidonvilles*."[67] Parliamentarians referred to specific local situations to support the inclusion of *bidonvilles* in the "unhealthy housing" category. In particular, a cohort of elected representatives from the Nord *département* raised the issue of the *courées*, a form of masonry housing built in city centers by late nineteenth-century textile factory owners. The minister told parliamentarians that they should "expect this law to enable us to tackle certain forms of unhealthy housing that have so far escaped the Loi Debré's scope,"[68] including the famous *courées*. How, in the space of only four years, had the *bidonvilles* become classified as just another type of insalubrious housing?

HOW THE *BIDONVILLES* BECAME A TYPE OF INSALUBRIOUS HOUSING

With the adoption of the 1970 law, the *bidonvilles* were expressly included in a broader category of "insalubrious housing," which inherited the legal tools of expropriation that had been forged since 1964 specifically for the *bidonvilles*. This evolution was legitimized during the parliamentary debates by a history of public intervention with roots stretching back to 1850, the year that France adopted a law authorizing expropriation for reasons of "public utility," thus providing a point of departure for the emergence of "insalubrious housing" as a category of public intervention.[69] A rapid review of this history helps us to understand both the many points that the two iterations of this category had in common and the reasons why the late 1960s marked their legal convergence. This process can be fully understood, however, only if we also take into account other concurrent shifts, including those taking place in the branches of state administration responsible for urban intervention.

Between 1850 and 1958, France gradually developed legal, financial, and conceptual tools that allowed for the renewal of areas that were already urbanized or built up. The first task was to facilitate expropriation for public use, initially by opening or extending roads. The scope of that mechanism was then extended to provide sufficient space for new construction. At the end of the nineteenth century, successive laws authorizing expropriation went hand in hand with the invention of the he notion of *ilôt insalubre* to justify it.

Understanding this notion is key because it lay at the heart of the 1970 law. Controversial from the outset, the category of the *ilôt insalubre* worked by categorizing entire groups of buildings as "insalubrious"—and therefore subject to expropriation and demolition—simply because a few buildings had been identified as unhealthy. This led many to protest the destruction of "healthy" buildings justified solely by their proximity to others deemed unfit for habitation. In the late nineteenth century, buildings would be declared unhealthy on the basis of morbidity statistics linked to the major epidemics of the time, cholera and tuberculosis. If statisticians registered an above-average death rate from one of these diseases, a building would be described as "murderous." These insalubrity criteria were debated during their progressive elaboration, but they remained at the heart of clearance policy for unhealthy buildings and *ilôts* throughout the first half of the twentieth century.[70] Between 1908 and 1920, seventeen *ilôts insalubres* were identified throughout the capital. However, none of these could be cleared without reducing the exorbitant cost of compensating the expropriated owners. In the end, the value of a condemned building was limited to that of the bare land it was situated on. Between 1938 and 1942, Parisian authorities increased this legislation's financial and administrative efficacy.[71]

The history of renewal projects involving the *ilôts insalubres* up to the 1950s is of course more complex than these legal and financial details convey.[72] However, even aside from being a constant in this well-documented history,[73] such legal and financial dimensions were at the heart of the laws passed to make *bidonville* clearance possible. The other point of convergence between these two notions of insalubrious housing lay in the coexistence of two defining criteria, one involving the material buildings and the other concerning the population. An analysis of the construction of the *ilôt insalubre* category reveals that perceived morbidity grew from a permanent interplay between these two types of causality. The first focused on the material characteristics of the buildings and their potential morbid effects. The second emphasized the allegedly deleterious impact that certain types of inhabitants—especially Jews and foreigners—could have on the buildings they occupied or even the air they breathed.[74]

In 1958, just as the *bidonvilles* that had sprung up around Paris, Lyon, and Marseille were beginning to be rehabilitated, a new stage began in the history of the *ilôts insalubres*. The legal and financial tools required for the clearance of the *ilôts* were formalized by an "urban renewal" program introduced by Decree 58-1465 of December 31, 1958. In terms of urban development, this renewal program was the counterpart of a "priority urbanization zone" program that was also created in 1958 to develop unurbanized areas and allow the construction of extensive housing estates that would bring together a large number of structures mainly devoted to social housing. Created and managed by the Ministry for Reconstruction, the program not only accelerated the clearance of some *ilôts insalubres* in Paris but also enabled the renewal of many other old city centers in both large and medium-sized cities throughout France. In 1965, however, financial constraints led to the program's abrupt suspension, leaving in the lurch municipalities that had embarked on more or less ambitious state-funded renewal schemes.

The northern city of Roubaix was one locale that bet big on the renovation of its old city center. In this textile capital, the plan had been to demolish the historic nineteenth-century working-class housing district famously known as the *courées*. Roubaix's elected representatives had hoped this would lead to a real urban transformation.[75] The suspension of state subsidies led to a large-scale local mobilization to have them reinstated or replaced. In 1968 and 1969, the municipality organized press conferences, ministerial visits, and even a colloquium on the *courées*, rallying support from many social sectors, including the academic community.[76] Minister of Housing Robert-André Vivien recalled two specific elements of this vast mobilization during the parliamentary debates of 1970. He noted that "on 26 June 1969, Mr Herman [senator for the Nord *département*], accompanied by a delegation of parliamentarians . . . discussed the problem of the *courées*, which unfortunately were not covered by the 'Loi Debré,'" commenting on how the "extensive use of an opinion issued by the Council of State of 19 June 1969 [had made it possible to] take action against this leprosy."[77]

This local political mobilization won the day after the adoption of the 1970 law, thanks to administrative shifts in urban planning and housing. The creation of the Ministère de l'Équipement in 1966 marked the start of major changes, which were consolidated amid political shifts stemming from the civil unrest of May 1968. The Ministère de l'Équipement represented a major upheaval because it unified two separate entities: the Building Ministry, responsible for housing construction and urban development, and the Transport and Public Works Ministry. The merger was part of the drive to "modernize" state administration following General de Gaulle's accession to power in 1959, and it was no cosmetic change. It sparked profound administrative transformations throughout the 1960s and 1970s. In particular, socialist activists rose to important administrative positions, playing a direct role in placing the *bidonville* issue on the governmental agenda in 1970.[78]

At the ministerial level, the *bidonville* problematic involved closely linked administrative and political issues. Administratively, one of the effects of the 1970 Law (Loi Vivien) was to place *bidonville* clearance under the remit of the new Ministère de l'Équipement, allocating specific budget lines and creating an ad hoc body called the Permanent Interministerial Group for the Absorption of Insalubrious Housing. This ministry could then take control of *bidonville* absorption operations, which had fallen for more than a decade under the jurisdiction of the Interior Ministry, municipal prefectures (especially that of the Seine), and various organizations that had been created during the War of Independence to administer large numbers of Algerian migrants or other formerly colonized populations.[79] The decision to define *bidonvilles* as Algerian and foreign housing was thus not merely symbolic. It meant that the administrative networks charged with addressing the *bidonville* issue—and later with *bidonville* clearance—now worked under the authority of the Interior Ministry, the same entity responsible for all matters relating to colonized Algeria and foreigners, including liaising with local authorities and maintaining law and order.

The Ministère de l'Équipement was well qualified to implement this program because some of its staff members had been involved for decades in the clearance of *ilôts insalubres* and the rehousing of their residents in transitional housing units.[80] However, these individuals emerged from social environments very different from those of the CTAMs, who had come from Algeria to work with migrants to mainland France in the 1950s. These included Catholic circles, associations linked to Emmaüs International and ATD Fourth World movements, social housing organizations, and design networks inside or outside of the Ministry of Public Works. A former CTAM who served as a project manager at the Val-de-Marne Prefecture, a linchpin of the *bidonvilles* clearance program in the Paris region, was astonished to read the biography of the first secretary-general of the Permanent Interministerial Group for the Absorption of Insalubrious Housing and discover that he had "demolished 20 large *garnis* and *bidonvilles* and rehoused 5,500 families" during twenty-five years of "combatting unhealthy housing in Rennes," as head of the city's social housing department.[81] The former CTAM had clearly just discovered that the network in which he had been operating since the 1950s, centered on the Interior Ministry and entities responsible for managing colonized populations in mainland France, had not been the only one dealing with the *bidonvilles*.

Finally, the Ministère de l'Équipement's appropriation of the legal and financial tools for *bidonville* clearance resulted from internal competition inherited from the Ministère de la Reconstruction. The rivalry pitted the Building Directorate, mainly responsible for housing and especially for the regulation and financing of social housing, and the Urban Planning Directorate, responsible for all urban planning instruments, in particular those focused since the 1950s on urban zoning. The 1970 law was in fact implemented under the authority of Building Directorate head Robert Lion, who collaborated directly with housing minister Robert-André Vivien. Lion thus assigned *bidonville* clearance (and that of other insalubrious housing) to his own Building Directorate, even though the urban renewal program that it replaced had been managed by the Urban Planning Directorate. Lion's account of the process that produced the 1970 law—which was completely silent on the fatal fire in the Aubervilliers *bidonville* that was usually highlighted as the catalyst for its adoption—makes clear the role that Roubaix's socialist elected representatives played in getting the urban renewal program replaced by the *bidonvilles* program.[82] Lion, a high-ranking civil servant, in fact exemplified the close links between political activism and the administrative developments. His connection with the Roubaix mobilization resulted not just from pure administrative opportunism (i.e., its use value in the drive to supplant the Urban Planning Directorate) but also from Lion's political activity as a socialist militant. This activism also explains why he became the head of a ministerial directorate that had until then been highly disparaged, despite the fact he had been part of one of France's most prestigious senior civil servant bodies, which was attached to the Ministère des Finances (Ministry of Finance).[83]

The official line was that the 1970 law was adopted as a result of the fatal fire on January 1 in the Aubervilliers *bidonville* in which four people died. But in reality it was the consequence of structural changes both in urban policies (the creation and then cancellation of the urban renewal program for the *îlots insalubres* in the space of fewer than ten years) and in the central administrations responsible for implementing them (renewal of management structures and their personnel).

Conclusion

By examining the participation of local elected representatives in the three parliamentary debates on the *bidonvilles*, and more importantly by identifying the actors who promoted the 1966 and 1970 laws and exploring their motives, this chapter has demonstrated how and why the definition of the *bidonville* evolved. The urban specificity of the *bidonville*—conceived as an agglomeration of self-built dwellings made of non-durable materials—was erased by the reemergence of the nineteenth-century category of "insalubrious housing," which had been originally created to condemn solid and legal structures that had deteriorated over time. This erasure was due to the evolution in the regulatory and administrative frameworks rather than to any changes in the *bidonvilles* observed by metropolitan public authorities in the 1950s. Under the 1970 Vivien Law, this erasure explains why *bidonvilles* continued to be identified by the supposed foreignness of their populations.

From the 1930s to the 1970s, the *bidonville* was progressively reformulated as a category of public intervention. The term originated to describe a doubly marginalized space that was reserved during the interwar period for colonized populations in the capitals of French colonial territories in North Africa. Later, in a modernized France stripped of its Empire, the *bidonville* retained its association with foreign populations but also came to symbolize "insalubrious housing," a category of public intervention first created in the nineteenth century to identify and eradicate urban spaces associated with that era's terrible epidemics.

The colonial origin of the notion of the *bidonville* explains why the term became established in metropolitan France, despite the existence of a previously established term, *zone*, that had been used since the beginning of the twentieth century to refer specifically to a self-built urban habitat constructed outside of accepted building standards and legal frameworks in the immediate periphery of a large urban center. The persistent definition of the *bidonville* as a habitat specific first to Algerians and then to foreigners more generally can be understood as a kind of colonial heritage transferred to the French mainland by personnel specialized in the management of foreign populations. From that perspective, the French case seems quite specific. But this colonial inheritance was reinforced by other factors, including the evolution of slum clearance policies put in place in the early twentieth century and the administrative and political dynamics of urban and housing policies in the late 1960s.

Finally, as we have seen, the administrative staff involved until 1970 in *bidonville* clearance were not so much specialists in housing or urban planning as they were in the management of colonized populations who had transferred their skills to dealing with France's migrant populations as Algeria gained its independence. As such, their approach was to define the *bidonvilles* essentially by their inhabitants' foreign characteristics. However, the tendency to define the *bidonville* as a national problem also undoubtedly owed much to the involvement of other actors. Indeed, the local elected representatives of the communes affected by the presence of *bidonvilles* were involved in identifying them as a public problem from the outset, both because the *bidonvilles* hampered their urban development projects and because of their local electorate's hostile reaction to this habitat and its residents.

Urban Risk?
Constructing Shantytowns as a Problem of Colonial Governance in Algiers and Casablanca, 1919–1962

JIM HOUSE

This comparative chapter examines the various ways a range of mostly European actors in colonial Algiers and Casablanca constructed shantytowns and their inhabitants as a problem of migration and mobility, public health, colonial urbanism and housing, urban poverty, and, latterly, as a political and security threat during the late-colonial era after 1918 and the crisis of decolonization after 1945. The largest in North Africa, these cities held acute symbolic as well as political value as "showcases" for French imperial rule, making them highly comparable and yet distinct. By the early 1950s, approximately one-third (i.e., one hundred thousand people) of the Muslim population in each city lived in shantytowns—the only population group to reside there—and their sociopolitical visibility was undeniable.

Some of the colonial rationalities behind representations of shantytowns might not only apply to these areas: for example, this was the case with the "social danger" that included a range of moralistic and often criminalizing, heavily gendered discourses that targeted socially mobile groups across the city. And although such discourses did not always originate in the colonial context, they were heavily influenced by it. Other discourses and policies, however, very specifically targeted shantytowns, such as regulation to contain informal settlements and policies using rehousing as social engineering to "modernize" shack dwellers. Within these spatializing discourses, there was always a close correlation between stigmatized areas and their inhabitants, implicitly or explicitly giving an ethnic dimension to this "othering."

Shantytowns constituted a screen onto which Europeans projected a range of anxieties and fears, which were often then reflected in urban governmentality. These anxieties related to a perceived loss of colonial control and hence the need for the reestablishment of colonial "order" that prioritized the health, social, economic, political, and security preoccupations of the dominant European population. Clearly, many Europeans were extremely, if not principally, worried about demography: in Casablanca, the Muslim Moroccan population increased from 52,134 in 1926 to 433,504 by 1950.[1] In greater Algiers, the Muslim Algerian population grew from 73,036 in 1926 to reach 293,665 by 1954.[2] This "demographic danger," with Muslims becoming the majority local population (Algiers) or considered likely to "invade" the European spaces of the city (especially Casablanca), is inseparable from the colonial situation and, especially, the crises of decolonization that marked these cities in particular, which witnessed urban guerrillas, mass street protests, and interethnic and intranationalist violence.[3] This chapter argues that a spatial reading of the social and political histories of the late-colonial period, and of decolonization, can arguably provide a new perspective on both colonial governmentalities and the sociopolitical agency of the local population.

To better show the evolution of European preoccupations and the policies they were designed to address, this chapter sets these developments within a longer-term perspective. It examines earlier key moments during which the shantytowns were made visible, such as the Popular Front (1936–1938), during Vichy (in North Africa, July 1940–November 1942), and the complex post-1945 chronology of welfare colonialism, as proindependence nationalists and communists constructed shantytowns as a symbol of socioeconomic inequality.

Although this chapter identifies many similarities between Algiers and Casablanca, the cities were nonetheless situated in different political spaces with distinct forms of colonial governmentality. Occupied by France since 1830, Algeria was a settler colony under direct rule and increasingly integrated into Metropolitan French governance structures. European preponderance was maintained, however, through a range of elected assemblies that, from the 1930s onward, strongly resisted the colonial administration's and Metropolitan politicians' attempted social and political reforms.[4] Algerians during this period gained greater political rights, notably with the Algerian statute in 1947, but remained unequal socially and economically as well as politically, with Algerian women in Algeria gaining the right to vote only in 1958.

Established in 1912, the Moroccan Protectorate, in contrast, constituted a dual political structure whereby the French ruled indirectly but in effect controlled the territory through a resident-general. The Moroccan sultan Mohammed V (ruled 1927–1961) kept his own administration (*makhzen*) but was reduced to largely symbolic statutory power, although in the 1940s, he became a figurehead for the independence movement.[5] In Morocco, the power differential between colonizer and colonized was arguably even greater than in Algeria, because little was ever implemented to allow Moroccans a meaningful say in how their country was run. Muslim Moroccans were therefore a population group upon which the French (or Moroccan) state could act almost unchecked, especially before 1945, and this helps explain the initially more interventionist, dualistic colonial urbanism in Casablanca as opposed to Algiers, for example.

This chapter argues that, if shantytowns were almost constantly being considered a problem for Europeans, what informed that problematization, and the number and "mix" of problems that shantytowns and their inhabitants were seen to represent, evolved considerably, as in the case of Mexico City. The respective weight of key themes similarly changed according to the wider sociopolitical context. This was true between Algiers and Casablanca, with the public health discourse being more prominent in the latter city, for example. Within each city, however, the "geography of urban risk" could be highly uneven between different shantytowns and other districts and indeed between different shantytowns themselves.[6] By focusing on each city's best-known informal settlements, respectively Carrières centrales in Casablanca and Mahieddine in Algiers, we can better trace the shifting categorizations and stigmatization of their inhabitants. After 1945, as the process of decolonization accelerated, Europeans' political and then security preoccupations increased because proindependence movements used shantytowns as a resource in the anticolonial struggle. European representations of shantytowns often created "problems" that were designed to perform political work, coming variously in the form of eradication, regulation, repression, and regrouping. This political work tells us much more about the dominant European society ascribing negative, essentializing characteristics than it reflects the experiences of subaltern groups targeted by such public discourses.[7] For this reason, the analysis here treats shantytowns as a politico-discursive arena as well as a physical space characterized by the precarious, self-built nature of the habitat, its non-publicly-authorized nature, the absence of minimal infrastructure, and hence the nonconformity to public health norms.

This study examines a range of mostly European actors: the central colonial administration, police, and military; municipal authorities and elected local representatives; public housing agencies; colonial ethnographers, sociologists and urban geographers; and journalists. The analysis draws on colonial archives, city council debates, contemporary studies and the press. But we will also see that some European left-wingers, alongside Moroccan or Algerian activists, sought to reframe the debate away from the problems that shantytown inhabitants supposedly posed and insisted, instead, on the everyday difficulties experienced by shack dwellers.

The different terms used to describe informal settlements exemplify the initially constrained agency of shantytown dwellers: for Europeans, as shantytowns were increasingly constructed as a problem, *bidonville* gradually became the established term from the 1930s onward, belatedly describing an urban phenomenon that had existed since the 1910s.[8] Due notably to this term's stigmatizing connotations, Algerians preferred to speak more of *barrārik*, the Arabicized form of *barraques*, the French word for "shacks." Similarly, many Moroccans frequently used the term *karyān*, stemming from the French term for quarry, *carrières*. This chapter therefore uses *shantytown* and not *bidonville* as a catchall and hopefully more neutral term to describe informal settlements.

Dominant Problematizing Themes in Algiers and Casablanca, 1918–1945

We can identify a first period until the mid or late 1940s when social discourses in both cities focused on shantytowns as a problem of migration, public health, urban control, and rehousing. The visible poverty in the cities was in fact often merely a transposition into an urban environment of the poverty in the countryside, and shantytowns first started to become socially visible through this link, established in both cities from the 1920s onward, between such settlements and migration.

Internal migrations within both North African territories, much less well known than the mass migration of firstly Algerians and latterly Moroccans to Metropolitan France from the 1910s, formed part of individual and collective strategies to survive the economic, social, legal, and political inequalities of the colonial regime.[9] Wide-scale land expropriation by Europeans, periodic famines, disease, and wider regional economic disparities continued to push migration to the main cities, as families strategized for the better access to food, jobs, education, and health that urban living provided.[10] With the traditional areas where migrants first settled, the Casbah (Algiers) and (Ancienne) Medina in Casablanca being full, migrants' residential strategies led them to other affordable city districts such as shantytowns, where it was possible to take advantage of chain migration and live close to jobs based in industrial areas, the port, and central markets and on building sites.

The two shantytown case studies in this chapter exemplify these processes: Mahieddine, the largest shantytown in Algiers until the mid-1950s, was situated near that city's port, market, and transport networks and had grown up from the 1910s around Algerian-owned Ottoman-era villas (fig. 10.1). The Carrières centrales (latterly Hāy Mohammadi) shantytown was within walking

Shantytowns
in Algiers(1954)

Mediterranean Sea

N.-D.
D' Afrique
Sup.

Bab-El-Oued

Ceinture Casbah

Upper
Casbah

Lower
Casbah

Climat De
France

Rue
D'isly

Rue
Michelet

Telemly
Sup.

Shantytowns
with more
than 1000
Inhabitants:

Hauteur
De
Mustapha

Mahieddine

Champ De
Manoeuvre

1. Aboulker
2. El Kettar
3. El Amal
4. Vinci
5. Legembre
6. Nador-Scala
7. Mahieddine

Pte Casbah-Belcourt Sup.

Redoute

Clos Salembier

Ruisseau

4   1   3   6

FIGURE 10.1. **Shantytowns in central Algiers, 1954.** Source: Adapted by Laurent Eisler from Robert Descloîtres, Jean-Claude Reverdy, and Claudine Descloîtres, *L'Algérie des bidonvilles: Le tiers-monde dans la cité* (Paris: Mouton, 1961), 43.

distance of Casablanca's fast-growing suburban industrial zone (fig. 10.2).[11] However, in Casablanca and, especially, Algiers, urbanization was accompanied by only limited industrialization, producing unemployment and underemployment. Very significant wage differentials with Europeans also explained low incomes and ethnic residential segregation.

Map of Casablanca
(Shantytowns)

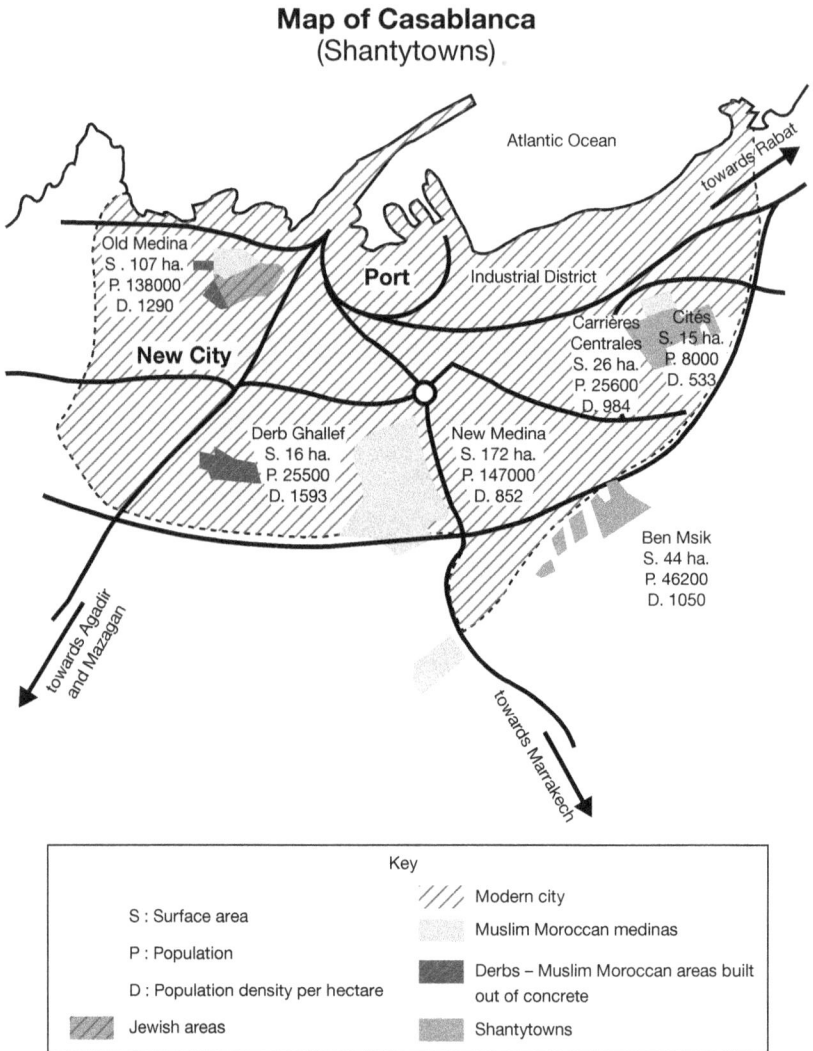

FIGURE 10.2. **Map of Casablanca, circa 1950.** Source: Adapted by Laurent Eisler from Robert Montagne, *Naissance du prolétariat marocain: Enquête collective 1948–1950* (Paris: Peyronnet, 1950), annex.

Economic migrants were not universally or necessarily considered a problem. In Casablanca, there was always the acknowledgment that the expanding economy needed labor. In both cities, however, individuals and families that European administrators and local councilors considered a burden on limited welfare budgets might be forcibly returned to their home regions, notably the unemployed, often single men often referred to as the "floating population" (*population flottante*). In Algiers, there were periodic roundups and forced returns (*refoulements*), as in 1923—including in the Mahieddine shantytown—and 1930.[12]

By the mid-1920s, migrations into Algiers were being problematized in more overtly spatialized ways as attention increasingly focused on where such newcomers lived. In turn, the presence of shacks was closely associated with a wider housing crisis that had previously been conceived of as affecting only Europeans. The link between migration and housing was also established through some local councilors and colonial officials who portrayed migrants as a health risk. Lemaire, head of the Algiers City Public Health Department, was concerned as early as 1923 that the overcrowded Casbah was already pushing Algerians into areas where large numbers of Europeans lived and expressed worry at the public health implications this had for Europeans, who always constituted the colonial administration's primary concern.[13]

An overtly "contaminationist" discourse emerged in the press and the Algiers city council debates in the first half of the 1930s. Councilor Tamzali, for example, critical of the inaction of the public authorities, complained in October 1930 that "Algiers is indeed in the process of being surrounded by blocks of foul slums, leprous, infected patches of land and by huts [*gourbis*] swarming with an emaciated native population."[14] Local (European) inhabitants protested against the presence of shacks near central Algiers, with Councilor Vial calling these districts "sources of infection" (*foyers d'infection*).[15] This question extended well beyond Algiers: the prominent urbanist Henri Prost's official report on colonial urbanism in 1932 portrayed informal settlements as a major new problem across the French empire.[16]

Despite such well-established hygienist rationalities, and the politicization and visibilization of Algerians' housing conditions during the 1930s, almost no rehousing was produced for Algerians before the late 1940s. How can we explain this? In the 1930s, the priority was to rehouse Europeans, who, for local councilors, represented the key electoral constituency.[17] We also see here what Stephen Legg calls the "tensions between the biopolitical and financial domains" that he identified in the governance of colonial Delhi.[18] In Algiers, the financial logics clearly won out.

Other factors intervened, however. For many Europeans, Algerians were triply "undeserving" of social housing: alongside that fact that priority went to Europeans, shantytown residents were often figured as newly arrived migrants, often without gainful employment (and hence requisite income), scrounging off poor relief, and thus not considered a legitimate urban presence. A third factor intervened, however, because most Algerians were essentialized by city councilors and housing agencies as culturally ill suited for social housing. As Algiers's Mayor Rozis declared to a parliamentary commission visiting Algeria in March 1937: "Most of the native Muslim population has a lower level of civilization than ours."[19] The colonial authorities' stated aim was to steer Algerians away from a relationship with vernacular forms of place, space, and housing (the tent and the hut) seen as hindering assimilation (here, the adoption of middle-class Metropolitan French lifestyles).

Like in Algiers, in Casablanca—on which we will now focus—colonial officials and the Casablanca Municipal Commission (an appointed body) established a link between population movement into and within Casablanca, the places where the poor lived, and the diseases they were believed to carry. This led to the targeting of migrants through roundups and, where relevant, *refoulement* back to "home regions." What Daniel Rivet has called a "public health dictatorship" (*dictature sanitaire*) targeting the "floating population" was undertaken on a much larger scale than in Algiers, justified by hygienist logics.[20] Until the late 1940s, the aim was to protect Europeans not from Moroccans considered a political and/or security risk but principally a medical danger.[21] For the moment, it was the countryside in the largely Berber south or other cities (Marrakech, Fez) that generated the most European political fears, and in Casablanca, it was the "old" and new medinas rather than the shantytowns.[22] In 1934, the journalist Léandre Vaillat encapsulated many of these European concerns in Morocco: "A real danger for Europeans lies in these 'shantytowns.' The enemy is at the gates of the city, but not an insurgent foe with rapid-fire rifles, but an awful, subtle, elusive opponent called typhus, cholera or plague."[23]

Shantytowns were in fact partly tolerated, because city authorities wanted to regroup them onto land with wider streets and numbered shacks to facilitate control: for example, Ben M'sīk shantytown was relocated at least three times.[24] Such policies were frequent in the protectorate due to the influence of Resident-General Hubert Lyautey, and his chief urbanist, Henri Prost, who, during the 1910s and 1920s, established residential zoning for the three main population groups (Muslim and Jewish Moroccans and Europeans).[25] Such intervention typically forced Moroccans farther and farther away from the central city to live in increasingly large (and densely populated) mainly Moroccan-only areas (e.g., the New Medina, shantytowns).[26]

Although the impact of the Popular Front in Morocco was strongly diluted in a conservative colonial context, socialists and anticolonial activists there started to place shantytowns as part of the social question, as in Algeria.[27] This eventually brought a response under the reformist resident-general Charles Noguès in 1937 and marked the first shift to national as opposed to city-level or employer-initiated intervention to house Moroccans.[28] Notwithstanding these measures taken in response to political pressure, in the

1930s, the public health imperative remained paramount. The serious typhus outbreak of 1936–1937 provided a convenient pretext to relocate up to sixty thousand Muslim Moroccans living in small shantytowns (termed *micro-bidonvilles*) and *derbs* (concrete-built informal housing, often with shacks in their midst) situated in urban pockets in or around Casablanca's new, central European-inhabited city center.[29] It was the shacks and *derbs* in these areas, not elsewhere, that the 1938–1939 measures targeted. As the city commission's rapporteur Michel Bon clearly put it, what was needed was an "operation to protect the European population" and the reimposition of colonial urban order.[30] Many of those living in shacks affected by the 1938–1939 operations re-housed themselves, swelling the already large Ben M'sīk shantytown, or what soon became Casablanca's other large shantytown under municipal management, Carrières centrales.[31] Carrières centrales, whose population soon rose to nineteen thousand, was relocated one final time in 1939–1940 onto municipal land.[32] Reenforcing ethnic separation was arguably the aim, rather than the indirect and hence unintended consequence, of the 1938–1939 destruction and regrouping measures. As we shall see, this policy came with significant spatial, social and political consequences. Initially, however, the idea was that larger shantytowns might be easier to control and police.[33]

The public health imperative also inspired a royal decree (July 1938) increasing the protectorate's ability to intervene on shantytowns. Further regulatory measures in May 1941 modified the 1938 decree to allow the *temporary* presence of shacks on municipal land pending rehousing.[34] In the absence of any mass rehousing of Moroccans (given financial considerations), it was improvement rather than eradication that became hygienists' main concern.[35]

In Carrières centrales, with ongoing migration, overcrowding worsened, as the informal settlement was also used to regroup people forcibly relocated from smaller shantytowns in the 1940s. By 1950, there were nearly forty-nine thousand people living across this informal settlement.[36] Such developments generated what we will call a "loss of control" narrative on urban growth. For if the authorities in Casablanca in the 1930s and 1940s tried to displace and reaffirm segregation, the speed of growth soon compromised such initiatives, as internal migration accelerated during and after World War II.[37] The scenario of the interwar years was therefore partially repeated, seeing the forcible return of nearly twenty thousand people from Casablanca between October 1945 and April 1946. After the last typhus epidemic of 1946, the official public health discourses targeting shantytowns became less prominent (though never disappeared), and forced returns became politically risky, because they contradicted the image of a benign colonial state.[38]

In Algiers—to which the discussion now returns—as we have seen, before the 1940s, there were few if any attempts to remove, relocate or regroup the many, but often smaller, shantytowns, and forced returns were less numerous than in Casablanca. While the colonial administration and city council had fended off many of the internal critiques of their strategic nonintervention, the shantytowns question was internationalized during the Vichy period in Algeria (1940–1942), this time inspiring an ambitious national plan to address the issue.[39] The Vichy regime was highly concerned about German and Italian propaganda that portrayed shantytowns as proof of the French state's inability to provide for its colonial subjects and was particularly sensitive about Algiers, "capital city of North Africa and French Africa."[40] In turn, such intervention chimed with the social reformism of the authoritarian Vichy regime. Maxime Weygand, writing in September 1941 as both Algeria's governor-general and delegate-general of the Vichy government in Africa, considered the destruction of shantytowns in Algeria as "a work of moral and social cleansing."[41] The focus in 1941 was clearly on central Algiers, initiated by a census of its shantytowns.[42]

Informal settlements across the colony were henceforth subjected to greater regulation and control.[43] On the regulatory side, the authorities in Algeria explicitly borrowed the Moroccan measures of 1938, which, in effect, criminalized some informal settlements and brought the largest Algiers shantytowns such as Mahieddine and El-Kettar under the administration of the local housing office and municipal authorities.[44] The internal bureaucratic and the external public discourses linked to these measures further problematized shantytowns as threats to public health, as housing that was unfit (*insalubre*) and/or unauthorized, alongside the socially dangerous profile and the exploitation of tenants.[45] It was agreed, however, that eradication could occur only once new accommodation was available for the "deserving poor."

For the city council, this category of "deserving poor" again covered regularly employed shantytown residents who had been in the city for years. The criteria for rehousing often remained informed by an essentializing culturalist ethos, however, especially because Mayor Rozis was still in power and the local housing office adopted similar standpoints.[46] The 1941 census explicitly also set out to exclude the recently arrived unemployed who were due to be forcibly returned.[47] Rozis also highlighted a further category of the undeserving, what he called "a mass of undesirables without honest employment or family who, when night comes, crowd into shacks and escape investigation."[48] In the mayor's view, these people were a danger and thus a matter for the police rather than the council and possible rehousing.[49]

Social Risks, 1930s–1950s

The fear of highly mobile single men was, even at this authoritarian point, more frequently associated with their supposed involvement in petty criminality than with anticolonial political activism. In similar ways to Casablanca, throughout the 1930s and into the early 1940s, the perceived political danger in Algiers, when spatialized, mostly centered on the nationalist hub of the Casbah and not the informal settlements.[50]

New themes emerged, or were reinforced, during the 1940s that underlined the social dangers allegedly posed by shantytown residents. Such representations henceforth occupied a more prominent place in the stigmatization of these areas, adding to rather than entirely replacing many of the negative themes of the 1930s. Mahieddine, in particular, was a center for the flourishing black market that developed in Algiers during World War II. After complaints to the Algiers prefect in May 1946 from residents' associations about the building of new shacks in Mahieddine for the purposes of stocking black market goods, the police officer in charge of the shantytown confirmed the practice, saying that shacks there were also being used for (illegal) betting purposes, and they described daily markets of clandestine goods.[51] An administrative trainee's report in 1944 had summarized Mahieddine as "a dodgy area where thieves and black market traffickers hide out, and where there are illegal butchers' stalls and cafés."[52] This example also illustrates how Algiers was a city at least partially coproduced by its Algerian inhabitants.

Shantytowns henceforth joined other majority-Algerian areas as criminalized spaces, albeit with their own specific repertoire of themes in the two cities. In Algiers, for example, sex work in the shantytowns does not appear to have been a major preoccupation of the authorities, as the Casbah was the true center of the city's sex industry, despite the fact that there was sex work also undertaken in shantytowns.[53] In contrast, in Casablanca, there was strong awareness of this public health issue extending into shantytowns for the thousands of women living there by the early 1950s who undertook regular or occasional nonregulated sex work. Carrières centrales figured prominently in such discussions, and raids on sex workers there by the public health authorities— very rare in Algiers shantytowns—were carried out from the early 1940s onward, as across other majority-Moroccan districts in Casablanca.[54] This problematization through criminalization often occurred despite the fact that some detailed contemporary studies emphasized that, beyond the question of unauthorized sex work, crime was relatively limited in both cities' shantytowns, which in their view remained essentially self-policing societies.[55]

Criminalization also occurred via further indirect routes. One such case was the fear of the youngest sectors of the "floating population," the *yaouleds*—several thousand boys and male adolescents in both cities who worked odd jobs as shoe shines, porters, and newspaper vendors to support themselves since orphaned or sent by their families. These street boys were systematically suspected of juvenile delinquency. While the heavily gendered *yaouled* question centered more on the Algiers Casbah, some *yaouleds* came from shantytowns.[56] By 1941, it had become a moral panic, with these boys' parents portrayed as "unfit" and charity scroungers.[57] The *yaouled* question was even more prominent in Casablanca and soon inflected with precise, as opposed to the previously more diffuse, political connotations.[58] According to European observers, Moroccan nationalists were using boys and young men, often recruited from ranks of petty criminals and the "floating population," for "intimidating" street demonstrations.[59]

The Post-1945 Configuration of Welfare Colonialism and Political and Security Risk

Before returning to the perceived political and/or security threats, which at the end of the 1940s became the principal way in which Europeans in Casablanca spoke about shantytowns, we need to situate local developments within their wider and fast-evolving national and imperial contexts. By 1945, the shantytown question had moved up the political agenda in both cities, becoming an essential element of the wider "social question" pressed home by nationalists and communists, to which colonial policy in North Africa sought to respond. France's aim to retain its colonies and hence rebuild its prestige after World War II came with a greater acceptance of the colonial state's social responsibilities.[60] For the central colonial authorities, however, the problem was that these often Paris-driven initiatives encountered strong local European resistance, making the housing situation critical. As a result, in both cities we often see a "loss of control" narrative from central and local authorities where, for example, figures of actually built or planned rehousing for shantytown dwellers are unfavorably compared to the number of people needing rehousing and/or still arriving in the city or projected to do so. The colonial archives reveal a sense of impending panic, quietly being kept at bay.[61]

Casablanca and the New Security Imperative

After 1945, European public discourses also increasingly reframed shantytowns a spaces of real or potential political resistance as part of a wider paradigm that came to dominate how *bidonvilles* were spoken about in Casablanca especially. A range of colonial officials, often involved in the everyday administration of urban Muslim Moroccans, wrote about what could be called the figure of the "neither-nor" (or *ni-ni*). According to this binary perspective, "politically naïve" displaced peasants had been largely desocialized from "traditional" society but were unable or unwilling to fully integrate themselves into urban modernity. Migration in this sense was both a chance and a potential risk for the colonial authorities. Socially, migrants were unused to urban Moroccan ways of life, and colonial officials essentialized them as being very different from European modernity.[62] For Captain Garnier in 1947, "this mass of natives," as he put it, "remains suspended between two opposite poles," that is, between "ancestral traditions" and "our modern ideas."[63]

Economically, migrants often faced partial employment and only a minority were considered stably and well-enough employed to socioeconomically integrate.[64] Many Moroccans, according to this viewpoint, found themselves in a situation of "anomie," lacking social, cultural and religious markers and were therefore easy prey for nationalist or communist campaigning. As Captain Maneville put it in his detailed monograph on the Carrières centrales shantytown (1950) that he oversaw, a political danger stemmed from "the large number of mobile, idle workers, professional beggars, prostitutes and crimes committed by this mass having lost its bearings and what's more that can be easily stoked up into a frenzy by the demagogic propaganda of political parties."[65]

Around 1948–1950 in Morocco, a new way of representing shantytown dwellers was thus born. French officials like Maneville had a keen sense of the acceleration of political and social change, the links between the two, and what that could mean for the future of French domination. Shantytowns were never the sole urban areas highlighted by such studies, but they usually figured prominently, as symbols of migration, of the housing crisis, of the nascent Moroccan proletariat, and, increasingly, of political danger and security risk.

By the late 1940s, while sometimes exaggerated, such political fears were certainly grounded. Casablanca was seeing the creation of a multicentered nationalist city that had come to include areas such as Carrières centrales as a result of astute, sustained efforts by the main proindependence party (Istiqlāl, or Independence, 1944–) and its influence in the communist-inspired trade union movement from where the Istiqlāl reached out to the urban poor. The latter constituted a new political target for the party. Casablanca, rather than Fez, Marrakech, or Rabat, was quickly becoming the key political center of Morocco, and Carrières centrales, alongside the New and "Old"

Medina—from which nationalism had radiated out during the 1940s—henceforth constituted one of the city's most militant nationalist areas.[66] From then on, it was the poor in the cities and not the protectorate's Berber south that constituted the political and security risk.

Robert Montagne's synthesis *Naissance du prolétariat marocain* (Birth of the Moroccan Proletariat; 1950) both reflected and solidified many of these European concerns.[67] Montagne, a military officer and ethnographer, was the most influential expert on North African colonial migrations.[68] In this volume, Montagne, worried by the rise of Arab nationalism, brought together the existing colonial knowledge on urban Morocco. This was colonial knowledge with an avowedly utilitarian purpose, designed to solve the worrying present "urban problem" that risked slipping out of French control.[69]

On June 1, 1950, Montagne wrote a confidential note to Resident-General Alphonse Juin as the *Naissance* project (researched from 1948 to 1950) was being finalized. In his *Note*, Montagne argued for a reformist strengthening of the colonial administration's urban presence across the protectorate. However, Casablanca is the only city that Montagne's letter directly mentions and that he discusses in detail. Montagne judged that "the huge mass of proletarians gathered around cities represents, in certain cases and especially in Casablanca, a great political and social danger for the near future. . . . In these very densely populated areas and that for the moment are beyond our real control—Carrières centrales and neighboring districts with 50,000 inhabitants, Ben M'sīk with 50,000, the Old Medina with 80,000 Muslims, without mentioning the 'compact block' of the New Medina (150,000 residents)—sudden and violent movements can unexpectedly develop among this peaceable and orderly population," and that it would be difficult to manage. "The consequences could be frightening," he added.[70]

Montagne argued that the French authorities probably had only one or two years to act.[71] In the short term, he outlined, colonial personnel should be increased and health, training, education, and shantytown rehousing be improved, defining the latter as "the key problem." Montagne's main focus was the "proletariat," and he was especially worried about the children of migrants, these "new generations born into the disorder of the cities," who lacked adequate social structures.[72] For Montagne, it was for the French to provide new markers for this "neither-nor" category.[73] As early as 1947, in fact, the protectorate had already introduced the *Délégations aux affaires urbaines* (Delegation for Urban Affairs, or DAU), staffed by army personnel who coordinated social, political, and administrative control of districts such as shantytowns.[74]

Resident-General Juin immediately seized on the fears formulated by

Montagne, but concentrated on the shantytowns. The following month, he wrote to other senior colonial officials of the need to "take back control over the shantytown population whose current state of abandon creates a considerable security danger in the four large cities [Casablanca, Fez, Marrakech and Rabat]."[75] Over the following eighteen months, further security measures were taken to protect Europeans.[76] Such European fears increased again during 1952 and sealed the advent of a new security imperative when, on December 7–8, 1952, Carrières centrales shantytown was the center of an urban uprising linked to nationalist-inspired strikes. At least one hundred deaths resulted from the ensuing militarized repression as the authorities, and many Europeans, wrongly feared a murderous "invasion" of the central European city by Moroccan men and responded on the basis of long-held Orientalist assumptions that Moroccans, as "Arabs," only respected force. This event was the pretext the authorities had long sought to further increase security personnel and ban the Istiqlāl, the Union générale des syndicats confédérés marocains (General CUGSCM) it had infiltrated and the Moroccan Communist Party. This repression was arguably so lethal because Carrières centrales provided a spatial focus for many Europeans' linked antinationalist and anticommunist hostility.[77] Internally, however, senior colonial officials openly admitted their inability to make Casablanca's nationalist city "legible" to the colonial state, despite the use of massive repressive force.[78] This was a problem that would continue in the next sequences of the independence struggle as resistance turned violent once the French exiled Mohammed V (August 1953).

Like many other mostly or uniquely Moroccan Muslim districts, Carrières centrales became a center of armed proindependence resistance during the last years of colonial rule (August 1953 through the summer 1956), and there were further, violently repressed street protests in that district (August 1953 and August 1955).[79] The previous overconcentration on Moroccan men in European public discourses inadvertently hid the role of women from the shantytowns in both the street demonstrations (during which many were shot) and the armed resistance that characterized this period.[80]

Just as the nationalist city had been constructed by linking up different Moroccan areas of Casablanca—New and "Old" Medinas, shantytowns, and the *derbs*, so the "underground city" of the armed guerrillas was similarly built, without there necessarily being any specific preponderance of the shantytowns in relation to other urban areas, even if colonial security discourses continued to focus on Carrières centrales.[81] To be sure, the banned party Istiqlāl had been more powerful in Carrières centrales than in the largest shantytown, Ben M'sīk, where its more moderate rival the Democratic

Independence Party, based less on working-class identity, was well implanted.[82] However, such distinctions were arguably more blurred during the subsequent armed resistance, with guerrilla recruitment streams broad. All large, densely populated Moroccan districts afforded cover for the hiding of militants, weapons, and supplies. During this crisis period of 1953–1956, mobility became a particular resource for nationalists and a problem for the security forces, with proindependence activists circulating between city and their home regions.[83]

The former colonial official and sociologist André Adam later reflected that Casablanca's segregationist policies illustrated "the drawbacks of mass-scale urbanism" that provided an ideal context for political opposition, armed or otherwise.[84] We see here the unintended consequences of initially confident imposition of colonial governance.

Countering this proindependence threat was also an intrinsic part of the shantytown rehousing program, which was in fact well underway by 1952 and provided the urban patchwork of shacks, new housing, and temporary prefabricated housing against which the crisis of decolonization played out. For example, reformist Resident-General Juin had written to the regional heads of the colonial administration on December 1, 1948, outlining the need for more rehousing and improved infrastructure, warning that "the shantytowns proliferating on the edges of Moroccan cities give those critical of France's accomplishments in this country a subject that can be easily used against us in the face of world opinion."[85] The time in office of Morocco's chief urbanist Michel Écochard (1946–1952) marked the peak of these efforts in Casablanca.[86] Unlike in Algeria, the conflict for independence in Morocco did not involve large refugee migrations into the cities, so the rehousing policies, although insufficient, were probably more successful than in Algiers.[87] However, in November 1953, there were fifty-six thousand people still living in fifteen thousand shacks in Carrières centrales alone, representing a key colonial legacy for the reindependent Moroccan state.[88]

Waging War on and in the Algiers Shantytowns

The forms taken by the crisis of decolonization in Algiers and the role of shantytowns in that process were similar but not identical. Like in Casablanca after 1946, in the space of only six years (1953–1959), an absence of state presence in the shantytowns had evolved into a situation in which the state asserted a new and significant role in both repression and reform.

As in Casablanca, a reformist rehousing wave in Algiers started prior to the political crisis that commenced in November 1954 with the start of the

War of Independence. The measures taken by Mayor Chevallier, who came into office in 1953, show the more powerful initiative of local assemblies in Algeria in relation to Morocco. Chevallier inherited the considerable legacies of his immediate predecessor, conservative mayor Pierre-René Gazagne and indeed those of Rozis before him (1935–1942) and the various reformist post-Vichy initiatives in 1943–1947, which had contained much Republican promise but little action on rehousing. This resulted in the de facto toleration of shantytowns. From the authorities' perspective, there were several key ongoing issues: slow recovery in postwar construction, continuing migrations, the need to also address unfit housing in non-shantytown districts, financial wrangling within the administration. First and foremost, however, as in the 1930s, was arguably the lack of sustained political will from local Europeans to commit money to rehouse Algerians in shantytowns, with these groups still considered variously undeserving. In addition, containing shantytown growth lacked requisite resource and personnel to implement.[89] Joëlle Deluz-La Bruyère and Jean-Jacques Deluz indicate that, between 1945 and 1953, only 650 social housing units for Algerians were completed within the city limits, with another 214 finished in the industrial suburbs.[90] Between 1942 and late 1954, the number of shantytowns in greater Algiers grew from 16 to 164, with a very conservative estimate of eighty-six thousand residents.[91] But it was difficult to accurately assess the situation when many small informal settlements were concealed from wider public view: there had been, and there remained, less resegregationist urbanism in Algiers than in Casablanca.

Between 1943 and 1953, shantytown rehousing was mostly limited to emergency situations after often-lethal fires, rockfalls, and mudslides, with the political opposition of the Algerian Communist Party (PCA) and proindependence nationalists (Algerian People's Party—Movement for the Triumph of Democratic Liberties, PPA-MTLD) looking on closely.[92] These parties' competition for the male urban poor's electoral support helped further politicize the shantytowns issue: the PCA supported residents to physically stop shack destructions, generally portraying shantytown residents not simply as victims but also as potential political actors.[93] Nationalists and communists in the French National Assembly portrayed shantytowns as a shocking indictment of the colonial regime that, on paper, had espoused greater political equality for Algerians in 1947.[94] For the colonial administration, the "loss of control" narrative on shantytowns was becoming ever stronger.[95] The period 1943–1953 in Algiers represents a striking example of how the chronologies of problematization were not always simultaneous with the chronologies of meaningful public intervention.

Chevallier therefore wanted to change the narrative on shantytowns and, through eradication and rehousing, make Algiers into a "showcase" city and welfare arena for local, international and Metropolitan French audiences.[96] Needing expertise, Chevallier then created a municipal urban planning agency in 1957 to advise the council, and that conducted its own aerial study as well as sophisticated assessments of shantytown population, estimated at 106,000 for greater Algiers.[97] Chevallier's first initiatives, designed by prominent architect Fernand Pouillon, were supported in Paris, and government ministers regularly visited—and were duly filmed and photographed visiting—the ambitious housing estates such as Climat de France and Diar El-Mahsūl, which were constructed at record speed from 1954 to 1955.[98]

Chevallier's rehousing drive was just getting going as the National Liberation Front (FLN) started its armed insurgency in November 1954. As the conflict spread, Chevallier's authority was eroded by the army, which in 1957 assumed policing in Algiers and in effect became the third, but increasingly powerful component of rehousing policy, alongside the council and Algiers public housing authority, notably through the military Sections administratives urbaines (Urban Administrative Units, or SAU). The SAU, not unlike the DAU in Casablanca, were responsible from 1957 for urban "pacification" in Algerian Muslim districts, and they ensured closer state contact with Algerians to bring them away from the FLN "counterstate."[99]

If the political danger certainly informed the Chevallier-inspired first wave of eradication, the new security imperative launched the second wave from 1957, which was as much about removing spaces of resistance as it was about welfare colonialism.[100] At the same time, however, by winning "hearts and minds," Algerians were to be coaxed away from the FLN—or its bitter nationalist rival the Algerian National Movement (MNA)—through a reformist agenda that also targeted young people and women through employment, education, and improved infrastructure in the shantytowns (termed *humanization*), pending those areas' destruction.[101]

Eradicating shantytowns and rehousing their inhabitants, especially in the most central districts such as Mahieddine, by 1957 with a population estimated at fifteen thousand, therefore moved from a local, municipal priority to representing state policy.[102] Entire shantytowns were bulldozed in this increasingly militarized context.[103] Such impetus was continued and indeed reinforced by the reformist Constantine Plan announced by Charles de Gaulle in October 1958, in which housing was allocated 17.3 percent of the plan's budget of 15 billion francs for 1958.[104] Politically, the French state wanted to avoid the notion that Algeria, rather than being an integral part of France, displayed characteristics of the "Third World."[105] Similarly accompanied by a repressive agenda, this rehousing and/or eradicationist drive targeting shantytowns in Algiers was simultaneously pursued in Metropolitan France, especially in the Paris suburbs, where many thousands of Algerians lived in informal settlements that the police considered nationalist hotbeds.[106]

In the Algiers region, the Constantine Plan also noticeably targeted suburban shantytowns, which, since the 1940s, had grown at faster rates because of accelerated socioeconomic development there, and also because the shantytowns in central Algiers were full and under closer, military surveillance. Of the 42,678 Algerians in Maison-Carrée (latterly El-Harrāch) in 1954, nearly half (20,600) were estimated to have been living in shantytowns, and that was before wartime migrations.[107]

The idea of shantytowns as a political and security danger in Algiers did not start entirely in 1954. We can find references to the nationalist PPA-MTLD and its clandestine, short-lived armed wing, the Special Organization (Organisation spéciale; 1947–1950) in the relatively central El-Kettar shantytown in 1950, for example.[108] The poor suburban area Maison-Carrée was already considered one of the most militant nationalist areas regionally in 1940, and it continued to be so.[109] However, the French archival trail regarding shantytowns as political risk before 1954 is inconclusive, perhaps for good reason, because, as we will now see, if the war of independence partly reconfigured the ways shantytowns were problematized in Algiers, this was arguably a more complex process than in Casablanca. In Algiers, shantytowns came to represent the social question, the housing crisis, a public health risk and internal migration and its consequences, being "overvisibilized" in many respects because of these processes. Yet before 1954, shantytowns in Algiers were much less central to the colonial state's political and security preoccupations than were shantytowns in Casablanca. This was probably because in Algiers, initial nationalist organizing and public commentary on it had tended to focus on other mainly Algerian districts (Casbah, Belcourt), even if the multicentered nationalist city here, as in Casablanca, ultimately came to include all areas.[110] We should also remember that most Algiers shantytowns were smaller than in Casablanca.

Nonetheless, once the urban nationalist guerrillas got going in Algiers in 1955, the French military became more influential in the production of discourses on the shantytowns as a security risk, without the Casbah ever losing its primacy. The partial shift occurred since the war situation in Algiers was not dissimilar to that in Casablanca from 1953 onward, with the underground city of highly mobile militants using monoethnic neighborhoods such as shantytowns to move around supplies and militants both within the city and between city and countryside, where the National Liberation Army (ALN), the armed wing of the FLN, was conducting guerrilla warfare against the French military.[111] The nature of the urban terrain in the central city also reinforced European fears, as residential ethnic segregation, likened by the social geographer Jean Pelletier to a Harlequin's jacket, with an archipelago of "Algerian" and "European" microdistricts, saw Algerians living in often closer proximity to Europeans than in Casablanca—in the case of Mahieddine shantytown, only thirty meters apart.[112] Algerians did not need to "invade" the central European city as Europeans feared in Casablanca—they were often already just next to European residential areas. In addition, shantytowns were often the sites on which intranationalist scores were played out, further underlining, for Europeans, the areas' reputation for violent lawlessness.[113]

Security forces were particularly worried that shantytowns could be bases for launching attacks against both security personnel and other European targets.[114] In November 1954, gendarmes had found an arms cache in the militant Boubsila (Bérardi) informal settlement in suburban Hussein-Dey.[115] The police intelligence services (PRG), which were renting out one of the Mahieddine villas—situated in the middle of the large shantytown—to conduct interrogations, feared a nationalist "raid" on the property in August 1955, and in March 1956, the head of the Algiers PRG reiterated such anxieties, calling for riot police to "usefully subdue Mahieddine shantytown where many dubious elements are constantly staying."[116] In September 1956, the Algiers prefecture announced a security operation in suburban Maison-Carrée and Hussein-Dey: "These areas are used as stopping-off points for a large number of terrorists operating in Algiers."[117] These linked fears therefore covered both central and suburban shantytowns, and also reflected the reality of informal settlements' integration into underground nationalist activities. This incorporation explained why, both before and especially during the Battle of Algiers (1957), state repression was implemented in shantytowns across all areas of Algiers alongside the more internationally visible operations in the Casbah.[118]

Within this new, security-dominated context, specific groups were prioritized. For example, the men in Mahieddine living without their families were slated for rehousing because, no longer simply considered problematic for their frequent changes of jobs, they figured as an acute security threat. Again, this security fear was partly justified—in Mahieddine, for example, some of the hostels and cafés where they stayed were indeed being used as FLN safe havens for operatives in transit.[119] In April 1957, the Mahieddine SAU chief had written to the Algiers prefect requesting money to rehouse an estimated five hundred men.[120] However, due to wartime refugee migrations, by September 1961, there were an estimated two thousand such single residents.[121]

In Algiers, as in Casablanca, mobility was therefore in and of itself a problem for the colonial administration, civilian and military. Additionally, the war saw tens of thousands of internally displaced mostly rural people arrive into safer, urban contexts, fleeing forced resettlement into military-run camps, the general economic fallout of war, and armed conflict in this multidimensional civil war.[122] Such arrivals of "unknown" individuals were difficult to stop, with forced returns—even those from Kabylia, who were considered a particular security threat and economic problem—being limited for legal reasons and their potentially negative impact on public opinion.[123] These refugee migrations often congregated in shantytowns. According to the local SAU, the shantytown population in suburban Maison-Carrée more than doubled between 1958 and 1960.[124] Such migrations also self-evidently compromised the rehousing drive that also struggled with the worsening security situation in 1961–1962, seriously compromising deliverability.[125] A leading SAU officer in Algiers estimated there to be 150,000 people living in shantytowns in greater Algiers in July 1961.[126] Against a backdrop of repression, it is unclear to what extent rehousing fulfilled its political objectives.

How did European observers refer to the social, cultural, political and economic identities of Algerian shantytown dwellers? The SAU officers, though instructed to produce monographs and sociological studies on their neighborhoods, were mostly too preoccupied by the chaos of war to write very lengthy studies, but they kept regular reports.[127] Their general approach was to see many shantytown residents as part of the politically naïve "Muslim masses" (*masses musulmanes*) displaying a wait-and-see attitude (*attentisme*), unwilling to commit to either side (French state and FLN or MNA) until 1961. Throughout, as in Casablanca, there was a preoccupation with mostly young men.[128] For most European observers, migrants from the countryside had difficulties adapting to city life, bringing representations close to the *ni-ni*, or "neither-nor," category we saw for Casablanca. In Algiers, discussions on the Algerian proletariat featured less prominently, as industrial-based employment was less established than in Casablanca, and arguably due to lesser degrees of anticommunism among observers. How shantytown inhabitants should be classified socioeconomically varied considerably, but *subproletariat* rather than *proletariat* was more commonly used. Such viewpoints traversed the SAU, wider colonial administration, and Algiers's more autonomous and influential field of sociological writing in relation to Casablanca, which included much discussion of shantytowns, for example by Pierre Bourdieu and Jean-Claude Reverdy.[129] Most famous, however, were the academic and political debates, initially between Bourdieu and Frantz Fanon, regarding whether the true revolutionary base of Algerian society was located in the proletariat, subproletariat, lumpen-proletariat or peasantry.[130]

The demonstrations of December 10–12, 1960 in Algiers, in which shanty-town residents participated very fully, provide a further window onto the po-litical and social integration of shantytown residents and their levels of mili-tancy. These protests were initially counterdemonstrations against Europeans mobilizing against de Gaulle's policy in Algeria that looked increasing like resulting in independence. Algerian demonstrators from across the city—female and male, young and old—soon converted this dynamic into a mass display for independence. There were violent clashes with the parachutists and armed Europeans, and at least one hundred people were killed.[131] These mobilizations were important because they showed the genuine popular en-thusiasm for and integration of all urban areas behind the cause for indepen-dence several years after the Battle of Algiers (1957) that had seriously eroded FLN structures. The French army from 1958 onward had arguably become complacent about its control over urban territory and population, missing the hyperlocal, underground, pro-FLN networks that remained in place.[132]

The SAU and other military reports openly recognized the significant role played by shantytown residents. During the protests in suburban Maison-Carrée, according to the SAU there, "the vast majority of demonstrators came from the shantytown areas."[133] A narrative of loss of control permeates the multiple security force reports that followed these December 1960 events, as colonial spatial containment, especially of young people, had failed: the Alge-rian demonstrators had been able to protest within but also beyond majority-Muslim areas, taking the arguments to majority European residential areas. Consequently, the army and riot police had struggled to protect Europeans' physical well-being and property.[134]

Yet two factors seem to have limited what could have brought a wider rec-ognition and visibility of the role of shantytowns and shantytown residents in the proindependence struggle beyond that of the French military. In central Algiers, press and wider political attention was often concentrated on where people congregated the most, that is, the "European" areas, rather than the sizable shantytowns nearby from where many demonstrators came.[135] Mean-while, in the suburbs such as Hussein-Dey and especially Maison-Carrée, where urban segregation was more clearly pronounced (rather like in Casa-blanca), shantytown dwellers marched toward the European areas. But these suburban areas were less socially visible and featured less prominently in Eu-ropean press reports and maps.[136]

Notwithstanding these and subsequent mass proindependence street protests, however, a senior army officer, with access to security reports from across Algiers, could state the next year: "We know very well that the trou-blemakers during the riots do not come from the shantytowns."[137] This mirrored some thinking within the SAU that shantytown residents, because they were hoping for rehousing, might hesitate in supporting the FLN.[138] From a French security perspective, therefore, the "mass" of shantytown dwellers—as opposed to the minority of proindependence militants viewed as harassing them—remained less radicalized than other categories such as the Casbah residents and former shantytown residents already rehoused; that is, the proletariat was more pro-FLN than the subproletariat. Such sources therefore give a different, complementary perspective on the security imperative in Algiers, emphasizing that, contrary to Casablanca, shantytowns in Algiers were not always considered the most dangerous districts, beyond their suspected role hiding militants and in launching attacks. In the rumor-driven European imaginary on shantytowns, Algiers never had its equivalent of Carrières centrales. But as Europeans vented their bitterness at impending French departure, shantytowns became "easy targets" (for bomb attacks or random assassinations): segregation for Algerians and Moroccans might be a political advantage for nationalist mobilization, but it could also attract violence, whether from the French state or radicalized Europeans.

Conclusion

This chapter has shown that, whereas the problematization of shantytowns and their residents was a constant, the "mix" of reasons behind such constructions evolved. Shantytowns were initially considered a minor, if not inexistent, political and security threat in the 1930s, and they were constructed mainly as a problem of migration and mobility, public health, urban containment, and a local, colonial, and international embarrassment on the "social question" and rehousing. Their location was therefore important, as the more central from a European perspective, the more visible they were to politicians and journalists and the more they threatened European public health.

Shantytowns then evolved to become in Casablanca the principle focus for the territorialization of the political and security risk that proindependence nationalism represented, without the other problematizations ever disappearing entirely. When understanding the strength of official and wider European security threat perceptions regarding Carrières centrales, however, this area's large size—initially encouraged by regrouping policies—resulting in some fifty thousand inhabitants by the early 1950s (three times the population of Mahieddine), should certainly be kept in mind, and many colonial officials ultimately agreed that such suburban relocations had backfired. However, size was never the sole explanatory factor: as well as antinationalism, deep-seated anticommunism within the French colonial apparatus also played its role in potentially exaggerating such fears, reminding us that decolonization and the Cold War were inseparable.

The picture in Algiers, which largely followed the same sequential development of increased political and security problematization as in Casablanca, is less clear-cut, because the primacy of the Casbah as a militant space was never superseded, at least in terms of media and political visibility. Seen by all military actors after 1954 as enclaves from which FLN attacks might be organized, some French military personnel nonetheless appear to have underestimated, perhaps through complacency, the wider political role played by the shantytowns and the districts' level of integration into the nationalist struggle.

State intervention in the shantytowns, this chapter has argued, occurred on a large scale only when these areas were viewed as a significant health, political, and/or security issue. This is consonant with the respective cases of Madrid and Rome also examined in this volume.

Shantytowns and their inhabitants navigated an unsteady course between social visibility and indeed overvisibility in some respects, and social invisibility in others, as nationalists, communists, and some socialists initially struggled to reframe the debate around the everyday problems faced by shantytown residents as opposed to the various difficulties they allegedly caused. European actors variously figured shantytown residents as migrants, workers, the unemployed or underemployed, proletariat or subproletariat, welfare scroungers, criminals, culturally "backward," suffering from anomie, sociologically and socioculturally indefinable, or indeed dangerous (or praised) armed revolutionaries and threatening street presence. Some of these stigmatizing and at times exoticizing themes clearly singled out shantytowns due to a housing type (shack) in need to destruction, families to rehouse, people to "civilize." Other imperatives, however, linked shantytowns to much wider concerns (security, migration, colonial urbanism, urban poverty, everyday criminality) that still often contained strongly spatialized dimensions. Overall, however, what emerges from this historical sequence of fifty years is a powerful expression of the colonial city as a coproduction between European and Algerian/Moroccan actors, and an assertion of political agency by local societies that so worried Europeans and successfully challenged the colonial rule they defended.

Notes

Introduction

1. United Nations, Department of Economic and Social Affairs, *World Urbanization Prospects: The 2018 Revision* (New York: United Nations, 2019), 9. On the inherent unreliability of these statistics, as well as the need for broader analytic conceptions of the "urban," see Neil Brenner and Christian Schmid, "The Urban Age in Question," *International Journal of Urban and Regional Research* 38 (2013): 731–55.

2. Edward Glaeser, *Triumph of the City: How Our Greatest Invention Makes Us Richer, Smarter, Greener, Healthier, and Happier* (New York: Penguin, 2011), 23.

3. Mike Davis, *Planet of Slums* (New York: Verso, 2007).

4. United Nations, Department of Economic and Social Affairs, Statistics Division, *Sustainable Development Goal 11, Sustainable Cities and Communities*, https://unstats.un.org/sdgs/report/2021/goal-11/.

5. The most influential example of this kind of presentist thinking is Hernando de Soto's *The Other Path* (New York: Harper & Row, 1989), later developed in *The Mystery of Capital* (New York: Basic Books, 2000). For critiques of Hernando de Soto, see Timothy Mitchell, "The Properties of Markets," in *Do Economists Make Markets*, ed. Lucia Siu, Donald MacKenzie, and Fabian Muniesa (Princeton, NJ: Princeton University Press, 2020); Alan Gilbert, "On the Mystery of Capital," *International Development Planning Review* 24, no. 1 (2009): 1–19. For reflections on the general issue of presentism and crisis, see Ananya Roy, "Slumdog Cities: Rethinking Subaltern Urbanism," *International Journal of Urban and Regional Research* 35, no. 2 (2011): 223–38; Brodwyn Fischer, "A Century in the Present Tense," in *Cities from Scratch: Poverty and Informality in Urban Latin America*, ed. Brodwyn Fischer, Bryan McCann, and Javier Auyero (Durham, NC: Duke University Press, 2014), 9–67. On the global intellectual history of the "slum," see Alan Mayne, *Slums: The History of a Global Injustice* (London: Reaktion Books, 2017).

6. The right to the city, first developed by Henri Lefebvre—in *Le droit à la ville* (Paris, Anthropos, 1968)—and later elaborated by Manuel Castells and many others, now generally refers to the idea that every urban resident should have full and equal access to all dimensions of urban life, from housing and public services to public space, public culture, and the formulation and enactment of public policy. It has acquired significant legal scaffolding, particularly in Latin American countries such as Brazil, Colombia, and Mexico, and it was adopted as a central tenet of UN-HABITAT III's Quito Declaration. See United Nations, *The New Urban Agenda* (New York: United Nations, 2017), point 11.

7. See Ananya Roy, "Why India Cannot Plan Its Cities," *Planning Theory* 8, no. 1 (2009): 76–87; Julie-Anne Boudreau and Diane Davis, "Introduction: A Processual Approach to Informalization," *Current Sociology Monograph* 65, no. 2 (2017): 151–66; Martjin Koster, "Assembling Formal and Informal Urban Governance: Political Brokerage in Recife, Brazil," *Anthropologica* 61 (2019): 25–34; Graham Denyer Willis, "City of Clones: Facsimiles and Governance in São Paulo, Brazil," *Current Sociology Monograph* 65, no. 2 (2017): 235–47; Jacquot Sébastien and Marie Morelle, "Comment penser l'informalité dans les villes 'du Nord,' à partir des théories urbaines 'du Sud'?," *Métropoles* 22 (2018): https://doi.org/10.4000/metropoles.5601; Richard Harris, "Modes of Informal Urban Development: A Global Phenomenon," *Journal of Planning Literature* 33, no. 3 (2017): 267–86.

8. A few social scientists have disrupted these patterns in recent years, some by rethinking the intellectual history of informality, and others by placing informality in the context of canonical histories of law, urbanism, or governance. Even here, however, it is rare to find the kind of archival research and critical evidentiary practices that open the social world of the past in the way that ethnography illuminates the present. For examples, see James Holston, *Insurgent Citizenship* (Princeton, NJ: Princeton University Press, 2008); Lícia Valladares, *The Invention of the Favela* (Durham, NC: Duke University Press, 2019); Boudreau and Davis, "Introduction"; Priscilla Connolly, "Latin American Informal Urbanism," in *Marginal Urbanisms*, ed. Felipe Hernández and Axel Becerra (Newcastle upon Tyne: Cambridge Scholars, 2017), 22–47; Jennifer Robinson, *Ordinary Cities* (New York: Routledge, 2006).

9. On the limitations of North Atlantic historical traditions, see Dipesh Chakrabarty, *Provincializing Europe* (Princeton, NJ: Princeton University Press, 2007). On the limitations of North Atlantic urban studies, see Robinson, *Ordinary*.

10. Programme Émergences, "The Informal City in the 20th Century: Urban Policy and Population Administration," supported by Ville de Paris.

11. This definition does not preclude the use of informality by state actors and state institutions; on the contrary, it embraces the concept that institutional actors can make use of informal networks and mechanisms of power, thus themselves entering the realm of informality even as they exercise formal power through legalized channels. In this way, our definition retains the important distinction between power relations that are sanctioned by law and power relations that are not, while also affirming that informality is a fundamental building block of power relations at every level or urban society. For succinct discussion of these issues (and different conclusions), see Diane Davis, "Informality and State Theory: Some Concluding Remarks," *Current Sociology Monograph* 65, no. 2 (2017): 315–24.

12. Keith Hart, "Informal Income Opportunities and Urban Employment in Ghana," *Journal of Modern African Studies* 11, no. 1 (1973): 61–89. For Hart's subsequent musings on the term's use and misuse—both in development debates and as a binary organizing neoliberalism and its contestations—see "Between Bureaucracy and the People: A Political History of Informality," Danish Institute for International Studies Working Paper 2008/7, Copenhagen, 2008.

13. For syntheses (often contrasting) of the concept's evolution and expansion, see, among many others, Ananya Roy and Nasir Alsayyad, *Urban Informality* (Lanham, MD: Lexington Books, 2003); Manuel Castells and Alejandro Portes, "World Underneath," in *The Informal Economy*, ed. Alejandro Portes, Manuel Castells, and Lauren Benton (Baltimore: Johns Hopkins, 1989), 11–37; Patricia Fernandez Kelly, *Out of the Shadows: Political Action and the Informal Economy in Latin America* (University Park: Penn State University Press, 2006); Adalberto Cardoso,

"Informality and Public Policies to Overcome It," *Sociologia & Antropologia* 6, no. 2 (2016): 321–49; Ann Varley, "Postcolonising Informality?," *Environment and Planning D: Society and Space* 31, no. 1 (2013): 4–22; Colin McFarlane, "Rethinking Informality: Politics, Crisis and the City," *Planning Theory & Practice* 13, no. 1 (2012): 89–208; Adriana Laura Massidda, "Cómo nombrar a la informalidad urbana," *QUID* 16, no. 10 (2018): 301–15; Rafael Soares Gonçalves, Nicolas Bautès, and Maria Maneiro, "A informalidade urbana em questão," *O Social em Questão* 21, no. 42 (2018): 9–26. For a summary of social science debates on broader economic informalities as positive or negative phenomena, see Davis, "Informality."

14. For a useful summary of debates about the formal-informal binary, see Alejandro Portes, "The Informal Sector: Definition, Controversy and Relation to National Development," *Review* 7, no. 1 (1983): 151–74; Cathy Rakowski, ed, *Contrapunto: The Informal Sector Debate in Latin America* (Albany: SUNY Press, 1994); Redento Recio, Iderlina Mateo-Babiano, and Sonia Roitman, "Revisiting Policy Epistemologies on Urban Informality," *Cities* 61 (2018): 136–44; Colin McFarlane and Michael Waibel, eds., *Urban Informalities* (London: Ashgate, 2012); Michele Acuto, Cecilia Dinardi, and Colin Marx, "Transcending Informal Urbanism," *Urban Studies* 56, no. 3 (2019): 475–87. See also Colin Marx and Emily Kelling, "Knowing Urban Informalities," *Urban Studies* 56, no. 3 (2019): 494–509, and Colin McFarlane's comment, "Thinking with and beyond the Informal-Formal Relation in Urban Thought," *Urban Studies* 56, no. 3 (2019): 620–23.

15. Debates about informality were in many ways the inheritors of earlier debates about social marginality in Latin America and elsewhere. See among many others, William Mangin, "Latin American Squatter Settlements," *Latin American Research Review* 2, no. 3 (1967): 65–98; Alejandro Portes, "Rationality and the Slum," *Comparative Studies in Society and History* 14, no. 2 (1972): 268–86; Anthony and Elizabeth Leeds, *A sociologia do Brasil urbano*, 2nd ed. (Rio: Editora FIOCRUZ, 2015); Janice Perlman, *The Myth of Marginality* (Berkeley: University of California Press, 1976); Mercedes González de la Rocha, "From the Marginality of the 1960s to the 'New Poverty' of Today," *Latin American Research Review* 39, no. 1 (2004): 183–203.

16. Alfred Brillembourg, *Informal City: Caracas Case* (Munich: Prestel, 2005); Felipe Hernández, Peter Kellett, and Lea Knudson-Allen, *Re-Thinking the Informal City: Critical Perspectives from Latin America* (New York: Berghahn Books, 2009); Agnès Deboulet, ed., *Repenser les quartiers précaires* (Paris: AFD, 2016).

17. John Turner, "The Squatter Settlement," *Architectural Design*, August 1968, 356–60; Rahul Mehrotra, "Negotiating the Static and Kinetic Cities," in *Other Cities, Other Worlds*, ed. Andreas Hyssen (Durham, NC: Duke University Press, 2008), 205–18; Rahul Mehrotra, *The Kinetic City and Other Essays* (Mumbai: ArchiTangle, 2021); Roy and Al-Sayyad, *Urban*; Robinson, *Ordinary*; Roy, "Slumdog"; Monika Grubbauer, "Postcolonial Urbanism across Disciplinary Boundaries," *Journal of Architecture* 24, no. 4 (2019): 469–86. This way of seeing informality also had its avatar in the Global North. See, e.g., Colin Ward and Dennis Hardy, "Plotlanders," *Oral History Journal* 13, no. 2 (1972): 57–70; Dennis Hardy and Colin H. Ward, *Arcadia for All: The Legacy of a Makeshift Landscape* (London: Mansell, 1984). For recent research, see Richard Bower, "Forgotten Plotlanders: Learning from the Survival of Lost Informal Housing in the UK," *Housing, Theory and Society* 34, no. 1 (2017): 79–105.

18. Holston, *Insurgent*; Luiz Antônio Machado da Silva, "A política na favela," *Cadernos Brasileiros* 9, no. 41 (1967): 33–47; Roy, "Why India."

19. Dipesh Chakrabarty's *Provincializing Europe* (Princeton, NJ: Princeton University Press, 2007) refers to a "hyperreal" Europe and India to distinguish the literal geographic reference

from an imagined ideal type. Here, we use the term to refer to idealized phenomena that are more significant as components of normative historical teleologies than as descriptions of historical processes.

20. "The civil law tradition" describes European-derived systems of law that emerged from the traditions of Roman law, canon law, and the Napoleonic traditions of code making; it is generally contrasted with the common law tradition of England and its former colonies, as well as with non-European legal systems around the world. See John Merryman and Rogelio Pérez-Perdomo, *The Civil Law Tradition*, 4th ed. (Stanford, CA: Stanford University Press, 2018). For a careful account of the interrelation of civil and common law, see Tamar Herzog, *A Short History of European Law* (Cambridge, MA: Harvard University Press, 2019).

21. See Connolly, "Latin American"; Fischer, "A Century."

22. Ángel Rama, *The Lettered City* (Durham, NC: Duke University Press, 1996); Richard Morse and Jorge Hardoy, *Rethinking the Latin American City* (Washington, DC: Woodrow Wilson Center, 1993); José Luis Romero, *Latinoamerica: Las ciudades y las ideas* (Mexico City: Siglo XXI, 1976).

23. On Mexico City, see Connolly, "Latin American"; Douglas Cope, *The Limits of Racial Domination* (Madison: University of Wisconsin Press, 1994); John Lear, "Mexico City: Space and Class in the Porfirian Capital," *Journal of Urban History* 22, no. 4 (1996): 454–92; Vera Candiani, *Dreaming of Dry Land* (Stanford, CA: Stanford University Press, 2014). On Salvador, Brazil, see Walter Fraga, *Mendigos moleques e vadios* (São Paulo: HUCITEC, 1996); João Reis, *Rebelião escrava* (São Paulo: Cia. Das Letras, 2003). On Buenos Aires, see Pancho Liernur, "Una ciudad efímera," *Estudios Sociales* 2 (1992): 103–21; Valeria Snitcofsky, *Historia de las villas de Buenos Aires* (Buenos Aires: Tejido Urbano, 2022), chap. 1. On Quito, see Cynthia Milton, *The Many Meanings of Poverty* (Stanford, CA: Stanford University Press, 2007). On Lima, see Charles Walker, *Shaky Colonialism* (Durham, NC: Duke University Press, 2008). On Bogotá, see Miguel Samper, *La miseria en Bogotá y otros escritos* (Bogotá: Universidad Nacional, 1969). On Caracas, see E. Jeffrey Stann, "Transportation and Urbanization in Caracas, 1891–1936," *Journal of Interamerican Studies and World Affairs* 17, no. 1 (1975): 82–100.

24. For further consideration of this issue in the Mexican and Chilean contexts, see Azuela and Antuñano and Giannotti and Cofré, in this volume.

25. See, e.g., Everardo Backheuser, *Habitações populares* (Rio de Janeiro: Imprensa Nacional, 1906); Sidney Chalhoub, *Cidade febril* (São Paulo: Cia. Das Letras, 1996); Lilian Fessler Vaz, *Modernidade e moradia* (Rio de Janeiro: 7 Letras, 2002); Valladares, *Invention*; Rafael Gonçalves de Almeida, "A emergência da favela como objeto da prática médica," *Terra Brasilis* 8 (2017): https://doi.org/10.4000/terrabrasilis.2082; José Tavares Correia de Lira, "Hidden Meanings," *Social Science Information* 38, no. 2 (1999): 297–327; Jeffrey Needell, *A Tropical Belle Époque* (Cambridge: Cambridge University Press, 1987); Lear, "Mexico City"; Claudia Agostini, *Monuments of Progress* (Calgary: University of Calgary Press, 2003); Matthew Vitz, *A City on a Lake* (Durham, NC: Duke University Press, 2018); Azuela and Antuñano, this volume; Edward Murphy, *For a Proper Home* (Pittsburgh, PA: University of Pittsburgh Press, 2015), esp. chap. 2; Richard Scobie, *Buenos Aires: Plaza to Suburb* (New York: Oxford University Press, 1974); Diego Armus, *The Ailing City* (Durham, NC: Duke University Press, 2011); Agnese Codebò, "La ciudad escenográfica," *Amerique Latine: Histoire & Memoire, Les Cahiers ALHIM* 29 (2015): https://doi.org/10.4000/alhim.5201.

26. By "hyperreal," we mean idealized forms that never exist in actuality yet become normative paradigms nonetheless.

27. For details of this process in Mexico, see Antuñano and Azuela, this volume. In Brazil, see Rafael Soares Gonçalves, *Favelas do Rio de Janeiro: História e direito* (Rio de Janeiro: Pallas/ PUC-Rio, 2013); Brodwyn Fischer, *A Poverty of Rights* (Stanford, CA: Stanford University Press, 2008) and "A ética do silêncio racial no contexto urbano: Políticas públicas e desigualdade social no Recife, 1900–1940," *Anais do Museu Paulista* 28 (2020): 1–45n31. For Chile, see Murphy, *For a Proper*; Giannotti and Cofré, this volume; T. Robert Burke, "Law and Development: The Chilean Housing Program," pts. 1 and 2, *Lawyer of the Americas* 2, no. 2 (1970): 173–79, and no. 3 (1970): 333–69.

28. On censuses and informality in Brazil, see Brodwyn Fischer, "From the Mocambo to the Favela," *Histoire et Mesure* 34, no. 1 (2019): 15–39; Rafael Soares Gonçalves, "Les favelas cariocas dans les recensements nationaux," *Histoire et Mesure* 34, no. 1 (2019): 41–63; Samuel Oliveira, "Informalidade urbana, classe trabalhadora e raça no Rio de Janeiro," *Revista de História* 180 (2021): 1–27; Samuel Oliveira, "A imaginação da informalidade urbana e dos trabalhadores no Rio de Janeiro e em Belo Horizonte," *Topoi* 23, no. 50 (2022): 540–62. For a survey of early sources for census information in Mexico, see Bernard Frieden, "The Search for Housing Policy in Mexico," *Town Planning Review* 36, no. 2 (1965): 75–94. For demographic analysis of later periods, see Connolly, "Latin American"; Priscilla Connolly, "Observing the Evolution of Irregular Settlement," *International Development Planning Review* 31, no. 1 (2009): 1–36; Emilio Duhau, *Habitat popular y política urbana* (Mexico City: Porrúa, 1998). For a summary of censuses after 1960 in Lima, see Jean-Claude Driant, *Las barriadas de Lima* (Lima: IFEA/DESCO, 1991); Julio Calderón Cockburn, "Los barrios marginales de Lima, 1961–2001," *Ciudad y Territorio: Estudios Territoriales* 35, nos. 136–37 (2003): 375–90. On early state quantification of *villas miseria* in Buenos Aires, see Adriana Massidda, Eva Camelli, and Valeria Snitcofsky, " 'Villas miserias' en Buenos Aires hacia mediados del siglo XX," *EURE* 49, no. 147 (2023): 1–21.

29. These processes were documented as they happened by a generation of Latin American and foreign social scientists. See, for example, the articles collected in Phillip Hauser, *Urbanization in Latin America* (New York: UNESCO, 1961), and Richard Morse's excellent bibliographical essays, "Recent Research on Latin American Urbanization: A Selective Survey with Commentary," *Latin American Research Review* 1, no. 1 (1965): 35–74, and "Trends and Issues in Latin American Urban Research," pts. 1 and 2, *Latin American Research Review* 6, no. 1 (1971): 3–52, and 6, no. 2 (1971): 19–75. For midcentury syntheses in Mexico see Frieden, "The Search for Housing Policy." In Venezuela, see Kenneth Karst, "Rights in Land and Housing in an Informal Legal System: The Barrios of Caracas," *American Journal of Comparative Law* 19, no. 3 (1971): 550–74. For synthetic analysis of these materials in Brazil, see Valladares, *Invention*; Fischer, "A Century."

30. See, among many others, Marcus Melo, "A cidade dos mocambos," *Espaço e Debates* 14 (1985): 44–66; Zélia Gominho, *Veneza Americana x. Mocambópolis* (Recife: CEPE, 1998); Luciano Parisse, *Favelas do Rio de Janeiro: Evolução e sentido* (Rio de Janeiro: PUC/CNPH, 1969); Marcelo Burgos, "Dos parques proletarios ao Favela-Bairro," in *Um século de favela*, by Alba Zaluar and Marcos Alvito (Rio de Janeiro: Editora FGV, 1998), chap. 1; Fischer, *Poverty*; Antonio Azuela and Maria Soledad Cruz Rodriguez, "La institucionalización de las colonias populares y la política urbana del DDF, 1940–1946," *Sociología* 9 (1989): 111–33; Connolly, "Latin American"; Emilio de Antuñano, "Planning a Mass City" (PhD diss., University of Chicago, 2017); Vitz, *City*; Jesse Horst, "Erasing las Yaguas," *Hispanic American Historical Review* 100, no. 3 (2020): 463–92; María José Bolaña, *Pobreza y segregación urbana: Cantegriles montevideanos, 1946–1973* (Montevideo: Rumbo, 2018); Lidia de la Torre, *Del conventillo a la villa miseria* (Buenos Aires:

Universidad Católica, 2008); Jorge Francisco Liernur, "De las 'nuevas tolderías' a la ciudad sin hombres," *Registros* 6 (2009): 7–24; Eduardo Blaustein, *Prohibido vivir aquí* (Buenos Aires: Punto de Encuentro, 2006); Maria Cristina Cravino, *Villa 31, entre el arraigo y el desalojo* (Buenos Aires: UNGS, 2009); Valeria Snitcofsky, *Historia*; Massidda, Camelli, and Snitcofsky, "Villas"; Burke, "Law and Development"; Murphy, *For a Proper* and "In and out of the Margins: Urban Land Seizures and Homeownership in Chile," in *Cities from Scratch: Poverty and Informality in Urban Latin America*, ed. Brodwyn Fischer, Bryan McCann, and Javier Auyero (Durham, NC: Duke University Press), 68–101; Alejandro Velasco, *Barrio Rising* (Durham, NC: Duke University Press, 2015); Serge Ollivier, this volume.

31. On political systems in Mexico and Venezuela, see Azuela and Antuñano, this volume; Velasco, *Barrio*. On Chile, see Murphy, *For a Proper*. For the role of informality in Brazilian national development, see Brodwyn Fischer, "Urban Informality, Citizenship, and the Paradoxes of Development," in *State and Nation Making in Latin America and Spain: The Rise and Fall of the Developmental State*, ed. Miguel Centeno and Agustín Ferraro (Cambridge: Cambridge University Press, 2019), 372–402.

32. For expanded discussion and related bibliography, see Fischer, "A Century"; Valladares, *Invention*. On Mexico, see Azuela and Antuñano, this volume.

33. On continuities across the political spectrum, see Horst, "Erasing."

34. Interestingly, revolutionary Cuba, unlike revolutionary Mexico, never incorporated self-generated urbanism into its formalized urban fabric. See Horst, "Erasing"; Sara Gómez, *De cierta manera* (Havana: Instituto Cubano de Arte e Industria Cinematográficos, 1974).

35. For Brazil, see Backheuser, *Habitações*; Otávio de Freitas, *O clima e a mortalidade* (Pernambuco: Imprensa Industrial, 1905); Recife, *Recenseamento 1913* (Recife: Collegio Salesiano, 1915); Pernambuco, *Recenseamento do Recife 1923* (Recife: Publicações Oficiais, 1924); Pernambuco, Comissão Censitária dos Mocambos, *Observações estatísticas sobre os mocambos* (Recife: Imprensa Oficial, 1939); Brasil, *Estatística predial do Districto Federal (1933)* (Rio de Janeiro: Diretoria Geral de Estatística, 1935); Brasil, Prefeitura do Distrito Federal, *Censo das Favelas* (Rio de Janeiro: Departamento de Geografia e Estatística, 1949). For Mexico, see Félix Sánchez, Ramón Ramírez, and Fernando Carmona de la Peña, "El problema de la habitación en la Ciudad de México" (Mexico City: Banco Nacional Hipotecario Urbano y de Obras Públicas, 1952); Instituto Nacional de la Vivienda, *Herradura de tugurios: Problemas y soluciones* (Mexico City: Instituto Nacional de la Vivienda, 1958); *Investigación nacional de la vivienda mexicana, 1961–2* (Mexico City: Instituto Nacional de la Vivienda, 1963). For Chile, see *El problema de la habitación en Chile* (Santiago: Caja de la Habitación, 1945); Instituto Nacional de Estadísticas, *Primer censo nacional de vivienda* (Santiago: Instituto Nacional de Estadísticas, 1952).

36. See, e.g., Lúcio Cardoso, *Salgueiro* (Rio de Janeiro: J. Olympio, 1935); A. C. Chagas Ribeiro, *Mocambos . . . romance* (Recife: Mozart, 1935); Bernardo Verbitsky, *Villa miseria también es América* (Buenos Aires: G. Kraft, 1957); Luis Buñuel, *Los olvidados* (Mexico City, 1950), film; Nelson Pereira dos Santos, *Rio 40 gráus* (Rio de Janeiro, 1955), film; David José Kohon, *Buenos Aires* (Buenos Aires, 1958), film, Lucas Demare, *Detrás de un largo muro* (Buenos Aires, 1958), film; John Turner, *A Roof of My Own* (New York, 1964), film; Gómez, *De cierta*; Gordon Parks, "Shocking Poverty Spurs Reds," *Life*, June 16, 1961.

37. A representative array of scholars of these generations (with an emphasis on those whose work is available in English) includes Oscar Lewis, Gino Germani, William Mangin, Anthony Leeds, Elizabeth Leeds, José Artur Rios, Lícia Valladares, Luís Antonio Machado da Silva, Janice Perlman, Larissa Lomnitz, Susan Eckstein, Helen Safa, Alejandro Portes, Wayne Cornelius, Alan

Gilbert, and Bryan Roberts. For ex post facto overviews of this work, see González de la Rocha, "From the Marginality"; Valladares, *Invention*; Fischer, "A Century"; Varley, "Postcolonising"; Connolly, "Latin American."

38. See, among many others (and in addition to several of the scholars in note 37 whose work spans many generations and themes), works by Manuel Castells, Cathy Schneider, Teresa Váldez, Elizabeth Jelin, Boaventura de Sousa Santos, Ruth Cardoso, Renato Boschi, Carlos Nelson Ferreira dos Santos, Lúcio Kowarick, Raquel Rolnick, Maria Celia Paoli, Teresa Caldeira, James Holston, Ann Varley, Antonio Azuela, Emilio Duhau, Juan Manuel Ramírez Sáiz, Jorge Alonso, Manuel Perlo Cohen, Mercedes González de la Rocha, and Pedro Moctezuma.

39. On de Soto, see *supra* note 5. Brazil has been an especially important site for this last group of studies. See, again among others and in addition to those previously noted, works by Alba Zaluar, Vera Telles, Keisha-Khan Perry, Jaime Alves, Gabriel Feltran, Michel Misse, Graham Denyer Willis, and Matthew Richmond.

40. For emblematic examples, see Hauser, "Urbanization"; Parisse, *Favelas*; Manuel Castells, *The City and the Grassroots* (Berkeley: University of California Press, 1983); Larissa Lomnitz, *Networks and Marginality* (New York: Academic Press, 1977); Alan Gilbert, *The Latin American City* (New York: Monthly Review, 1994); Holston, *Insurgent*.

41. Valladares, *Invention*; Perlman, *Myth*; Hermano Vianna, *The Mystery of Samba* (Chapel Hill: University of North Carolina Press, 1999); Nísia Trindade Lima, "O movimento de favelados do Rio de Janeiro" (MA thesis, IUPERJ, 1989).

42. Carlos G. Vélez-Ibáñez, *Rituals of Marginality: Politics, Process, and Culture Change in Urban Central Mexico, 1969–1974* (Berkeley: University of California Press, 1983); David Yee, "Shantytown Mexico: The Democratic Opening in Ciudad Nezahualcóyotl, 1969–1976," *The Americas* 78, no. 1 (2021): 119–47; Vitz, *City*; Antuñano, "Mexico City as an Urban Laboratory," *Journal of Urban History* 45, no. 4 (2018): 813–30.

43. See citations *supra* note 30.

44. For full discussion and citation of this literature, please see chapters 1 and 5–8 of this volume.

45. Emmanuel Leroy-Ladurie, ed., *La ville classique*, in *Histoire de la France urbaine*, ed. Georges Duby (Paris: Seuil, 1981), 3:656; Olivier Zeller, ed., *La ville moderne XVIᵉ–XVIIIᵉ siècle*, part of the book series *Histoire de l'Europe urbaine*, ed. Jean-Luc Pinol (Paris: Seuil, 2003), vol. 3. Even in periods when demographic pressure was not an overriding consideration, some historians believe that these spaces were consubstantial with cities, housing people and activities that had no place in the urban core. On this point, see Yannick Jambon, *Aux marges des villes modernes: Les faubourgs dans le royaume de France du XVIᵉ au début du XIXᵉ siècle*, new ed. (Lyon: Presses Universitaires, 2017); Arnaud Exbalin and François Godicheau, eds., *Los arrabales del imperio: Administrar los suburbios de las urbes en la Monarquía católica (siglos XVI–XIX)* (Buenos Aires: Prohistoria, 2022).

46. Urbanization, in this context, refers to the alignment of streets and the provision of urban services.

47. See, e.g., Paul Lecat, "La fabrique d'un quartier ordinaire: Le quartier de la Réunion entre Charonne et Paris des années 1830 aux années 1930" (PhD diss., Université Gustave Eiffel, 2021); Alexandre Frondizi, "Paris au-delà de Paris: Urbanisation et révolution dans l'outre-octroi populaire, 1789–1860" (PhD diss., Sciences Po, Paris, 2018).

48. The "Zone" was a military protection zone outside the fortifications. For military reasons, it was a *non aedificandi* zone, but authorities tolerated landowners who temporarily built

"light building" (wooden huts and *roulottes*). So from its creation in the 1830s, the zone was covered by structures inhabited by a stigmatized population. The zone has generated abundant literature. See Anne Granier, "La Zone et les zoniers de Paris, approches spatiales d'une marge urbaine (1912–1946)" (PhD diss., Lyon University, 2017); James Cannon, *The Paris Zone: A Cultural History, 1840–1940* (Burlington, VT: Ashgate, 2015); Isabelle Backouche, "La Zone et les zoniers parisiens: Un territoire habité, un espace stigmatisé," in *Genres urbains: Autour d'Annie Fourcaut*, ed. Emmanuel Bellanger, Thibault Tellier, Loïc Vadelorge, Danièle Voldman, and Charlotte Vorms (Paris: Créaphis, 2019), 49–66; Isabelle Backouche, "La fabrique d'un espace urbain qui fait peur: La zone de Paris (1900–1950)," in *Peurs urbaines XVIᵉ–XXIᵉ siècle*, ed. Philippe Chassaigne, Adèle Delaporte, and Caroline Le Mao (Pessac: MSHA, 2022).

49. Rubén Pallol, *El ensanche norte: Chamberí, 1860–1931: Un Madrid moderno* (Madrid: Los Libros de la Catarata, 2015). Photos of the Magallanes Street are in César Chicote, *La Vivienda insalubre en Madrid* (Madrid: Imprenta Municipal, 1914).

50. For a Parisian example, see Marie-Christine Volovitch-Tavares, *Portugais à Champigny, le temps des baraques* (Paris: Autrement, 1995).

51. Manuel Charpy, "L'apprentissage du vide. Commerces populaires et espace public à Paris dans la première moitié du XIXᵉ siècle," *Espaces et sociétés* 144–45, no. 1 (2011): 15–35.

52. Laurent Coudroy de Lille, "L'ensanche de población en Espagne, invention d'une pratique d'aménagement urbain, 1840–1890" (PhD diss., Université de Paris X, 1994); Laurent Coudroy de Lille, "La question des ensanches (1860–1910): Problème d'histoire et d'historiographie urbaine en Espagne," in *Recherches sur l'histoire de l'État dans le monde ibérique (XVᵉ–XXᵉ siècles)*, ed. Jean-Frédéric Schaub (Paris: Rue D'Ulm, 1993), 263–83.

53. Elia Canosa Zamora and Isabel Rodríguez Chumillas, "Urbanización marginal en la periferia noreste de Madrid," *Ciudad y Territorio* 66 (October–December 1985): 11–14; Ramón López Lucio, "En torno a los procesos reales de desarrollo urbano: Las tipologías de crecimiento en la formación de la periferia de Madrid," *Ciudad y Territorio* 2–3 (1976): 153–58; Charlotte Vorms, *La forja del extrarradio: La construcción del Madrid popular (1860–1936)* (2012; Granada: Comares, 2022).

54. Marcel Roncayolo, ed., *La ville à l'âge industriel*, in *Histoire de la France urbaine*, ed. Georges Duby (Paris: Seuil, 1983), 4:670; Gérard Jacquemet, *Belleville au XIXᵉ siècle: Du faubourg à la ville* (Paris: École des Hautes Études en Sciences Sociales, 1984).

55. Annie Fourcaut, *La banlieue en morceaux: La crise des lotissements défectueux en France dans l'entre-deux-guerres* (Grâne: Créaphis, 2000).

56. Luciano Villani, *Le borgate del fascismo: Storia urbana, politica e sociale della periferia romana* (Milan: Ledizioni, 2012).

57. Vorms, *Bâtisseurs*; Fourcaut, *La banlieue*; Charlotte Vorms, "Mal-lotis de la banlieue parisienne et des faubourgs de Madrid," in *Genres urbains: Autour d'Annie Fourcaut*, ed. Emmanuel Bellanger, Thibault Tellier, Loïc Vadelorge, Danièle Voldman, and Charlotte Vorms (Paris: Créaphis, 2019), 69–91.

58. See Charlotte Vorms, this volume. See also Tiago Luis Lavandeira Castela, "A Liberal Space: A History of the Illegalized Working-Class Extensions of Lisbon" (PhD diss., University of California, Berkeley, 2011). On the new labels, see Jean-Charles Depaule, ed., *Les mots de la stigmatisation urbaine* (Paris: Maison des Sciences de l'Homme, 2006); Christian Topalov, Laurent Coudroy de Lille, Jean-Charles Depaule, and Brigitte Marin, eds., *L'aventure des mots de la ville* (Paris: Bouquins/R. Laffont, 2010); Richard Harris and Charlotte Vorms, eds., *What's in a Name? Talking about Urban Peripheries* (Toronto: University of Toronto, 2017).

59. Françoise de Barros and Charlotte Vorms, "Favelas, bidonvilles, *baracche*, etc.: Recensements et fichiers," *Histoire & Mesure* 34, no. 1 (2019): 3–14.

60. Ildefonso Cerdà, *Monografía estadística de la clase obrera Barcelona—Teoría general de la urbanización y aplicación de sus principios y doctrinas a la reforma y ensanche de Barcelona* (Madrid: Impr. Española, 1867); Philippe Hauser, *Madrid bajo el punto de vista médico-social* (Madrid: Editora Nacional, 1902); Ayuntamiento de Madrid, *Información sobre la ciudad, Madrid* (Madrid: Imprenta Municipal, 1929); Chicote, *La Vivienda*; Maurice Bonnefond, "Les colonies de bicoques de la région parisienne," *Vie Urbaine* 25 (1925): 525–62 and 26 (1925): 597–626; Georges Bisson, "Les lotissements dans la région parisienne" (PhD diss., Institut d'urbanisme de l'Université de Paris, 1929–1930).

61. Comune di Roma—Ufficio di statistica e censimento, *Alloggi precari a Roma*, supplement to the statistical bulletin (Rome: Tip. Operaia Romana, 1958); Rogelio Duocastella, *Los suburbios 1957: Semana del Suburbio* (Barcelona: Gráf. Levante, 1957); Miguel Siguán, *Del campo al suburbio: Un estudio sobre la inmigración interior en España* (Madrid: CSIC, 1959).

62. Luciano Villani, "Recenser les baraques et leurs habitants à Rome, de la fin du XIXᵉ siècle aux années 1960," *Histoire & Mesure* 34, no. 1 (2019): 65–92.

63. Fernando Salsano, "La sistemazione degli sfrattati dall'area dei Fori Imperiali e la nascita delle borgate nella Roma fascista," *Città e Storia* 5, no. 1 (2010): 207–28; Fernando Salsano, "Il ventre di Roma: Trasformazione monumentale dell'area dei fori e nascita delle borgate negli anni del governatorato fascista" (PhD diss., Università degli studi Roma, 2007).

64. Charlotte Vorms, "Madrid années 1950: La question des baraques," *Le mouvement social* 245 (October–December 2013): 43–57.

65. Raffaele Cattedra, "Bidonville: Paradigme et réalité refoulée de la ville du XXᵉ siècle," in *Les mots de la stigmatisation urbaine*, ed. Jean-Charles Depaule (Paris: UNESCO, 2006), 123–63. The construction of "European cities" in the Maghreb (and Indochina) relegated indigenous cities to the status of suburbanity in need of reform. On this, see Xavier Huetz de Lemps and Odile Goerg, eds., "La ville coloniale," in *Histoire de l'Europe urbaine*, ed. Jean-Luc Pinol (Paris: Seuil, 2003), vol. 5. This ethno-racial division would evolve into a social division after independence. On this, see Rachid Sidi Boumedine, *Bétonvilles contre bidonvilles: Cent ans de bidonvilles à Alger* (Algiers: APIC, 2016).

66. Jim House, "L'impossible contrôle d'une ville coloniale? Casablanca, décembre 1952," *Genèses* 86, no. 1 (2012): 78–103; Jim House, "Shantytowns in the City, Algiers and Casablanca as a (Post)Colonial Archive," *Francosphères* 3, no. 1 (2014): 43–62; Emmanuel Blanchard, *La police parisienne et les Algériens, 1944–1962* (Paris: Nouveau Monde Éditions, 2011).

67. Annie Fourcaut, "De la classe au territoire ou du social à l'urbain," *Le Mouvement social* 200 (July–September 2002): 170–76.

68. Michel Lescure, *Les banques, l'État et le marché immobilier en France à l'époque contemporaine, 1820–1940* (Paris: École des hautes études en sciences sociales, 1982); Alexia Yates, *Selling Paris: Property and Commercial Culture in the Fin-de-Siècle Capital* (Cambridge, MA: Harvard University Press, 2015), Alexia Yates, *Real Estate and Global Urban History* (Cambridge: Cambridge University Press, 2021).

69. Rogelio Duocastella, *Mataró 1955: Estudio de sociología religiosa sobre una ciudad industrial española* (Madrid: Centro de Estudios de Sociología Aplicada, 1961); Jesús María Vázquez and Pablo López Rivas, *Palomeras: Una parroquia suburbana* (Madrid: CSIC, Instituto Balmes, 1966). Influenced especially by approaches developed by Father Lebret's economy and humanism movement (based in Lyon) and by Belgian religious sociology (developed in Louvain),

clerics and Catholic activists investigated the work, education, lifeways, and cultural and spiritual practices of first-generation urbanites. Father Lebret and other leaders of these movements circulated on both sides of the Atlantic, helping to develop one of the clearest truly transatlantic convergences of thought about what would come to be known as the informal city. On his work in Brazil, see Lícia Valladares, "Louis-Joseph Lebret et les favelas de Rio de Janeiro (1957–1959): Enquêter pour l'action," *Genèses* 60, no. 3 (2005): 31–56.

70. Constancio de Castro, "El Pozo del Tío Raimundo," *Estudios Geográficos* 22, nos. 84–85 (1961): 501–26; Miguel Siguán, *Del campo*; P. Montes Mieza, M. Paredes Grosso M., and A. Villanueva Paredes, "Los asentamientos chabolistas en Madrid," *Ciudad y Territorio* 2–3 (1976): 159–72; Franco Alasia and Danilo Montaldi, *Milano, Corea: Inchiesta sugli immigrati negli anni del miracolo* (Milan: Feltrinelli, 1960).

71. Giovanni Berlinguer and Piero Della Seta, *Borgate di Roma* (Rome: Riuniti, 1960); Monique Hervo, *Bidonvilles, l'enlisement* (Paris: F. Maspero, 1971).

72. Ramón López Lucio, "Génesis y remodelación de una parcelación marginal madrileña: El Pozo del Tío Raimundo (Vallecas)," *Ciudad y Territorio* 76 (April–June 1988), 55–70; Joan Busquets y Grau, *La urbanización marginal* (Barcelona: UPC, 1999); Federico Zanfi, *Città latenti: Un progetto per l'Italia abusiva* (Milan: Bruno Mondadori, 2008); Federico Zanfi, "The Città Abusiva in Contemporary Southern Italy: Illegal Building and Prospects for Change," *Urban Studies* 50, no. 16 (2013): 3428–45; Colette Pétonnet, *On est tous dans le brouillard* (Paris: CTHS, 2012).

73. The use of the term *marginal* in this context was distinct from its use in transnational debates about the culture of poverty. The Barcelona architect Joan Busquets chose this expression to refer to the subject of his PhD dissertation and kept this label for the later publication of part of it in 1999. Joan Busquets, "Las coreas de Barcelona: Estudio sobre la urbanización marginal" (PhD diss., Barcelona University, 1974); Joan Busquets, *La urbanización*. Informal urbanization was a central subject for the Laboratorio de Urbanismo, created in 1969 around Manuel de Solà-Morales in Barcelona's school of architecture, where Busquets studied and worked. Although his research demonstrated that in the "urbanización marginal" "the 'marginal' (or 'informal') was in its process and mechanisms, but not necessarily in its population nor final results" (*La urbanización*, 9), Busquets doesn't explain the choice of this expression.

74. Abdelmalek Sayad and Éliane Dupuy, *Un Nanterre algérien: Terre de bidonvilles* (Paris: Autrement, 1995); Natacha Lillo, *La petite Espagne de la Plaine-Saint-Denis 1900–1980* (Paris: Autrement, 2004); Volovitch-Tavares, *Portugais*; Vincent Lemire and Stéphanie Samson, eds., *Baraques: L'album photographique du dispensaire La Mouche-Gerland, 1929–1936* (Lyon: ENS Lyon, 2003); Melissa K. Byrnes, "Liberating the Land or Absorbing a Community," *French Politics, Culture & Society* 31, no. 3 (Winter 2013): 1–20.

75. For an overview of the general European scholarship on twentieth-century informal urbanization, including both midcentury studies and the historiography written by historians that we consider here, see Noel Manzano Gómez, "La urbanización informal en Europa en el siglo XX: Una historiografía," *O Social em Questão* 21, no. 42 (2018): 27–56.

76. Jacquemet, *Belleville*; Jean-Paul Burdy, *Le Soleil noir: Un quartier de Saint-Étienne 1840–1940* (Lyon: PU, 1989); Maurizio Gribaudi, *Itinéraires ouvriers: Espaces et groupes sociaux à Turin au début du XXᵉ siècle* (Paris: EHESS, 1987); Alain Faure, *Les premiers banlieusards: Aux origines de la banlieue de Paris, 1860–1940* (Paris: Créaphis, 1991); Annie Fourcaut, *Bobigny, banlieue rouge* (Paris: Éditions Ouvrières, 1988).

77. Françoise de Barros and Muriel Cohen. "Entre politiques urbaines et contrôle des migrants: La décolonisation inachevée des recensements des bidonvilles en France (années 1950–

années 1970)," *Histoire & Mesure* 34, no. 1 (2019): 151–84; Françoise de Barros, "L'État au prisme des municipalités: Une comparaison historique des catégorisations des étrangers en France (1919–1984)" (PhD diss., Université de Paris 1, 2004); Françoise de Barros, "Des 'Français musulmans d'Algérie' aux 'immigrés': L'importation de classifications coloniales dans les politiques du logement en France (1950–1970)," *Actes de la recherche en sciences sociales* 159, no. 4 (2005): 26–53; Marie-Claude Blanc-Chaléard, *En finir avec les bidonvilles* (Paris: Publications de la Sorbonne, 2016); Muriel Cohen, *Des familles invisibles* (Paris: Publications de la Sorbonne, 2020); Victor Collet, *Nanterre, du bidonville à la cité* (Marseille: Agone, 2019); Cédric David, "La résorption des bidonvilles de Saint-Denis: Politique urbaine et redéfinition de la place des immigrants dans la ville (années 1960–1970)," *Histoire Urbaine* 27, no. 1 (2010): 121–42.

78. Maurizio Gribaudi, *Paris, ville ouvrière—une histoire occultée: 1789–1848* (Paris: Découverte, 2014); Frondizi, *Paris*; Lecat, "La fabrique"; Anne Granier, "Une politique d'abandon surveillé: La zone de Boulogne-sur-Seine pendant l'entre-deux-guerres (1919–1933)," *Espaces et Sociétés* 171, no. 4 (2017): 19–36; Margot Delon, "Un espace à trois dimensions," *SociologieS*, http://sociologies.revues.org/5542; Jim House, "Shantytowns and the Disruption of Colonial Order in Late-Colonial Algiers and Casablanca," in *Francophone Cultures and Geographies of Identity*, ed. Adlai Murdoch and Zsuzsanna Fagyal (Newcastle: Cambridge Scholars, 2013), 76–92; Boumedine, *Bétonvilles*; Roseanna Webster, "Women and the Fight for Urban Change in Late Francoist Spain," *Past & Present* 260 no. 1 (2023): 158–99; Carlos Hernández Quero, "El desborde de la ciudad liberal: Cultura política y conflicto en los suburbios de Madrid (1880–1930)" (PhD diss., Universidad Complutense de Madrid, 2020); Francisco Andrés Burbano Trimiño, "La urbanización marginal durante el franquismo: El chabolismo madrileño (1950–1960)," *Hispania Nova* 18 (2020): 301–43; Inbal Ofer, "La Guerra de Agua: Notions of Morality, Respectability, and Community in a Madrid Neighborhood," *Journal of Urban History* 35, no. 2 (2009): 220–35; Inbal Ofer, *Claiming the City/Contesting the State: Squatting, Community Formation and Democratization in Spain (1955–1986)* (London: Routledge, 2017); Xavier Domènech, ed., "Movimiento vecinal y cambio político," special issue, *Historia del Presente*, n.s., 16 (2010); Mercè Tatjer Mir and Cristina Larrea Killinger, eds., *Barracas: La Barcelona informal del siglo XX* (Barcelona: MUHBA, 2010); Xavier Camino Vallhonrat, Òscar Casasayas Garbí, Pilar Díaz Giner, Maximiliano Díaz Molinaro, Cristina Larrea Killinger, Flora Muñoz Romero, and Mercè Tatjer Mir, eds., *Barraquisme, la ciutat (im)possible* (Barcelona: Generalitat de Catalunya, 2011); José Luis Oyón, Manel Guàrdia, Maribel Rosselló, David H. Falagán, and Joan Roger, eds., *La revolució de l'habitatge a les perifèries obreres i populars* (Barcelona: MUHBA, 2021).

79. Fabrizio Maccaglia, *Palerme, illégalismes et gouvernement urbain d'exception* (Lyon: ENS, 2009); Thomas Aguilera, *Gouverner les illegalismes urbains* (Paris: Dalloz, 2017); Thomas Aguilera, "L'informalité urbaine aux marges de la connaissance: Statistiques, cartographie et politiques des bidonvilles à Madrid," *Anthropologica* 61 (2019): 35–50.

80. An early attempt to overcome a national understanding of informal urbanization, though restricted to a specific region supposed to share some sociocultural features, is Lila Leontidou's *The Mediterranean City in Transition* (Cambridge: Cambridge University Press, 1990).

81. For further discussion, see, among others, Gonçalves, this volume; Charlotte Vorms, "Le franquisme vu des baraques," unpublished manuscript, 2024; Lícia Valladares, "Louis-Joseph Lebret"; Bryan McCann, *Hard Times in the Marvelous City* (Durham, NC: Duke University Press, 2014); Cathy Schneider, *Shantytown Protest in Pinochet's Chile* (Philadelphia: Temple University Press, 2010).

Chapter One

1. The literature is extensive, but we draw on Brodwyn Fischer, "Historicizing Informal Governance in 20th Century Brazil," *Contemporary Social Science* 17, no. 3 (2022): 205–21; Ananya Roy, "Urban Informality: The Production of Space and the Practice of Planning," in *The Oxford Handbook of Urban Planning*, ed. Rachel Weber and Randall Crane (Oxford: Oxford University Press, 2012), 691–705; Ananya Roy, "Why India Cannot Plan Its Cities," *Planning Theory* 8, no. 1 (2009): 76–87; Ann Varley, "Postcolonising Informality?," *Environment and Planning D: Society and Space* 31, no. 1 (2013): 4–22; Oren Yiftachel, "Theoretical Notes on 'Gray Cities': The Coming of Urban Apartheid?," *Planning Theory* 8 (2009): 88–100.

2. John Comaroff and Jean Comaroff, eds., *Law and Disorder in the Postcolony* (Chicago: University of Chicago Press, 2008).

3. José Luis Romero, *Latinoamerica: Las ciudades y las ideas* (Mexico City: Siglo XXI, 1976); Richard Morse, "Recent Research on Latin American Urbanization: A Selective Survey with Commentary," *Latin American Research Review* 1, no. 1 (1965): 35–74; Ángel Rama, *The Lettered City* (Durham, NC: Duke University Press, 1996); Edmundo O' Gorman, "Reflexiones sobre la distribución colonial de la ciudad de México" (1938), in *Seis estudios históricos de tema mexicano* (Xalapa: Universidad Veracruzana, 1960), 11–40. For a discussion of this historiography, see Adrián Gorelik, "Miradas sobre Buenos Aires: Los itinerarios urbanos del pensamiento social," in *Miradas sobre Buenos Aires: Historia cultural y crítica urbana* (Buenos Aires: Siglo XXI, 2004), 113–39.

4. Connolly, "Latin American."

5. Óscar Calvo Isaza, *Urbanización y revolución en América Latina: Santiago de Chile, Buenos Aires y Ciudad de México (1950–1980)* (Mexico City: El Colegio de México, Universidad Nacional de Colombia, 2023).

6. Figures are from Sonia Pérez Toledo, "Formas de gobierno local, modelos constitucionales y cuerpo electoral, 1824–1867," in *Historia política de la ciudad de México*, ed. A. Rodríguez Kuri (Mexico City: El Colegio de México, 2012), 221–86, 225; Ariel Rodríguez Kuri, *La experiencia olvidada: El Ayuntamiento de México: Política y gobierno, 1876–1912* (Mexico City: Universidad Autónoma de México, El Colegio de México, 1996), 82.

7. We cite this historiography later. For an introduction to the relationship between the city and the revolution, see John Lear, *Workers, Neighbors, and Citizens: The Revolution in Mexico City* (Lincoln: University of Nebraska Press, 2001).

8. The historiography on this topic is extensive and has grown in recent years. For classic approaches, see Jorge H. Jiménez Muñoz, *La traza del poder: Historia de la política y los negocios urbanos en el Distrito Federal: de sus orígenes a la desaparición del Ayuntamiento (1824–1928)* (Mexico City: Secretaría de Cultura del Distrito Federal, UACM, 2012); Carol McMichael, "The Urban Development of Mexico City, 1850–1930," in *Planning Latin America's Capital Cities*, ed. Arturo Almandoz (London: Routledge, 2002), 139–52; Erika Berra, "La expansión de la Ciudad de México y los conflictos urbanos, 1900–1930" (PhD diss., El Colegio de México, 1983).

9. Lear, *Workers*.

10. Claudia Agostini, *Monuments of Progress* (Calgary: University of Calgary Press, 2003), 57–64.

11. Such adoption is noted by Jiménez Muñoz, *La traza*, 35, and Ernesto Aréchiga Córdoba, "Lucha de clases en la ciudad: La disputa por el espacio urbano, ca. 1890–1930," in *Los trabajadores de la ciudad de México, 1860–1950: Textos en homenaje a Clara E. Lida*, ed. Carlos Illades and Mario Barbosa Cruz (Mexico City: El Colegio de México, Universidad Autónoma Metro-

politana, Campus Cuajimalpa, 2013), 31. Note the existence of an earlier regulation, from 1875, the "Bases a las que se sujetarán las colonias que se formen dentro del radio de la municipalidad de México" (reproduced in Jiménez Muñoz, *La traza*, 34).

12. Public Works Commission, cited by Berra, "La expansión," 187.

13. Art. 5. The agreement is reproduced in Berra, "La expansión," 196–99.

14. The term *colonia* referred, in nineteenth-century Mexico, to colonization. In the context of Porfirian Mexico City, colonization signified the incorporation of communal lands, ranches, and agrarian estates into a thriving real estate market.

15. Archivo Histórico de la Ciudad de México (AHCM), Fondo Ayuntamiento, Colonias, vol. 519, file 22.

16. Neighborhood organizational petitions for public services between 1890 and 1910 reflect this ambivalence. See Aréchiga Córdoba, "Lucha," 42–43.

17. This description pertains to Colonia Morelos. Consejo Superior de Salubridad, *Informes rendidos por los inspectores sanitarios de cuartel y los de distrito al Consejo Superior de Salubridad* (Mexico City: Imprenta de Gobierno en el Ex-Arzobispado, 1895), 11.

18. Thus, for example, the city council approved the construction of Colonia El Rastro in 1897 without committing to distribute public services: "This special case [the City Council] believes that it should receive the Colonia . . . for having constructed the City Hall a building that requires a special service as is the Rastro, and where it is necessary to facilitate the means for the numerous people who have business in the establishment to settle nearby; for that reason it proposes the admission of the Colonia as forming part of the City; but it believes that this Colonia being outside the perimeter for which it is calculating the sanitation of the city and being by special circumstances in a situation where it requires a special drainage service, it believes that for the time being the City Hall should not take the commitment to make municipal service." "García Teruel y Pablo Macedo solicitan establecer una Colonia en los terrenos del Rastro," AHCM, Fondo Ayuntamiento, Colonias, vol. 519, file 12.

19. Cited in Jiménez Muñoz, *La traza*, 191–92.

20. Lear, *Workers*; María Soledad Cruz Rodríguez, *Crecimiento urbano y procesos sociales en el Distrito Federal (1920–28)* (Mexico City: UAM, 1994).

21. Cruz Rodríguez, *Crecimiento*; María Cristina Montaño, *La tierra de Ixtapalapa: Luchas sociales desde las chinampas hasta la transformación urbana* (Mexico City: Universidad Autónoma Metropolitana, 1984); Ann Varley, "¿Propiedad de la revolución? Los ejidos en el crecimiento de la ciudad de México," *Revista Interamericana de la Planificación* 22 (1989): 125–55.

22. Antonio Azuela and Camilo Saavedra, "Uso, desgaste y reuso de la expropiación en la ciudad de México," in *Expropiación y conflicto social en cinco metrópolis latinoamericanas*, ed. Antonio Azuela (Mexico City: UNAM, Lincoln Institute of Land Policy, 2013), 409–54.

23. Aréchiga Córdoba, "Lucha"; Matthew Vitz, *A City on a Lake* (Durham, NC: Duke University Press, 2018); Ariel Rodríguez Kuri, *Historia del desasosiego: La Revolución en la Ciudad de México, 1911–1922* (Mexico City: El Colegio de México, 2010).

24. On the 1922 tenant strike, see Vitz, *City*, chap. 2. On tenant movements, see also Lear, "Mexico City."

25. "Sindicato de Colonos y Vecinos de Portales al General Lázaro Cárdenas, Presidente de la República, México, D.F., 25 August 1935," quoted in "Las condiciones de vida en las colonias populares," *Boletín del Archivo General de la Nación, México* 6, no. 2, April–June 1982, 17.

26. José Manuel Puig Causaranc, "Por qué y en qué extensión faltan los servicios de urbanización en el Distrito Federal," *Obras Públicas* 4 (April 1930): 225–31, 227.

27. "Sindicato de Colonos y Vecinos de Portales al General Lázaro Cárdenas, Presidente de la República, México, D.F., 21 December 1937," AGN, Fondo Lázaro Cárdenas, file 418.2/1.

28. "Sindicato de Colonos y Vecinos de Portales al General Lázaro Cárdenas . . . 21 December 1937."

29. Jiménez Muñoz, *La traza*, 255–59. See also Cruz Rodríguez, *Crecimiento*.

30. Sergio Miranda Pacheco, *La creación del Departamento del Distrito Federal: Urbanización, política y cambio institucional* (Mexico City: UNAM, 2008).

31. On the rise of the planning movement in Mexico, see Gerardo Sánchez Ruiz, *Planificación y urbanismo de la Revolución mexicana: Los sustentos de una nueva modernidad en la Ciudad de México* (Mexico City: UAM, 2002); Alejandrina Escudero, *Una ciudad noble y lógica: Las propuestas de Carlos Contreras Elizondo para la Ciudad de México* (Mexico City: UNAM, 2018).

32. "Actas de la Comisión de adiciones y reformas al Reglamento de Construcciones," AHCM, Fondo Departamento del Distrito Federal (DDF), Obras Públicas (OP), box 274, file 2.

33. One example, from February 1947 (approximate date), when the Office of Public Works reported that "Mr. Pedro Rojas has been selling land to various interested parties, without being subject to the approved planning project, and possibly without having authorized any subdivision blocking the street projected to the north of the Pilcomayo River; a situation that requires an inspection of the land, to determine if the facts in question are true, so that if so, the respective regulations in force will be followed." AHCM, DDF, OP, box 254, file 1.

34. The plan not only remained unfinished; its legal meaning had a remarkable ambiguity. Antuñano, "Planning."

35. There were ten offices or committees in the baroque municipal bureaucracy in charge of city planning, in the opinion of Enrique Guerrero, "Urbanismo oficial," *Arquitectura y lo Demás* 1 (1945): 16–22.

36. Ing. Luis Guzmán Castillo (Chief of the Coordination Section of the Office of the Regulatory Plan) to Chief of the Office of the Regulatory Plan, November 2, 1947, AHCM, DDF, OP, box 161.

37. City Growth Regulatory Commission, July 29, 1947, AHCM, DDF, OP, box 598, file 2.

38. Beginning in the 1970s, scholars documented how the Mexican political regime (what Wayne Cornelius called the "PRI-government apparatus") gained the support of the urban poor in exchange for urban services and land titles. Some scholars stressed the accomplishment of the Mexican state in meeting the demands of the urban poor, while others focused on its authoritarian character and its successful control over the "urban masses" for the sake of capitalist development. For examples of the first perspective, see Susan Eckstein, "The State and the Urban Poor," in *Authoritarianism in Mexico*, ed. José Luis Reyna and Richard S. Weinert (Philadelphia: Institute for the Study of Human Issues, 1977), 23–46; Wayne Cornelius, *Politics and the Migrant Poor in Mexico City* (Stanford, CA: Stanford University Press, 1975). Examples of the second perspective include Juan Manuel Ramírez Sáiz, *El movimiento urbano popular en México* (Mexico City: Siglo XXI, 1986); Jorge Alonso, ed., *Los movimientos sociales en el Valle de México* (Mexico City: SEP, 1986); Manuel Perlo Cohen, "Política y vivienda en México, 1910–1952," *Revista Mexicana de Sociología* 41, no. 3 (1981): 769–835.

39. Rodrigo Reyes Meneses, "Los efectos materiales del constitucionalismo mexicano: Una perspectiva de la sociología del derecho," in *La herencia del constitucionalismo mexicano y sus desafíos* (Mexico City: Suprema Corte de Justicia de la Nación, 2017), 301–29.

40. Brodwyn Fischer, *A Poverty of Rights* (Stanford, CA: Stanford University Press, 2008).

41. On the regime of government of the proletarian colonias, see Perló Cohen, "Política," *Revista Mexicana de Sociología* 41, no. 3 (1981): 769–835; Antonio Azuela and Maria Soledad Cruz Rodriguez, "La institucionalización de las colonias populares y la política urbana del DDF, 1940–1946," *Sociología* 9 (1989): 111–33; Cristina Sánchez Mejorada, *Rezagos de la modernidad: Memorias de una ciudad presente* (Mexico City: UAM, 2005).

42. On Ramos Millán, see Antuñano, "Planning," esp. chap. 5. On Escuadrón 201, see Ezequiel Cornejo Cabrera, "La colonia proletaria Escuadrón 201," *Estudios Sociológicos* 2 (1956): 170–73.

43. Instituto Nacional de la Vivienda, *Características, problemas y programa de acción en beneficio de las colonias proletarias* (Mexico City: Instituto Nacional de la Vivienda, 1957), 1.

44. Antuñano, "Planning." Still in 1975 the *Diario Oficial de la Federación* (*DOF*)published agreements on "planning projects" for Colonia Valle Gómez and others (*DOF*, March 23, 1975).

45. Of the 279 colonias proletarias that existed in 1955, 105 were formed during the presidency of Manuel Ávila Camacho (1940–1946). A further 52 were established during the presidency of Miguel Alemán Valdés (1946–1952), especially before 1950. Numbers and dates of the establishment of *colonias proletarias* can be seen in David Cymet Lerer and Guillermo Ortiz, *El problema de las colonias proletarias, Ciudad de México* (Mexico City: Escuela Superior de Ingeniería y Arquitectura, IPN, 1955), 68–72.

46. *Gaceta Oficial del Gobierno del Distrito Federal*, May 10, 1946.

47. Antonio Azuela and Rodrigo Reyes Meneses, "The Everyday Formation of Urban Space: Law and Poverty in Mexico City," in *The Expanding Spaces of Law*, ed. Irus Braverman, Nicholas Blomley, David Delaney, and Alexander Kedar (Stanford, CA: Stanford University Press, 2014), 167–89. See also Reyes Meneses, "Los efectos."

48. For example, the "National Law of Proletarian Colonization" presented in the Chamber of Deputies in December 1951 recognized the proletarian colonies as an "effective means for the widening and progress of the city, and the community that constitutes it . . . a positive social need, which must be satisfied by the State through adequate and timely legislation." Chamber of Deputies, "Diario de Debates de la Cámara de Diputados," December 30, 1951. Around the same time, in 1951 and 1952, DDF officials drafted a new planning law that would take effect in 1953. Initial versions of the law included "formation of proletarian colonies and expansion of existing ones" as one of the government's planning responsibilities. This reference would disappear in the final version of the law. Different versions of the law are found in AHCM, Gobernación, box 175.

49. The most important legal provisions to pursue this purpose were the Planning Act of 1953 and the Subdivisions Bylaw of 1941.

50. "Bases for the conclusion of agreements that are suspended," May 11, 1954, AHCM, DDF, OP, box 258, file 1.

51. See, for example, the case of the Fraccionamiento Presidentes de América, AHCM, DDF, OP, box 258, file 1.

52. Jorge Legorreta, "Renovación urbana para erradicar la herradura de tugurios del Centro Histórico," *La Jornada*, October 26, 2001.

53. *Mañana*, June 11, 1955.

54. On the history of Ciudad Nezahualcóyotl, see Vélez-Ibañez, *Rituals*; David Yee, "Shantytown Mexico: The Democratic Opening in Ciudad Nezahualcóyotl, 1969–1976," *The Americas* 78, no. 1 (2021): 119–47.

55. Paula López Caballero, *Indígenas de la nación: Etnografía histórica de la alteridad en México (Milpa Alta, siglos XVII–XXI)* (Mexico City: Fondo de Cultura Económica, 2017).

56. Montaño, *La tierra.* On the construction of Ciudad Universitaria, see UNAM, *Ciudad Universitaria: Crisol del México moderno* (Mexico City: UNAM, ICA, Fundación Miguel Alemán, Banco de México, 2009).

57. María Soledad Cruz Rodríguez, *Propiedad, poblamiento y periferia rural en la Zona Metropolitana de la Ciudad de México* (Mexico City: UAM-Azcapotzalco, RNIU 2001), 150.

58. The information presented here on *colonias* and *ejidos* was elaborated based on a specialized cartographic analysis by Isaías Torres and Andrea Villasís. We are grateful to María Soledad Cruz Rodríguez for the enormous amount of information she made available to us for this exercise.

59. In addition to the fact that the government was unable to prevent clandestine subdivisions on privately owned land and even land invasions, it was also unable to prevent the settlers from demanding their "recognition" (for the case of Colonia Ajusco, in the Coyoacán pedregales, see Jorge Alonso, *Lucha urbana y acumulación de capital* [Mexico City: Ediciones de la Casa Chata, 1980]). But it is also true that they were not viewed with sympathy and that an attempt was made to impose a policy of restricting the growth of the city.

60. María Soledad Cruz, "Las tierras ejidales y el proceso de poblamiento," in *Dinámica urbana y procesos sociopolíticos: Lecturas de actualización sobre la Ciudad de México*, ed. René Coulomb and Emilio Duhau (Mexico City: OICM, UAM-Azcapotzalco, 1993), 148.

61. This was provided for in the Agrarian Codes of 1934 and 1942, as well as in the Federal Agrarian Reform Law in force since 1972.

62. The AHCM contains evidence of this legal prosecution. AHCM, DDF, OP, file 658, bundle 1.

63. Antonio Azuela, "Avatares de un cronotopo: El ejido en el fin del orden postrevolucionario," in *Si persisten las molestias*, ed. Fernando Escalante (Mexico City: Cal y Arena, 2018), 53–88.

64. Arturo Warman, *Los campesinos, hijos predilectos del régimen* (Mexico City: Editorial Nuestro Tiempo, 1972).

65. This was illustrated by the work of Julio Calderón, who studied thirty-six settlers' mobilizations in *colonias* created in ejidos in Mexico City between 1980 and 1984. In none of them did settlers demand services from those who had sold them their plots. Julio Calderón, *Luchas por la tierra, contradicciones sociales y sistema político: El caso de las zonas ejidales comunales en la Ciudad de México*, mimeo (1986).

66. An emblematic case of those years was that of the Santa Cruz Acatlán ejido, near Ciudad Satélite, which became known as "The Golden Ejido" because of the profits some *ejidatarios* obtained from the expropriation of their lands. See Fernando Benítez, *Viaje al fondo de México* (Mexico City: Fondo de Cultura Económica, 1975).

67. Alberto Rébora, "Políticas de suelo urbano en México: Experiencias y perspectivas," in *Los pobres de la ciudad y la tierra*, ed. Alfonso Iracheta Cenecorta and Martim Smolka (Mexico City: El Colegio Mexiquense, Lincoln Institute of Land Policy, 2000), 215–27.

68. At least one-third of Pedregal de San Ángel was developed on land of Ejido de San Jerónimo Aculco.

69. Ann Varley, "La zona urbana ejidal y la urbanización de la Ciudad de México," *Revista A* (Universidad Autónoma Metropolitana-Azcapotzalco) 6, no. 15 (1985): 72.

70. Varley, "La zona," 74.

71. The government intervened and followed this conflict closely, as can be seen in a copious

file in the Archivo General de la Nación (AGN), Dirección General de Investigaciones Políticas y Sociales, box 1705-A, file 2.

72. Alonso, *Lucha.*

73. See the cases of Colonia Providencia, Nueva Atzacoalco, and Quinta María Elena, to the north of the city, and Olivar de los Padres and Molino de Rosas, to the south, in AHCM, DDF, OP, box 658, file 1.

74. Carlos Contreras, *El plano regulador del Distrito Federal* (Mexico City: Talleres Gráficos de la Nación, 1933), quoted in Sánchez Ruiz, *Planificación*, 98.

75. Mario Pani, "El problema de la habitación en la ciudad de México," June 1952, AHCM, DDF, OP, box 658, file 1.

76. Enrique Cervantes, *Tlalnepantla: Desarrollo metropolitano de la zona norte de la ciudad de México* (Mexico City: Ayuntamiento de Tlalnepantla, 1969).

77. Lane Simonian, *Defending the Land of the Jaguar: A History of Conservation in Mexico* (Austin: University of Texas Press, 1995); Humberto Urquiza, "Ciencia forestal, propiedad y conservación para el desarrollo nacional: Los estudios y trabajos ambientales de Miguel Ángel de Quevedo: Una historia de su influencia en las políticas de conservación" (PhD diss., UNAM, 2014); Vitz, *City.*

78. Although the most fragile ecosystems—the *chinampas* and the *pedregales*—are only a small proportion of this immense territory, the prohibition of urbanization applies without distinction to the whole of it.

79. AGN, Dirección General de Investigaciones Políticas y Sociales, box 1705-A, file 2.

80. Note by Elvia Sánchez Navarro on January 9, in unidentified newspaper, in AGN, Dirección General de Investigaciones Políticas y Sociales, box 1705-A, file 2.

81. For example, in a collective work on environmental problems in Mexico and Latin America, the contribution of the specialist in "irregular settlements" made no reference to the environmental dimension of the urbanization of popular sectors. Jorge Montaño, *Los pobres de la ciudad en los asentamientos espontáneos: Poder y política* (Mexico City: Siglo XXI, 1976). Neither for the journalist Arturo Sotomayor, author of an alarmist work on environmental problems, did the *colonias* represent an environmental problem. *La metrópoli mexicana y su agonía* (Mexico City: UNAM, 1973). It was the "smog" that attracted most of the attention.

82. Thus, for example, the "ecological preservation zones of population centers" were defined as an integral element of such centers, together with the urbanized area and the area susceptible to urbanization.

83. It should be noted that at the UN Summit on Human Settlements in Vancouver (1976), the environment was not highlighted as part of the urban agenda. Marta Schteingart and Clara Salazar, *Expansión urbana, sociedad y ambiente* (Mexico City: El Colegio de México, 2005).

84. Plan General del Plan Director del Distrito Federal, *Diario Oficial de la Federación*, November 30, 1976.

85. Plan General del Plan Director del Distrito Federal, *Diario Oficial de la Federación*, March 18, 1980. Two years later, the Declaration of Uses and Destinations for the Ecological Conservation Area of the Federal District was issued to specify and reinforce the restrictions to urbanization. *Diario Oficial de la Federación*, November 29, 1982.

86. Gabriel Quadri, "Una breve crónica del ecologismo en México," in *Servicios urbanos, gestión local y medio ambiente*, ed. Martha Schteingart and Luciano D'Andrea (Mexico City: El Colegio de México, 1991), 337-53.

87. "Plantea el DDF el rescate de la capital, con el PRUPE y sin recursos," *Proceso*, August 26, 1985.

88. See Programa de Control y Ordenamiento de los Asentamientos Humanos en el Suelo de Conservación, http://www.paot.org.mx/centro/programas/asentamientos/ase_resu.html. For a historical analysis of covenants, see Schteingart and Salazar, *Expansión*.

89. "Lomas de Seminario desalojada," *Proceso*, November 5, 1988.

90. The issue caused the first major split in the Pacto de Grupos Ecologistas, as part of it opposed the use of force. Gabriel Quadri, "Una breve."

91. Since then, it could be said that there was a "tower of babel in the Ajusco," but the tendency to reiterate the status of conservation land continues to this day. Antonio Azuela, "Una torre de babel para el Ajusco: Territorio, urbanización y medio ambiente en el discurso jurídico mexicano," in *Servicios urbanos, gestión local y medio ambiente*, ed. Martha Schteingart and Luciano D'Andrea (Mexico City: El Colegio de México, 1991), 205–29.

92. Still, in 2014 it was established, among the environmental policy goals, that the Ministry of Environment "will recover 600 hectares occupied by irregular human settlements" in conservation land. Programa Institucional de la Procuraduría Ambiental y del Ordenamiento Territorial, 2014–2018, *Gaceta Oficial del Distrito Federal*, May 13, 2016.

93. Many times, those who come to live in these rural areas also face discrimination from those who present themselves as the "original" inhabitants of these areas. See Paula López Caballero, *Indígenas de la nación* (Mexico City: Fondo de Cultura Económica, 2017).

94. Jill Wigle, "The 'Graying' of 'Green' Zones: Spatial Governance and Irregular Settlement in Xochimilco, Mexico City," *International Journal of Urban and Regional Research* 38, no. 2 (2014): 573–89.

95. Once again, it should be remembered that the creation of the conservation land referred to above includes only the territory of the nation's capital. That is, the strength of the environmentalist discourse in the Federal District did not prevent the State of Mexico from continuing to be the setting for the formation of new irregular settlements. Priscilla Connolly, "La urbanización irregular y el orden urbano en la Zona Metropolitana del Valle de México," in *Irregular: Suelo y mercado en América Latina*, ed. Clara Salazar (Mexico City: El Colegio de México, 2012), 379–425. However, because it has not been our intention to examine urban informality in the entire metropolitan zone of Mexico City, we can close our account of the four types of informalization that marked the history of the capital of the Mexican Republic in the twentieth century.

96. Patrick Joyce, *The Rule of Freedom: Liberalism and the Modern City* (London: Verso, 2003).

97. Ariel Rodríguez Kuri, *Museo del universo: Los Juegos Olímpicos y el movimiento estudiantil de 1968* (Mexico City: El Colegio de México, 2019), 414.

Chapter Two

1. Law of June 22, 1865, no. 2359, Art. 86.

2. The economic historian Paolo Malanima, estimating the resident population in cities with over ten thousand inhabitants, found that at the beginning of the sixteenth century, the urbanization rate in north-central Italy, the most urbanized region of the country, was around 16.4 percent; in Western Europe, it averaged just 5.6 percent (15.8 percent in the Netherlands, 3.2 percent in England and Wales). By the time of political unification in 1861, the rate had fallen to 13.3 percent, and in Western Europe it had risen to 16.7 percent (29.5 percent in the Netherlands, 40.8 percent in England and Wales). Paolo Malanima, "Urbanisation and the Italian

Economy during the Last Millennium," *European Review of Economic History* 9, no. 1 (2005): 97-122, tables 1 and 2. For a summary of the history of Italian urbanization in the modern and contemporary eras, see Marzio Barbagli and Maurizio Pisani, *Dentro e fuori le mura: Città e gruppi sociali dal 1400 a oggi* (Bologna: Il Mulino, 2012).

3. Carlo Cattaneo, one of the most acute observers of Italian urban life, wrote in 1836: "In Italy we are already rich enough in vast and empty buildings, in markets without merchants, in streets without travelers. In most of our beautiful and large cities we are similar to men who, thin from illness, sometimes go to the seaside in loose, floppy clothes, with trousers that flutter in place of the lost flesh." Cattaneo, "Ricerche sul progetto di una strada di ferro da Milano a Venezia," *Annali universali di statistica, economia pubblica, storia, viaggi e commercio* 47 (1836): 292.

4. Stefano Gallo, *Senza attraversare le frontiere: Le migrazioni interne dall'Unità a oggi* (Rome: Laterza, 2012), 56-74, 113-31.

5. See Vorms, this volume.

6. See Brodwyn Fischer, "From the Mocambo to the Favela," *Histoire et Mesure* 34, no. 1 (2019).

7. On the relationship between Italian urban planners and the fascist regime, see Giorgio Ciucci, *Gli architetti e il fascismo: Architettura e città 1922-1944* (Turin: Einaudi, 1989); Paolo Nicoloso, *Mussolini architetto: Propaganda e paesaggio urbano nell'Italia fascista* (Turin: Einaudi, 2008).

8. On illegal construction in Italy, see Alberto Clementi and Francesco Perego, eds., *La metropoli "spontanea": Il caso di Roma. 1925-1981: Sviluppo residenziale di una città dentro e fuori dal piano* (Bari: Dedalo, 1983); Marco Cremaschi, "L'abusivismo meridionale: Realtà e rappresentazione," *Meridiana* 9 (1990): 127-53; Federico Zanfi, "The Città Abusiva in Contemporary Southern Italy: Illegal Building and Prospects for Change," *Urban Studies* 50 (2013): 3428-45; Federico Zanfi, *Città latenti: Un progetto per l'Italia abusiva* (Milan: Bruno Mondadori, 2008); Fabrizio Maccaglia, *Palerme, illégalismes et gouvernement urbain d'exception* (Lyon: ENS, 2009); Paolo Berdini, *Breve storia dell'abusivismo in Italia: Dal ventennio fascista al prossimo futuro* (Rome: Donzelli, 2010).

9. On the transnational circulation of sanitarism, see Pierre-Yves Saunier and Shane Ewen, eds., *Another Global City: Historical Explorations into the Transnational Municipal Moment 1850-2000* (New York: Palgrave Macmillan, 2008); Martin V. Melosi, *The Sanitary City: Environmental Services in Urban America from Colonial Times to the Present* (Pittsburgh, PA: University of Pittsburgh Press, 2008); Jean-François Eck and Pierre Tilly, eds., *Innovations, réglementations et transferts de technologie en Europe du Nord-Ouest aux XIXᵉ et XXᵉ siècles* (Berlin: Lang, 2011). On the Italian case, see Claudio Pogliano, "L'utopia igienista (1870-1920)," in *Storia d'Italia: Annali 7* (1984): 587-631; Carla Giovannini, *Risanare le città: L'utopia igienista di fine Ottocento* (Milan: Franco Angeli, 1996); Guido Zucconi, *La città contesa: Dagli ingegneri sanitari agli urbanisti (1855-1942)* (Milan: Jaca Book, 1999); Guido Zucconi, *La città degli igienisti: Riforme e utopie sanitarie nell'Italia umbertina* (Rome: Carocci, 2022).

10. Quoted in Giulio Sabbatini, *Commento alle leggi sulle espropriazioni per pubblica utilità* (Turin: Unione Tipografico-Editrice Torinese, 1913), 2: 628.

11. Ministero di Agricoltura, Industria e Commercio, Direzione generale della statistica, *Censimento della popolazione del Regno d'Italia al 31 dicembre 1881: Relazione generale e confronti internazionali* (Rome: Tipografia Eredi Botta, 1885), xxvi-xxx.

12. Ministero di Agricoltura, *Censimento*, xxvii.

13. Ministero di Agricoltura, *Censimento*, xxx-xxxiii.

14. Law of January 15, 1885, no. 2892.

15. Atti Parlamentari, *Raccolta degli atti stampati della Camera*, session 1882–86, vol. 22, no. 261: *Disposizioni per provvedere alla pubblica igiene della città di Napoli*, 2. On the cholera epidemic of 1884 in Naples, see Frank M. Snowden, *Naples in the Time of Cholera, 1884–1911* (Cambridge: Cambridge University Press, 1995), 99–154.

16. Law of December 22, 1888, no. 5849, art. 39.

17. *Istruzioni ministeriali sull'igiene del suolo e dell'abitato*, June 20, 1896, no. 20000. These parameters were not binding but put in order various provisions in the municipal regulations that, according to the municipal and provincial law of 1889 (Royal Decree of February 10, 1889, no. 5921), established rules to ensure the solidity, hygiene, and aesthetics of buildings.

18. Direzione generale della statistica, *Risultati dell'inchiesta sulle condizioni igieniche e sanitarie nei Comuni del Regno: Relazione generale* (Rome: Tipografia in San Michele, 1886), xciv–cxii.

19. See Giovannini, *Risanare*, 67–73, 197–206. There is no trace of *baracche* in another ministerial investigation into Rome either: Ministero di Agricoltura, Industria e Commercio, Direzione generale di statistica, *Notizie sulle condizioni edilizie e demografiche della città di Roma e di alcune altre grandi città italiane ed estere nel 1888* (Rome: Tipografia eredi Botta, 1889).

20. See Paola Somma, "Le inchieste municipali sulle abitazioni nel primo decennio del '900," *Storia Urbana* 21(1982): 177–207 (quotation at 200 from a report by the Comune of Venice from 1910); Antonio Calò and Giulio Ernesti, "Casa e città nell'Italia giolittiana: Questione urbana e case popolari," *Storia Urbana* 82–83 (1998): 117–96.

21. Ministero di Agricoltura, Industria e Commercio, Direzione generale della statistica, *Censimento della popolazione del Regno d'Italia al 10 febbraio 1901*, vol. 5, *Relazione sul metodo di esecuzione e sui risultati del censimento, raffrontati con quelli dei censimenti italiani precedenti e di censimenti esteri* (Rome: Tipografia Nazionale di G. Bertero and C., 1904), xxxiv.

22. Comune di Roma, Servizio di statistica, *Il censimento 10–11 giugno 1911 nel comune di Roma e confronti con i risultati dei censimenti precedenti* (Rome: Tipografia Cecchini, 1915), 50–56. See also Colette Vallat, *Rome et ses borgate 1960–1980: Des marques urbaines à la ville diffuse* (Rome: École Française de Rome, 1995), 96–98.

23. Comune di Roma, *Il censimento*, 54.

24. See Vorms and House, both in this volume.

25. See Gallo, *Senza*, 117. On internal migration during the fascist period, see also Anna Treves, *Le migrazioni interne nell'Italia fascista: Politica e realtà demografica* (Turin: Einaudi, 1976); Ercole Sori, *L'emigrazione italiana dall'Unità alla Seconda guerra mondiale* (Bologna: Il Mulino, 1979), 441–73; Stefano Gallo, "Migrazioni interne al Meridione e politiche della mobilità tra le due guerre," *Meridiana* 92 (2018): 143–68.

26. Luigi Einaudi, "Censimento, collegio nazionale e collegio uninominale," *Corriere della Sera*, June 15, 1923, quoted in Einaudi, *Cronache economiche e politiche di un trentennio (1893–1925)* (Turin: Einaudi, 1965), 7: 272.

27. See Giuseppe Barone, "Sull'uso capitalistico del terremoto: Blocco urbano e ricostruzione edilizia a Messina durante il fascismo," *Storia Urbana* 19 (1982): 47–104; Antonino Checco, "Messina dal terremoto del 1908 al fascismo: La ricostruzione senza sviluppo," *Storia Urbana* 46 (1989): 161–92; Giacomo Parrinello, *Fault Lines. Earthquakes and Urbanism in Modern Italy* (New York: Berghahn, 2015), 84–118.

28. See Villani, this volume; Stefano Chianese, "The Baraccati of Rome: Internal Migration, Housing, and Poverty in Fascist Italy (1924–1933)," *HHB Working Paper Series* 6 (2016): 1–43; Brunero Liseo and Marco Teodori, "Emergenza abitativa e baracche a Roma tra le due guerre,"

in *Istituzioni, disuguaglianze, economia in Italia: Una visione diacronica*, ed. Donatella Strangio (Milan: Franco Angeli, 2018), 99–137.

29. See, e.g., Renato Ricci, "Baracche e sbaraccamenti," *Capitolium* 3 (1930): 142–49.

30. Gaetano Minnucci, "Baracca," in *Enciclopedia italiana di scienze, lettere ed arti* (Milan: Istituto Giovanni Treccani, 1930), 6:104–6.

31. Istituto centrale di statistica del Regno d'Italia, *Indagine sulle abitazioni al 21 aprile 1931–anno IX, parte prima: Testo relazione del Prof. Alfredo Niceforo* (Florence: Stabilimenti Grafici A. Vallecchi, 1936), 14.

32. Istituto centrale, 41.

33. Istituto centrale, table 2.

34. Istituto centrale di statistica del Regno d'Italia, *Indagine sulle abitazioni al 21 aprile 1931–anno IX, parte seconda: Tavole* (Florence: Stabilimenti Grafici A. Vallecchi, 1934), 35.

35. Along with operations in Rome described in this volume by Luciano Villani, events in Parma's Otretorrente district, which became subject to an urban redevelopment project because it was seen as an antifascist lair, are exemplary in this regard. See Margherita Becchetti and Paolo Giandebiaggi, eds., *I capannoni a Parma: Storie di persone e di città* (Parma: Mup, 2020).

36. See Vorms, Fischer, and House, all in this volume.

37. Royal Decree of July 27, 1934, no. 1265.

38. Law of July 6, 1939, no. 1092; Law of August 17, 1942, no. 1150.

39. On transformations in the legal concept of habitability between the end of the nineteenth century and the 1970s, see esp. Carmela Decaro Bonella, *La licenza di abitabilità* (Naples: Jovene, 1978).

40. Ministero dei Lavori Pubblici, *Commissione per lo studio del problema della casa* (Rome: Istituto Poligrafico dello Stato, 1949), 13.

41. This category was also present in subsequent censuses, albeit with some important changes, testifying to recognition of the peculiarity of a phenomenon that's evolution was to be monitored. Between 1951 and 1971, the number of "other lodgings" surveyed increased from 252,080 with 876,903 inhabitants, to 79,401 with 236,737 inhabitants.

42. Istituto centrale di statistica, *IX Censimento generale della popolazione 4 novembre 1951*, vol. 6, *Abitazioni* (Rome: Abete, 1957), 5.

43. Law of March 28, 1952, no. 200.

44. See Michela Morgante, "'The Little People Who Live in the Dark': Gli abitanti delle grotte di Napoli nella lente dell'UNRRA," in *Inchieste sulla casa in Italia: La condizione abitativa nelle città italiane nel secondo dopoguerra*, ed. Daniela Adorni and David Tabor (Rome: Viella, 2019), 247–65.

45. Atti Parlamentari, Senato della Repubblica, "Disegno di legge no. 1788: Autorizzazione della spesa di lire 6 miliardi per la costruzione in Napoli di case ultrapopolari," session of July 13, 1951, 2.

46. Atti Parlamentari, 2.

47. On the history and characteristics of the *Sassi*, see, esp., Amerigo Restucci, *Matera, i Sassi* (Turin: Einaudi, 1991); Angelo Del Parigi and Rosalba Demetrio, *Antropologia di un labirinto urbano: I Sassi di Matera* (Venosa: Edizioni Osanna Venosa, 1994); Alfonso Pontrandolfi, *La vergogna cancellata: Matera negli anni dello sfollamento dei Sassi* (Matera: Altrimedia, 2002); Anne Parmly Toxey, *Materan Contradictions: Architecture, Preservation and Politics* (Farnham: Ashgate, 2011); Pietro Laureano, *Giardini di pietra: I Sassi di Matera e la civiltà mediterranea* (Turin: Bollati Boringhieri, 2012).

48. Atti Parlamentari, Camera dei Deputati, "Disegno di legge n. 2141: Risanamento dei 'Sassi' di Matera," session of August 9, 1951, 2.

49. Atti Parlamentari, 2.

50. In April 1948, the communist leader Palmiro Togliatti had visited Matera and given a speech denouncing living conditions in the *Sassi*.

51. Law of May 17, 1952, no. 619.

52. The discussion in the Commissione Lavori Pubblici della Camera dei Deputati between February and March 1952 was also significant. See Atti Parlamentari, Camera dei Deputati, Settima Commissione Lavori Pubblici, "Discussione del disegno di legge 2144 e della proposta di legge di iniziativa del deputato Bianco," sessions of February 6, 1952 (572–76), February 8, 1952 (577–82), and March 14, 1952 (601–12).

53. For an analysis of this inquiry, see Gianluca Fiocco, *L'Italia prima del miracolo economico: L'inchiesta parlamentare sulla miseria, 1951–1954* (Manduria: Lacaita, 2004); Paola Rossi, ed., *Povertà, miseria e servizio sociale: L'inchiesta parlamentare del 1952* (Rome: Viella, 2018).

54. Camera dei Deputati, *Atti della commissione parlamentare di inchiesta sulla miseria in Italia e sui mezzi per combatterla*, vol. 1, *Relazione generale* (Rome: Camera dei Deputati, 1953), table 22.

55. Camera dei Deputati, *Atti della commissione*, vol. 6, *Indagini delle delegazioni parlamentari: La miseria nelle grandi città* (Rome: Camera dei Deputati, 1953), 13, 81, 174.

56. Camera dei Deputati, 6: 32.

57. Camera dei Deputati, 6:144.

58. Camera dei Deputati, 6:81–82.

59. Atti Parlamentari, Camera dei Deputati, "Disegno di legge n. 620: Provvedimenti per l'eliminazione delle abitazioni malsane," session of January 26, 1954, 1.

60. Atti Parlamentari, Senato del Regno, "Disegno di legge n. 2827: Lotta contro il tugurio e costruzioni di case per il popolo," session of February 24, 1953, 3.

61. Law of August 9, 1954, no. 640.

62. See Ministero dei Lavori Pubblici, *Prescrizioni tecniche relative ai progetti tipo di alloggi popolari, per accogliere le famiglie allocate in grotte, baracche, scantinati, edifici pubblici, locali malsani e simili* (Rome: Istituto Poligrafico dello Stato, 1954).

63. Law of August 9, 1954, n. 640, arts. 12–13.

64. UNRRA-CASAS, Prima Giunta, Ufficio distrettuale della Sicilia, *Inchiesta sulle abitazioni malsane in Sicilia*, vol. 1, *Relazione generale e allegati* (Catania, n.p., 1955), 3. UNRRA-CASAS was established in Italy in 1946 as an executive body of the UN Relief and Rehabilitation Administration with the purpose of assisting the homeless.

65. UNRRA-CASAS, 26.

66. UNRRA-CASAS, 41–42.

67. UNRRA-CASAS, 93.

68. UNRRA-CASAS, 42.

69. Comune di Roma, Ufficio di statistica e censimento, *Alloggi precari a Roma: Indagine disposta dalla Commissione consiliare speciale per lo studio del problema della casa sugli abitanti delle grotte dei ruderi e delle baracche*, supplement to the statistical bulletin (Rome: Comune di Roma, 1958), 17–18. On the origin and development of this survey, see Luciano Villani, "'Alloggi precari a Roma': Dibattito politico e indagine sull'abitazione informale alla vigilia di un passaggio cruciale nell'evoluzione dell'abusivismo nella capitale (1947–1957)," in *Inchieste*, ed. Daniela Adorni and Davide Tabor (Rome: Viella, 2019), 369–90.

70. Comune di Roma, *Alloggi precari*, 14.

71. Comune di Roma, 76.

72. Berlinguer and Della Seta, *Borgate*.

73. Berlinguer and Della Seta, 77.

74. Berlinguer and Della Seta, 78.

75. Franco Alasia and Danilo Montaldi, *Milano, Corea: Inchiesta sugli immigrati negli anni del miracolo* (Milan: Feltrinelli, 1960), 60.

76. Alasia and Montaldi, 75–76.

77. Leone Diena, *Borgata milanese* (Milan: Franco Angeli, 1963), 154–55. For a reconstruction of the historical origins of the Milanese *coree*, see John Foot, "Dentro la città irregolare: Una rivisitazione delle coree milanesi, 1950–2000," *Storia Urbana* 108 (2005): 139–56.

78. See Italo Insolera, *Roma moderna: Da Napoleone I al XXI secolo* (Turin: Einaudi, 2011), 279–95; Vallat, *Rome*, 117–23.

79. For a reconstruction of the debate on illegal construction in Rome in the 1950s, see Leonardo Benevolo, "Le discussioni e gli studi preparatori al Nuovo Piano Regolatore," *Urbanistica* 28–29 (1959): 91–126.

80. In this regard, the case of Palermo is especially interesting. See Maccaglia, *Palerme*, 125–57.

81. For a reconstruction of the story, see Bruno Bonomo, "Sviluppo urbano, pianificazione e governo del territorio negli anni della grande trasformazione: La frana di Agrigento," *Storia e Futuro*, 43 (2017): https://storiaefuturo.eu/sviluppo-urbano-pianificazione-e-governo-del -territorio-negli-anni-della-grande-trasformazione-la-frana-di-agrigento/.

82. Ministero dei Lavori Pubblici, *Commissione di indagine sulla situazione urbanistico-edilizia di Agrigento: Relazione al Ministro, on. Giacomo Mancini* (Rome: Ministero dei Lavori Pubblici, 1966), 76.

83. For the Italian urbanist Federico Zanfi, "the illegal city is the largest collective project ever carried out in our country: the projection into space of a certain family model, an imaginary and an implicit self-organization policy that has dramatically influenced Italian urban structure." Federico Zanfi, *Città latenti: Un progetto per l'Italia abusiva* (Milan: Bruno Mondadori, 2008), xiv.

Chapter Three

1. The literature on the history of the *chabolas* in the Franco era is relatively limited. There were a small number of studies carried out at the time of the *chabolas* and then a flurry of interest in the early 1980s, when the first democratic municipalities were remodeling these areas and rehousing their inhabitants. More recently, a team of anthropologists and geographers has studied the history of the phenomenon in Barcelona. Mercè Tatjer Mir and Cristina Larrea Killinger, eds., *Barracas: La Barcelona informal del siglo XX* (Barcelona: MUHBA, 2010); Xavier Camino Vallhonrat, Òscar Casasayas Garbí, Pilar Díaz Giner, Maximiliano Díaz Molinaro, Cristina Larrea Killinger, Flora Muñoz Romero, and Mercè Tatjer Mir, eds., *Barraquisme, la ciutat (im)possible* (Barcelona: Generalitat de Catalunya, 2011). On the phenomenon in Madrid, noteworthy studies include Inbal Ofer, *Claiming the City/Contesting the State: Squatting, Community Formation and Democratization in Spain (1955–1986)* (London: Routledge, 2017); Francisco Burbano Trimiño, "La autoconstrucción de Madrid durante el franquismo: El Pozo del Tío Raimundo" (MA thesis, Universidad Complutense de Madrid, 2015); Francisco

Andrés Burbano Trimiño, "La urbanización marginal durante el franquismo: El chabolismo madrileño (1950–1960)," *Hispania Nova* 18 (2020): 301–43. I am currently preparing a book on the history of the *chabolas* in Madrid and their administration by the public authorities under Francoism.

2. These figures were produced by the town planning authority in Madrid, which also managed informal urbanization in the city. The number of inhabitants has been extrapolated from the number of *chabolas*. These figures should be taken mainly as an order of magnitude. Apart from the fact that counting informal housing, as with any illegal or clandestine activity, is complicated, the definition of *chabolas* is very vague and varies from one actor to the next. On the counting of informal settlements, see Françoise de Barros and Charlotte Vorms, "Favelas, bidonvilles, *baracche*, etc.: Recensements et fichiers," *Histoire & Mesure* 34, no. 1 (2019): 3–14. On the counting of Madrid's *chabolas* and the definition of this category, see Charlotte Vorms, "La périphérie sous surveillance: Le recensement des baraques et de leurs habitants à Madrid sous le franquisme," *Histoire & Mesure* 34, no. 1 (2019): 93–120.

3. See Françoise de Barros's chapter in this volume.

4. Madrid's *ensanche* plan was adopted in 1860 and the national framework for *ensanches* (Ensanche de Población Act) in 1864. On the different *ensanches de población*, see Laurent Coudroy de Lille, "L'*ensanche de población* en Espagne, invention d'une pratique d'aménagement urbain, 1840–1890" (PhD diss., Université de Paris X, 1994); Laurent Coudroy de Lille, "La question des *ensanches* (1860–1910): Problème d'histoire et d'historiographie urbaine en Espagne," in *Recherches sur l'histoire de l'État dans le monde ibérique (XVᵉ-XXᵉ siècles)*, ed. Jean-Frédéric Schaub (Paris: Rue D'Ulm, 1993), 263–83.

5. These characteristics can also be found in many Latin American cities. Agustín E. Ferraro and Miguel A. Centeno, *State and Nation Making in Latin America and Spain: The Rise and Fall of the Developmental State* (New York: Cambridge University Press, 2019).

6. Antonio Azuela de la Cueva, "Low Income Settlements and the Law in Mexico City," *International Journal of Urban and Regional Research* 11, no. 4 (1987): 522–42; Priscilla Connolly, "Latin American Informal Urbanism," in *Marginal Urbanisms*, ed. Felipe Hernández and Axel Becerra (Newcastle upon Tyne: Cambridge Scholars, 2017), 22–47.

7. Data taken from the municipal registers.

8. On the suburb of Chamberí, see Elia Canosa Zamora, Jesús Ollero Carrasco, Julio Penedo Cobo, and Isabel Rodríguez Chumillas, *Historia de Chamberí* (Madrid: Ayuntamiento de Madrid, 1988); Rubén Pallol, *El ensanche norte: Chamberí, 1860–1931: Un Madrid moderno* (Madrid: Los Libros de la Catarata, 2015).

9. Tortosa and Gandia, for example. See Laurent Coudroy de Lille, "Los ensanches españoles vistos desde fuera: Aspectos ideológicos de su urbanismo," *Ciudad y Territorio Estudios Territoriales (CyTET)* 119–20 (1999): 235–51.

10. On land prices in the *ensanche*, see Rafael Mas, "La actividad inmobiliaria del Marques de Salamanca en Madrid (1862–1875)," *Ciudad y Territorio* (1978): 47–70. On land prices in the *extrarradio*, see Charlotte Vorms, *Bâtisseurs de banlieue à Madrid: Le quartier de la Prosperidad (1860–1936)* (Paris: Créaphis, 2012). The term *extrarradio* originally had a fiscal meaning, because the *ensanche*'s perimeter followed the city's octroi wall. Use of the term to refer to this ring located beyond the *ensanche* became widespread, first in administrative vocabulary and then in everyday language. On the history of the term *extrarradio*, see Charlotte Vorms, "Extrarradio," in *L'aventure des mots de la ville*, ed. Christian Topalov, Laurent Coudroy de Lille,

Jean-Charles Depaule, and Brigitte Marin (Paris: Bouquins/R. Laffont, 2010): 459–64; Charlotte Vorms, "Naming Madrid's Working-Class Periphery 1860–1970: The Construction of Urban Illegitimacy," in *What's in a Name? Talking about Urban Peripheries*, ed. Richard Harris and Charlotte Vorms (Toronto: University of Toronto, 2017): 209–30.

11. Ayuntamiento de Madrid, *Ensanche de las poblaciones: Disposiciones oficiales de carácter general relativas al ensanche de Madrid desde el Real decreto de 8 de Abril de 1857* (Madrid: Imprenta Municipal, 1917).

12. E.g., Archivo de Villa de Madrid (AV), *Secretaría* 4–261–66.

13. AV *Secretaría* 5–68–76.

14. See, e.g., AV *Secretaría* 5–68–5.

15. See, e.g., AV *Secretaría* 7–245–32.

16. Underlining appears in original. AV *Secretaría* 5–66–82.

17. On how the illegalization of informal urbanization neighborhoods was shaped by law in Mexico, see Antonio Azuela, "Low Income."

18. Pedro Núñez Granés, *El problema de la urbanización del Extrarradio de dicha Villa desde los puntos de vista técnico, económico, administrativo y legal* (Madrid: Imprenta Municipal, 1920), 12.

19. This mechanism is well documented in the case of Brazil: Brodwyn Fischer, *A Poverty of Rights* (Stanford, CA: Stanford University Press, 2008); Rafael Soares Gonçalves, *Favelas do Rio de Janeiro: História e direito* (Rio de Janeiro: Pallas/PUC-Rio, 2013). It is also evident, albeit to varying degrees in Mexico: Connolly, "Latin American."

20. On the role of the construction of a welfare system in defining nationality and controlling migration, see, in particular, Paul-André Rosental, "Migrations, souveraineté, droits sociaux. Protéger et expulser les étrangers en Europe du XIXe siècle à nos jours," *Annales: Histoire, Sciences Sociales* 66 (2011): 335–73.

21. Alejandro Pérez-Olivares, *Madrid cautivo: Ocupación y control de una ciudad (1936–1948)* (Valencia: Universitat de València, 2020); Gutmaro Gómez Bravo and Jorge Marco, *La obra del miedo: Violencia y sociedad en la España Franquista (1936–1950)* (Madrid: Península, 2011).

22. On the politicization of the peripheral neighborhoods in the first third of the twentieth century, see Carlos Hernández Quero, "El desborde de la ciudad liberal: Cultura política y conflicto en los suburbios de Madrid (1880–1930)" (PhD diss., Universidad Complutense de Madrid, 2020).

23. Ley de base para la Ordenación urbana de Madrid of November 25, 1944, published in *Boletín Oficial del Estado* (*BOE*) of November 26, 1944.

24. *BOE*, October 17, 1947.

25. Marco Ferreri, *El pisito* (Documento Films, 1959).

26. Ley de 12 de mayo de 1956 sobre Régimen de Suelo y Ordenación Urbana.

27. On the Land Law, see José María Baño León, *Derecho urbanístico común* (Madrid: IUSTEL, 2009); Martín Bassols Coma, *Génesis y evolución del derecho urbanístico español (1812–1956)* (Madrid: Montecorvo, 1973); Luciano Parejo Alfonso, *La ordenación urbanística: El período 1956–1975* (Madrid: Montecorvo, 1979); Luciano Parejo Alfonso, "L'évolution du cadre juridique de la production de la ville depuis 1956," in *L'urbanisme espagnol depuis les années 1970: La ville, la démocratie et le marché*, ed. Laurent Coudroy de Lille, Céline Vaz, and Charlotte Vorms (Rennes: Presses Universitaires de Rennes, 2013): 25–38.

28. They nevertheless retained a large share of the profits from the transactions.

29. On Francoist housing policy and the rise of land developers, see Céline Vaz, "Le franquisme et la production de la ville: Politiques du logement et de l'urbanisme, mondes professionnels et savoirs urbains en Espagne des années 1930 aux années 1970" (PhD diss., Université de Paris 10, 2013).

30. With the introduction of the zoning principle, the urban planning documents drawn up by the public authorities ultimately determined what could be done on each piece of land, with heavy consequences for real estate prices.

31. This was certainly the case with one of the most prominent developers, José Banús. Banús came from a humble background—his father was a bricklayer and small building contractor and he himself had left school early. He joined Franco's fifth column in Madrid. He was arrested and sentenced to death by the Republican justice system. His subsequent social rise was founded on the relationships he had built up during the war. Together with his brother, he set up a construction company that was awarded several public construction projects, including work on the pharaonic Valle de los Caídos monument project, which was built using prison labor. He then moved into property development, first in Madrid and then in Marbella on the Mediterranean coast of Andalusia. On the wealth of the regime's oligarchy, see Mariano Sánchez Soler, *Ricos por la guerra de España: El enriquecimiento de la oligarquía franquista desde 1936 hasta la transición* (Madrid: Raíces, 2007).

32. Decree of the presidency of the government of August 23, 1957.

33. See Luciano Villani's chapter in this volume.

34. See Jim House's chapter in this volume.

35. This period of rural exodus took place in a context in which public investment was directed far more to the cities than the countryside. See Ferraro and Centeno, *State and Nation.*

36. Archivo Regional de la Comunidad de Madrid (ARCM), Comisaría General de Ordenación Urbana de Madrid y de Sus Alrededores (CGOUMA), 252414/1: Servicio de Inspección, September 2, 1957.

37. ARCM 252414/1.

38. Preserved in the town planning board collection at the ARCM.

39. Antonio Ferres, *La Piqueta* (Barcelona: Destino, 1959). Curiously, the novel escaped censorship, unlike the author's later works, which forced him to go into exile.

40. The municipal engineer Pedro Núñez Granés was preoccupied by this problem, which inspired a major urban design competition in 1928. See Núñez Granés, *El problema.*

41. Frédéric Dufaux and Annie Fourcaut, *Le monde des grands ensembles* (Grâne: Créaphis, 2004).

42. On the Restoration regime, see, in particular, José Varela Ortega, *Los amigos políticos, partidos, elecciones y caciquismo en la Restauración (1875–1900)* (Madrid: Alianza Editorial, 1977); Antonio Robles Egea, ed., *Política en penumbra: Patronazgo y clientelismo políticos en la España contemporánea* (Madrid: Siglo XXI, 1996); "Historia social: Clientelas, caciquismo y poder en la Restauración," special issue, *Historia Social* 36 (2000). On caciquism in Madrid, see Javier Moreno Luzón, *Romanones: Caciquismo y política liberal* (Madrid: Alianza Editorial, 1998).

43. Universal male suffrage was introduced in 1890 in Spain.

44. In Latin America, the same kind of process, whereby informal districts appear and are then progressively integrated into the urban fabric and its networks, can be found in Mexico. See Connolly, "Latin American"; Azuela and Antuñano, this volume.

45. The military engineer Eduardo Gallego, who sat on the town planning board as a representative of the ministry of the armed forces, tended to defend the informal suburbs against

a repressive policy. See the acts of the Comisión de Urbanismo de Madrid, preserved in what is currently called the Centro de Documentación de Medio Ambiente y Ordenación del Territorio de la Comunidad de Madrid.

46. This figure is based on the analysis of a sample of 365 households evacuated during the operations carried out in 1954–1955—the first such operations to be undertaken. However, the families listed had been registered by the authorities one or two years earlier, and these were the only families that the authorities considered to have a right. Those who had managed to settle under the police surveillance radar in the meantime were not counted.

47. Events would be staged for the press showing the housing minister or his representative ceremoniously handing over the keys to a family or families moving into their modern new homes. A priest would also be present to bless the public housing complex.

48. This figure results from an analysis of demolition records. ARCM, Coplaco, 903142/2.

Chapter Four

1. Livio Toschi, "Edilizia economica e popolare a Roma (V): L'amministrazione Nathan e le casette comunali per i baraccati," *Edilizia Popolare* 252–53 (1997): 4–15.

2. Comune di Roma-servizio di statistica, *Il censimento 10–11 giugno 1911* (Rome: Tip. Cecchini, 1915), 54; Archivio storico capitolino (ASC), Ripartizione VIII Igiene e sanità (1871–1940), Carteggio, series 1, b. 26, f. 1, n.d. but assumed to be 1913.

3. Edoardo e Duilio Susmel, ed., *Opera omnia di Benito Mussolini* (Florence: La Fenice, 1951–1963), 22:48.

4. Vittorio Vidotto, "La capitale del fascismo," in *Roma Capitale: Storia di Roma dall'Antichità ad oggi*, ed. Vittorio Vidotto (Rome: Laterza, 2002), 379–413; Vittorio Vidotto, "I luoghi del fascismo a Roma," *Dimensioni e problemi della ricerca storica* 2 (2005): 39–51.

5. Vittorio Vidotto, "La Roma di Mussolini," in *La modernità totalitaria: Il fascismo italiano*, ed. Emilio Gentile (Rome: Laterza, 2008), 159–71, esp. 163–64; Emilio Gentile, *Fascismo di pietra* (Rome: Laterza, 2007).

6. Gentile, "Fascismo," 159–63.

7. I Congresso Nazionale di Urbanistica, *Discorso inaugurale di S. E. Giuseppe Bottai* (Rome: Tipografia delle Terme, 1937), 5.

8. For a related example, see Charlotte Vorms's account of Francoist Spain, in this volume.

9. The governorate was created to administer the capital under fascism, replacing the mayor, the municipal government, and the municipal council. The governor was appointed directly by the head of the national government and thus had no autonomy.

10. Emilio Gentile, *Le origini dell'ideologia fascista (1918–1925)* (Bari: Laterza, 1975); Pier Giorgio Zunino, *L'ideologia del fascismo: Miti, credenze e valori nella stabilizzazione del regime* (Bologna: Il Mulino, 2005).

11. On Cremonesi and his experience leading the Capitoline administration, see Mario Belardinelli, "Filippo Cremonesi e l'amministrazione capitolina dal liberalismo al fascismo (1922–1926)," *Roma moderna e contemporanea* 1–2 (2013): 7–33; Paola Salvatori, *Il Governatorato di Roma, L'amministrazione della capitale durante il fascismo* (Milan: Franco Angeli, 2006).

12. SPQR, *Memoriale di Roma al Governo Nazionale—February 1923* (Rome: Tipografia Centenari, 1923), 24.

13. Archivio storico capitolino (ASC), Ripartizioni, Ripartizione V LLPP/Ispettorato edilizio, 1922/5151/1922, report from August 24, 1922.

14. ASC, Ripartizioni, Ripartizione V LLPP/Ispettorato edilizio, 1922/5151/1922, report from August 24, 1922.

15. Vittorio Vidotto, *Roma contemporanea* (Rome: Laterza, 2001), 178–85.

16. Emilio Gentile, *Il culto del littorio: La sacralizzazione della politica nell'Italia fascista* (Rome: Laterza, 2005), 130. See also Andrea Giardina and André Vauchez, *Il mito di Roma: Da Carlo Magno a Mussolini* (Rome: Laterza, 2000).

17. Susmel, *Opera*, 22:48. Cremonesi was among those who credited Mussolini with resurrecting "the ancient spirit of *romanità*" in the new fascist Italy. Cremonesi, "Premessa," *Capitolium* 1 (1925): 2.

18. Appio II, "Roma nell'ultimo triennio," *Capitolium* 7 (1925): 437.

19. ASC, Ripartizione V, LLPP-Ispettorato edilizio, 1924/29218/1924, notice of August 24, 1924.

20. ASC, Ripartizione V, LLPP-Ispettorato edilizio, 1924/29218/1924, notice of August 24, 1924.

21. Archivio centrale dello Stato (ACS), Presidenza del consiglio dei ministri (Pcm), 1927, f. 3.19.872.

22. Nello Ciampi, "Le nuove case per i baraccati," *Capitolium* 12 (1926): 761–65.

23. Ciampi. "Le nuove," 762.

24. For the importance of the sanitarist tradition in defining the idea of habitability in Italy, see Francesco Bertolini, this volume.

25. "I trogloditi di fuori Porta del Popolo," *Il Messaggero*, February 3, 1923.

26. "I trogloditi di fuori Porta del Popolo," *Il Messaggero*, February 25, 1923.

27. "I trogloditi," February 25, 1923.

28. "I trogloditi fuori Porta del Popolo," *Il Messaggero*, January 17, 1923.

29. One article complained that faced with the *baracche*, foreign tourists could not resist the temptation to photograph them, collecting "documents, which to our disgrace, travel the world, giving us an unenviable reputation abroad," "I trogloditi di fuori Porta del Popolo," *Il Messaggero*, January 24, 1923.

30. "Una testimonianza d'inciviltà che occorre distruggere," *La Tribuna*, November 16, 1924.

31. This campaign was orchestrated several times by the newspaper of Arnaldo Mussolini, Benito's brother. For the period preceding the speech of May 26, 1927, see "L'ora delle grandi città," *Il Popolo d'Italia*, January 3, 1926, quoted in in Treves, *Le migrazioni*, 68–69.

32. Susmel, *Mussolini*, 12:366.

33. In particular, in the magazines and in the positions expressed by reformist socialism, without ever being opposed, however, to the central role assumed by cities in the organization of economic and social life. See Danilo Breschi, *Mussolini e la città: Il fascismo tra antiurbanesimo e modernità* (Milan: Luni Editrice, 2018), 83–154.

34. Angelo Ventrone, *La seduzione totalitaria: Guerra, modernità, violenza politica* (Rome: Donzelli, 2004), 10–12.

35. In reality, regardless of ambiguity about what should be considered urban or rural, it is not certain that rural fertility was higher than that recorded in the urban environment. See Carl Ipsen, *Demografia totalitaria: Il problema della popolazione nell'Italia fascista* (Bologna: Il Mulino, 1997), 190.

36. Oswald Spengler. *Il tramonto dell'occidente*, trans. and introduced by Julius Evola (Milan: Longanesi, 1957).

37. Renzo De Felice, *Mussolini il duce: I—Gli anni del consenso 1929–1936* (Turin: Einaudi, 1974), 38–42. Spengler and Mussolini wrote the prefaces to the Italian version of Richard Korherr's *Regresso delle nascite: Morte dei popoli* (Rome: Libreria del Littorio, 1928). When Spengler

published *Jahre der Entscheidung* in 1933, Mussolini had it translated into Italian. Spengler, *Anni decisivi*, translated and introduced by Vittorio B. Brocchieri (Milan: Bompiani, 1934).

38. For a summary verification of the results, see the judgement of Renzo De Felice, *Mussolini il duce*, 151–57.

39. On the first, see Valerio Castronovo, *Lo sviluppo economico e sociale*, in *Torino 1920–1936: Società e cultura tra sviluppo industriale e capitalismo* (Turin: Ed. Progetto, 1976), 5–11. On the multiple objectives and meanings of fascist ruralism, see Andrea Di Michele, "I diversi volti del ruralismo fascista," *Italia contemporanea* 199 (1995): 243–67; Mauro Stampacchia, *Ruralizzare l'Italia: Agricoltura e bonifiche tra Mussolini e Serpieri 1928–1943* (Milan: Franco Angeli, 2000). On the second, see Mario Isnenghi, *Il ruralismo nella cultura italiana*, in *Storia dell'agricoltura italiana in età contemporanea*, ed. Piero Bevilacqua (Venice: Marsilio, 1991), 3:898.

40. Piero Melograni, *Gli industriali e Mussolini: Rapporti tra Confindustria e fascismo dal 1919 al 1929* (Milan: Longanesi, 1980), 263, quoted in Breschi, *Mussolini*, 353.

41. Michele Sernini, "Le circoscrizioni amministrative nella politica di controllo degli insediamenti in Italia dal 1925 ad oggi," *Storia Urbana* 6 (1978): 22–55.

42. In this regard, the interview with the governor of Rome, Boncompagni Ludovisi, was significant. In distinguishing between "pathological" and "physiological" urbanism, he counted as the main cause of the first "the influx of undesirable guests." "L'urbanesimo a Roma: I compiti del Governatorato," *Il Popolo d'Italia*, December 6, 1928, quoted in Breschi, *Mussolini*, 353. In the same way, before the law of December 24, 1928, was promulgated, the leaders of the Capitoline administration requested the intervention of police headquarters for the "repatriation of undesirables," in compliance with government directives. ASC, Ufficio di assistenza sociale (UAS), *carteggio con titolario* (c.t.), *classe* 7, b. 92, f. 11, note from December 23, 1927.

43. The paper began publishing in October 1925 to replace the Roman edition of *Il Popolo d'Italia*, the national organ of the fascist party, becoming the voice of the regime in the capital. A newspaper attentive to urban events, it was sometimes the promoter of initiatives that found effective realization, as in the case of the *sbaraccamento* of October 28, 1927.

44. Ippolito Bastiani, "Un ignobile sfruttatore della povertà inviato al confino," *Il Popolo di Roma*, July 17, 1927; "Una protesta di 47 famiglie," July 16, 1927; "Da Neroni a Carrai: L'uno vale l'altro," July 23, 1927.

45. Ippolito Bastiani, "Dentro e fuori Porta S. Giovanni: Eccellenza, bisogna provvedere!," *Il Popolo di Roma*, July 5, 1927. The same day, governor Potenziani went to visit via Alba, accompanied by journalists. "Col governatore fra la povera gente," July 6, 1927.

46. Ippolito Bastiani, "Case degli sfrattati o casette operaie?," *Il Popolo di Roma*, July 14, 1927. *Domicilio coatto* was a form of internal exile originally adopted in 1863 and later adapted by the fascist regime.

47. Ippolito Bastiani, "Non diminuzione di affitti; ma demolizione," *Il Popolo di Roma*, July 30, 1927.

48. Ippolito Bastiani, "Case a tipo operaio," *Il Popolo di Roma*, September 15, 1927.

49. "Dalle baracche alle strade," *Il Popolo di Roma*, September 25, 1927.

50. "Monte Gallo rimediare al passato," *Il Popolo di Roma*, March 14, 1928.

51. In a letter addressed to the ICP's Alberto Calza Bini, Mussolini attached a clipping of the article "Per l'Annuale della Marcia su Roma oltre 2 mila vani saranno pronti a sostituire le baracche," which appeared in *Il Popolo di Roma* on September 14, 1927, asking: "Can you confirm the enclosed news that—needless to say—made me very pleased? Demolition of a total of 2,000 rooms would be a beautiful celebration of the fifth annual. I would also be satisfied with

1,500 to start, or rather continue," ACS, Segreteria particolare del duce (SPD), *carteggio ordinario* (c.o.), f. 509813, Mussolini to Calza Bini, September 14, 1927. The previous day the same newspaper ran the headline "Per volere di Benito Mussolini le baracche saranno abbattute," even claiming that what was planned was "the complete demolition of all the Abyssinian villages," *Il Popolo di Roma,* September 13, 1927. It seems, however, that it was the paper that promoted the initiative, as clarified in the article "Oltre 5000 famiglie nelle baracche," September 9, 1927.

52. ACS, SPD, c.o., f. 509813, note from Mussolini to Calza Bini, September 16, 1927.

53. ASC, UAS, c.t., classe 7, b. 92, f. 21, communication from Mussolini to Boncompagni, November 25, 1928.

54. Benito Mussolini, "Cifre e deduzioni: Sfollare le città," *Il Popolo d'Italia,* November 22, 1928.

55. Law of December 24, 1928, n. 2961. The prefect was the state's local representative.

56. See Charlotte Vorms, this volume.

57. ASC, UAS, c.t., classe 7, b. 90, f. 7, note from UAS to the *questura* in Rome, March 1929.

58. ASC, UAS, c.t., classe 7, b. 90, f. 4, handwritten note from the delegate for welfare services to the secretary-general of the governorate.

59. Ippolito Bastiani, "Case da abbattere, uomini da salvare," *Il Popolo di Roma,* November 23, 1928.

60. "Le baracche in muratura," *Il Popolo di Roma,* January 10, 1929. See also "Una piccola abitante di un 'villaggio abissino' annegata nel Tevere," *Il Popolo di Roma,* July 19, 1927.

61. "Interessi cittadini: Torrespaccata-Santa Maura," *Il Popolo di Roma,* August 3, 1927; "Baracche in legno e baracche in muratura," August 5, 1927; "Case a tipo operaio," September 15, 1927.

62. "Le baracche in muratura e il nuovo piano regolatore," *Il Popolo di Roma,* August 11, 1927.

63. "Baracche in legno e baracche in muratura"; "Case a tipo operaio"; "La casa e l'igiene," *Il Popolo di Roma,* October 14, 1927; "Baracche e casette esempio ammonitore," October 25, 1927.

64. However, these aspects also refer to the social and material conditions of inhabitants: only those able to afford it could restore their own houses.

65. On the *borgate ufficiali,* see Villani, *Le borgate;* Luciano Villani and Milena Farina, *Borgate romane: Storia e forma urbana* (Melfi: Libria, 2017).

66. In 1930, around 300 *baracche* were demolished. In 1931, 514 were demolished by the governorate, plus another 126 by private individuals, ASC, UAS, c.t., *classe* 6, b. 74, f. 4, handwritten note.

67. ASC, Gabinetto del Sindaco, 1938, b. 1621, *titolo* 1, *classe* 9–1. The summary table indicates the presence of both masonry and wooden *baracche* but does not specify the material of those demolished or cleaned.

68. ASC, UAS, c.t., *classe* 7, b. 95, f. 2, document from Raffaello Ricci to Governor Boncompagni, January 18, 1930.

69. Alberto Calza Bini, "Difficoltà grande," *Il Popolo di Roma,* November 29, 1928.

70. Alberto Calza Bini, "L'Istituto per le case popolari e la crisi degli alloggi," December 1928, ASC, SPD, c.o., 1922–43, f. 509813.

71. Archivio Ater, attachments to the minutes of the CdA, 1936, Calza Bini, "Programma e politica generale in tema di case per le classi meno abbienti," June 25, 1936.

72. Ippolito Bastiani, "La casa e la delinquenza," *Il Popolo di Roma,* March 29, 1928.

73. Bastiani.

74. Giuseppe Bottai, "Appelli all'uomo," *Critica Fascista*, January 1, 1934, quoted in Emilio Gentile, *Fascismo: Storia e interpretazione* (Rome: Laterza, 2007), 241.

75. Originally, the fascist New Man appeared in the guise of the *squadrista* and subsequently assumed different traits and features in relation to changes over the Ventennio. See Gentile, *Fascismo*, 235–64. See also Patrick Bernhard and Lutz Klinkhammer, eds., *L'uomo nuovo del fascismo: La costruzione di un progetto totalitario* (Rome: Viella, 2018).

76. I have drawn this conclusion after consulting hundreds of archival documents, such as requests for subsidies, recommendations, and administrative and judicial proceedings concerning the *baracche* and their inhabitants.

77. These characteristics are attributable to *borgate* built from 1930 to 1934 and not to subsequent ones built by the ICP after 1935.

78. ASC, UAS, c.t., *classe 7*, b. 102, f. 1, Boncompagni a Mussolini, n.d., but from March 1933.

79. ASSC, Consulta di Roma, *verbali*, vol. 2, meeting of September 10, 1930.

80. Raffaello Ricci, "Baracche e abitazioni malsane," *Capitolium* 2 (1931): 84.

81. Archivio Ater, attached to the minutes of CdA, 1935, Alberto Calza Bini, "Programma per nuovi lavori e per la sistemazione della popolazione sfrattata o baraccata nella capitale," March 1935.

82. "Borgate rurali e alloggi minimi a Roma," *La Casa* (1936): 123–29.

83. The most imaginative picture was given by a reporter from the governmental magazine. G. Zucca, "Delenda baracca," *Capitolium* 1 (1931): 44–48.

84. Acs, Spd, c.o., b. 840, f. 500.019–1, report from CCRR to governor Boncompagni, August 6, 1934.

85. ASC, UAS, c.t., *classe 6*, b. 84, f. 3, letter from Riccardo Moretti to Edmondo Rossoni; see also ASC, Segretariato generale, *carteggio*, b. 416, note from Moretti to Boncompagni, May 8, 1933.

86. In the *borgate* built between 1930 and 1934, water, electrical, and sewage systems were often absent (especially in the early years) or in a perennial state of disrepair.

87. Regio Decreto, February 4, 1915, n. 148.

88. ASC, UAS, *classe 7*, b. 107, f. 3, correspondence between Ripartizione V and Ufficio legale, June 1933.

89. On this, see Villani, *Le borgate*, 292–99.

90. On the contrary, in 1933 governor Boncompagni Ludovisi suggested that Mussolini abandon other *borgate ufficiali* projects, as those existing could already be bankrupt, although he was not listened to. ASC, UAS, c.t., *classe 7*, b. 102, f. 1, note from Boncompagni to S. E. Il Capo del Governo, March 9, 1933.

91. Autonomous Fascist Institute for public housing, Health and Hygiene Office, Office for Surveillance and Repression of Illegal Buildings.

92. "In fact, it appears that morbidity in isolated *baracche*, however primitive, usually presents more modest rates than in *casermoni alveari*, where the chain of contagion strengthens more quickly." ASC, Ripartizione VIII—Igiene e sanità, 1871–1940, *carteggio*, series 2, b. 186, f. 2, "Stato dell'edilizia popolare," October 1939.

93. ASC, Ripartizione VIII—Igiene e sanità, 1871–1940, *carteggio*, series 2, b. 186, f. 2, IFACP della provincia di Roma, "Dati riassuntivi sul movimento demografico dell'inquilinato nell'anno 1939," April 24, 1940.

94. Raffaello Ricci, "Baracche e sbaraccamenti," *Capitolium* 3 (1930): 145.

95. ASC, UAS, c.t., *classe* 7, b. 102, f. 1, "Censimento delle famiglie ricoverate in baracche nel territorio del Governatorato di Roma città e suburbio," March 1933.

96. For a broader analysis conducted at a national level, see Gallo, *Senza*.

97. ASC, Ripartizione VIII—Igiene e sanità, 1871–1940, *carteggio*, series 2, b. 182, f. 2.

98. Legge, July 6, 1939, n. 1092.

99. On this argument, see Pietrenzo Piazzo, *Roma: La crescita metropolitana abusiva* (Rome: Officina Edizioni, 1982); Alberto Clementi and Francesco Perego, eds., *La metropoli "spontanea": Il caso di Roma, 1925–1981: Sviluppo residenziale di una città dentro e fuori dal piano* (Bari: Dedalo, 1983). On the various settlement processes that have mostly affected the area close to the Grande raccordo anulare—the motorway around Rome—over the past twenty years, and on transformations in living conditions, see Carlo Cellamare, ed., *Fuori raccordo: Abitare l'altra Roma* (Rome: Donzelli, 2016); Alessandro Lanzetta, *Roma informale: La città mediterranea del GRA* (Rome: Manifestolibri, 2018).

100. ASC, Deliberazioni del Governatore, resolution no. 5390, July 25, 1935.

Chapter Five

1. Brazil was governed by a military dictatorship from 1964 until the indirect election of the first postdictatorship civilian president in 1985. The dictatorship actively participated in housing policy by establishing the Banco Nacional de Habitação to promote housing production. The dictatorship participated directly or indirectly in removal policies that impacted Rio's favelas during the 1960s and 1970s. Ermínio Maricato, *Política habitacional no regime militar: Do milagre brasileiro à crise econômica* (Petrópolis: Vozes, 1987); Mario Brum, "Ditadura civil-militar e favelas: Estigma e restrições ao debate sobre a cidade (1969–1973)," *Cadernos Metrópole* 14, no. 28 (2013): 357–79; Marco Marques Pestana, *Remoções de favelas no Rio de Janeiro: Empresários, Estado e movimento de favelados: 1957–1973* (Rio de Janeiro: Arquivo Nacional, 2022).

2. On the FLXIII, see Reginaldo Scheuermann Costa, "A Fundação Leão XIII educando os favelados (1947–1964)" (PhD diss., Universidade Federal do Rio de Janeiro, 2015); Igor Martins Medeiros Robaína, "Assistência social ou controle sócio-espacial: Uma análise das espacialidades políticas da Fundação Leão XII sobre as favelas cariocas (1947–1962)," *Revista Espacialidades* 6, no. 5 (2013): 176–96; Emanuel Giannotti and Rafael Soares Gonçalves, "La Guerra Fría en las favelas y las poblaciones, 1945–1964: Una disputa entre comunistas e Iglesia Católica," *Izquierdas* 49 (2020): 642–62.

3. Fundação Leão XIII, *Favelas, compromisso que vamos resgatar* (Rio de Janeiro: FLXIII, 1962).

4. Previous works include Bart Slob, "Do barraco para o apartamento: A humanização e a urbanização de uma favela situada em um bairro nobre do Rio de Janeiro" (undergraduate thesis, National Museum/UFRJ, 2002); Soraya Silveira Simões, *Histoire et ethnographie d'une cité de Rio: La Cruzada São Sebastião* (Paris: Karthala, 2010). This material was previously covered in Rafael Soares Gonçalves, "Trabalhadores e as favelas cariocas: O caso da Favela da Praia do Pinto no período do segundo pós-guerra," in *Trabalhadores e trabalhadoras: Capítulos de história social*, ed. Fabiane Popinigis and Deivison Amaral (Rio de Janeiro: Paco Editorial, 2022). The Social Service Department files of the FLXIII, as well as those of the Cruzada São Sebastião Social Service, were located in a closet in the parish hall of the Santos Anjos Church, in Leblon. After cleaning and cataloging, we transferred this material to the Pastoral de Favelas, which is located in the Catholic diocese of Rio de Janeiro in Glória. The collection contains 622 files from

the FLXIII and 1,120 files from the São Sebastião Crusade. This chapter is based on data from the first group.

5. Founded by Bishop Dom Helder Câmara, on October 29, 1955, the Cruzada São Sebastião was a private Catholic entity, whose objective was to offer human and Christian solutions to solve the problem of the favelas. It counted on public donations and subsidies and intended to urbanize all the favelas in Rio de Janeiro. On the Cruzada São Sebastião, see Emanuel Giannotti and Rafael Soares Gonçalves, "La Guerra Fría en las favelas y las poblaciones, 1945–1964: Una disputa entre comunistas e Iglesia Católica," *Izquierdas* 49 (2020): 642–62; Simões, *Histoire.*

6. These files were preserved only because they were sent to the Social Service of the Cruzada São Sebastião, which kept track of the transferred families. If the largest number of files are from residents of Praia do Pinto (581 files, or 93 percent of the total), there are, however, a smaller number of files from residents of other favelas around Lagoa Rodrigo de Freitas: Ilha das Dragas (10 files), Areinha (14 files) and Pedra do Baiano (17 files), who were also transferred to the Cruzada São Sebastião complex.

7. Cezar Honorato explains that the first Social Service Department programs offered a technical training course for *visitadoras,* whereas full-fledged social workers had to attain a college degree. Cezar Honorato, "O assistente social e as favelas (1945/64)," in *Favelas cariocas: Ontem e hoje,* ed. Marco Antonio da Silva Mello, Luiz Antônio Machado da Silva, Letícia de Luna Freire, and Soraya Silveira Simões (Rio de Janeiro: Garamond, 2012), 141–68. See also Maria José Valença, "Como trabalhar numa favela carioca através da experiência da Fundação Leão XIII" (undergraduate thesis, PUC Rio, 1953). Besides working in the Niemeyer slum removal, Valença also worked at the FLXIII agency in Praia do Pinto.

8. Valença, "Como trabalhar," 8.

9. Brasil, Officina de Estatística, *Recenseamento do Rio de Janeiro de 1906 (Districto Federal)* (Rio de Janeiro: Officina da Estatística, 1907).

10. According to the city hall's 1948 census of favelas, "The largest nuclei are Jacarezinho, Mangueira and Praia do Pinto, true cities of shanties." Brasil, Prefeitura do Distrito Federal, Censo das Favelas, 10. For the 1950 census, see Alberto Passos Guimarães, "As favelas do Distrito Federal," *Revista Brasileira de Estatística* 55 (1953): 250–78.

11. Guimarães, "As favelas," 259.

12. Rafael Soares Gonçalves, *Favelas do Rio de Janeiro: História e direito* (Rio de Janeiro: Pallas/PUC-Rio, 2013); Brodwyn Fischer, *A Poverty of Rights* (Stanford, CA: Stanford University Press, 2008).

13. See Janice Perlman, *The Myth of Marginality* (Berkeley: University of California Press, 1976); Lícia Valladares, *The Invention of the Favela* (Durham, NC: Duke University Press, 2019).

14. Getúlio Vargas governed the country after 1930 and carried out a self-coup on November 10, 1937, imposing a dictatorial regime called the Estado Novo that lasted until 1945.

15. Rio de Janeiro was Brazil's Federal District until 1960, when the national capital was transferred to the planned city of Brasília. As Brazil's capital, Rio's local policies influenced and were also influenced by national political debates. Although the municipal council was elected, Rio's prefect was appointed by the president of the Republic.

16. Even without the presence of communists, the city council was very combative in the debates involving the favelas during the 1950s and became a relevant actor in these issues, providing important negotiation channels. See Maria Lais Pereira da Silva, *Favelas cariocas (1930–1964)* (Rio de Janeiro: Contraponto, 2005), 63; Brodwyn Fischer, "The Red Menace Reconsidered: A Forgotten History of Communist Mobilization in Rio de Janeiro's Favelas, 1945–1964," *Hispanic*

American Historical Review 94, no. 1 (2014): 1–33; Giannotti and Gonçalves, "La guerra." The Communist Party was very active in other Latin American cities, as can be seen in this volume, especially in Giannoti and Cofré's chapter on Santiago, Ollivier's on Caracas, and Fischer's on Recife.

17. Gonçalves, *Favelas*.

18. Antonio Luigi Negro, and Fernando Teixeira Silva, "Trabalhadores, sindicatos e política (1945–1964)," in *O Brasil republicano: O tempo da experiência democrática*, ed. Jorge Ferreira and Lucilia de Almeida Neves Delgado (Rio de Janeiro: Civilização Brasileira, 2003), 155; Paulo Fontes, "The Local and the Global: Neighborhoods, Workers and Associations in São Paulo (1945–1964)," *International Review of Social History* 62 (2017): 191–216; Fischer, "Red Menace."

19. Rafael Soares Gonçalves, Manuella Thereza Cabral Pessanha, and Géssica Martins Mororó, "Pelo direito de permanecer: Mobilização política e o acesso a serviços de água e luz nas favelas cariocas no período pós-estado novo," *Revista Libertas* 15, no. 2 (2015): 295–314.

20. The Uniões Femininas were one of the many communist-inspired organizations that developed in the postwar period and played a central role in the political strategies of the PCB after its outlawing in May 1947. See Rafael Soares Gonçalves and Manuella Theresa Cabral Pessanha, "Mulheres na luta: A mobilização política das Uniões Femininas nas favelas cariocas no pós-guerra," *Revista Izquierdas* 50 (2021): 1–16. On the campaign against soldiers in Korea, see Jayme Fernandes Ribeiro, *Combatentes da paz* (Rio de Janeiro: 7 Letras, 2011).

21. Nísia Trindade Lima, "O movimento de favelados do Rio de Janeiro" (MA thesis, IUPERJ, 1989), 79.

22. Fischer, "Red Menace," 23.

23. Samuel Silva Rodrigues de Oliveira, "A Câmara Municipal do Rio/DF e a política para as favelas," in *Anais do XXVI Simpósio Nacional de História* (São Paulo: ANPUH, 2011): 1–16. *Morro* (hill) is Rio slang for a favela.

24. Fischer, "Red Menace," 8.

25. Marcos Cesar de Oliveira Pinheiro, "O PCB e os Comitês Populares democráticos na cidade do Rio de Janeiro (1945–1947)" (MA thesis, UFRJ, 2007), 43.

26. Luciano Parisse, *Favelas do Rio de Janeiro: Evolução e sentido* (Rio de Janeiro: PUC/CNPH, 1969), 88.

27. On this census, see Brodwyn Fischer, "From the Mocambo to the Favela," *Histoire et Mesure* 34, no. 1 (2019): 15–39; Rafael Soares Gonçalves, "Les favelas cariocas dans les recensements nationaux," *Histoire et Mesure* 34, no. 1 (2019): 41–63; Samuel Oliveira, "Informalidade urbana, classe trabalhadora e raça no rio de Janeiro," *Revista de História* 180 (2021): 1–27.

28. Samuel Silva Rodrigues de Oliveira, "As 'Batalhas do Rio': As metáforas de guerra e as políticas para as favelas cariocas (1946–1961)," *Sociologias* 23, no. 58 (2021): 418–43.

29. The Comissão de Favelas operated until 1956, when it was replaced by the Service for the Recovery of Slums and Unhygienic Housing (SERFHA).

30. Oliveira, "As 'Batalhas.'"

31. Parisse, *Favelas*, 124.

32. Juan Cruz Esquivel, "Da sociedade política à sociedade civil: A presença política da Igreja Católica Brasileira num período de instabilidade política (1952–2004)," *Projeto História* 29 (2004): 201.

33. The Catholic influence in the field of social service aimed to build a third-way discourse, with the formulation of a capitalism permeated by Christian communitarianism and free of

liberal exaggerations, to serve as a counterweight to socialism. See Marilda Vilela Iamamoto and Raul de Carvalho, *Relações sociais e serviço social no Brasil: Esboço de uma interpretação histórico-metodológica* (São Paulo: Cortez, 2006), 241.

34. Arlete Alves Lima, *Serviço social no Brasil: A ideologia de uma década* (São Paulo: Cortez, 1987), 55.

35. Rafael Soares Gonçalves, Soraya Silveira Simões, and Leticia de Luna Freire, "A contribuição da Igreja Católica na transformação da habitação popular em problema público na França e no Brasil," *Cuadernos de Antropología Social* 31 (2010): 97–120.

36. SAGMACS, *Aspectos humanos da favela carioca*, supplement to *O Estado de S. Paulo*, April 13 and 15, 1960, 28. On the SAGMACS report, see Valladares, *Invention*; Lucas Ricardo Cestauro, "A atuação de Lebret e da Sagmacs no Brasil (1947–1964): Ideias, planos e contribuições" (PhD diss., Institute of Architecture and Urbanism/USP, 2015); Marco Antonio da Silva Mello, Luiz Antônio Machado da Silva, Letícia de Luna Freire, and Soraya Silveira Simões, eds., *Favelas cariocas: Ontem e hoje* (Rio de Janeiro: Garamond, 2012).

37. Valença, "Como trabalhar," 2.

38. The Abrigo Cristo Redentor was created in 1936 by Raphael Levy Miranda, the "apostle of Brazilian social assistance" and a friend of President Getúlio Vargas. After being managed by religious institutions, the shelter became a public agency in 1991. See Gonçalves et al, "A contribuição."

39. Oliveira, "As 'Batalhas.'"

40. Igor Martins Medeiros Robaína, "Diferentes conflitos, poderes e disputas territoriais: O papel da Igreja Católica no Espaço das favelas na cidade do Rio de Janeiro (1947–1962)," *Scripta Nova* 16, no. 52 (2012): 6.

41. Valença, "Como trabalhar," 5.

42. Gonçalves et al., "A contribuição."

43. Honorato, "O assistente," 162.

44. After the transfer of the capital to Brasília in 1960, the former Federal District became the state of Guanabara, equivalent to the municipality of Rio de Janeiro. In 1975, the states of Guanabara and Rio de Janeiro merged and the capital became Rio. See Samuel Oliveira, " 'Trabalhadores favelados': Identificação das favelas e movimentos sociais no Rio de Janeiro e em Belo Horizonte" (PhD diss., PPGHPBC-CPDOC/FGV, 2014), 67.

45. Cited by Oliveira, 68.

46. Valença, "Como trabalhar," 5.

47. Oliveira, "As 'Batalhas.'"

48. Fundação Leão XIII, *Favelas*. Maria Luiza Moniz de Aragão, director of the Social Service of the FLXIII, reported in a 1947 work that a União Feminina was unable to install itself in Barreira do Vasco thanks to the presence of a FLXIII Social Action Center. Iamamoto and Carvalho, "Relações," 284.

49. Parisse, *Favelas*, 55.

50. Sidney Chalhoub, *Trabalho, lar e botequim* (Campinas: UNICAMP, 1986), 50–51.

51. Valença, "Como trabalhar," 4.

52. Valença, 6.

53. The Pernambuco physician Victor Tavares de Moura took on the job of studying and eradicating Rio de Janeiro's favelas in the early 1940s. He conducted statistical studies and promoted the construction of at least three "Provisional Proletarian Parks" to resettle favela residents.

Such parks assumed a disciplinary zeal and a strong moralistic propensity. On his performance, see Fischer, "From the *Mocambo*."

54. Slob, "Do barraco."

55. On SERFHA's performance, especially under the command of José Arthur Rios in the early 1960s, in which the agency strengthened its urbanizing perspective and support to neighborhood associations, see Lima, "O movimento," 135.

56. Anthony Leeds and Elizabeth Leeds, *A sociologia do Brasil urbano* (Rio de Janeiro: Zahar, 1978). On debates about marginality in relation to Rio's favelas, see Perlman, *Myth*; Luis Antonio Machado da Silva, "Vida e morte da teoria da marginalidade," in *Porque Marx?*, ed. Leandro Konder (Rio de Janeiro: Ediciones Graal, 1983), 217–32; Rafael Soares Gonçalves and Carolina Rocha dos Santos, "Favelas cariocas: Da noção de marginalidade à ideia de margens urbanas," *Revista de Direito da Cidade* 14, no. 3 (2022): 1884–1905.

57. Brodwyn Fischer, "A Century in the Present Tense," in *Cities from Scratch*, ed. Brodwyn Fischer, Bryan McCann, and Javier Auyero (Durham, NC: Duke University Press, 2014), 9–67.

58. Perlman, *Myth*, 114.

59. Flávia Brito do Nascimento, "Lar e família: O discurso assistencialista sobre habitação popular nos anos 40 e 50," *Risco* 3, no. 2 (2006): 43–55.

60. On IPEME, see Danielle Lopes Bittencourt, "O morro é do povo: Memórias e experiências de mobilização e favelas cariocas" (MA thesis, UFF, 2012); Marco Marques Pestana, "Ampliação seletiva do Estado e remoções de favela no Rio de Janeiro: Embates entre empresariado do setor imobiliário movimento de favelados (1957–1973)" (PhD diss., UFF, 2018).

61. Valença, "Como trabalhar," xii.

62. Maria Luiza Muniz de Aragão, "Favela—vivem ou vegetam as 1.111 famílias da Barreira do Vasco?" *Serviço Social* 54 (1949): 69.

63. Brasil, Prefeitura do Distrito Federal, *Censo*, 8. About the racist propositions of the Federal District's 1948 favela census, see Brodwyn Fischer, "Quase pretos de tão pobres? Race and Social Discrimination in Rio de Janeiro's Twentieth-Century Criminal Courts," *Latin American Research Review* 39, no. 1 (2004): 31–59; Fischer, *Poverty*; Gonçalves, "Les favelas."

64. Brasil, "Censo," 11.

65. Valença, "Como trabalhar," 44.

66. File 23, Fundo Fichas FLXIII, Arquivo da Pastoral de Favelas.

67. File 23, Fundo Fichas FLXIII. *Macumba* was a slang term for syncretic Afro-diasporic religious practices in Brazil and elsewhere in the Southern Cone.

68. File 23, Fundo Fichas FLXIII.

69. Valença, "Como trabalhar," 56.

70. Brodwyn Fischer, "A ética do silêncio racial no contexto urbano: Políticas públicas e desigualdade social no Recife, 1900–1940," *Anais do Museu Paulista* 28 (2020): 1–45, 4–5. On racial debates in an urban context, see also Fischer, this volume.

71. Marcos Chor Maio, "Modernidade e racismo: Costa Pinto e o projeto Unesco de relações raciais," in *Projeto UNESCO no Brasil: Textos críticos*, ed. Cláudio Luiz Pereira and Lívio Sansone (Salvador: EDUFBA, 2007), 19.

72. Maio, "Modernidade," 21.

73. Luiz de Aguiar Costa Pinto, *O Negro no Rio de Janeiro: Relações de raças numa sociedade em mudança* (São Paulo: Editora Nacional, 1953), 134.

74. Iamamoto e Carvalho, "Relações," 288.

75. Valença, "Como trabalhar," 44.

76. Valéria Lima Guimarães, *O PCB cai no samba* (Rio de Janeiro: APERJ, 2009); Lima, "O movimento," 84.

77. See Michael Conniff, *Urban Politics in Brazil* (Pittsburgh, PA: University of Pittsburgh Press, 1981); Rafael Soares Gonçalves, "E o prefeito sobe o morro: As intervenções da gestão Pedro Ernesto nas favelas cariocas," in Rafael Soares Gonçalves, Mario Brum, and Mauro Amoroso, *Pensando as favelas cariocas* (Rio de Janeiro: PUC and Pallas, 2021), 57–86.

78. Leeds and Leeds, *A sociologia*, 175. About the *jogo do bicho*, see Amy Chazkel, *Laws of Chance* (Durham, NC: Duke University Press, 2011).

79. José Alípio Goulart, *Favelas do Distrito Federal* (Rio de Janeiro: Ministério da Agricultura, 1957), 33.

80. Leeds and Leeds, *A sociologia*, 99.

81. File 23 (August 10, 1948), Fundo Fichas FLXIII, Arquivo da Pastoral de Favelas.

82. File 23 (February 27, 1950), Fundo Fichas FLXIII, Arquivo da Pastoral de Favelas.

83. Leeds and Leeds, *A sociologia*, 106.

84. Silva, *Favelas*, 115.

85. Silva, 119.

86. Oliveira, "Informalidade."

87. File 8b (May 2, 1951), Fundo Fichas FLXIII, Arquivo da Pastoral de Favelas.

88. Of the 1,307 workers, we did not identify reference to sex in seven forms. Regarding the professions, the forms did not present uniform data. The ways of designating them varied according to how *visitadoras* filled out the forms, which makes it difficult to tabulate the data. We are still building a more homogeneous classification of the information. In any case, it is possible to identify that besides workers in domestic service and in civil construction, there were many workers in the region's factories, in commerce and the service sector, odd jobbers, street sellers, and even civil servants.

89. File 19 (January 18, 1962), Fundo Fichas FLXIII, Arquivo da Pastoral de Favelas.

90. IPEME (Institute of Market Research and Studies), *Favelas e favelados do DF* (Rio de Janeiro: IPEME, 1957).

91. Iamamoto and Carvalho, "Relações," 290.

92. Leeds and Leeds, *A sociologia*, 101.

93. Report of June 11, 1954, file 16, Collection FLXIII Files, Arquivo da Pastoral de Favelas.

94. File 1043 (September 20, 1949), Fundo Fichas FLXIII, Arquivo da Pastoral de Favelas.

95. File 42 (July 3, 1958), Fundo Fichas FLXIII, Arquivo da Pastoral de Favelas.

96. Report of August 7, 1948, file 8b, Fundo FLXIII Files, Arquivo da Pastoral de Favelas.

97. Goulart, *Favelas*, 7.

98. IPEME, *Favelas*, 12.

99. On the UTF, see Lima, "O movimento"; Brodwyn Fischer, "Democracy, Thuggery and the Grassroots: Antoine Magarinos Torres and the União dos Trabalhadores Favelados in the Age of Carioca Populism," *Nuevo Mundo Mundos Nuevos* (2013): https://doi.org/10.4000/nuevo mundo.64840; Rafael Soares Gonçalves and Mauro Amoroso, "União como acesso à cidade: A UTF entre a história e a memória do movimento associativo de favelas do Rio de Janeiro," *Revista do Arquivo Geral da Cidade do Rio de Janeiro* 7 (2013): 175–90; Marco Pestana, *A União dos Trabalhadores Favelados e a luta contra o controle negociado das favelas cariocas (1954-1964)* (Niterói: EdUFF, 2016).

100. Although Vargas imposed a dictatorial regime between 1937 and 1945, he retained significant political influence among workers and was elected president in 1950.

101. File 18, Collection FLXIII, Arquivo da Pastoral de Favelas.

102. Rafael Soares Gonçalves, "L'informalité comme une ressource urbaine ? Le cas des favelas de Rio de Janeiro," *EchoGéo* 39 (2017): 1–16.

103. Valença, "Como trabalhar," 36.

104. Valença, 74.

105. Valença, 75.

106. File 1356, Fundo Fichas FLXIII, Arquivo da Pastoral de Favelas.

107. File 16, Fundo Fichas FLXIII, Arquivo da Pastoral de Favelas.

108. File 6, undated report, Fundo Fichas FLXIII, Arquivo da Pastoral de Favelas.

109. Register of March 8,1949. File #1409. Leão XIII Foundation Archives. Archive of the Pastoral of Favelas.

110. File 8b, Fundo Fichas FLXIII, Arquivo da Pastoral de Favelas.

111. File 1409, FLXIII/Arquivo da Pastoral de Favelas.

112. The FLXIII's Social Service mediated land sales and shack exchanges but did not interfere in Leblon's Parque Proletária, which was next to the Praia do Pinto favela. Dona Ruth, for example, went to the agency to ask to exchange her shack, but the *visitadora* informed her that there was nothing she could do because the exchange with a house in the *parque* required the approval of park administrators. Record of August 26, 1950, File 1285, Fundo Fichas FLXIII, Arquivo da Pastoral de Favelas.

113. File 42, Fundo Fichas FLXIII, Arquivo da Pastoral de Favelas.

114. File 8b, Fundo Fichas FLXIII, Arquivo da Pastoral de Favelas. It is not clear if Sr. Serafim, who appears frequently in the files, was an employee of the FLXIII itself or represented some other public agency.

115. This was the aforementioned 1937 Building Code of the Federal District, which imposed strict rules for any favela construction and provided for their replacement with "minimum-type housing."

116. Undated record, file 1281, Fundo Fichas FLXIII, Arquivo da Pastoral de Favelas.

117. There are numerous attempts by residents to circumvent the control of FLXIII. In some cases, this resistance manifested itself in a more organized way. Danielle Bittencourt, quoting the SAGMACS report, describes the formation of the União de Defesa e Melhoramentos da Barreira do Vasco as an act of resistance against the control exercised by the FLXIII in that favela, especially regarding the prohibition of the improvement of shacks or their substitution with masonry houses. Bittencourt, "O morro," 92–93.

118. File 5, Fundo Fichas FLXIII, Arquivo da Pastoral de Favelas.

119. Rafael Soares Gonçalves, "Da política da 'contenção' à remoção: Aspectos jurídicos das Favelas Cariocas," in Mello et al., *Favelas cariocas*, 253–78.

120. Goulart, *Favelas*, 33.

121. Gonçalves, "Da política," 33.

122. Goulart, *Favelas*, 43–44.

123. Silveira was elected councilman for the UDN (National Democratic Union) in 1947, and he was elected federal deputy and took office in February 1951, when he transferred to the PSB. He was elected federal deputy several times until his mandate was revoked in 1969 by the Military Government's AI5. See Fischer, *Poverty*, 268–95.

124. File 5, Fundo Fichas FLXIII, Arquivo da Pastoral de Favelas.

125. Goulart, *Favelas*, 43.

126. Fernanda Barcellos, *As favelas: Estudo sociológico* (Rio de Janeiro: Aurora, 1951), 12.

127. Barcellos, 19.

128. Goulart, *Favelas*, 44.

129. Valença, "Como trabalhar," xii.

130. Register of May 30, 1956, file 1471, Fundo Fichas FLXIII, Arquivo da Pastoral de Favelas.

131. Oliveira, "Trabalhadores," 2014.

132. Bittencourt, "O morro," 87.

133. Bittencourt, 87.

134. Goulart, *Favelas*, 45.

135. Breno Botelho Ribeiro, "Manu militari: A ação jurídica católica nos conflitos fundiários urbanos do Rio de Janeiro, uma etnografia com a Pastoral de favelas" (MA thesis, UFF, 2020), 66–67.

136. Esquivel, "Da sociedade," 203–4.

137. Enny Guarnieri, *Uma experiência de promoção social* (Rio de Janeiro: CBCISS, 1965), 2–3.

138. The residents of the Bairro São Sebastião could have access to the apartment, after paying installments for fifteen years, which ranged from 8 percent to 15 percent of the minimum wage, as long as they respected certain conditions, such as a prohibition on renting, transferring, or modifying the properties without the express authorization of the Cruzada São Sebastião. Gonçalves, *Favelas*.

139. Luiz Antonio Machado da Silva, "A continuidade do 'problema da favela,'" in *Cidade: Histórias e desafios*, ed. Lúcia Lippi Oliveira (Rio de Janeiro: FGV, 2002), 220–37.

Chapter Six

1. While the word *barrio* means "neighborhood" in Spanish, it has evolved to mean "slum" in Venezuela. This term has been generically applied since the twentieth century to all working-class neighborhoods with buildings characterized by a range of irregularities (in terms of real estate, the law, and construction).

2. Republic of Venezuela, "Ley Orgánica de Ordenación Urbanística," *Gaceta Oficial*, no. 33.868, December 16, 1987. Unless otherwise indicated, all quotations from Venezuelan sources have been translated into English via French.

3. Between 40 percent and 60 percent of the inhabitants of the Venezuelan capital of Caracas lived in the *barrios* at this time, that is, between 1.1 million and 1.5 million people. Teolinda Bolívar, "Los agentes sociales articulados a la producción de los barrios de ranchos," *Coloquio Vivienda* (Universidad Central de Venezuela) 1, no. 1 (1989): 143–61, 146; Antonio de Lisio, "La evolución urbana de Caracas: Indicadores e interpretaciones sobre el desarrollo de la interrelación ciudad-naturaleza," *Revista Geográfica Venezolana* 42, no. 2 (2001): 203–26, 215; Teolinda Bolívar and Yves Pedrazzini, "La Venezuela urbana: Una mirada desde los barrios," *Revista Bitácora Urbano Territorial* 12, no. 1 (2008): 55–76, 64.

4. Pedro Nikken and Rogelio Pérez Perdomo, *Derecho y propiedad de la vivienda en los barrios de Caracas* (Caracas: UCV, 1979), 81.

5. Records show that only 28.2 percent of the *barrios* housing was freehold in 1973. See Kenneth L. Karst, Murray L. Schwartz, and Audrey J. Schwartz, *The Evolution of Law in the Barrios of Caracas* (Los Angeles: Latin American Center, University of California, 1973), 98. In fact, these authors pointed out, it is possible that none of the land was freehold because the validity of the titles was not proven.

6. Nikken and Pérez Perdomo, *Derecho*, 90.

7. The word *Adeco* is used to refer to AD. Similarly, *copeyano* is the adjective referring to the Christian Democratic Party COPEI.

8. Beatriz Meza, "Contra el rancho en Venezuela: De la campaña de 1946 a la batalla de 1951," *Diseño y Sociedad* (2010): 48–57; Juan José Martín Frechilla, "Vivienda popular e iniciativa municipal en Caracas, 1908–1958 (o como algunos pioneros no estaban equivocados)," in *La cuestión de los barrios*, ed. Teolinda Bolívar and Josefina Baldó (Caracas: Monte Avila Latinoamericana, 1996), 189–201.

9. Martín Frechilla, "Vivienda."

10. Meza, "Contra el rancho."

11. Venezuela, Ministerio de Fomento, *Cuarto Censo Nacional de Población*, 1920, quoted in Angélica Cedeño González, "Estructura espacial del AMDC año 1966" (BA thesis, Universidad Central de Venezuela, 1984), 31.

12. Venezuela, Ministerio de Fomento, *Quinto Censo Nacional de Población*, 1936, and *Sexto Censo Nacional de Población*, 1941, quoted in Cedeño González, *Estructura*.

13. Martín Frechilla, "Vivienda."

14. Martín Frechilla. The prohibition was drawn up by the Dirrección de Sanidad Nacional (National Health Directorate), which came under the Ministerio de Relaciones Interiores (Interior Ministry) and the Comisión de Estudios de la Red de Cloacas y Colectores de Caracas (Commission for the Study of Caracas's Sewage and Drainage System), which came under the Ministerio de Obras Públicas.

15. Martín Frechilla.

16. Martín Frechilla.

17. Venezuela, Ministerio de Fomento, 1947, T.VII, CV, quoted in Meza, "Contra el rancho."

18. Venezuela, quoted in Meza.

19. Venezuela, T1, XXII, quoted in Meza, "Contra el rancho."

20. Meza, "Contra el rancho."

21. Oficina Metropolitana de Planeamiento Urbano (OMPU), "Crecimiento histórico de los ranchos de Caracas: Lapso 1949–1971," pamphlet (Caracas: OMPU, 1974).

22. Nikken and Pérez Perdomo, *Derecho*.

23. Ley Orgánica del Distrito Federal, Art. 13, *ordinal* 6, V, quoted in Nikken and Pérez Perdomo, *Derecho*.

24. Meza, "Contra el rancho."

25. Martín Frechilla, "Vivienda."

26. Martín Frechilla.

27. Martín Frechilla.

28. Meza, "Contra el rancho."

29. Alejandro Oropeza Castillo, "Informe General [BO]" (mimeo), in INFODOC, Caracas, Facultad de Arquitectura y Urbanismo, Universidad Central de Venezuela (1946); Alejandro Oropeza Castillo, "Proyecto N° 6. VIVIENDA MINIMA [BO]" (mimeo), in INFODOC, Caracas, Facultad de Arquitectura y Urbanismo, Universidad Central de Venezuela, both quoted in Meza, "Contra el rancho."

30. Rómulo Betancourt, *Venezuela, política y petróleo* (1956; Mexico City: Seix Barral, 1979), 523.

31. Meza, "Contra el rancho."

32. Martín Frechilla, "Vivienda."

33. Oficina Metropolita de Planeamiento Urbano (OMPU), "Crecimiento," quoted in Meza, "Contra el rancho."

34. For insights into Pérez Jiménez's economic policy, see Charles W. Anderson, *Politics and Economic Change in Latin America* (Princeton, NJ: D. Van Nostrand, 1967).

35. Juan José Martín Frechilla, "La construcción de una capital: Del primer proyecto moderno a la metrópoli desquiciada," in *Caracas, memorias para el futuro*, ed. Giuseppe Imbesi and Elisenda Vila (Rome: Gangemi Editore, 1995), 77–102.

36. Banco Obrero, "Reurbanización de Ciudad Tablitas: Un nuevo mundo para la clase trabajadora, Banco Obrero Vanguardia de la vivienda venezolana," pamphlet (Caracas: Banco Obrero, 1952), quoted in Meza, "Contra el rancho."

37. The report, which was headed by Leopoldo Martinez Olavarria, was commended in 1996 by Juan José Martín Frechilla. He highlighted the fact that the urban planners of the 1990s had finally come around to such recommendations. Martín Frechilla, Vivienda; Meza, "Contra el rancho."

38. Banco Obrero, "Informe preliminar sobre el cerro piloto presentado por el Banco Obrero y la Governación del Distrito Federal" (Caracas, 1954), quoted in Martín Frechilla, "Vivienda."

39. Iraida Montaño, "Les invasions de terres urbaines au Venezuela: Un problème . . . ou une solution?" (PhD diss., Université de Paris Val-de-Marne, 1980), 155.

40. Juan José Martín Frechilla, *Planes, planos y proyectos para Venezuela: 1908–1958 (apuntes para una historia de la construcción del país)* (Caracas: Fondo Editorial Acta Científica Venezolana, 1994).

41. Martín Frechilla, "Vivienda."

42. Antonio de Lisio, "La evolución."

43. Esther Marcano, *Evaluación de las inversiones del sector público en las áreas de ranchos de Caracas* (Caracas: UCV-FAU, 1972) quoted in Montaño, Les invasions, 155.

44. I. Montaño, *Les invasions*, 158; Fundacomun, *Inventario de los barrios pobres del área metropolitana de Caracas y el dpto. Vargas* (Caracas: Fondo Editorial Común, 1978), 19–20.

45. Ocarina Castillo d'Imperio, *Los años del buldozer: Ideología y política, 1948–1958* (Caracas: Fondo Editorial Tropykos, 2003), 58–59.

46. See Talton Ray, *The Politics of the Barrios in Venezuela* (Berkeley: University of California Press, 1969), 16–17.

47. Arturo Uslar Pietri, "El alba de la democracia," *Revista Billiken*, January 25, 1958.

48. This democratization was formalized in the famous Punto Fijo Pact, which was signed in Caracas by Rómulo Betancourt (AD), Jóvito Villalba (URD), and Rafael Caldera (COPEI).

49. The Fourth Republic of Venezuela, known in Venezuela as the Cuarta República or simply the "Cuarta."

50. This account of the events in San Agustín is based on a double-page spread in the January 31, 1959, edition of the communist daily *Tribuna Popular*. It commemorates the previous year's "battles" of San Agustín under the title "Valiente 'Hornos de Cal'" (valiant 'Hornos de Cal'). While the report was, of course, already an appropriated memory of the great event, it is rich in valuable factual details on the actors in this sudden working-class radicalization: "Valiente 'Hornos de Cal'!," *Tribuna Popular*, January 31, 1959. See also Ramón J. Velásquez, "Aspectos de la evolución política de Venezuela en el último medio siglo," in *Venezuela moderna: Medio siglo de historia, 1926–1976*, ed. Ramón J. Velásquez (Caracas: Fundación Eugenio Mendoza, 1979), 200; Carlos Gimenez, interviewed by Serge Ollivier in July 2013, Caracas; photographic archives of the Fundación Fotografía Urbana, http://prodavinci.com/galeria/?gid=51&pid=1483.

51. Alejandro Velasco, *Barrio Rising* (Durham, NC: Duke University Press, 2015), 377.

52. "18 horas de jubilo frenético en Caracas por la caída del dictador," *El Nacional*, January 24, 1958.

53. Ramón Velásquez, "Aspectos," 208–10. Archive footage from Universal International News showing clips of Nixon's brief official visit to Caracas is available online: "May 13, 1958— Vice President Richard Nixon Attacked in Venezuela," YouTube video, 3:53, posted by Helmer-Reenberg, https://www.youtube.com/watch?v=nvigX1doz2U.

54. Ramón Velásquez, "Aspectos," 218. The daily *El Universal* reported ten dead and eighty-four injured. See *El Universal*, September 8, in José Rivas Rivas, ed., *Historia gráfica de Venezuela: El gobierno de Larrazábal: 1958* (Caracas: Ediciones Torán, 1982), 7:173.

55. Blas Lamberti, interviewed by Agustín Blanco Muñoz, in Agustín Blanco Muñoz, *Venezuela 1958: Otra derrota popular* (Caracas: Universidad Central de Venezuela, 1991), 98.

56. Edgar Sanabria, interviewed by Agustín Blanco Muñoz, in Agustín Blanco Muñoz, *El 23 de enero: Habla la conspiración* (Caracas: Editorial Ateneo de Caracas, 1980), 223. Following Wolfgang Larrazábal's resignation from the junta to concentrate on his presidential campaign, Edgar Sanabria assumed the interim presidency of the Republic from November 18, 1958, to February 18, 1959.

57. "Ministro del interior informo sobre plan mínimo de urgencia para solucionar el desempleo," *El Universal*, March 14, 1958, and in Rivas Rivas, *Historia*, 7:85.

58. Ministerio de Obras Públicas, "Memoria y cuenta que el Ministerio de Obras Públicas presenta al Congreso nacional," 1960, xiv.

59. Ministerio de Obras Públicas, "Memoria," xv–xvi.

60. "Informe sobre el Programa a realizar por el Plan de Obras Extraordinarias," unpaginated, quoted in OMPU, *Censo Socio-Económico de los barrios del Área metropolitana de Caracas* (1959; Caracas: OMPU, 1967).

61. Ministerio de Obras Públicas, "Memoria y cuenta," xiv.

62. "Informe sobre el Programa a realizar por el Plan de Obras Extraordinarias," unpaginated; "Comenzó ayer el reenganche de los trabajadores cesantes del 'Plan de Emergencia,'" *El Independiente*, January 13, 1959.

63. Ministerio de Obras Públicas, "Memoria y cuenta," xiv.

64. More than 210 million bolivares per year. Ministerio de Obras Públicas, xv.

65. *La Religion*, February 23, 1958.

66. Ray, *The Politics*, 33–36.

67. "El Rancho y El superbloque," annex 12, in Banco Obrero, "Proyecto de Evaluación de los Superbloques," (Caracas: Banco Obrero, 1959), 12; OMPU, *Censo*, unpaginated.

68. From 1,180,934 to 1,478,628 inhabitants. Dirección General de Estadística, quoted in OMPU, *Censo* (unpaginated).

69. Biblioteca Nacional de Venezuela, Partido Comunista de Venezuela (hereafter, BNV), *caja* 5.

70. These requests came from the El Millo and Los Mecedores *barrios*: Gallegos Mancera to Presidencia del Cuerpo, Caracas, June 2, 1958, BNV, *caja* 5. On the construction program on behalf of the inhabitants of the Las Brisas de Pro-Patria *barrio*, see the report presented by Gallegos Mancera to Concejo Municipal, Caracas, July 1, 1958, BNV, *caja* 5. For the Turiamo *barrio*: Armando Vegas to Gallegos Mancera, Caracas, November 14, 1958, BNV, *caja* 5.

71. Velasco, *Barrio*, 78–79.

72. "Fundan Confederación de Juntas Pro-Fomento más de doscientas organizaciones populares," *Tribuna Popular*, June 28, 1958.

73. Report, Celula no. 6 to the Comité de Radio, Caracas, July 2, 1958, BNV, *caja* 5.

74. Resolutions, Comité de Radio, Caracas, July 6, 1958, BNV, *caja* 5.

75. Bulletin, Comité Regional del DF, Caracas, August 1958, BNV, *caja* 5.

76. Bulletin, Sec. de Org. del CR, Caracas, October 1958, BNV, *caja* 5.

77. Ángel E. Álvarez, "COPEI: La triste historia de un partido sin vocación de poder," in *Los partidos políticos venezolanos en el siglo XXI*, ed. José E. Molina and Ángel E. Álvarez (Caracas: Vadell Hermanos Editores, 2004), 170.

78. Organizational plan, CR del DF, Caracas, 30 July 1959, BNV, *caja* 5.

79. Héctor Pérez Marcano, interviewed by Agustín Blanco Muñoz, in *La lucha armada: La izquierda revolucionaria insurge*, ed. Agustín Blanco Muñoz (Caracas: Universidad Central de Venezuela, 1981), 293; Simón Sáez Mérida, interviewed by Agustín Blanco Muñoz, in Muñoz, 102 and 121; Lino Martínez, interviewed by Agustín Blanco Muñoz, in Muñoz, 22.

80. According to Gabriel Moro, "Por que perdió A.D. en Caracas?," *Momento*, May 5, 1963, 30–31.

81. Moro, 29–30.

82. Bulletin, CR del DF, Caracas, November 1958, BNV, *caja* 5.

83. Moro, "Por que," 30.

84. Velásquez, "Aspectos," 205.

85. Consejo Supremo Electoral, *Los partidos políticos y sus estadísticas electorales (1946–1984)* (Caracas: Consejo Supremo Electoral, 1987), 1:55.

86. Consejo Supremo Electoral, *Resultad de las votaciones efectuadas el 7 de diciembre de 1958* (Caracas: Consejo Supremo Electoral, 1959), 5.

87. Consejo Supremo Electoral, *Los partidos*, 347.

88. Acción en Venezuela, Departamento de Estudios e Investigaciones, "Informe para la comisión especial del congreso sobre el problema de los barrios a nivel nacional," presided over by Dr. Raúl Ramos Calles, Caracas, 1969, 3. These estimates were subsequently revised downward.

89. See James Hanson, "Cycles of Economic Growth and Structural Change since 1950," in *Venezuela: The Democratic Experience*, ed. John. D. Martz and David Myers (London: Praeger, 1977), 76–77.

90. Under the Punto Fijo Pact, employers' organizations had to be represented in the national coalition government. See Presidencia de la República, *Documentos que hicieron historia* (Caracas: Publicaciones de la Presidencia de la República, 1962), 2:444 and 2:445; Margarita López Maya, Luis Calcaño Gómez, and Thaís Maingón, *Del pacto de Punto Fijo al pacto social: Desarrollo, hegemonía y actores políticos en la Venezuela actual* (Caracas: Fondo Editorial Acta Científica Venezolana, 1989), 109.

91. See Luis Lander, *La vivienda popular en Venezuela: Especulación de tierras como un obstáculo para el desarrollo urbano* (Caracas: Cendes, UCV, 1976), 20.

92. "La Ley de Ventas de Parcelas de 1960," *Revista del Ministerio de Justicia* (n.d.), 10:36.

93. See Arturo Sosa and Eloi Lengrand, *Del garibaldismo estudiantil a la izquierda criolla: Los origines marxistas del proyecto de Acción Democrática, 1928–1935* (Caracas: Centauro, 1981).

94. Velasco, *Barrio*, 105–8.

95. In *Boletín*, Comité Regional del DF, Caracas, September 18, 1960, BNV, *caja* 7.

96. This is apparent in a letter from the junta of the *barrio* La Sabana to Eduardo Gallegos Mancera, *Junta Pro-Mejoras à Concejo*, August 28, 1959, BNV, *caja* 5.

97. Ray, *The Politics*, 116.

98. *Boletín*, Comité Regional del DF, Caracas, November 3, 1959, BNV, *caja* 5.

99. CORDIPLAN, "II Plan de la Nación," Oficina Central de Coordinación y Planificación de la Presidencia de la República, 1960, chap. 5, synthesized in Maritza Izaguirre and Carola Ravell, *Nuevo enfoque en el desarrollo de la comunidad* (Buenos Aires: Humanitas, 1968).

100. The *desarrollo de la comunidad* long remained a special interest of Charlita Muñoz. He published a book at the end of the 1980s to popularize the concept, but it had already largely fallen out of favor in public policy. Rubén Charlita Muñoz, *Desarrollo de la comunidad: Definición, interpretación, teoría y práctica* (Caracas: Ediciones Centauro, 1987).

101. Moro, "Por que perdió AD," 34; Ray, *The Politics*, 117.

102. On July 4, 1962. See Teolinda Bolívar and Iris Rosas, "Los caminos de la investigación de los asentamientos humanos precarios," in *La ciudad: De la planificación a la privatización*, ed. Teolinda Bolívar, Juan José Martín Frechilla, and Alberto Lovera (Caracas: Universidad Central de Venezuela, Consejo de Desarrollo Científico y Humanístico Fondo Editorial Acta Científica Venezolana, 1994), 122.

103. According to information provided to the US embassy by Muñoz himself. See Ray, *The Politics*, 122.

104. See FUNDACOMUN, *Memoria y Cuneta, 1963* (Caracas: El Cojo, 1964).

105. Iraida Montaño, *Les invasions*.

106. The Junta Comunal of the working-class parish of El Valle issued fifty-one such documents relating to *barrios* housing during the first six months of 1975. Nikken and Pérez Perdomo, *Derecho*, 56.

107. The majority of the life stories collected—except for those of communist militants— described the 1960s as a golden age of community spirit unthreatened by political cleavages within the *barrios*. Such opinions were certainly shaped both by the narrators' nostalgia and by Venezuela's political polarization at the time of the investigation. These memories were also historically consistent with the phase of *barrio* consolidation, when local junta entrepreneurs used party cronyism for the "community"; this contrasts with memories of the 1980s, when leaders of the new neighbors' associations tended to use the "community" of already-serviced *barrios* to legitimate their careers in municipal administration.

108. Nikken and Pérez Perdomo, *Derecho*, 38.

109. Azuela and Antuñano, this volume.

110. Giannotti and Cofré, this volume.

111. With Decree No. 332, the president of the Republic established a "programme to put in order the areas occupied by the poor districts of the country's cities" (*Programa para el ordenamiento de las areas ocupadas por los barrios pobres de las ciudades del país*). Presidencia de la República, *Gaceta Oficial* No. 30.472, August 13, 1974.

Chapter Seven

1. CORVI was the acronym for Corporación de la Vivienda, a state institution in charge of the housing problem between 1953 and 1976.

2. The term *población* in Chile refers to a residential settlement. Over the decades, it has

been increasingly associated with working-class neighborhoods, generally located on the periphery. The word *poblador* came to indicate the inhabitants of these urban spaces.

3. Vicente Espinoza, *Para una historia de los pobres en la ciudad* (Santiago: Ediciones SUR, 1988); Mario Garcés, *Tomando su sitio: El movimiento de pobladores de Santiago, 1957–1970* (Santiago: LOM, 2002); Alexis Cortes, "El movimiento de pobladores chilenos y la población La Victoria: Ejemplaridad, movimientos sociales y el derecho a la ciudad," *EURE* 40, no. 119 (2014): 239–60.

4. Manuel Castells, *Luttes urbaines et pouvoir politique* (Paris: Masperio, 1973).

5. Gabriel Salazar, *Movimientos sociales en Chile: Trayectoria histórica y proyección política* (Santiago: Uqbar, 2012); María José Castillo and Rossana Forray, "La vivienda, un problema de acceso al suelo," *ARQ* 86 (2014): 48–57. See, among others, Raúl Zibechi, *Territorios en resistencia: Cartografía política de las periferias urbanas latinoamericanas* (Buenos Aires: Lavaca Editora, 2007).

6. Joaquín Duque and Ernesto Pastrana, "La movilización reivindicativa urbana de los sectores populares en Chile: 1964–1972," *Revista Latinoamericana de Ciencias Sociales* 4 (1972): 259–93; Cecilia Urrutia, *Historia de las poblaciones callampas* (Santiago: Quimantu, 1972); Jorge Giusti, *Organización y participación popular en Chile: El mito del "hombre marginal"* (Santiago: FLACSO, 1973); Manuel Castells, "Movimiento de pobladores y lucha de clase en Chile," *EURE* 3, no. 7 (1973): 9–35; Peter Cleaves, *Bureaucratic Politics and Administration in Chile* (Berkeley: University of California Press, 1974).

7. Beatríz Aguirre and Francisco Sabatini, *Discusión sobre políticas de desarrollo en las áreas de asentamiento precario de Santiago* (Santiago: ECLAC, 1981); Teresa Valdés, *El problema de la vivienda: Políticas estatales y movilización popular* (Santiago: FLACSO, 1983); Armando de Ramón, "La población informal: Poblamiento de la periferia de Santiago. 1920–1970," *EURE* 16, no. 50 (1990): 5–17; Augusto Vergara, "Como nació la idea de la ocupación de terrenos en las poblaciones 'Lautaro San Pablo,' en año 45 al 46, para establecerse definitivamente en 'población Los Nogales,'" n.d., http://poblacionlosnogales.cl/wp-content/uploads/2017/01/TEX1 .pdf; "Cómo se organizó la toma de Zañartu," in *Lo que se teje en La Legua*, ed. María Angélica Rodríguez and Mario Garcés (Santiago: Fosis, Red de Organizaciones Sociales de La Legua, ECO, 1999), 86–92.

8. Jorge Rojas, "La lucha por la vivienda en tiempos de González Videla: Las experiencias de las poblaciones Los Nogales, Lo Zañartu y Luis Emilio Recabarren en Santiago de Chile, 1946–1947," *Revista Izquierdas* 39 (2018): 1–33.

9. Charles Tilly, *Contentious Performances* (New York: Cambridge University Press, 2008).

10. See, among others, David Collier, *Squatters and Oligarchs. Authoritarian Rule and Policy Change in Peru* (Baltimore: Johns Hopkins, 1976); Alan Gilbert and Peter Ward, *Housing, the State and the Poor: Policy and Practice in Three Latin American Cities* (Cambridge: Cambridge University Press, 1985); Antonio Azuela and María Soledad Cruz Rodríguez, "La institucionalización de las colonias populares y la política urbana del DDF, 1940–1946," *Sociología* 9 (1989): 111–33; Brodwyn Fischer, *A Poverty of Rights* (Stanford, CA: Stanford University Press, 2008); Rafael Soares Gonçalves, *Favelas do Rio de Janeiro: História e direito* (Rio de Janeiro: Pallas/PUC-Rio, 2013); Edward Murphy, *For a Proper Home* (Pittsburgh, PA: University of Pittsburgh Press, 2015); Emilio de Antuñano, "Planning a Mass City" (PhD diss., University of Chicago, 2017); Fischer and Vorms, this volume.

11. Gilbert Joseph and Daniela Spenser, *In from the Cold: Latin America's New Encounter*

with the Cold War (Durham, NC: Duke University Press, 2008); Tania Harmer and Alfredo Riquelme, *Chile y la Guerra Fría global* (Santiago: RIL Editores, 2014).

12. Simon Collier and William F. Sater, *A History of Chile, 1808-1994* (Cambridge: Cambridge University Press, 1996); Sofía Correa, Consuelo Figueroa, Alfredo Jocelyn-Holt, Claudio Rolle, and Manuel Vicuña, *Historia del siglo XX chileno* (Santiago: Editorial Sudamericana, 2001); Tomás Moulian, *Fracturas: De Pedro Aguirre Cerda a Salvador Allende (1938-1973)* (Santiago: LOM, 2006); Isabel Torres, *La crisis del sistema democrático: Las elecciones presidenciales y los proyectos excluyentes: Chile, 1958-1970* (Santiago: Editorial Universitaria, 2014).

13. Armando de Ramón, *Santiago de Chile (1541-1991): Historia de una sociedad urbana* (Madrid: Mapfre, 1992).

14. Gabriel Salazar, *Labradores, peones y proletarios: Formación y crisis de la sociedad popular chilena del siglo XIX* (Santiago: SUR, 1985); Sergio Grez, *De la "regeneración del pueblo" a la huelga general: Génesis y evolución histórica del movimiento popular en Chile (1810-1890)* (Santiago: DIBAM, 1997); Macarena Ponce de León, *Gobernar la pobreza: Prácticas de caridad y beneficencia en la ciudad de Santiago, 1830-1890* (Santiago: DIBAM, 2011).

15. Armando de Ramón, "Suburbios y arrabales en un área metropolitana: el caso de Santiago de Chile, 1872-1932," in *Ensayos históricos-sociales sobre la urbanización en América Latina*, ed. Jorge Hardoy, Richard Morse, and Richard Schaedel (Buenos Aires: SIAP, 1978), 113-30.

16. Luis Alberto Romero, *Qué hacer con los pobres: Elites y sectores populares en Santiago de Chile, 1840-1895* (Buenos Aires: Sudamericana, 1997); Salazar, *Labradores*; De Ramón, *Santiago*.

17. Macarena Ibarra, "Higiene y salud urbana en la mirada de médicos, arquitectos y urbanistas durante la primera mitad del siglo XX, Chile," *Revista Médica de Chile* 144, no. 1 (2016): 116-23.

18. Peter DeShazo, *Urban Workers and Labor Unions in Chile 1902-1927* (Madison: University of Wisconsin Press, 1983); Isabel Torres, "Los conventillos en Santiago (1900-1930)," *Cuadernos de Historia* 6 (1986): 67-85; Alejandra Brito, "Del rancho al conventillo: Transformaciones de la identidad popular-femenina, Santiago de Chile 1850-1920," in *Disciplina y desacato: Construcción de identidad en Chile, siglos XIX y XX*, ed. Elizabeth Hutchison, Karin Rosemblatt, and María Soledad Zárate (Santiago: SUR-CEDEM, 1995), 27-69; Grez, *De la "regeneración."*

19. Armando de Ramón, "Estudio de una periferia urbana: Santiago de Chile 1850-1900," *Historia* 20 (1985): 199-294.

20. The *comuna* is a basic administrative unit throughout Chile; its size falls somewhere between an urban district and a county. A large urban area such as Santiago contained many *comunas*.

21. de Ramón, *Santiago*.

22. René León, *Ñuñohue: Historia de Ñuñoa, Providencia, Las Condes y La Reina* (Buenos Aires: Francisco Aguirre, 1972); Ana María Farías, "Urbanización, política de vivienda y pobladores organizados en Las Barrancas: El caso de la población Neptuno, 1959-1968" (BA thesis, Santiago, Pontificia Universidad Católica de Chile, 1992); Waldo Vila, "La urbanización obrera en Santiago sur, 1905-1925: De arrabal decimonónico a periferia proletaria" (PhD diss., Santiago, Pontificia Universidad Católica de Chile, 2014).

23. Ronn Pineo and James Baer, eds., *Cities of Hope. People, Protests, and Progress in Urbanizing Latin America, 1870-1930* (New York: Routledge, 2001); James Baer, "Tenant Mobilization and the 1907 Rent Strike in Buenos Aires," *The Americas* 49, no. 3 (1993): 343-68; Andrew Wood, "Urban Protest and the Discourse of Popular Nationalism in Postrevolutionary Mexico: The Case of the Veracruz Rent Strike," *National Identities* 2, no. 3 (2010): 265-76; Carlos Álvarez, "La Huelga de Inquilinos de 1907 en Rosario: Una aproximación," *Sociohistórica* 49 (2022): 1-13.

24. Espinoza, *Para una historia*; Nicky Cerón, "Por una vivienda digna de ser ocupada por seres humanos: Movimiento social arrendatario: Dinámicas asociativas y de politización popular (1914–1925)" (undergraduate thesis, Santiago, Universidad de Chile, 2017).

25. Espinoza, *Para una historia*; Simón Castillo and Waldo Vila, *Periferia: Poblaciones y desarrollo urbano en Santiago de Chile 1920–1940* (Santiago: Ediciones Universidad Alberto Hurtado, 2022).

26. Espinoza, *Para una historia*; Cerón, *Por una vivienda*.

27. Luis Bravo, *Chile: El problema de la vivienda a través de su legislación* (Santiago: Editorial Universitaria Católica, 1959); Rodrigo Hidalgo, *La vivienda social en Chile y la construcción del espacio urbano en el Santiago del siglo XX* (Santiago: DIBAM, 2005); Castillo and Vila, *Periferia*.

28. José Fernández, "Historia del derecho urbanístico chileno," *Revista de Derecho Público* 77 (2012): 79–97. Eduardo Cordero, "La formación del derecho urbanístico chileno a partir del siglo XIX: De la legislación urbanística al derecho urbanístico integrado," *Revista de Derecho* (Valdivia) 30, no. 1 (2017): 127–52.

29. *Karl Brunner desde el bicentenario* (Santiago: Facultad de Arquitectura y Urbanismo, Universidad de Chile, 2009); José Rosas, Germán Hidalgo, Wren Strabucchi, and Pedro Bannen, "El plano oficial de urbanización de la comuna de Santiago de 1939: Trazas comunes entre la ciudad moderna y la ciudad preexistente," *ARQ* 91 (2015): 83–93.

30. Bravo, *Chile*; Hidalgo, *La vivienda*; Luis Valenzuela, "Mass Housing and Urbanization: On the Road to Modernization in Santiago, Chile, 1930–60," *Planning Perspective* 23, no. 3 (2008): 263–90.

31. de Ramón, "La población."

32. Oscar Álvarez, "Aspecto higiénico del problema de la vivienda popular," *Urbanismo y Arquitectura* 4 (1939): 8–10. The author does not specify the source of the figures given. A 1944 study by the Commissariat provided similar data. See "En Santiago faltan 100 mil viviendas," *El Siglo*, March 19, 1944, 1 and 7.

33. Caja de la Habitación, *El problema de la habitación en Chile* (Santiago: Imp. Guternberg, 1945), 15. See also the results of a census carried out in a popular sector of Santiago: Ricardo Mitchell, "Censo la ribera norte del Mapocho," *La Vivienda* 1 (1945): 12–14.

34. "10,000 arrendatarios amenazados de lanzamiento," *El Siglo*, April 29, 1944, 8.

35. "Varias familias fueron lanzadas ayer," *El Siglo*, April 12, 1944, 8.

36. Espinoza, *Para una historia*; Rodrigo Henríquez, *In "Estado sólido": Políticas y politización en la construcción estatal. Chile 1920–1950* (Santiago: Ediciones UC, 2014).

37. Espinoza, *Para una historia*.

38. "Los pobladores de Valdés Barros Luco impidieron 3 lanzamientos," *El Siglo*, May 12, 1945, 1; "Aún están bajo amenazada de lanzamiento 100 familias de Valdés de Barros Luco!" *El Siglo*, May 14, 1945, 5; "El lunes lanzaron a 300 pobladores de Varas Mena," *El Siglo*, February 24, 1945, 7; "Todos están amenazados de lanzamiento en población Varas Mena," *El Siglo*, February 26, 1945, 7; "Se gastaron sus mejores energías para tener viviendas: Las defenderán a cualquier costo, la población Varas Mena," *El Siglo*, October 10, 1945, 5; "Vecinos de población Varas Mena dispuestos a defender sus casas," in *La Opinión* (Santiago), October 10, 1945, 2.

39. María Soledad Gómez, "Factores nacionales e internacionales de la política interna del Partido Comunista de Chile (1922–1952)," in *El Partido Comunista en Chile*, ed. Augusto Varas (Santiago: FLACSO-CESOC, 1988), 65–139; Alfonso Salgado, "The Court Is Open for Criticism and Self-Criticism: Power Struggle and Radicalization of the Communist Party of Chile, 1945–1946," *Historia* 51, no. 1 (2018): 165–200.

40. Elías Lafferte, "El XIII congreso del partido," *Principios* 55 (1946): 5. See also Luis Reinoso, "Cumplir las resoluciones del V congreso regional de Santiago," *Principios* 44 (1945): 13–15; Humberto Abarca, "Organicemos la lucha contra el golpe de Estado," *Principios* 56–57 (1946): 3–10.

41. Luis Reinoso, "La solución de los problemas nacionales a través de la movilización de las masas—enseñanzas del XIII congreso" *Principios* 56–57 (1946): 15–19.

42. "Amenazan con lanzan a 200 personas en Chacra El Pino," *El Siglo*, June 16, 1945, 6; "200 familias amenazadas de ser lanzadas en Población El Pino," *El Siglo*, July 8, 1945, 6.

43. In 1945 there are several agreements of the Council of the Caja de la Habitación Popular to buy land to build the housing project, including the plot where the *mejoreros* had settled. See Acuerdo No. 4125, Santiago, May 23, 1945, Archivo Nacional de la Administración (ARNAD), Fondo Caja de la Habitación Popular, Acuerdos del Consejo, vol. 4.

44. Letter from the "El Pino" committee to President Juan Antonio Ríos, Santiago, July 7, 1945, ARNAD, Ministry of Labor Fund, Providencias, vol. 883.

45. Executive Vice President of the Caja de la Habitación Popular, Informe memorial mejoreros chacra "El Pino" al Señor Ministro del Trabajo (providencia no. 07067), Santiago, August 14, 1945, ARNAD, Fondo Ministerio del Trabajo, Providencias, vol. 883.

46. "Salieron a la calle los pobladores de El Pino," *El Siglo*, November 6, 1945, 1.

47. "1.500 personas amenazadas de lanzamiento," *La Opinión*, November 6, 1945, 8.

48. "Suspendido lanzamiento de ocupantes de Pob. 'El Pino,'" *La Opinión*, November 7, 1945, 8; "Caja de la Habitación se niega a protejer a 1.500 personas que serán lanzadas en 'El Pino,'" *La Opinión* (Santiago), November 9, 1945, 1 and 8; "Entrevista con el presidente Ríos gestionan pobladores de El Pino," *El Siglo* (Santiago), December 5, 1945, 8.

49. "Hoy se realizará el desalojo de 1500 pobladores de El Pino," *El Siglo*, December 10, 1945, 9.

50. "El congreso comunista llama a impedir el lanzamiento de El Pino y protesta de la inseguridad de la Braden," *El Siglo*, December 13, 1945, 4.

51. "Intentaron lanzamiento en El Pino: Impedido otra vez," *El Siglo*, December 14, 1945, 1; "Sindicatos y organismos obreros impiden el lanzamiento de los pobladores de 'El Pino,'" *La Opinión* (Santiago), December 14, 1945, 8.

52. "A la chacra Acevedo serán trasladado los pobladores de El Pino: Triunfaron," *El Siglo*, December 17, 1945, 6; "Ubicados desde ayer en la chacra Acevedo los pobladores de 'El Pino,'" in *La Opinión* (Santiago), December 21, 1945, 4. A smaller number of the families, contrary to the agreement, remained in El Pino: "Los propios pobladores desmienten a 'El Chileno': Nos querellaremos criminalmente, nos declararon," *El Siglo*, February 18, 1946, 8.

53. "Más de 2 mil personas están amenazadas de lanzamiento," *La Opinión*, Santiago, October 25, 1945, 8; "Angustioso llamado a la opinión pública hacen los mejoreros de la población El Pino," *El Siglo*, October 29, 1945, 6; "No somos usurpadores de terrenos, nos estimularon para que levantáramos una población y valorizarla: Ahora nos echan," *El Siglo*, November 12, 1945, 7; "Habría ubicación para ocupantes de predio El Pino," *El Diario Ilustrado* (Santiago), November 16, 1945, 4.

54. "Brota una nueva lacra en la ciudad," *El Diario Ilustrado* (Santiago), November 21, 1945, 1.

55. Gómez, "Factores nacionales"; Andrew Barnard, "Chile," in *Latin America between the Second World War and the Cold War 1944–1948*, ed. Leslie Bethell and Ian Roxborough (Cambridge: Cambridge University Press, 1992), 66–91; Carlos Huneeus, *La Guerra Fría chilena: Gabriel González Videla y la ley maldita* (Santiago: Debate, 2009); Jody Pavilack, *Mining for the Na-*

tion. The Politics of Chile's Coal Communities from the Popular Front to the Cold War (University Park: Penn State University Press, 2011).

56. "Intendente René Frías no dará fuerza pública para lanzamiento en Zañartu," *El Siglo*, June 13, 1947, 8.

57. Espinoza, *Para una historia*.

58. "Ola de lanzamientos continua en Santiago," *El Siglo*, August 12, 1947, 8.

59. Huneeus, *La guerra*; Pavilack, *Mining*.

60. "Violando domicilios y sin orden competente, ayer detuvieron a 3 personas en Población 'Zañartu,'" *El Siglo*, September 29, 1947, 8.

61. "Director de la Vivienda, comandante Riesle, visitó ayer la Población 'Zañartu,' que ha surgido en Ñunoa," *El Diario Ilustrado* (Santiago), October 31, 1947, 7.

62. Articles with these accusations can be found in *El Diario Ilustrado*, December 19, 1947, 4; January 7, 1948, 4 and 8; January 14, 1948, 2; February 18, 1948, 5; and *La Opinión*, January 15, 1948, and February 18, 1948.

63. Huneeus, *La guerra*.

64. Gabriela Mistral was a Chilean educator, poet, and diplomat. In 1945, she was awarded the Nobel Prize in Literature.

65. "Hay orden de desalojo contra 140 pobladores," *El Siglo*, August 27, 1947, 1. "El gobierno debe evitar lanzamientos de 1,200 personas de Población 'Gabriela Mistral,'" *El Siglo*, August 28, 1947, 8; "Se logró suspender transitoriamente lanzamiento de Pob. Gabriela Mistral," *El Siglo*, August 29, 1947, 8.

66. "Insisten en desmentir lo de la Población 'Gabriela Mistral,'" *El Siglo*, November 23, 1947, 9.

67. See, e.g., *La Opinión*, October 16 and 26, 1947, and January 13, 1948; and *El Diario Ilustrado*, November 10, 1947.

68. Acuerdo No. 9016, Santiago, May 28, 1948, ARNAD, Fondo Caja de la Habitación Popular, Acuerdos del Consejo, vol. 35; "Más de 1.200 personas serán lanzadas hoy en población 'Gabriela Mistral,'" *El Siglo*, January 8, 1948, 8; "Comenzó ayer desalojo en masa de los habitantes de población 'G. Mistral,'" *El Siglo*, January 9, 1948, 8; "Hoy trasladan a Los Nogales familias lanzadas de Castro," *El Siglo*, February 3, 1948, 1.

69. Daniel Fauré and Cristina Moyano, eds., *Memoria social de la población Los Nogales (1947–2015)* (Santiago: Corporación Cultural USACH, 2016).

70. Ordinary session of the municipal council, Barrancas, April 24, 1942, minute book 1939–1947, 67–68.

71. Ordinary sessions of the municipal council, Barrancas, September 1, 1945, and October 6, 1945, minute book 1939–1947, 221–22 and 224–27.

72. This is what is stated in a letter from the site purchasers sent to the municipal council. See Ordinary session of the municipal council, Barrancas, March 18, 1948, minute book 1947–1950, 197–203.

73. "Subsiste el peligro de desalojo para 50 familias de pobladores," *El Siglo*, June 22, 1946, 8.

74. Ordinary session of the municipal council, Barrancas, November 11, 1947, minute book 1947–1950, 98–100. Carlos Balbotin later raised similar accusations again. See Ordinary session of the municipal council, Barrancas, February 12, 1948, minute book 1947–1950, 166–80.

75. Ordinary sessions of the municipal council, Barrancas, January 8, 1948, February 12, 1948, March 4, 1948, March 18, 1948, and April 1, 1948, minute book 1947–1950, 132–38, 166–80, 186–96, 197–204, and 204–10.

76. "La población Lautaro trabaja para su progreso," *La Voz de las Barrancas*, no. 2, Santiago, second half of October 1949, 2.

77. "Dos niños perecieron carbonizados en un incendio en población Zañartu," *La Nación* (Santiago), January 10, 1948, 2.

78. "Algunas experiencias sobre organización de pobladores," *Vivienda Popular* (Santiago), February 19, 1948, 2.

79. "Se entregó terrenos a vecinos de manzana n° 1 de Población Zañartu," *El Siglo*, March 14, 1948, 2.

80. Several newspapers covered the transfers during the first months, among them *El Siglo, La Opinión*, and *El Diario Ilustrado*. During the following months, operations began to disappear from the press, also as a result of the closing of *El Siglo* in mid-1948.

81. "Informe sobre población 'Zañartu'" (oficio 06902), Santiago, August 4, 1947, ARNAD, Fondo Caja de la Habitación Popular, Antecedentes de acuerdos, vol. 24.

82. "Se acerca el día del desalojo de 300 familias en población Zañartu," *El Siglo*, March 27, 1946, 8. Other news was published by the same newspaper on March 21 and 22, 1946.

83. Sessions of the municipal council, Ñuñoa, April 10, 1947, and May 28, 1947, book of Minutes of Municipal Sessions 1946–1948, 291–96 and 323–31. See also "Mil personas amenazadas de desalojo por alcalde oligarca de Ñuñoa," *El Siglo*, April 24, 1946, 8.

84. Another complaint, reported by the historian Jorge Rojas, was made by the owner of a property located in Población Zañartu. Carabineros found that 160 people were living in forty small houses, and they were ordered to leave. See Rojas, *La lucha*.

85. "Fundo de la Caja de Seguro Obligatorio que está en arriendo, ha sido ocupado ilegalmente por más de 100 familias," *El Diario Ilustrado* (Santiago), June 12, 1947, 5; "Bajo métodos comunistas perfectamente ideados se están produciendo ocupaciones ilegales de terrenos en pleno Santiago," *El Imparcial* (Santiago), June 18, 1947, 1.

86. "Suman 900 familias las amenazadas de desalojo en la población Zañartu: Queremos casas de emergencia, dicen al gobierno," *El Siglo*, June 12, 1947, 8; "Lucharemos hasta tener las casas de emergencia," *El Siglo*, June 14, 1947, 2; "Se pidió casas de emergencia en la población: Concentración hubo ayer," *El Siglo*, June 16, 1947, 8.

87. "Persiguen a 200 familias en 'Lo Valdivieso,' negándoles derecho a vivir en modestos ranchos," *El Siglo*, July 11, 1947, 8; "Carabineros destrozaron casas de Pob. Valdivieso" *El Siglo*, July 24, 1947, 1; "El Intendente comprobó destrozos en la Población Valdivieso" *El Siglo*, July 25, 1947, 8.

88. "800 families of Pob. Zañartu ask for help to build houses," *El Siglo*, August 30, 1947, 8; "Pobladores de 'Zañartu' han hecho méritos suficientes para que la Caja expropie terrenos," *El Siglo*, October 18, 1947, 4; "Caja de la Habitación debe expropiar terrenos de la población Zañartu," *El Siglo*, October 20, 1947, 8. Other articles appeared on October 21, 25, and 27.

89. "El Nuevo problema de las poblaciones 'fantasmas' estudia director del depto de la vivienda, comandante Riesle," *El Diario Ilustrado* (Santiago), November 5, 1947, 7.

90. This information is taken from articles published by *El Diario Ilustrado* on October 31, 1947, 7; November 5, 1947, 7; November 6, 1947, 8; and November 20, 1947, 4. They also seem consistent with two articles that appeared on November 14, 1947, in *La Nación* and *La Opinión*.

91. Paul Drake, *Socialismo y populismo: Chile 1936–1973* (Valparaíso: Universidad Católica de Valparaíso, 1992); Cristian Pozo, "Ocaso de la unidad obrera en Chile: Confrontación comunista-socialista y la división de la CTCH (1946–1947)" (MA thesis, Santiago, Universidad de Chile, 2013).

92. Rojas, *La lucha*.

93. "Quieren dividir movimiento de pobladores para impedir que obtengan terrenos," *El Siglo*, June 22, 1947, 11. Among the towns adhering to the Front were Zanjón de la Aguada, Mapocho Norte, El Pino, Areneros, Sudamérica, La Marquesita, Zañartu, Bolívar.

94. "Grupo de estafadores comunistas están engañando bajo el nombre Frente Nacional de la Vivienda," *El Diario Ilustrado* (Santiago), June 21, 1947, 1; "Declaraciones del auténtico Frente Nacional de la Vivienda," *El Diario Ilustrado* (Santiago), January 4, 1948, 22.

95. Pozo, *Ocaso*.

96. The activities of the Frente Nacional de la Vivienda, led by Pedro Cáceres, can be found in its official organ, *Vivienda*. In addition, the socialist newspaper *La Opinión* devoted rather attentive coverage to it.

97. "Acuerdos del Frente Nacional de la Vivienda," *El Siglo*, December 19, 1947, 9.

98. "Hoy se inaugura se inaugura congreso de pobladores comuna de San Miguel" *El Siglo*, March 26, 1948, 8; "Títulos de dominio para pobladores," *El Siglo*, March 28, 1948, 8; "Congreso de la vivienda inaugúrese" *El Siglo*, June 27, 1948, 1; "80 delegados participan en el congreso de la vivienda," *El Siglo*, June 28, 1948, 1.

99. "Pobladores se unificaran en un solo potente organismo," *Democracia*, April 24, 1950, 4–5.

100. "We Are Not Communists!," *Vivienda* 7 (1951): 1; "Porque y quienes atacan el Frente Nacional de la Vivienda," *Vivienda* 8 (1951): 1; "Nuestros enemigos," *Vivienda* 10 (1951): 3.

101. The congress was covered by *Democracia* and *La Opinión*.

102. "Esta noche se inaugura congreso de pobladores," *El Siglo*, January 15, 1954, 5; "Se inició el Congreso de Pobladores," *El Siglo*, January 16, 1954. 8; "Hoy será clausurado el Congreso de Pobladores," *El Siglo*, January 17, 1954, 7; "Luchar por termino de lanzamientos," *El Siglo*, January 18, 1954, 8. See also Manuel Loyola, "Los pobladores de Santiago; 1952–1964: Su fase de incorporación a la vida nacional" (BA thesis, Pontificia Universidad Católica de Chile, 1989).

103. Moulian, *Fracturas*; Correa et al., *Historia*.

104. "Desaparecerán poblaciones callampas: Del Pedregal," *La Nación*, Santiago, November 12, 1952, 2; "300 casas construyán para callamperos en noventa días," *La Nación* (Santiago), November 12, 1952, 5.

105. The commission was formed with Decree No. 6077 of the Ministry of the Interior, dated November 27 and published in the *Diario Oficial* on December 30, 1952. See also "Comenzó la ofensiva contra las poblaciones callampas," *La Nación* (Santiago), November 21, 1952, 4.

106. Pedro Gallo, "Las poblaciones callampas como problema sanitario," *Revista Chilena de Higiene y Medicina Preventiva* 15, nos. 1–2 (1953): 39–42; Juan Astica and Mario Vergara, *Antecedentes para la evaluación del problema de las poblaciones callampas en Chile* (paper presented at the Second Inter-American Meeting on Housing and Planning, Lima, 1958); Mario Valencia, *Las poblaciones callampas: Un aspecto del problema habitacional chileno* (thesis to qualify for the title of civil engineer, Universidad de Chile, 1959).

107. The law empowered the Caja de la Habitación to buy land, parcel it out, and sell it to low-income people. It also facilitated loans so that the beneficiaries could buy materials and build on the land. Existing obligations regarding the formation of new towns, such as the obligation to carry out urbanization works before selling the land, were not applicable to these operations. See Law No. 10.254, enacted on February 4, 1952, and published on February 20, 1952. See, e.g., issues 18, 20 and 24 of *Vivienda*, for the Housing Front; and the issues of *El Siglo* of January 1, 1953; January 29, 1953; and February 3, 1953, for the Agrupación de Pobladores.

108. "Inmediato plan para viviendas populares," *La Nación* (Santiago), November 6, 1952, 2; "Constituida comisión que estudiará el problema integral de la vivienda," *La Nación* (Santiago), January 17, 1953.

109. Bravo, *Chile*; Hidalgo, *La vivienda*; Boris Cofré, "El sueño de la casa propia: Estado, empresarios y trabajadores ante el problema de la vivienda y urbanización residencial, Santiago de Chile, 1952–1973" (PhD diss., Pontificia Universidad Católica de Chile, 2016).

110. *Agregados*, or *allegados*, were families living in others' families houses or lots, a very common situation in Chile and other Latin American countries.

111. "Nuevo organismo se formó en la población Nueva La Legua," *Democracia* (Santiago), April 3, 1950, 3; "500 familias de población callampa no tienen donde levantar sus mejoras," *La Opinión* (Santiago), April 14, 1951, 4; "700 familias de Nueva La Legua tramitadas hace más de dos años," *El Poblador*, no. 2, May 31, 1952, 2; "Los agregados de Nueva La Legua piden sitios y escuelas," *El Siglo*, December 3, 1952, 6; "El problema de los agregados en población Nueva La Legua," *El Siglo*, April 12, 1953, 5.

112. Adrián Escalona, "Comité 'Agregados de Nueva La Legua': Hoy 'Población Germán Riesco,'" in *Constructores de ciudad: Nueve historias del primer concurso "Historia de las Poblaciones,"* ed. David Avello, Paulina Matta, Alfredo Rodríguez, and Alex Rosenfeld (Santiago: SUR, 1989), 36–48.

113. "Violentamente desalojados agregados que ocuparon casas de Pob. Aníbal Pinto," *El Siglo*, March 15, 1954, 1. See also "Familias sin hogar intentaron tomar por asalto una población que está en construcción," *Las Noticias de Última Hora* (Santiago), March 14, 1954, 8; Santiago Danús Peña to the Minister of the Interior (Oficio No. 600), Santiago, March 15, 1954, ARNAD, Ministry of the Interior Fund, Providencias, vol. 15586; Santiago Danús Peña to the Minister of the Interior with transcription of the report of the 1st Police Station of Carabineros (Oficio No. 602), Santiago, March 15, 1954, ARNAD, Ministry of the Interior Fund, Providencias, vol. 15586.

114. "Permanecen en la calle los agregados de Nueva La Legua," *El Siglo*, March 16, 1954, 5.

115. "Permanecen." In relation to the minister's promise, on March 17, he requested a study on the fiscal sites where the *callampas* populations could be relocated. See Minister of the Interior to the Minister of Land and Colonization, Santiago, March 17, 1954, ARNAD, Ministry of the Interior Fund, Oficios, vol. 15569.

116. "618 son las familias de agregados que permanecen en calles de Nueva La Legua," *El Siglo*, March 17, 1954, 5.

117. "3,000 sitios acordó distribuir la corporación de la vivienda," *El Siglo*, March 19, 1954, 2; "Prometieron iniciar el traslado de agregados el miércoles próximo," *El Siglo*, March 20, 1954, 2.

118. "La experiencia lo confirma: Solo a través de la lucha conquistaran un hogar," *El Siglo*, March 21, 1954, 3. Similar arguments were repeated at the end of August, in a public act that inaugurated the Población Germán Riesco. See "Ayer se iniciaron actos de inauguración de la población Germán Riesco de San Miguel," *El Siglo*, August 28, 1954, 8.

119. "Con desfiles y concentración despidieron a agregados los pobladores de Nueva La Legua," *El Siglo*, March 29, 1954, 5; "19 días llevan durmiendo en la calle 700 familias," *El Siglo*, March 31, 1954, 8; "Tragedia provocó temporal en agregados de Nueva La Legua," *El Siglo*, April 9, 1954, 1.

120. "Pobladores ocuparon anoche 174 sitios," *El Siglo*, May 29, 1954, 1.

121. Bravo, *Chile*; Escalona, "Comité."

122. Rolando Guerra Arredondo to the general manager of the Housing Corporation, Santiago, December 2, 1954, ARNAD, Ministry of the Interior Fund, Providencias, vol. 15599. Among the occupants were some families from the Población Germán Riesco whom the official convinced to return to their properties while waiting for the promised sites to be delivered to them.

123. "Familias desalojadas ocuparon terrenos en la calle San Joaquin," *El Siglo*, December 3, 1954, 1 and 8.

124. "Hoy se concentran pobladores de la nueva población callampa," *El Siglo*, December 5, 1954, 6.

125. Moulian, *Fracturas*; Sofía Correa, "Algunos antecedentes históricos del proyecto neoliberal en Chile (1955–1958)," *Revista del Centro de Estudios de la Realidad Contemporánea* 6 (1986): 106–46.

126. Bravo, *Chile*.

127. "100 families se 'tomaron' terrenos del SSS en P. Alto," *El Siglo*, October 2, 1956, 1.

128. Orlando Millas, *Memorias 1957–1991: Una digresión* (Santiago: CESOC, 1996).

129. "Las 11 familias de Santa Teresa siguen durmiendo a la intemperie," *El Siglo*, January 13, 1957, 1 and 9.

130. "Queremos maderas para edificar," *El Siglo*, January 15, 1957, 4.

131. Dafne Marticorena, "Algunas soluciones al problema de las poblaciones callampas" (BA thesis, Universidad Católica, 1959).

132. "Queremos maderas."

133. "De callamperos a propietarios," *La Tercera de La Hora* (Santiago), September 13, 1956, 16; "Cerro Blanco muestra llagas y miseria de miles de chilenos" and "Pobladores de Cerro Blanco quieren ser trasladados a los terrenos que el SSS compró en el Huanaco," *El Siglo*, October 14, 1956, 6; "Traslado antes de las elecciones piden pobladores de Cerro Blanco," *El Siglo*, January 27, 1957, 12; Council of the Housing Corporation, ordinary session, Santiago, May 2, 1957, ARNAD, CORVI fund, minutes, vol. 221, 23D–24D.

134. "Pobladores del Cerro Blanco huyeron de la mugre: Gobierno los hizo regresar a la fuerza," *El Siglo*, February 10, 1957, 1 and 9.

135. "Comicio contra la carestía y los desalojos," *El Siglo*, January 17, 1957, 6; "Pobladores participan en lucha contra la carestía," *El Siglo*, January 18, 1957, 4; "Arrendatarios acordaron no pagar las alzas," *El Siglo*, January 18, 1957, 5; "Arrendatarios presentan pelea a las alzas," *El Siglo*, March 21, 1957, 4; "Entrega de casas, sitios y urbanización total, abordará congreso de pobladores," *El Siglo*, March 24, 1957, 12; "Hoy finaliza el quinto congreso de pobladores," *El Siglo*, March 31, 1957, 9.

136. Pedro Milos, *Historia y memoria, 2 de abril de 1957* (Santiago: LOM, 2007).

137. "Violencia policial desalojó 40 familias en Quinta Normal," *El Siglo*, May 20, 1957, 6; Clodomiro Bustamante Acuña, Carabineros Colonel, to the Ministry of the Interior, Santiago, May 20, 1957, ARNAD, Ministry of the Interior Fund, Oficios, vol. 16570; "Aclaración a publicaciones formula intendente de Stgo," *Diario Ilustrado*, May 21, 1957, 10.

138. The bibliography on La Victoria is extensive. For a detailed account of the *toma*, see Espinoza, *Para una historia*; Garcés, *Tomando*. Two recent texts, with fairly complete bibliographies, are: Cortes, *El movimiento* and Emanuel Giannotti, "Una ciudad de propietarios: El caso de la Población La Victoria," *AUS* 15 (2014): 40–45.

139. Sobre ocupación ilegal de terrenos de la CORVI en el sector "La Feria," Union Memo No. 505, Santiago, October 30, 1957, ARNAD, Fondo del Ministerio del Interior, Oficios, vol. 16578.

140. Giannotti, "Una ciudad."

141. "'Queremos hacer un Chile mejor' dijeron pobladores de 'La Feria,'" *El Siglo*, November 2, 1957, 5.

142. Consejo de la Corporación de la Vivienda, Consideraciones sobre la ocupación clandestina de terrenos de la Corporación de la Vivienda denominado 'La Feria norte' y ubicados en Santiago, ordinary session, Santiago, November 6, 1957, ARNAD, file CORVI, Actas, vol. 225, 2D.

143. Consejo de la Corporación de la Vivienda, 3D.

144. "Pobladores callampas de La Granja se tomaron sitios de 'San Gregorio,'" *El Siglo*, November 4, 1957, 12. See also "Otra invasión callampas: Mil familias desalojadas hacia Fundo San Gregorio," *Las Noticias de Última Hora*, November 3, 1957, 8; "Gobierno echó a callamperos," *Las Noticias de Última Hora*, November 4, 1957, 1; "Fueron expulsados los ocupantes de San Gregorio," *El Siglo*, November 5, 1957, 1.

145. Garcés, *Tomando*; Manuel Castells, *The City and the Grassroots* (Berkeley: University of California Press, 1983); Murphy, *For a Proper*.

146. However, this representation was constructed only through the party newspaper, *El Siglo*. Throughout the 1950s and part of the 1960s, the *pobladores* and the *tomas* were absent from the party's magazine, *Principios*, as well as from official speeches and documents. According to Mario Garcés, this could be explained by the difficulty of Marxist theories, oriented toward production, to conceptualize the world of the *pobladores*. Garcés, *Tomando*.

147. Antonio Azuela, "Los asentamientos populares y el orden jurídico en la urbanización periférica de América Latina," *Revista Mexicana de Sociología* 55, no. 3 (1993): 133–68. See also Alan Gilbert, "Pirates and Invaders: Land Acquisition in Urban Colombia and Venezuela," *World Development* 9, no. 7 (1981): 665–78.

148. Fischer, *Poverty*; Gonçalves, *Favelas*.

149. This contrasts with other Latin American cases, where the tolerance was higher, although it changed over time. See Ollivier and Fischer, in this volume.

150. Carlos Hirth, "Los loteos brujos y la comunidad nacional" (thesis seminar, Universidad Católica de Chile, 1967).

151. Garcés, *Tomando*; Emanuel Giannotti and Hugo Mondragón, "La inestabilidad de la forma: Proyectos para barrios populares en Santiago de Chile, 1953–1970," *Bitácora Urbano-territorial* 27, no. 1 (2017): 35–46.

152. Alfonso Torres, *La ciudad en la sombra: Barrios y luchas populares en Bogotá 1950–1977*, 2nd ed. (Bogotá: Universidad Piloto de Colombia, 2013).

153. Ray, *The Politics*; Collier, *Squatters*; Henry Dietz, "Land Invasion and Consolidation: A Study of Working Poor / Governmental Relations in Lima, Peru," *Urban Anthropology* 6, no. 4 (1977): 371–85; Azuela and Cruz, "La institucionalización"; Antuñano, "Planning"; Ollivier, this volume.

154. Adriana Massidda, "Shantytowns and the Modern City: Examining Urban Poverty in South-Western Buenos Aires (1958–1967)" (PhD diss., Cambridge University, 2016); Valeria Snitcofsky, *Historia de las villas de Buenos Aires* (Buenos Aires: Tejido Urbano, 2022); María José Bolaña, *Pobreza y segregación urbana: "Cantegriles" montevideanos 1946–1973* (Montevideo: Editorial Rumbo 2018); Brodwyn Fischer, "The Red Menace Reconsidered: A Forgotten History of Communist Mobilization in Rio de Janeiro's Favelas, 1945–1964," *Hispanic American Historical Review* 94, no. 1 (2014): 1–33; Samuel Oliveira, "Associativismos de trabalhadores favelados no Rio de Janeiro e em Belo Horizonte (1954–1964)," *Estudos Históricos* 31, no. 65 (2018): 349–68; Emanuel Giannotti and Rafael Soares Gonçalves, "La Guerra Fría en las favelas y las

poblaciones, 1945–1964: Una disputa entre comunistas e Iglesia Católica," *Izquierdas* 49 (2020): 642–62.

155. Among others, see Wayne Cornelius, *Politics and the Migrant Poor in Mexico City* (Stanford, CA: Stanford University Press, 1975); Castells, *The City*; Gilbert and Ward, *Housing*.

Chapter Eight

1. Translated as *Brazil: Mixture or Massacre: Essays on the Genocide of a Black People* (Dover, MA: Majority Press, 1979).

2. "Racial democracy" in Brazil (and in Latin America more broadly) posited that Latin America's racial inequalities resulted from structural and material conditions created by slavery and colonialism but were not sustained by institutional or ideological commitments to racism and were destined to fade with miscegenation and economic development. In Brazil, this idealized notion was based heavily in a long-standing set of beliefs about the supposed fluidity of Brazilian social and sexual relationships, which developed from the nineteenth century forward as a cornerstone of Brazil's national imaginary. After World War II, when the term itself was first used, *racial democracy* became Brazil's international calling card and a central element of Brazilian domestic politics. For relatively recent synthetic and critical analysis, see Antonio Sérgio Guimarães, "Democracia racial: O ideal, o pacto e o mito," *Novos Estudos CEBRAP* 61 (2001): 147–62; Antonio Sérgio Guimarães, "A democracia racial revisitada," *Afro-Ásia* 60 (2019): 9–44; Paulina Alberto, "Of Sentiment, Science and Myth," *Social History* 37, no. 3 (2012): 261–96; Paulina Alberto and Jesse Hoffnung-Garskof, "Racial Democracy and Racial Inclusion," in *Afro-Latin American Studies*, ed. Alejandro de la Fuente and George Reid Andrews (Cambridge: Cambridge University Press, 2018), 264–300; de la Fuente, "'From Slaves to Citizens?,'" *International Labor and Working Class History* 77, no. 1 (2010): 154–73; Jessica Graham, *Shifting the Meaning of Democracy* (Berkeley: University of California Press, 2019); Marcos Chor Maio and Ricardo Ventura Santos, *Raça, ciência e sociedade* (Rio de Janeiro: Fundação Oswaldo Cruz, 1996); Robin Sheriff, "Exposing Silence as Cultural Censorship," *American Anthropologist* 102, no. 1 (2000): 114–32.

3. Nascimento, *O genocidio*, 83–87.

4. Carolina Maria de Jesus, *Child of the Dark* (New York: Dutton, 1962). For historical statistics on race and *favelas*, see Brodwyn Fischer, "From the Mocambo to the Favela," *Histoire et Mesure* 34, no. 1 (2019): 15–39 and "Partindo a cidade maravilhosa," in *Quase cidadão*, ed. Olívia Gomes da Cunha and Flávio dos Santos Gomes (Rio de Janeiro: FGV, 2007), 419–50. In midtwentieth-century Rio, Afro-descendants were 30 percent of the city but 67 percent of the *favela* population; we lack hard data for other cities, but scattered research indicates similar patterns.

5. Thales de Azevedo, *Democracia racial: Ideologia e realidade* (Petrópolis: Vozes, 1976); Paulina Alberto, *Terms of Inclusion* (Chapel Hill: University of North Carolina Press, 2011); Jerry Dávila, *Hotel Trópico* (Durham, NC: Duke University Press, 2010).

6. Hebe Mattos, "Prefácio," in *Além da escravidão*, ed. Fred Cooper, Thomas Holt, and Rebecca Scott (Rio de Janeiro: Civilização Brasileira, 2004); Brodwyn Fischer, Keila Grinberg, and Hebe Mattos, "Law, Silence, and Racialized Inequalities in the History of Afro-Brazil," in, *Afro-Latin American*, ed. Alejandro de la Fuente and Reid Andrews (Cambridge: Cambridge University Press, 2018), 130–78; Brodwyn Fischer, "A ética do silêncio racial no contexto urbano: Políticas públicas e desigualdade social no Recife, 1900–1940," *Anais do Museu Paulista* 28 (2020), 1–45; Sheriff, "Exposing."

7. Ramos, *The Negro in Brazil* (Washington, DC: Associated Publishers, 1939), 173. Ramos referred to regions with significant Afro-Brazilian population.

8. Donald Pierson, *Negroes in Brazil: A Study of Race Contact in Bahia* (Chicago: University of Chicago Press, 1942), 17, 348. Thales de Azevedo reinforced Pierson's view in *As elites de cor* (São Paulo: Editora Nacional, 1955), 71.

9. L. A. Costa Pinto, *O Negro no Rio de Janeiro*, 2nd ed. (Rio de Janeiro: UFRJ, 1998), 35, 132.; Chor Maio, *Raça*, introduction.

10. Roger Bastide and Florestan Fernandes *Brancos e negros em São Paulo*, 4th ed. (São Paulo: Global, 2006), esp. 71–90. Fernandes, Bastide, and Costa Pinto worked on a series of influential UNESCO-sponsored studies from the 1950s that were widely recognized as central to subsequent critiques of racial democracy but generally either relied on psychosocial analysis of Black people or retained a structuralist-materialist frame to explain the persistence of racial inequality. See Marcos Chor Maio, "O projeto UNESCO e a agenda das ciências sociais no Brasil dos anos 40 e 50," *Revista Brasileira de Ciências Sociais* 14, no. 41 (1999): 141–58; Marcos Chor Maio, "Florestan Fernandes, Oracy Nogueira, and the UNESCO Project on Race Relations in São Paulo," *Latin American Perspectives* 38, no. 3 (2011): 136–49; Cláudio Pereira and Livio Sansone, *O Projeto UNESCO no Brasil* (Salvador: EdUFBA, 2007).

11. Fischer, "Ética."

12. This literature is vast. For English syntheses and analyses, see Michael Hanchard, *Racial Politics in Contemporary Brazil* (Durham, NC: Duke University Press, 1999); Rebecca Reichmann, *Race in Contemporary Brazil* (University Park, PA: Penn State University Press, 1999); Edward Telles, *Race in Another America* (Princeton, NJ: Princeton University Press, 2014); Tianna Paschel, *Becoming Black Political Subjects* (Princeton, NJ: Princeton University Press, 2016); Jaime Alves, *The Anti-Black City* (Minneapolis: University of Minnesota, 2018); Jan French, "Rethinking Police Violence in Brazil," *Latin American Politics and Society* 55, no. 4 (2013): 161–81; Keisha-Khan Perry, *Black Women against the Land Grab* (Minneapolis: University of Minnesota Press, 2013). In Portuguese, see Renato Meirelles and Celso Athayde, *Um país chamado favela* (São Paulo: Gente, 2014); Renato Emerson dos Santos, *Questões urbanas e racismo* (Petrópolis: DP and Alii, 2012); Verena Alberti and Amilcar Araujo Pereira, *Historias do movimento Negro no Brasil* (Rio de Janeiro: CPDOC, 2007); Antonia dos Santos Garcia, *Desigualdades raciais e segregação urbana em antigas capitais* (Rio de Janeiro: Garamond, 2009); Mara Silva, "Propriedades, negritude e moradia na produção da segregação racial da cidade" (MA thesis, UFMG, 2018); Josemeire Alves Pereira and Mara Silva, "O estigma do invasor na produção do espaço urbano," in *Periferias em rede*, ed. Clarice Libânio and Josemeire Alves Pereira (Belo Horizonte: Favela é Isso Aí, 2018).

13. See, e.g., Sidney Chalhoub, *Cidade febril* (São Paulo: Cia. Das Letras, 1996); Andrelino Campos, *Do quilombo à favela* (Rio de Janeiro: Bertrand, 2005); Fischer, "Partindo" and "Ética"; Ynaê Lopes dos Santos, *Além da senzala* (São Paulo: Hucitec, 2010) and "Escravidão, moradia e resistência," *Nuevo Mundo/Mundos Nuevos* (2010): https://doi.org/10.4000/nuevomundo.58448; Reinaldo José de Oliveira and Regina Marques de Souza Oliveira, "Origens da segregação racial no Brasil," *Amérique Latine* 29 (2015): http://doi.org/10.4000/alhim.5191; Marcus Carvalho, *Liberdade* (Recife: UFPE, 2001); Raquel Rolnik, "Territorios Negros nas cidades brasileiras," *Revista de Estudos Afro-Asiáticos* 17 (1989): 1–17; Lourdes Carril, *Quilombo, favela, e periferia* (São Paulo: Annablume, FAPESP, 2006); George Reid Andrews, "Inequality," in de la Fuente and Andrews, *Afro-Latin American*, 52–91; George Reid Andrews, *Blacks and Whites in São Paulo* (Madison: University of Wisconsin Press, 1991); Petrônio Domingues, *Uma história não contada*

(São Paulo: Senac, 2003); Celso Castilho, *Slave Emancipation in Brazil* (Pittsburgh, PA: University of Pittsburgh Press, 2016); Maria Helena Machado, "From Slave Rebels to Strikebreakers," *Hispanic American Historical Review* 86, no. 2 (2006): 247–74; Maria Helena Machado, *O plano e o pânico* (Rio de Janeiro: UFRJ, 1994); Flávio Gomes and Petrônio Domingues, *Políticas da Raça* (São Paulo: Selo Negro, 2014).

14. Social science exceptions include Meirelles and Athayde, *Um país*; Perry, *Black*; and Rolnik, "Territorios." Some histories of the *favela* have also begun to reconsider the racialization of *favelas*. See Fischer, "Ética," as well as Ana Barone and Flávia Rios, eds., *Negros nas cidades brasileiras* (Intermeios: Casa de Artes e Livros, 2019); Ana Barone, ed., "Dossiê: Dimensões raciais da cultura material urbana no Brasil," special issue, *Anais do Museu Paulista* 28 (2020); Oliveira, "Informalidade urbana, classe trabalhadora e raça no rio de Janeiro," *Revista de História* 180 (2021): 1–27; Samuel Oliveira, "Relações raciais e o movimento de trabalhadores favelados de Belo Horizonte," *Varia História* 38, no. 77 (2022): 559–91; Josemeire Alves Pereira, "Para além do horizonte planejado" (PhD diss., UNICAMP, 2019); Rómulo Costa Mattos, "Shantytown Dwellers' Resistance in Brazil's First Republic," *International Journal of Labor and Working-Class History* 83 (2013): 54–69; Rómulo Costa Mattos, "Pelos pobres!" (PhD diss., UFF, 2008).

15. One of the most significant strains of innovative scholarship that is exceptional in this vein documents the history of *favelas* in Belo Horizonte; see especially Alves Pereira, "Para além."

16. Brazilian slavery was abolished in 1888, the latest date in the Western Hemisphere.

17. Fischer et al., "Law, Silence." Brazilian informality resembled slavery in the sense that it created systems of power in which small mobilities were deeply precarious and often failed to overturn inequality's scaffolding. See Chalhoub, "The Precariousness of Freedom in a Slave Society," *International Review of Social History* 56 (2011): 405–39. There are significant parallels between the ideology of informality and the individualistic Black property claims explored by Nathan Connolly in twentieth–century Miami. Writing about the function of property and individualism across the racial spectrum, Connolly writes: "Driven by individual self-interest and, often, communal ideals about race, people of every complexion made Jim Crow work. And they did so by pursuing frail promises about the benefits of property ownership, the acceptability of state violence, and the potentially reparative power of urban redevelopment. Through projects as everyday as paved streets in the city or new houses in the suburbs, even Jim Crow's most beleaguered and maligned people placed their hopes in one day morally perfecting American capitalism." Connolly, *A World More Concrete* (Chicago: University of Chicago Press, 2019), 4–5.

18. On the notion that informality is characteristic of city building across social classes, see Ananya Roy, "Why India Cannot Plan Its Cities," *Planning Theory* 8, no. 1 (2009): 76–87; James Holston, *Insurgent Citizenship* (Princeton, NJ: Princeton University Press, 2008). On wealthy people's use of informality in Rio, see Brodwyn Fischer, *A Poverty of Rights* (Stanford, CA: Stanford University Press, 2008).

19. For an elegant summary of this scholarship, see Flávio Gomes, "Quilombos," in *Dicionário da escravidão e Liberdade*, ed. Flávio Gomes and Lília Schwarcz (São Paulo: Cia. das Letras, 2018), 367–73.

20. On cultural and intellectual underpinnings of the urban imagination, see Jennifer Robinson, *Ordinary Cities* (New York: Routledge, 2006).

21. For the influence of these in Brazil, see Lília Schwartz, *O espectáculo das raças* (São Paulo: Cia. das Letras), 1993.

22. Nicolau Sevcenko, *Orfeu extático na metropole* (São Paulo: Cia. das Letras, 1992); Nicolau Sevcenko, "A capital irradiante," in *História da vida privada no Brasil*, ed. Nicolau Sevcenko (São Paulo: Cia. das Letras, 1999), 3: 513–619; Luiz Cesar de Quieroz Ribeiro and Roberto Pechman, *Cidade, povo, nação* (Rio de Janeiro: Civilização Brasileira, 1996); Jeffrey Needell, *A Tropical Belle Époque* (Cambridge: Cambridge University Press, 1987); Teresa Meade, *Civilizing Rio* (University Park, PA: Penn State University Press, 1997); Nísia Trindade Lima and Gilberto Hochman, "Condenado pela raça, absolvido pela medicina: O Brasil descoberto pelo movimento sanitarista da Primeira República," in Maia and Santos, *Raça*, 23–40. Antonio Rezende, *(Des)encantos modernos* (Recife: UFPE, 2016); Ciro Flávio Bandeira de Mello, "A noiva do trabalho," in *BH: Horizontes históricos*, ed. Eliana Dutra (Belo Horizonte: C/Arte, 1996), 11–47.

23. For an early summary of these regulations in Rio, Recife, Belo Horizonte, Niterói, and São Paulo, see Everardo Backheuser, *Habitações populares* (Rio de Janeiro: Imprensa Nacional, 1906). For later accounts of legal evolution, see Lilian Fessler Vaz, *Modernidade e moradia* (Rio de Janeiro: 7 Letras, 2002); Mauricio de Almeida Abreu, *Evolução urbana do Rio de Janeiro* (Rio de Janeiro: Zahar, 1988); Jaime Benchimol, *Pereira Passos* (Rio de Janeiro: Biblioteca Carioca, 1990); Sidney Chalhoub, *Cidade febril* (São Paulo: Cia. Das Letras, 1996); Fischer, *A Poverty of Rights* (Stanford, CA: Stanford University Press, 2008); Rafael Soares Gonçalves, *Favelas do Rio de Janeiro: História e direito* (Rio de Janeiro: Pallas/PUC-Rio, 2013); Meade, *Civilizing*; Luiz Quieroz Ribeiro, *Dos cortiços aos condomínios fechados* (Rio de Janeiro: Civilização Brasileira, 1996); Alves Pereira, "Para além"; Daniel McDonald, "The Origins of Informality in a Brazilian Planned City," *Journal of Urban History* 47, no. 1 (2019): 29–49; Marcus Melo, "A cidade dos mocambos," *Espaço e Debates* 14 (1985): 44–66; Raquel Rolnik, *A cidade e a lei* (São Paulo: Studio Nóbel, 1997). On São Luis, see Maria da Conceição Pinheiro de Almeida, "Porões, sótãos e palhoças: Moradias dos pobres sob a mira do serviço sanitário em São Luís/MA nos primeiros anos da República," in *Histórias da pobreza no Brasil*, ed. Fabiano Quadros Rückert, Jonathan Fachini da Silva, José Carlos da Silva, and Tiago da Silva César (Rio Grande do Sul: FURG, 2019), 5–106.

24. Lícia Valladares, *The Invention of the Favela* (Durham, NC: Duke University Press, 2019); José Tavares de Lira, "O urbanismo e o seu outro: Raça, cultura e cidade no Brasil (1920–1945)," *Revista Brasileira de Estudos Urbanos e Regionais* 1, no. 1 (1999): 47–78.

25. In addition to works cited in note 18, *supra*, see Luciano Parisse, *Favelas do Rio de Janeiro: Evolução e sentido* (Rio de Janeiro: PUC/CNPH, 1969); Anthony Leeds and Elizabeth Leeds, *A sociologia do Brasil urbano* (Rio de Janeiro: Zahar, 1978); Samuel Oliveira, " 'Trabalhadores favelados': Identificação das favelas e movimentos sociais no Rio de Janeiro e em Belo Horizonte" (PhD diss., PPGHPBC-CPDOC/FGV, 2014); Zélia Gominho, *Veneza Americana x. Mocambópolis* (Recife: CEPE, 1998); Costa Mattos, "Pelos pobres!"

26. On Catholicism, see Gonçalves, in this volume. In this respect, housing campaigns in Brazil echoed those in Spain and Italy.

27. The idea that tolerance is at the center of Brazil's informal politics has been essential to recent scholarship of informality in Brazil, which developed the term in conversation with mid-twentieth-century legal and political debates. Some of the concept's foundations can be found in the classic Brazilian literature on *favela* hierarchy and negotiation. Luiz Antônio Machado da Silva, "A política na favela," *Cadernos Brasileiros* 9, no. 41 (1967): 33–47; Boaventura de Souza Santos, "The Law of the Oppressed," *Law and Society Review* 12, no. 1 (1977): 5–126; Leeds and Leeds, *A sociologia*. For a contemporary history of "the politics of legal tolerance," see Fischer, *Poverty*, chaps. 2 and 7; Brodwyn Fischer, "Urban Informality, Citizenship, and the

Paradoxes of Development," in *State and Nation Making in Latin America and Spain: The Rise and Fall of the Developmental State*, ed. Miguel Centeno and Agustín Ferraro (Cambridge: Cambridge University Press, 2019), 372–402; and Brodwyn Fischer, "Favelas and Politics in Brazil," *Oxford Research Encyclopedia of Latin American History* (2019): https://doi.org/10.1093/acre fore/9780199366439.013.420. On the parallel notion of precarious tolerance as a feature of the Rio *favelas*' legal status in the mid-twentieth century, see Rafael Soares Gonçalves, *Favelas*; Rafael Soares Gonçalves and Caroline dos Santos, "Gestão da informalidade urbana e tolerância precária," *Revista Brasileira de Estudos Urbanos e Regionais* 23 (2021): https://doi.org/10.22296/2317 -1529.rbeur.202103; Rafael Soares Gonçalves, this volume. Historiographical iterations of Brazilian "tolerance" should be read in conversation with James Holston's discussion in *Insurgent* of the role of legal uncertainty in generating Brazilian inequality; the concept is also usefully paired with Alisha Holland's "Forbearance," *American Political Science Review* 110, no. 2 (2016): 232–46.

28. Statistical estimates are difficult in this era because different cities measured different aspects of informality: Recife's pioneering *mocambo* census, for example, measured individual dwellings built from rustic or improvised materials, while national censuses and Rio's 1933 building census measured construction materials and public services, and Rio's private and city-wide *favela* censuses measured only agglomerations of fifty or more low-income improvised structures. In São Paulo, where few places were labeled *favelas* until the mid-twentieth century and low-income housing was concentrated in *cortiços* and auto-construction in unregulated peripheries, it is even harder to trace the proportion of residents who lived in informality. See Fischer, "From the *Mocambo*"; Samuel Oliveira, "A imaginação da informalidade urbana e dos trabalhadores no Rio de Janeiro e em Belo Horizonte," *Topoi* 23, no. 50 (2022): 540–62; Rafael Soares Gonçalves, "Les favelas cariocas dans les recensements nationaux," *Histoire et Mesure* 34, no. 1 (2019): 41–63; Berenice Guimarães, "Favelas em Belo Horizonte," *Análise e Conjuntura* 7, nos. 2–3 (1992): 11–18.

29. Leeds and Leeds, *A sociologia*; Vaz, *Modernidade*; Maria Lais Pereira da Silva, *Favelas cariocas (1930–1964)* (Rio de Janeiro: Contraponto, 2005); Fischer, *Poverty* and "Urban Informality"; Gonçalves, *Favelas*.

30. On the quantification of Brazilian informality, see Fischer, "From the *Mocambo*," Gonçalves, "Favelas"; Oliveira, "Informalidade" and "A imaginação." Correlations between racial and geographies were quite strong in the 1933 and 1940 Rio censuses. Unpublished censuses of Rio *favelas*, a generation of midcentury social science research, and subsequent censuses of *favela* populations that included racial data in Rio and Belo Horizonte further substantiated those claims. In recent years, these patterns have if anything become stronger. In addition to census data from Rio and Belo Horizonte, see Pierson, *Negroes*; Costa Pinto, *O negro*; Bastide and Fernandes, *Brancos*; Telles, *Race*. In the community-led Censo de Maré from 2014, of 140,000 people, 52.9 percent were *pardo*, 9.2 percent *preto*, and 36.6 percent *branco*. On public services and race, see Fischer, "Partindo."

31. See esp. Lorraine Leu, *Defiant Geographies* (Pittsburgh, PA: University of Pittsburgh Press, 2020).

32. José Tavares de Lira, "A construção discursiva da casa popular no Recife (década de 30)," *Análise Social* 29, no. 3 (1994): 733–53; Tavares de Lira, "O urbanismo."

33. L. F. de Tollenare, *Notas dominicais tomadas durante uma residencia em Portugal e no Brasil nos annos de 1816, 1817, e 1818* (Recife: Jornal do Recife, 1905), 42.

34. G. W. Freyreiss, *Viagem ao interior do Brazil* (São Paulo: Diário Oficial, 1906), 226, also cited in Mary Karasch, *Slave Life in Rio de Janeiro* (Princeton, NJ: Princeton University Press, 1987), 186.

35. Lima Barreto, *O Moleque* (Niterói: Itapuca, 2020), discussed in Romulo da Costa Mattos, "As *favelas* na obra de Lima Barreto," *URBANA* 2, no. 1 (2007): 1–27; Freyre, *Sobrados e mocambos* (São Paulo: Global, 2004), 350, 413.

36. Karasch, *Slave*, 105, 403, 405, 407.

37. For classification, see Backheuser, *Habitações*.

38. Sandra Lauderdale-Graham, *House and Street* (Austin: University of Texas Press, 1988), 16 and 26. For tenement owners who deliberately blurred the line between huts and tenement rooms to avoid municipal prohibitions, see Chalhoub, *Cidade*, 43–44.

39. Lauderdale-Graham, *House*, 128. Chalhoub, *Cidade*, esp. 45; Santos, *Além*.

40. The *cidade negra* is elaborated on later in this chapter. On *zungus* and the *cidade negra*, see Santos, *Além*; Luiz Carlos Soares, *O "povo de cam" na capital do Brasil* (Rio de Janeiro: 7 Letras, 2007); Juliana Barreto Farias, Flávio dos Santos Gomes, Carlos Eugênio Líbano Soares, and Carlos Eduardo de Araújo Moreira, eds., *Cidades Negras* (São Paulo: Alameda, 2006). On living on one's own account as a challenge to slavery, see Chalhoub, *Visões da liberdade* (São Paulo: Cia. das Letras, 1990), esp. 233–48.

41. Santos, *Além*; Chalhoub, *Cidade*; Karasch, *Slave*; Soares, *O povo*.

42. Karasch, *Slave*, 185 and 534n46.

43. Lauderdale-Graham, *House*, 49.

44. On the blackening of white bodies in *favelas*, see Leu, *Defiant*.

45. The concept of the *cidade negra* relates to Raquel Rolnik's *território negro*.

46. Chalhoub explores how the *cidade negra* served to "erode" "slavery's politics of domination." *Visões*, 185.

47. In modern Portuguese, *coito* means intercourse, but in the nineteenth century it was a common spelling for *couto*, which implies a den of criminals or animals. On June 27, 1871, for example, the *Jornal do Recife* reported the discovery of a "coito de escravos" in the city of Olinda, where police arrested an escaped enslaved woman named Rita and her companions used "herbs" to "cast spells, which were evidently worthless since she was captured."

48. Chalhoub, *Visões*, 238. On the legal importance of "possessing" freedom, see Beatriz Mamigonian and Keila Grinberg, "The Crime of Illegal Enslavement and the Precariousness of Freedom in Nineteenth-Century Brazil," in *The Boundaries of Freedom*, ed. Brodwyn Fischer and Keila Grinberg (Cambridge: Cambridge University Press, 2022), 35–56.

49. For examples in English, see Marcus Carvalho, "Hellish Nurseries," in Fischer and Grinberg, *Boundaries*, 57–82; see also Chalhoub, *Visões* and *A força da escravidão* (São Paulo: Cia. das Letras, 2012). On wet nurses, see Maria Helena Machado, "Body, Gender, and Identity," in Fischer and Grinberg, *Boundaries*, 163–82. On poison, see Chalhoub, *Visões*, 205. On mass uprising, see João Reis, *Rebelião escrava* (São Paulo: Cia. Das Letras, 2003).

50. Chalhoub, *Visões*, 212, 216.

51. For ways of conceptualizing similar spaces outside of Brazil, see Katherine McKitterick, *Demonic Grounds* (Minneapolis: University of Minnesota Press, 2006); Rashauna Johnson, *Slavery's Metropolis* (New York: Cambridge University Press, 2016); Marisa Fuentes, *Dispossessed Lives* (Philadelphia: University of Pennsylvania Press, 2016).

52. See note 18, *supra*.

53. In the 1850s, Brazil finally ended its Atlantic slave trade; in 1871 the country passed a free-womb law; and in 1888 the Imperial government abolished legalized slavery. For overview and bibliography, see Herbert Klein and Francisco Vidal Luna, *Slavery in Brazil* (New York: Cambridge University Press, 2010); Fischer and Grinberg, *Boundaries*, "Introduction."

54. This process sometimes pierced the seigneurial logic that had often governed Brazilian emancipation. See Machado, *O plano*; Chalhoub, *Visões*. But continuities also remained. See Chalhoub, *A força*; Wlamyra Albuquerque, "The Life and Times of a Free Black Man in Brazil's Era of Abolition," in Fischer and Grinberg, *Boundaries*, 264-86. Already in 1850 the majority of Brazil's Afro-descendant population was legally free and by final abolition, more than half of the 1.5 million people enslaved in 1872 had attained their freedom.

55. Wlamyra Albuquerque, *O jogo da dissimulação* (São Paulo: Cia. das Letras, 2009).

56. This was especially explicit in São Paulo: Domíngues, *Uma história*.

57. Valladares, *Invenção*; Chalhoub, *Cidade*; Costa Mattos, "Pelos pobres!"

58. Kim Butler, *Freedoms Given, Freedoms Won* (New Brunswick, NJ: Rutgers University Press, 1998); Bastide and Fernandes, *Brancos*; Rolnik, "Territorios"; Renata Monteiro Siqueira, "O viaduto e o samba: O Largo da Banana, urbanização e relações raciais em São Paulo" (PhD diss., 2021), esp. chap. 1; Marcelo Vitale Teodoro da Silva, "Territórios negros em trânsito" (MA thesis, USP, 2018); Domingues, *Uma história*; José Carlos Gomes da Silva, "Os sub-urbanos e a outra face da cidade" (MA thesis, UNICAMP, 1990); Fábio Dantas, "Saindo das sombras: Classe e raça na São Paulo pós-abolição (1887-1930)" (MA thesis, UFSP, 2018).

59. Backheuser, *Habitações*, 108-9. As in most texts for this period, racial markers generally appeared only when individuals were racialized as black or brown.

60. Lira, "A construção," and "O urbanismo." *Mocambo*'s parallel meaning, as a *quilombo* or space of resistance, has a connected history and etymology. See Flávio Gomes, *Mocambos e quilombos* (São Paulo: Claro Enigma, 2015); Beatriz Nascimento, *Uma história feita por mãos negras* (Rio de Janeiro: Zahar, 2021), chap. 12.

61. One of the first mentions of this transposition is in the *Jornal do Brasil*, July 5, 1901. On the Canudos myth, see Valladares, *Invenção*. For a thoughtful critique of pairing the conceptual *favela* with Canudos, see Rafael Gonçalves de Almeida, "A resignificação do mito de origem da *favela* pela arte de Mauricio Hora," *Espaço e Cultura* 46 (2019): 45-60.

62. Oliveira, "Informalidade"; McDonald, "The Origins"; Alves Pereira, "Para Além."

63. Some accounts date the racialization of Rio's *favela* somewhat later; see Rafael Cardoso, *Modernity in Black and White* (New York: Cambridge University Press, 2021), 46. While Cardoso argues convincingly that there was a narrowing in the visual representation of race in the *favelas* in the 1920s and 1930s, as this section and the authors it cites document, racialization existed from the beginning in visual, journalistic, and political discourse. White people also continued to appear in some representations of the *favela* in those later years, the best-known example internationally being that of Gordon Parks's "Flávio" series for *Life* magazine.

64. In the public sphere and in most legal documentation, white people during this era were rarely identified by race, but Black people most often were, unless their social status entitled them to polite racial silence.

65. *Gazeta de Noticias*, April 2, 1902; *Jornal do Brasil*, June 10, 1907. *Bahiano* was technically a regional label but used in this context it had a clear racial meaning. These articles frequently referenced European literature and high culture, thus indicating that their intended public did not include the vast masses of Brazil's population who had not been thus schooled. This oddly

paralleled a tendency throughout the Americas to give enslaved people names that referenced Shakespeare or the classics.

66. Cardoso discusses João do Rio as the article's potential author in *Modernidade*, 35n27.

67. *Gazeta de Notícias*, May 21, 1903. *Capoeira* is a Brazilian martial art born of slave resistance; *capoeiras* were practitioners of capoeira, who often played a role in the violent political conflicts of the late nineteenth century.

68. "As Mulheres Detentas," *Gazeta de Notícias*, September 6, 1905.

69. For discussion, see Mayra Cristine Pessôa Antas, "A construção de uma imagem" (MA thesis, UFRRJ, 2018).

70. *O Malho*, July 27, 1907; Antas, "A construção," 57–58.

71. Oliveira, "Trabalhadores," 145; Alves Pereira, "Para Além."

72. See, e.g., *Jornal do Recife*, February 8, 1878.

73. See, e.g., *Jornal do Recife*, March 10, 1880; September 7, 1924; April 29, 1927; *Jornal do Recife*, November 28,1937. *Batuque* refers to Afro-Brazilian musical practices, which overlapped also with dance, spiritual practice, and resistance.

74. *Diario de Pernambuco*, September 30 and November 25, 1921.

75. "Os forames da pobresa do Recife," *Jornal do Recife*, February 8, 1923, 3. These kinds of characterizations persisted well past the putative peak of scientific racism and could coexist with pragmatic acceptance; in 1931, a group of self-described property owners decried unhealthy *mocambos* that "dão à cidade do Recife uma apparencia da daldeiamento africano e semi-selvagem" but also accepted them as "ainda a formula possível encontrada para resolver a necessidade da habitação do pauperismo." *Jornal do Recife*, February 5, 1931.

76. Postcards held in the Col. Josebias Bandeira collection, Fundação Joaquim Nabuco, Recife.

77. For a more detailed account of racial silence and the *mocambos*, see Fischer, "A ética"; on the deceptiveness of racial silence in Belo Horizonte, see Alves Pereira, "Para além."

78. See, e.g., "Um enemigo das casas de palha," *Jornal Pequeno*, June 8, 1915 and February 13, 1920.

79. Melo, *A cidade*, 49.

80. *A Hora Social*, April 19, 1920.

81. Israel Ozanam, "Foi metido num tronco," in *Fronteiras culturais no Recife repúblicano*, ed. Augusto Neves da Silva, 91–116.

82. Freitas, *O clima*, 50.

83. Arthur Orlando, *Porto e cidade do Recife* (Recife: Jornal do Recife, 1908), 117–18.

84. *Jornal Pequeno*, April 16, 1920. This approach was apparent in Rio, too, and is discussed by Rafael Gonçalves de Almeida, "A emergência."

85. On Rio in this sense, see Cardoso, *Modernity*, 46.

86. *Jornal do Brasil*, April 25, 1907. Interestingly, Innocêncio was aware of Paris's strategy vis-à-vis Belle Époque auto-construction, suggesting that Rio follow its example and create informal areas outside of the urbanized limits along the same lines as had happened in La Zone.

87. *Jornal do Brasil*, June 13, 1907.

88. *Gazeta de Notícias*, April 20, 1916; *Correio da Manhã*, April 20 and May 26, 1916; *A Época*, May 26, 1916; *Gazeta de Notícias*, May 27 and May 30, 1916; *Correio da Manhã*, May 27 and June 3, 1916.

89. *Correio da Manhã*, May 26 and 27, 1916.

90. *Correio da Manhã*, June 3, 1916.

91. Backheuser, *Renascença*, 94.

92. *Jornal do Brasil*, June 8, 1907. The third was José Mariano (Recife's best-known abolitionist with Joaquim Nabuco).

93. *Gazeta de Notícias*, May 27; *Correio da Manhã*, May 28 and September 11, 1916.

94. Thiago Pereira Francisco, "Habitação popular, reforma urbana e periferização no Recife, 1920-1945" (MA thesis, UFPE, 2013), 52-56.

95. *Fon-fon*, January 27, 1912, p 45.

96. *Fon-fon*, June 3, 1916, 21.

97. On Rio, see André Reyes Novaes, "*Favelas* and the Divided City," *Social & Cultural Geography* 15, no. 2 (2014): 201-25; this article is a prime example of excellent contemporary urban scholarship that analyzes Rio's spatial inequality while making only a single mention of Brazilian racial dynamics. For Recife, see Fischer, "Do *mocambo*"; Pereira Francisco, "Habitação." For Belo Horizonte, see Alves Pereira, "Para além."

98. This emerged especially clearly in the wake of the 1907 eviction threat against the Morro da Favella in Rio, when the sympathetic politician Lopes Trovão said that he could go to the courts to stay the eviction order but preferred "out of respect" to work "personally." *Jornal do Brasil*, June 9, 1907.

99. See for example the comments of João Nogueira Jaguaribe in debates surrounding one of the earliest proposed subsidies for worker housing in 1906. *Annaes da Camara de Deputados*, 1906, no. 3, 481. Jaguaribe, originally from Recife, was the son of the conservative Visconde de Jaguaribe and spent much of his career in rural São Paulo. The notion of urban overpopulation and rural labor scarcity was a central trope from Brazil's postabolition period right through the mid-twentieth century, when transnational debates about rural marginality reached their peak. Brodwyn Fischer, "A Century in the Present Tense," in *Cities from Scratch*, ed. Brodwyn Fischer, Bryan McCann, and Javier Auyero (Durham, NC: Duke University Press, 2014), 9-67. In Brazil's Belle Époque public sphere, rural people (overtly racialized in the elite imagination) were portrayed as an anathema to Brazilian civilization. This trope is best exemplified by Euclides da Cunha's *Os sertões*. See Nísia Trindade Lima, *Um sertão chamado Brasil* (Rio de Janeiro: Revan, IUPERJ, 1999). This kind of thinking was similar to Italian justifications for forced deportation in the fascist period and would fuel similar proposals in Brazil in the 1930s. See chapters by Villani and Bartolini, this volume.

100. *Jornal do Recife*, June 28, 1875. For a similar case half a century later, see "Revoltante," *Jornal do Recife*, January 3, 1930.

101. *Jornal do Recife*, quoting city council report, February 7, 1915.

102. The political art of granting exceptions was especially entrenched in Recife, where city officials at every level received so many requests for legal exceptions that they sometimes sought to simply exempt all poor people from the taxes and fines that were meant to limit informality. See, e.g., *Jornal do Recife*, January 31, 1915.

103. Manuela Carneiro da Cunha, "Silences of the Law," *History and Anthropology* 1, no. 2 (1985): 427-43; Chalhoub, *Visões* and *A força*.

104. *Gazeta de Notícias*, December 15, 1902.

105. *Gazeta de Notícias*, May 21, 1903.

106. See, for example, notices and letters penned by the Recife's Liga Mixta dos Proprietários Pobres da Villa São Miguel in the early 1930s or articles about the Morro da Favella and the Morro da Santo Antônio in early twentieth century Rio.

107. *Gazeta de Notícias*, May 21, 1903.

108. *Gazeta de Notícias*, November 8, 1917.

109. "Radiomania na aldeia do Brum," *Diário de Pernambuco*, March 15, 1936.

110. Martha Abreu, *Da senzala ao palco* (Campinas: UNICAMP, 2017); Marc Hertzman, *Making Samba* (Durham, NC: Duke University Press, 2013); Hermano Vianna, *The Mystery of Samba* (Chapel Hill: University of North Carolina Press, 1999); Bryan McCann, *Hello Hello Brazil* (Durham, NC: Duke University Press, 2004); Bruno Carvalho, *Porous City* (Liverpool: Liverpool University Press, 2013).

111. This was true even of *sambas* whose authors did not live in the *favelas*, but especially characteristic of those who spent extensive time in the communities.

112. For an early example, see Manuel Dias's "Morro da Mangueira" (1926). For further discussion of these themes, see Claudia Matos, *Acertei no milhar* (Rio de Janeiro: Paz e Terra, 1982); Fischer, *Poverty*, chap. 2.

113. Oliveira Dias, "Vagabundo (samba de Gambôa)," Casa Bevilaquia, 1928. For similar themes, see "O trabalho me deu o bolo" (Antonio Moreira da Silva and João Golo, 1936); "Trabalhar eu não!" (Anibal Alves, 1946); "O pobre vive de teimoso" (Donga c/David Nasser, 1948); "Falta um Zero no meu Ordenado" (Benedito Lacerda and Ary Barroso, 1947); "O dinheiro que eu ganho" (Assis Valente, 1951).

114. See, e.g., Bide e Francisco Alves, "A malandragem" (1928).

115. See also Custodio Mesquita and Heber Boscoli, "O morro começa aí" (1941); Dunga and Mario Rossi, "Morro" (1941).

116. The samba was written by the Bahia-born Afro-descendant composer Assis Valente and sung (improbably) by Carmen Miranda, in one example of the ways samba was whitened for public consumption. For further discussion, see Fischer, "From the *Mocambo*."

117. Although Assis Valente was not born or raised in a *favela*, *favelas* were a constant theme in his considerable catalog, perhaps because he had experienced much of the stigma associated with them as a child domestic laborer in his native state.

118. Boaventura de Sousa Santos, "The Law of the Oppressed," *Law & Society Review* 12, no. 1 (1977): 5-126.

119. Document registered with the Delegacia de Vigilancia Geral e Costumes (political police) in May 1931, held in the Arquivo Público Estadual Jordão Emerenciano (APEJE). The São Miguel case is perhaps Recife's best-known early example of organized resistance to forced removal; it was probably the inspiration for a communist novel in the 1930s and is described by Mello and Gominho as well as in popular education pamphlets distributed at the height of Recife's progressive cycle preceding the 1964 military coup.

120. "Mostardinha—Senhor Feudal de um povoado de Lama," *Folha do Povo*, July 24, 1935. There was also a complaint against São Miguel along these lines in the 1940s. For discussion of the complaint against one Rio lawyer who was simultaneously a champion of local democracy and accused of local authoritarianism, see Brodwyn Fischer, "Democracy, Thuggery and the Grassroots: Antoine Magarinos Torres and the União dos Trabalhadores Favelados in the Age of Carioca Populism," *Nuevo Mundo Mundos Nuevos* (2013): https://doi.org/10.4000/nuevomundo.64840.

121. See reports of the "commission of residents and families" that approached politicians in 1907, *Jornal do Brasil*, June 8, 1907. For later cases in Rio, see, e.g., the *Gazeta de Notícias* and the *Correio da Manhã* on April 20, 1916; *Gazeta de Notícias*, November 8, 1917; and the numerous cases documented in Fischer, *Poverty*. For Recife, see discussion later in this chapter.

122. "O Comartello no Pombal," *Jornal do Recife*, December 27, 1924.

123. "A favella vai abaixo." On Agache, see Denise Stuckenbruck, *O Rio de Janeiro em questão* (Rio de Janeiro: Observatório de Políticas Urbanas e Gestão Municipal, 1996); Valladares, *Invenção*; Gonçalves, *Favelas*; Fischer, *Poverty*.

124. Brazilian National Archive (AN), records of the Secretaria da Presidência da República (SPR), series 17.4, *caixa* 33, pasta 1934.

125. For further discussion, see Sergio Cabral, *Escolas de samba do Rio de Janeiro* (Rio de Janeiro: Lazuli, 2016), 87; da Silva, *Favelas*, 199; Fischer, *Poverty*, 261–63.

126. AN, SPR, series 17.1, *caixa* 41. Salgueiro also offers evidence of one of the most sophisticated and multi-pronged histories of struggle that Rio witnessed during these years.

127. By Brazilian law, all coastal land belonged to the Marine Corps, a point that was central to *favela* and *mocambo* struggles in Rio and Recife throughout the twentieth century.

128. Note from Delegado Auxiliar to the Delegado of Recife's 1st Police District, August 6, 1934, APEJE, SSP 474.

129. *Folha do Povo*, August 22, 1935.

130. For late twentieth-century iterations, see Robin Sheriff, *Dreaming Equality* (New Brunswick, NJ: Rutgers University Press, 2001).

131. William Mangin, "Latin American Squatter Settlements," *Latin American Research Review* 2, no. 3 (1967): 65–98; Janice Perlman, *The Myth of Marginality* (Berkeley: University of California Press, 1976); Fischer, "A Century"; Gonçalves, this volume.

132. Gabriel Feltran, *The Entangled City* (Manchester: Manchester University Press, 2020).

133. On the romanticism of Tarsila do Amaral's painting, see Cardoso, *Modernity*.

134. This can also be seen in transnational discussions of Brazil in Black press outlets such as the *Chicago Defender*; see especially Robert Abbott's articles from the early 1920s.

135. Maria Nascimento, "Morro e Favela," June 1949.

136. Alberti and Pereira, *Histórias*.

137. On the *favela* as *quilombo*, see Beatriz Nascimento, *Uma história*, esp. chap.12. See also Adrelino Campos, *Do quilombo*.

138. Nascimento, *Uma história*, 71.

139. Connolly, *A World*; Keeanga Yamahtta Taylor, *Race for Profit* (Chapel Hill: University of North Carolina Press, 2019); Thomas Sugrue, *The Origins of the Urban Crisis* (Princeton, NJ: Princeton University Press, 2005).

140. Nascimento, *Uma história*, 169.

Chapter Nine

1. This space has since been filled with various developments, including social housing complexes and the ring road that runs around the capital.

2. Anne Granier, "La Zone et les zoniers de Paris, approches spatiales d'une marge urbaine (1912–1946)" (PhD diss., Lyon University, 2017).

3. Granier, "La zone," 13–14. Unless otherwise indicated, all quotations from French sources have been translated into English.

4. Marie-Claude Blanc-Chaléard, *En finir avec les bidonvilles* (Paris: Publications de la Sorbonne, 2016), 24–27.

5. A number of authors can be consulted on these dimensions of *bidonvilles*. See Muriel Cohen, Cédric David, Margot Delon, and Victor Colet for the Paris region and Ed Naylor and Antonin Gay-Dupuy for Marseille.

6. Other *bidonvilles* in the Paris region also housed Spanish migrants.

7. During French colonial rule in Algeria from 1865 to 1944, Algerians were given the specific legal status of *sujet* (subject), which meant they could be declared French nationals but not citizens. In 1944, this "colonial hybridization" was abolished for all Algerians residing in Metropolitan France, giving them the same right to vote as any other French citizen. However, a distinction continued to exist in practice, if only through the introduction of the new legal term *Français musulman d'Algérie* (French Muslims of Algeria).

8. See Jim House's contribution to this volume.

9. These were identified based on maps of tuberculosis mortality. Yankel Fijalkow, *La construction des îlots insalubres, Paris 1850–1945* (Paris: L'Harmattan, 1998).

10. Léandre Vaillat, *Le visage français du Maroc* (Paris: Horizons de France, 1931); Jean Royer, *L'urbanisme aux colonies et dans les pays tropicaux* (La Charité-sur-Loire: Delayance, 1932); Daniel Rivet, "Hygiénisme pasteurien et exclusion des pauvres dans la ville coloniale: Exemple du Maroc du début des années 1930 à 1945," *Revue d'histoire maghrébine* 83–84 (1986): 689–703; Claude Liauzu, "Un aspect de la crise en Tunisie: La naissance des bidonvilles," *Outre-Mers: Revue d'histoire* 63, no. 232 (1976): 607–21; Claude Liauzu, "L'Afrique et la crise de 1930 (1924–1938)," *Revue française d'histoire d'outre-mer* 232–33 (1976): 607–21 (in support of this "Tunisian" thesis, the author cited Adam, *Casablanca*); Robert Descloîtres, Jean-Claude Reverdy, and Claudine Descloîtres, *L'Algérie des bidonvilles: Le tiers-monde dans la cité* (Paris: Mouton, 1961), 84–87. For a recent review, especially concerning the Moroccan and Tunisian contexts of this genesis, see Cattedra, "Bidonville: Paradigme" and also "Bidonville," in *L'Aventure des mots de la ville*, ed. Christian Topalov, Laurent Coudroy de Lille, Jean-Charles Depaule, and Brigitte Mari (Paris: R. Laffont, 2010), 125–31.

11. Jim House, "Shantytowns and Rehousing in Late Colonial Algiers and Casablanca," in *France's Modernising Mission: Citizenship, Welfare and the Ends of Empire*, ed. Ed Naylor (London: Palgrave Macmillan, 2018), 133–63. See also House's chapter in this volume.

12. Descloîtres, Reverdy, and Descloîtres, *L'Algérie*; Tony Socard, "L'urbanisme en Algérie" and "Logement musulman," *Documents Algériens* (Service du Cabinet du Gouverneur Général d'Algérie, Série Culture 9 1946); Jean Pelletier, "Un aspect de l'habitat à Alger: Les bidonvilles," *Revue de Géographie de Lyon*, no. 3 (1955): 286.

13. Benjamin Stora, *Ils venaient d'Algérie: L'immigration algérienne en France (1912–1992)* (Paris: Fayard, 1992); Emmanuel Blanchard, *Histoire de l'immigration algérienne en France* (Paris: La Découverte, 2018).

14. Pierre Laroque and Pierre Ollive, Le problème de l'émigration des travailleurs nord-africains en France (Paris: Haut Comité méditerranéen et d'Afrique du Nord, 1938); Georges Mauco, *Les étrangers en France* (Paris: A. Colin, 1932); Alain Bernard, *L'Afrique française* (1930), quoted in Andrée Michel, *Les travailleurs algériens en France* (Paris: CNRS, 1957); Robert Sanson, "Les travailleurs nord-africains de la région parisienne," in *Documents sur l'immigration* (Paris: INED, Travaux et documents, 1947), cahier no. 2, 162–93.

15. On ignoring the *bidonville*, see ESNA, "Le logement des Nord-africains," *Cahiers Nord-Africains* (January–February 1951); Jean-Jacques Rager, *L'émigration en France des musulmans d'Algérie: Principaux aspects démographiques, économiques et sociaux*, Report commissioned by the Haut Comité consultatif de la Population et de la Famille (Alger: Service d'Information du Cabinet du Gouverneur Général d'Algérie, 1956) Documents Algériens, Série sociale, no. 49. Other types of housing included hostels built and financed by employers, social housing linked to the public authorities, or the *garnis*, and other furnished hotels. As indigenous housing, see

Louis Chevalier, *Le problème démographique nord-africain* (Paris: INED, Travaux et documents, 1947), *cahier* no. 6, 151.

16. Generally speaking, all the Paris suburbs experienced significant demographic growth at some point from the end of the nineteenth century onward as a result of foreign and more especially provincial migration, which transformed what had essentially been rural communes into urban spaces. Nanterre, which is situated approximately ten kilometers from Paris, did not begin to expand until after World War I, but it then did so at a faster rate than any other part of the Paris region. This is one of the factors that led to the continued construction of vast *bidonvilles* until the end of the 1960s. After World War II, despite its growth, the substantial territory of Nanterre still comprised large areas of nonurbanized land.

17. Françoise de Barros, "Les municipalités face aux Algériens: Méconnaissances et usages des catégories coloniales en métropole avant et après la Seconde Guerre mondiale," *Genèses* 53 (2003): 69–92, 85–87.

18. The *garnis*, or *meublés* as they were also called, were hotels whose clientele were permanent residents rather than travelers. These were mainly poor populations, including French nationals for a long time, who were not able to access their own private accommodation. The *garnis* therefore constituted an urban working-class habitat. This form of housing remained widespread until the 1980s, when the extremely inadequate social housing stock in France began to improve. They nevertheless still exist today to accommodate people who cannot access social housing. The impoverished and often unhealthy nature of this accommodation stemmed from frequent overcrowding (one or more families per room) and the abusive practices of proprietors who sought to maximize profits by not equipping or maintaining the rooms properly. Proprietors who took abusive practices to the extreme were known as "sleep merchants." In the worst cases, the "rooms" (which were sometimes actually cellars) would in fact be dormitories where the "tenants" would take turns sleeping in the same bed on a rolling eight-hour basis.

19. The Ministère de l'Intérieur appointed the CTAMs in 1952 to work in a number of prefectures in Metropolitan France. Their number increased with the start of the insurrection in 1954 and grew throughout the War of Independence, rising from four to thirty-four in the space of a decade. Their powers evolved accordingly. Charged on their arrival with facilitating both "the organization of moral, material, and social assistance to the Muslim population" and their "adjustment to life in metropolitan France and professional and social advancement," the CTAMs were ultimately given express authority in 1958 over "all questions relating to Muslim affairs." Françoise de Barros, "Contours d'un réseau administratif 'algérien' et construction d'une compétence en 'affaires musulmanes': Les conseillers techniques pour les affaires musulmanes en métropoles (1952–1965)," *Politix* 76 (2006): 97–117.

20. To my knowledge, no study has ever been conducted on the activities in practice of the North African social advisors. For a description of their official attributions, see Vincent Viet, *La France immigrée: Construction d'une politique* (Paris: Fayard, 1997), 180–84.

21. Choukri Hmed, "Loger les étrangers 'isolés' en France: Socio-histoire d'une institution d'État: La Sonacotra (1956–2006)" (PhD diss, Paris Panthéon-Sorbonne, 2005).

22. Françoise de Barros, "Des 'Français musulmans d'Algérie' aux 'immigrés': L'importation de classifications coloniales dans les politiques du logement en France (1950–1970)," *Actes de la recherche en sciences sociales* 159, no. 4 (2005): 26–53.

23. Emmanuel Blanchard, *La police parisienne et les Algériens, 1944–1946* (Paris: Nouveau Monde Éditions, 2011), 322.

24. This section is largely based on Françoise de Barros, "La guerre d'indépendance

algérienne dans des espaces politiques locaux métropolitains: Quelle spécificité communiste?," in *Les territoires du communisme: Élus locaux, politiques publiques et sociabilités militantes*, ed. Emmanuel Bellanger and Julian Mischi (Paris: Armand Colin, 2013), 131–50.

25. Benjamin Stora, *La gangrène et l'oubli: Mémoire de la guerre d'Algérie* (Paris: La Découverte, 1991), 52–55.

26. Danielle Tartakowsky, "Les manifestations de rue," in *La guerre d'Algérie et les Français*, ed. Jean-Pierre Rioux (Paris: Fayard, 1990), 132.

27. During French colonial rule in Algeria from 1865 to 1944, Algerians were given the specific legal status of *sujet* (subject), which meant they could be declared French nationals but not citizens. In other communes where large numbers of Algerians lived in slums rather than *bidonvilles*, interventions took the form of urban renewal operations, but they ultimately had the same consequences, as in Roubaix, a northern industrial city in the Nord *département*, in 1957. Social class logics were also found to be a factor in neighborhood tensions around a *bidonville* in Champigny (eastern suburb of Paris located in what is now the Val-de-Marne *département*) that had no Algerians living in it and where politicization did not begin until 1964. For a comparative study of local mobilizations against the *bidonvilles* according to whether they were inhabited by Algerian (Nanterre) or Portuguese (Champigny) migrants, see Françoise de Barros, "Protests against Shantytowns in the 1950s and 1960s: Class Logics, Clientelist Relations and 'Colonial Redeployments,'" in Naylor, *France's*, 199–224.

28. Archives Municipales de Nanterre (AMN), "Immigrés-bidonville 1955–1961," letter from Raymond Barbet, May 31, 1960, my emphasis. While the two sides are not named, they are nevertheless explicitly implied through the words highlighted.

29. At the time, the Nanterre district of Petit Nanterre was cossetted by the communist elected representatives because it contained the first new social housing estates, which they were proud of, and because it adjoined La Folie, one of the largest *bidonvilles* in Nanterre.

30. Stora, *Ils venaient*, 109 and 151–70; Muriel Cohen, "Les Algériens des bidonvilles de Nanterre pendant la guerre d'Algérie: Histoire et mémoire" (MA thesis, Université de Paris I, 2003).

31. Monique Hervo, *Chroniques du bidonville: Nanterre en guerre d'Algérie* (Paris: Le Seuil, 2001), 143; Viet, *La France*, 188.

32. This mobilization of local actors in 1965 took place after numerous complaints had been addressed to the municipality in 1964 both by neighboring inhabitants (mainly female) and by the staff of a primary school located next to the extensive La Folie *bidonville*. AMN, "Immigrés-bidonvilles 1962–70," unclassified.

33. "A Gerland [Lyon], la zone est appelée bidonville dès lors que des Algériens isolés y remplacent des familles des années 1930," Blanc-Chaléard, *En finir*, 38.

34. Françoise de Barros and Muriel Cohen. "Entre politiques urbaines et contrôle des migrants: La décolonisation inachevée des recensements des bidonvilles en France (années 1950–années 1970)," *Histoire & Mesure* 34, no. 1 (2019): 151–84.

35. The Paris suburb of Champigny, the provincial city of Rouen, and the southeastern city of Marseille. Blanc-Chaléard, *En finir*, 191.

36. Sénat, parliamentary debates, October 15, 1964, 1090–91.

37. Jean Ithurbide, *député* for Champigny-sur-Marne, UNR, Assemblée Nationale, parliamentary debates, June 14, 1964, 2005.

38. Robert-André Vivien, Assemblée Nationale, parliamentary debates, June 10, 1970, 2450.

39. Assemblée Nationale, parliamentary debates, June 10, 1970, 2450.

40. Louis Deschizeaux, deputy mayor of Châteauroux, Assemblée Nationale, parliamentary debates, November 12, 1964, 5347.

41. Fijalkow, *La construction.*

42. André Fanton *député* for Paris's Eleventh Arrondissement, UNR, Assemblée Nationale, parliamentary debates, first sitting on June 26, 1964, 2254.

43. Raymond Barbet, deputy mayor of Nanterre, PCF, Assemblée Nationale, parliamentary debates, first sitting on June 26, 1964, 2254.

44. Pierre Pasquini, *député* for Nice, deputy mayor, UNR, Assemblée Nationale, parliamentary debates, first sitting on June 26, 1964, 2255.

45. Modeste Zussy, senator of Haut-Rhin, honorary mayoral president of Haut-Rhin, UNR, Sénat, parliamentary debates, October15, 1964, 1090–91.

46. Rapporteur to the Assemblée Nationale, parliamentary debates, June 14, 1966, 2005.

47. Roland Nungesser, Assemblée Nationale, parliamentary debates, June 14, 1966, 2007.

48. Raymond Barbet, deputy mayor of Nanterre, PCF, Assemblée Nationale, parliamentary debates, June 14, 1966, 2009.

49. Fernand Grenier, deputy mayor of Saint-Denis, PCF, Assemblée Nationale, parliamentary debates, June 14, 1966, 2009.

50. Assemblée Nationale, parliamentary debates, June 10, 1970, 2450.

51. Blanc-Chaléard, *En finir*, 11.

52. Blanc-Chaléard, *En finir.*

53. Édouard Le Bellegou, mayor of Toulon from 1953 to 1959, member of the socialist party Section Française de l'Internationale Ouvrière, Sénat, parliamentary debates, October 15, 1964, 1093.

54. Edmond Desouches, deputy mayor of Lucé (Eure-et-Loir), vice-president of the FGDS group in the Assemblée Nationale, Assemblée Nationale, parliamentary debates, November 12, 1964, 5347.

55. There were always political issues at play behind the general considerations relating to this matter (the *préfet*'s and the commune's legal powers, financial responsibility for the expropriations), because the elected representatives from communes affected by the presence of *bidonvilles* were often opponents of the government. This was particularly the case with the 1966 law. The Gaullist minister who promoted it, Roland Nungesser, was at that time the electoral rival of the communist mayor of a commune situated in the east of Paris that contained one of the most densely populated *bidonvilles* in metropolitan France at approximately fifteen thousand Portuguese inhabitants.

56. Sénat, parliamentary debates, 22/06/66, 908.

57. Sénat, parliamentary debates, 22/06/66, 913.

58. Assemblée Nationale, parliamentary debates, 10/06/70, 2449.

59. Assemblée Nationale, parliamentary debates, 10/06/70, 2449.

60. Assemblée Nationale, parliamentary debates, 10/06/70, 2450.

61. Eugène Claudius-Petit was notably the former president of SONACOTRAL (Société Nationale de Construction pour les Travailleurs Algériens), a public organization created in 1956 to participate in the absorption of the *bidonvilles* by building and managing hostels for isolated Algerian men, in other words men who were single or living in metropolitan France without their family. The involvement of this organization thus suggests that the *bidonvilles* were associated with Algeria until 1965. SONACOTRAL then became SONACOTRA (Société Nationale de

Construction pour les Travailleurs). Its hostels took in *bidonville* inhabitants of all foreign nationalities. On Debré, see Institut Paul Delouvrier, *L'aménagement de la région parisienne (1961–1969): Le témoignage de Paul Delouvrier, accompagné par un entretien avec Michel Debré* (Paris: Presses de l'École Nationale des Ponts et Chaussées, 2003), 214–15. In reality, Debré's interest and motivation in elaborating a proposal for this bill remain obscure due to a lack of sources on the subject. Blanc-Chaléard, *En finir*, 188.

62. In fact, the 1966 law was partly the result of this intense rivalry. Nungesser's electoral district as a *député* was being impacted by the *bidonville* in Champigny-sur-Marne, a commune run by the communist elected representative Louis Talamoni. Exploiting the fact that there were local protests against this *bidonville*, Nungesser (even before he became minister) made sure that the 1964 law was not applied in Champigny. Instead, he sought to introduce a new law on the *bidonvilles* in his own name and to have it implemented in his electoral district so that he could make electoral gains from the absorption. When the "Loi Nungesser" was adopted in 1966, expropriation procedures were quickly initiated for the city of Paris's Office Public d'HLM (social housing department) but not for Champigny. Similarly, the "government plan" adopted at the same time provided for a range of financial resources that were initially reserved for only six communes, all located in the Paris suburbs. The resources destined for Champigny were the first to be deployed.

63. Sénat, parliamentary debates, June 22, 1966, 909.

64. Sénat, parliamentary debates, June 22, 1966, 910.

65. R. Nungesser, Assemblée Nationale, parliamentary debates, 14/06/66, 2007–8.

66. Assemblée Nationale, parliamentary debates, June 10, 1970, 2448.

67. Assemblée Nationale, parliamentary debates, June 10, 1970, 2452.

68. Assemblée Nationale, parliamentary debates, June 10, 1970, 2452.

69. Assemblée Nationale, parliamentary debates, 10/06/70, 2448.

70. Fijalkow, *La construction*.

71. Isabelle Backouche, "Rénover un quartier parisien sous Vichy: Un Paris expérimental plus qu'une rêverie sur Paris," *Genèses* 4, no. 73 (2008): 12–13.

72. The clearance progressed very slowly. By the end of this decade, of the seventeen blocks identified in the period up to 1920, there were still "some 4,800 buildings occupied by more than 180,000 inhabitants" remaining in Paris, Claire Lévy-Vroelant, "Le diagnostic d'insalubrité et ses conséquences sur la ville: Paris, 1894–1960," *Population* 54, nos. 4–5 (1999): 707–43. For example, on the legal and financial details, another obstacle to the demolition of the *îlots insalubres* that also held up the absorption of the *bidonvilles* was the need to build new housing for the inhabitants that would be financially accessible to them.

73. See, in particular, Isabelle Backouche, *Paris transformé: Le Marais 1900–1980: De l'îlot insalubre au secteur sauvegardé* (Paris: Créaphis, Lieux Habites, 2016); Alain Faure, "La pioche du démolisseur: Les logiques et les masques de la rénovation urbaine," *Métropolitiques*, February 17, 2016; Fijalkow, *La construction*; Lévy-Vroelant, "Le diagnostic."

74. Fijalkow, *La construction*, 146–89; Lévy-Vroelant, "Le diagnostic."

75. This urban renewal program, which was famous as much for its urban scope as for its political dimensions, has been the subject of numerous studies since the 1970s. See, e.g., Jean Descamps, lawyer at the Lille bar, "La résorption des courées dans la métropole Nord" (PhD diss., Lille, n.d. [late 1970s]); Marie-France Larthomas, *De la mise en œuvre d'une politique de résorption de l'habitat insalubre dans la métropole Nord* (Report commissioned by ORSUCOMN, Lille, October 1972); Marie-France Larthomas, "L'habitat insalubre en métropole Nord: Les

données du problème" (Diplôme d'Étude Approfondies diss., Université des Sciences et Techniques de Lille, 1977); Didier Cornuel and Bruno Duriez, *Centre d'analyse du développement, Transformations économiques, évolution des rapports politiques et restructuration urbaine: Roubaix 1960–1975* (Research report for the Ministère de l'Équipement, December 1975); Didier Cornuel and Bruno Duriez, *Le Mirage urbain: Histoire du logement à Roubaix* (Paris: Éditions Anthropos, 1983).

76. CREGE (Centre de Recherches Économiques et de Gestion), *Étude sur l'habitat insalubre dans les courées de la métropole-nord* (Report commissioned by ORSUCOMN, Lille, April–June 1971); Jacques Prouvost, "Les courées à Roubaix," *Revue du Nord* 51, no. 201 (1969): 307–16.

77. Assemblée Nationale, parliamentary debates, 10/06/70, 2450.

78. Françoise de Barros, "Genèse de la politique de développement social des quartiers: éléments de formalisation d'un 'problème des banlieues'" (Diplôme d'Études Approfondies diss., Université de Paris I, 1994).

79. For Algerian migrants, these included FAS, SONACOTRAL, and LOGIREP. Bernard Bret, "Contribution à l'étude de l'habitat provisoire dans la banlieue parisienne: Les bidonvilles de Nanterre" (PhD diss., Faculté des Lettres et Sciences Humaines de Paris, 1968), 171. For Africans, CETRAFA managed migrant hostels.

80. Jean-Paul Tricart, "Genèse d'un dispositif d'assistance: Les 'cités de transit,'" *Revue Française de Sociologie* 18, no. 4 (1977): 601–24.

81. This phrase came at the end of a biographical article on Guy Houist published in the press. It had been annotated with a large question mark by the project manager, who had cut the article out and kept it. ADVM, 1050W1*, "Résorptions des bidonvilles, réunions de 1967 à 1970."

82. Testimonies collected by Blanc-Chaléard, *En finir*, 286.

83. On the different dimensions of the rivalry between these two directorates operating under the Ministère de l'Équipement during the 1970s and on its impact on urban policies, see Françoise de Barros, "Genèse."

Chapter Ten

1. Archives nationales de France (ANF), Pierrefitte-sur-Seine, Premier ministre / organismes rattachés directement / Centre des hautes études sur l'Afrique et l'Asie modernes (CHEAM), 20000046/63, Article 1712, Roger Maneville, "Prolétariat et bidonvilles," 1950, 15.

2. Robert Descloîtres, Jean-Claude Reverdy, and Claudine Descloîtres, *L'Algérie des bidonvilles: Le tiers-monde dans la cité* (Paris: Mouton, 1961), 81.

3. Henceforth, the terms *Algerian* and *Moroccan* refer to the respective local Muslim populations. Where relevant, the terms *Jewish Algerian* and *Jewish Moroccan* are used. The term *European* covers both settlers from Metropolitan France or mostly southern Europe and colonial personnel.

4. James McDougall, *A History of Algeria* (Cambridge: Cambridge University Press, 2017), 182–86.

5. See Daniel Rivet, *Histoire du Maroc: De Moulay Idriss à Mohammed VI* (Paris: Fayard, 2012).

6. Stephen Legg, *Spaces of Colonialism: Delhi's Urban Governmentalities* (London: Blackwell, 2007), 82.

7. See Abdelmalek Sayad, *La double absence: Des illusions de l'émigré aux souffrances de l'immigré* (Paris: Seuil, 1999), 257, 259.

8. Cattedra, "Bidonville: Paradigme." In Algiers, it took until the mid-late 1940s, as opposed to the mid- to late 1930s in Casablanca, for European administrators, politicians, and many journalists to systematically use the term *bidonville*. As Françoise de Barros's contribution in this volume shows, the term *bidonville* was then used in Metropolitan France, initially to describe the informal housing of North African migrants.

9. Neil MacMaster, *Colonial Migrants and Racism: Algerians in France, 1900–1962* (Basingstoke: Macmillan, 1996); Elkebir Atouf, *Aux origines historiques de l'immigration marocaine en France 1910–1963* (Paris: Éditions Connaissances et Savoirs, 2009).

10. André Adam, *Casablanca: Essai sur la transformation de la société marocaine au contact de l'Occident*, 2 vols. (Paris: CNRS, 1968); Boumedine, *Bétonvilles*; Descloîtres et al., *L'Algérie*.

11. Georges Torres, *Les bidonvilles d'Alger* (Marseille: Université Aix-Marseille 1, 1953); Najīb Taki, *Jawānib Min Dhākiret Krayyān Sentrāl-al-Ḥaiyy al-Muḥammadiyy fī al-Qarn al-ʿIshrīn*, 2 vols. (al-Dār al-Baiḍāʾ: Mouʾassasat Masjid al-Ḥassan al-Thāniyy bi-al-Dār al-Baiḍāʾ/Les Éditions La Croisée des Chemins, 2014).

12. Archives nationales d'outre-mer (ANOM), Aix-en-Provence, Algérie, Département d'Alger, Préfecture, Administration des Indigènes, 10I/7, *Annexe au rapport mensuel: Situation économique de l'Algérie*, March 31, 1923; *Annexe au Bulletin municipal officiel de la Ville d'Alger* (hereafter *BMOVA*) of April 5–20, 1930, session of April 4, 1930, 88 (Kerrad).

13. Ville d'Alger, *Compte-rendu des travaux du Bureau municipal d'Hygiène pour 1922 et 1923 inclus* (1925), 127.

14. Original text: *Alger, est en effet en voie d'être encerclée d'îlots de taudis infects et de taches lépreuses et pesteuses, de gourbis où grouille une population indigène famélique.*

15. *Annexe BMOVA* of November 5–20, 1930, session of October 24, 1930, 248 (and 247–49 more generally).

16. Henri Prost, "Rapport général," in Jean Royer, ed., *L'Urbanisme aux colonies et dans les pays tropicaux: Communications & Rapports du Congrès international de l'urbanisme aux colonies et dans les pays de latitude intertropicale* (Paris: Éditions de l'urbanisme, 1932), 1:21–24, here 24.

17. Boussad Aïche, "Des cités indigènes aux cités de recasement en Algérie (1930–1950)," in *Villes maghrébines en situations coloniales*, ed. Charlotte Jelidi (Paris: Karthala; Tunis: IRMC, 2014), 97–111; Mahfoud Kaddache, *La vie politique à Alger de 1919 à 1939* (Algiers: SNED, 1970); Jean-Louis Planche, "Alger: Urbanisation et contrôle ethnique 1930–1962," in *Alger, lumières sur la ville*, ed. Naïma Chabbi-Chemrouk, Nadia Djelal-Assari, Madani Safar Zeitoun, and Rachid Sidi Boumedine (Algiers: Dalimen, 2004), 110–20.

18. Legg, *Spaces*, 215.

19. Original text: *La plus grande partie du peuple indigène est à un stade de civilisation inférieur au nôtre.* ANOM, Algérie, Gouvernement général d'Algérie, 3CAB/83, Dossier Commission d'Enquête parlementaire, March 5, 1937, Rozis audition, 2.

20. Daniel Rivet, *Lyautey et l'institution du Protectorat français* (Paris: L'Harmattan, 1988), 2:237.

21. Rivet, *Lyautey*, 2:232–37; Daniel Rivet, "Hygiénisme pasteurien et exclusion des pauvres dans la ville coloniale: Exemple du Maroc du début des années 1930 à 1945," *Revue d'histoire maghrébine* 83–84 (1986): 689–703.

22. See Ministère des Affaires Étrangères, Centre des archives diplomatiques de Nantes, Archives du Protectorat du Maroc (CADN, APM), Direction de l'Intérieur (DI), DI348, Directeur des services de sécurité, *note*, January 30, 1944.

23. Original text: *Un véritable danger pour la cite européenne gît dans ces "Bidonvilles."* *L'ennemi est aux portes de la ville, non un ennemi de dissidence, avec ses carabines à tir rapide, mais un terrible seigneur, subtil, insaisissable, qui a nom typhus, choléra ou peste.* Léandre Vaillat, *Le périple marocain* (Paris: Flammarion, 1934), 91.

24. André Adam, "Le 'Bidonville' de Ben Msīk à Casablanca," *Annales de l'Institut d'Études orientales de la Faculté de Lettres d'Alger* 8 (1949–1950): 61–199.

25. On these questions, see Jean-Louis Cohen and Monique Eleb, *Casablanca: Mythes et figures d'une aventure urbaine* (Paris: Hazan, 2004); Janet L. Abu-Lughod, *Rabat: Urban Apartheid in Morocco* (Princeton, NJ: Princeton University Press, 1980).

26. On colonial urbanism before 1945, see ANF, CHEAM, 20000002/32, Article 841, Paul Hubert, *Tableau du commandement de la Ville de Casablanca au 1er janvier 1945*, 1946.

27. See Guillaume Denglos, *La Revue Maghreb (1932–1936). Une publication franco-marocaine engagée* (Paris: L'Harmattan, 2015), 42–43, 196–97, 221.

28. Both Douar Debbagh and Douar Doum, Rabat's largest shantytowns, were relocated. See ANF, CHEAM, 20000002/58, Article 1523, J. Roux, *Essai monographique sur le bidonville de la cité Yacoub El Mansour.*

29. On the largest of these *derbs*, see M. Bérenguier, "Monographie d'un quartier de Casablanca: 'le Derb Ghalef,'" *Bulletin économique et social du Maroc* 28, no. 63 (1954): 391–42.

30. Original text: *Dispositif de protection de la population européenne.* Moroccan National Archives (MNA), Rabat, E831, Michel Bon, *Rapport général sur l'assainissement de la Ville de Casablanca: Bidonvilles et derbs. Exercices 1938–1939*, February 27, 1939, 12.

31. Yvonne Mahé, *L'extension des villes indigènes au Maroc* (PhD diss., Imprimerie J. Bière, Bordeaux, 1936), 41.

32. Taki, *Jawānib*, 1:211–20.

33. MNA, E831, Bon, *Rapport général*, 34; Mahé, *L'extension*, 79, 101, 114; Hubert, *Tableau*, 71.

34. Taki, *Jawānib*, 1:220.

35. Cattedra, "Bidonville: Paradigme," 132–33.

36. Adam, *Casablanca*, 1:88; Maneville, "Prolétariat," 8.

37. See CADN, APM, 1MA/280/41, *Bulletins économiques*, 1945–46; Adam, *Casablanca*, 1:216; Maneville, "Prolétariat," 37–38; Taki, *Jawānib*, 1:224.

38. CADN, APM, DI622, 624 and 626.

39. On the wider context, see Jacques Cantier, *L'Algérie sous le régime de Vichy* (Paris: Odile Jacob, 2002), 33–35, 106–17, 346–54.

40. Original text: *Métropole de l'Afrique du Nord et de l'Afrique française.* ANOM, Algérie, Administration des Indigènes, 101/Io, intervention by the Secretary General of Algiers Prefecture, *Le problème des "bidonvilles": Commission du 13 mars 1941.* See also Cantier, *L'Algérie*, 117n42; Cantier, "1939–1945: Une métropole coloniale en guerre," in *Alger 1940–1962: Une ville en guerres*, ed. Jean-Jacques Jordi and Guy Pervillé (Paris: Autrement, 1999), 16–61, here 44.

41. Original text: *Une œuvre d'assainissement moral et social.* Algerian national archives, Algiers (ANA), Direction des Travaux publics (DTP), 1286, Gouverneur général d'Algérie to Ministre secrétaire d'État à l'Intérieur, September 1941, *Arrêté du 13 septembre 1941 destiné à faciliter l'assainissement des agglomérations algériennes.*

42. On the census, see Jim House, "Intervening on 'Problem' Areas and Their Inhabitants: The Socio-Political and Security Logics behind Censuses in the Algiers Shantytowns, 1941–1962," *Histoire & Mesure* 34, no. 1 (2019): 121–50, esp. 127–32.

43. For this extensive correspondence, see ANOM, Algérie, 10I/9 and 10I/10; ANA, DTP, 1286.

44. ANOM, Algérie, 10I/10, Gubernatorial decree of September 13, 1941, Algiers municipal decrees of October 28 and November 28, 1941.

45. Governor General Abrial's letter of June 9, 1941, to the Prefects of Oran and Constantine contains these themes, and lists the "security danger" (ANA, DTP, 1286).

46. ANOM 10I/10, Algérie, President of Algiers Public Housing Office to Algiers Prefect, March 17, 1941. On the 1941 measures, see Descloîtres et al., *L'Algérie*, 67–68; Jean-Claude Isnard, *Les problèmes du logement dans l'agglomération algéroise* (Paris: Mémoire de stage, École nationale d'administration, 1949), 15–17.

47. ANA, DTP, 1286, *Problème de l'habitat indigène et plus spécialement des "bidonvilles" à Alger*, April 11, 1941.

48. Original text: *Une masse d'indésirables sans profession avouable, sans famille qui, la nuit venue, s'entassent dans les baraques et échappent aux investigations.*

49. *Annexe BMOVA*, April 5–20, 1941, session of April 4, 1941, 177–80, here 178.

50. For journalism on the Casbah, see Lucienne Favre, *Dans la Casbah* (Paris: Grasset, 1937), 251–354. On Algiers during the 1930s, see Omar Carlier, *Entre nation et jihad: Histoire sociale des radicalismes algériens* (Paris: Presses de la FNSP, 1995); Christian Phéline, *La terre, l'étoile, le couteau: Le 2 août 1936 à Alger* (Vulaines-sur-Seine: Éditions du Croquant, 2021).

51. ANOM, Algérie, Département d'Alger, Police et maintien de l'ordre, 1F/443, Gardien de la Paix de la Cité Mahieddine, *Rapport à Monsieur le Commissaire du 9ème arrondissement*, May 22, 1946. See also Danielle Beaujon, "The Algerian Enemy Within. Policing the Black Market in Marseille and Algiers, 1939–1950," *French Historical Studies* 47, no. 2 (2024): 289–318.

52. Original text: *Un endroit louche où se réfugient des voleurs, des trafiquants du marché noir; où existent des boucheries clandestines, des cafés illégaux.* ANF, CHEAM, 20000046/23, Article 693, Henri Weiler, *Prolétariat musulman et Grand Alger*, 1944, 14.

53. See Favre, *La Casbah*; Christelle Taraud, *La prostitution coloniale. Algérie, Tunisie, Maroc (1830–1962)* (Paris: Payot, 2003).

54. Taraud, *La prostitution*, 69–70, 167–68, 205–7; Jean Mathieu and P. H. Maury, *Bousbir. La prostitution dans le Maroc colonial: Ethnographie d'un quartier résérve* (1951; Paris: Éditions Paris-Méditerranée, 2003), 69–71.

55. Adam, "Le 'Bidonville,'" 162–64; Fouad Benseddik, *Syndicalisme et politique au Maroc* (Paris: L'Harmattan, 1990), 668–69; Torres, *Les bidonvilles*, 131–32, 133–34.

56. See Kaddache, *La Vie politique*, 127–28; 204; *Annexe BMOVA*, July 5–20, 1920, session of July 2, 1920, 251 (Billion du Plan); Christelle Taraud, "Les *yaouleds*: Entre marginalisation sociale et sédition politique," *Revue d'histoire de l'enfance "irrégulière"* 10 (2008): 59–74.

57. For 1941–1942 on the *yaouleds*, see ANOM, Algérie, Préfecture d'Alger, Cabinet du Préfet d'Alger, 1K/178. I am very grateful to Kalthoum Meidane for indicating these files to me.

58. CADN, APM, DI622.

59. Bruno Rotalier, "Les *yaouleds* (enfants des rues) de Casablanca et leur participation aux émeutes de décembre 1952," *Revue de l'histoire de l'enfance "irrégulière"* 4 (2002): 207–22, here 221. See also CADN, APM, DI380, Capitaine de la Porte des Vaux, *Le Parti de l'Istiqlal à Casablanca*, January 1953, 35.

60. On this wider context, see Ed Naylor, ed., *France's Modernising Mission: Citizenship, Welfare and the Ends of Empire* (London: Macmillan, 2018).

61. For Algiers, see Isnard, *Les problèmes*; Agence urbaine de la Ville d'Alger (AUVA), *Les bidonvilles: L'immigration musulmane à Alger et dans l'agglomération algéroise*, 1957 (personal archives of Rachid Sidi Boumedine). For Casablanca, see ANF, CHEAM, 20000046/42, Article 1225, Capitaine Paul Garnier, *Étude sur le prolétariat indigène de Casablanca*, October 1947, 57–58; Maneville, "Prolétariat," 209–16.

62. See ANF, CHEAM, 2000002/65, Article 1700, J. Ratier, *Étude sociologique du bidonville des Carrières centrales de Casablanca*, June 1949, 67.

63. Original text: *Cette masse indigène . . . reste suspendue entre deux pôles opposés . . . traditions ancestrales et nos conceptions modernes.* Garnier, *Étude sur le prolétariat indigène*, 88.

64. Abdelmajid Arrif, "Présentation," in Mathieu and Maury, *Bousbir*, 11–35, here 17.

65. Original text: *L'importance de la main-d'œuvre flottante des désœuvrés, des mendiants professionnels, de la prostitution, des délits commis par cette masse désencadrée au surplus facile à émouvoir et à exciter par la propagande démagogique des partis politiques.* Maneville, "Prolétariat," 39.

66. CADN, APM, DI478; Benseddik, *Syndicalisme et politique au Maroc*; Taki, *Jawānib*; ʿAbd al-Rraḥmān al-Yūsufiyy, *ʾAḥādīth fī mā Jarā. Mudhakkarrāt min Sīratiyy Kamā Rawaytuhā Libou Darqah* (ʿIn al-Sabiʿ al-Dār al-Baiḍāʾ: Dār al-Nasher al-Maghrebiyyah, 2018), 1:51–55.

67. Robert Montagne, *Naissance du prolétariat marocain: Enquête collective 1948–1950* (Paris: Peyronnet, 1950).

68. On Montagne, see François Pouillon and Daniel Rivet, eds., *La sociologie musulmane de Robert Montagne* (Paris: Maisonneuve et Larose, 2000).

69. See Michèle Jolé, "Les villes et la politique de recherche française au Maroc," *Bulletin économique et social du Maroc* 147–48 (1983): 149–83, here 156–58, 166–67; Arrif, "Présentation," 16–18.

70. Original text: *Dans ces agglomérations très denses, et pour l'instant hors de notre emprise efficace, que sont les Carrières centrales (et leurs dépendances) avec 50.000 âmes, Ben M'sik avec 50.000, la vieille Médina avec 80.000 musulmans, pour ne pas parler du 'bloc compact' de la Nouvelle Médina (150.000) peuvent à l'improviste, se développer, au sein d'un peuple paisible et discipliné, des mouvements soudains et violents.* And: *Les conséquences peuvent en être redoutables.*

71. CADN, APM, DI478, Montagne to General Juin, June 1, 1950.

72. Original: *Nouvelles générations nées dans le désordre des cités.* Montagne, *Naissance*, 263. In his later book, Montagne repeated fears about male youth. Montagne, *Révolution au Maroc* (Paris: Éditions France Empire, 1954), 274, 323–28.

73. Montagne, *Naissance*, 42, 220, 244, 248–51.

74. See CADN, APM, DI305, dossier Contrôle urbain.

75. Original: *Reprendre en mains la population des bidonvilles dont l'abandon actuel fait peser sur la sécurité des quatre grandes villes un grand danger.* CADN, APM, DI300, Juin to Secretary-General of Moroccan Protectorate, *Problème des agglomérations urbaines*, July 12, 1950.

76. Jim House, "L'impossible contrôle d'une ville coloniale? Casablanca, décembre 1952," *Genèses* 86, no. 1 (2012): 78–103, 88–89.

77. House.

78. CADN, APM, DI380, De la Porte des Vaux, *Le Parti de l'Istiqlal à Casablanca*, 6, 11, 48.

79. Taki, *Jawānib*, 2:319–20, 323–27, 434–41; CADN, APM, Contrôle civil Casablanca, 5.

80. Alison Baker, *Voices of Resistance: Oral Histories of Moroccan Women* (Albany: State University of New York Press, 1998).

81. Mohammed Zade, *Résistance et Armée de Libération au Maroc (1947–1956)* (Rabat: Haut Commissariat aux anciens résistants et anciens membres de l'Armée de libération, 2007); Taki, *Jawānib*, 2:323–450. On the "underground city," see Christopher E. Goscha, "Colonial Hanoi and Saigon at War: Social Dynamics of the Viet Minh's Underground City," *War in History* 20, no. 2 (2013): 222–50.

82. Najīb Taki, "Musāhamat Krayyān Ibn Msīk fi al-Muqāwamah al-Musallahah bi-l-Dār al-Baiḍāʾ: Khaliyyet al-Yad al-Sawdāʾ Namaudhajan," in *al-Dār al-Baiḍāʾ fi Māʾat Sannah (1907–2007)*, ed. Muḥammed al-Falaḥ al-ʿAlawiyy (al-Dār al-Baiḍāʾ: Kulliyyet al-ʾĀdāb wa al-ʿUlūm al-ʾInsāniyyah Ibn Msīk, 2010), 136–49. On the Democratic Independence Party, see CADN, APM, Région de Casablanca, 989, *Le Parti démocratique de l'indépendance à Casablanca*, June 29, 1953.

83. On urban-rural mobility, see Jim House, "Double présence: Migrations, liens ville-campagne et luttes pour l'indépendance à Alger, Casablanca, Hanoi et Saigon," *Monde(s): Histoire, espaces, relations* 12 (2017): 95–120.

84. Original: *Les inconvénients du gigantisme spatial.* Adam, *Casablanca*, 1:95.

85. Original: *Les bidonvilles qui prolifèrent en bordure des Cités marocaines ne sont pas sans offrir aux détracteurs de l'œuvre française en ce pays un sujet de critique facile à exploiter auprès de l'opinion mondiale.* CADN, APM, DI302, "Bidonvilles."

86. See Écochard's *Note sur l'habitat* (July 1949) in CADN, APM, Cabinet du Délégué à la résidence générale, 131.

87. For an overview of shantytown rehousing, see Cohen and Eleb, *Casablanca*, 288–348; Taki, *Jawānib*, 1:395–484.

88. CADN, APM, Secrétaire général du Protectorat, 237, DAU de Casablanca, *Note sur le déplacement et le recasement des bidonvilles de Casablanca*, November 21, 1953.

89. See the extensive documentation in ANOM, Algérie, Département d'Alger, Préfecture, Administration des Indigènes, 10I/9 and 10I/10.

90. Joëlle Deluz-La Bruyère and Jean-Jacques Deluz, "L'Allogio sociale a Algeri durante il periodo coloniale (1920–1962)," *Storia Urbana* 10, nos. 35–36 (1986): 107–52, here 149. The most detailed analysis on these questions is Thierry Guillopé, *Le logement social en Algérie à la période coloniale (années 1920–1960)* (PhD diss., Université Paris-Est, 2023).

91. Descloîtres et al., *L'Algerie*, 86.

92. See ANOM, Algérie, Préfecture d'Alger, Cabinet du Préfet d'Alger, 1K/495, 1K/478, and 1K/952.

93. Emmanuel Sivan, *Communisme et nationalisme en Algérie: 1920–1962* (Paris: Presses de la FNSP, 1976), 168–75, 184–205; ANOM, Algérie, 10I/10, President of Algiers Public Housing Office to Prefect of Algiers, January 16, 1950; Sadek Hadjerès, articles in *Liberté*, July 6, 16, and 29, 1950.

94. See *Journal officiel, débats parlementaires*, August 21, 1947, minutes of session 1, August 20, 1947, 4454 and 4485 (Mezerna, Marty).

95. ANOM, Algérie, Cabinet du Gouverneur Général, 9CAB/115, Note pour Monsieur le Directeur du Cabinet, *Les "bidonvilles" d'Alger / Situation au mois de Mai 1948*, May 14, 1948.

96. See "La Ville-pilote de l'Afrique du Nord vient porter témoignage," *Alger-Revue* (December 1955), 26–31.

97. AUVA, *Les bidonvilles. L'immigration musulmane à Alger et dans l'agglomération algéroise*, 1957.

98. On Chevallier, see Zeynep Çelik, *Urban Forms and Colonial Confrontations: Algiers under French Rule* (Berkeley: University of California Press, 1997), 117–20, 143–57.

99. On the SAU, see Samia Henni, *Architecture of Counterrevolution: The French Army in Northern Algeria* (Zürich: Verlag, 2017), 149–60.

100. On the new rehousing agenda in 1957, see Algiers Wilāya Archives (AWA), 5K85, Préfecture d'Alger, Bureau du Plan, *Réunion d'information et de travail du 21 janvier 1957 concernant les mesures à prendre en vue de la résorption des bidonvilles de l'agglomération algéroise*, January 22, 1957.

101. See Neil MacMaster, *Burning the Veil: The Algerian War and the 'Emancipation' of Muslim Women, 1954–1962* (Manchester: Manchester University Press, 2009).

102. AWA, 4L136, SAU de la Cité Mahieddine, *Travaux d'intérêt communal: Demande d'ouverture de crédits. Exposé général*, undated but 1957.

103. Marie-Monique Robin, *Escadrons de la mort, l'école française* (Paris: La Découverte, 2004), 99–101; Çelik, *Urban Forms*, 211n57.

104. Çelik, *Urban Forms*, 120–21.

105. The most detailed preindependence published study (1961) for Algiers carried a subtitle and argument to that effect: Descloîtres et al., *L'Algerie*.

106. See the chapter by Françoise de Barros, in this volume.

107. See Marie-Renée Chéné, *Treize ans d'histoire d'un bidonville algérien: "Bubsila" 1950–1963*, unpublished study, March 1963 (Glycines Library, Algiers).

108. ANOM, Algérie, Service des liaisons nord-africaines (SLNA), 4i/224, Organisation spéciale, 1949–1954.

109. ANOM, Algérie, SLNA, 4i/4, PPA Alger 1936–1945, dossier Maison-Carrée; ANOM, Algérie, Cabinet du Gouverneur Général, 11CAB36, Maison-Carrée Police d'État. *Rapport mensuel sur l'état d'esprit des populations (24 novembre–23 décembre 1955)*.

110. See Jim House, *Shantytowns and the City: Colonial Power Relations in Algiers and Casablanca* (Oxford: Oxford University Press, in preparation).

111. See McDougall, *A History*, 198–222.

112. Jean Pelletier, *Alger 1955: Essai d'une géographie sociale* (1959; Algiers: Apic Éditions, 2015), 109.

113. See ANOM, Algérie, SAU, 2SAS64, SAU Mahieddine. Similar themes of spatial proximity and intranecine Algerian violence also concerned neighbors of Algerian shantytowns in suburban Paris, as Françoise de Barros shows in her chapter in this volume.

114. For example, see AWA, 5K84, *Rapport No.385/4 du Commandant de Brigade d'Alger (6 août 1956) sur bidonville sis avenue de Bourmont*.

115. See ANOM, Algérie, Cabinet du Gouverneur Général, 10 CAB/54.

116. Original: *Dominer utilement le Bidonville où gîtent en permanence de nombreux éléments douteux*. ANOM, Algérie, Préfecture d'Alger, Cabinet du Préfet d'Alger, 1K/577, Chef de la Police des Renseignements généraux du District d'Alger to Préfet d'Alger (Cabinet), *Au sujet Villa Mahiéddine*, March 16, 1956.

117. Original: *Ces localités servent en effet de relais à un grand nombre de terroristes qui opèrent à Alger*. ANOM, Algérie, Préfecture d'Alger, Cabinet du Préfet d'Alger, 1K/670, Préfecture d'Alger communiqué of September 30, 1956.

118. See, for Maison-Carrée and Clos-Salembier, ANOM, 1K/670. For such operations across the city in late July 1955, see ANOM, Algérie, Cabinet du Gouverneur Général, 11CAB36, Commissaire divisionnaire, Benhamou G, Commissaire Central, Chef de la Circonscription de Police d'Alger to Préfet—Police générale / Alger, July 30, 1955.

119. These observations are based on the author's forty interviews (2012–2022) with former

residents of the Mahieddine shantytown, including the widow of a former hostel manager in Mahieddine (Algiers, April 8, 2014).

120. AWA, 5K84, Chef de la SAU de la Cité Mahieddine to M. le Préfet d'Alger, April 8, 1957.

121. ANOM, Algérie, SAU, 2SAS64, Mahieddine, report, September 20, 1961.

122. For the urban impact of these migrations across Algeria, see Pierre Bourdieu and his team, *Travail et travailleurs en Algérie* (Paris: Mouton, 1963), esp. 451–557.

123. ANOM, Algérie, SAU, 2SAS59, Clos-Salembier, Chef de la SAU du Clos-Salembier, *Rapport sur les populations kabyles du Clos-Salembier*, June 22, 1960.

124. ANOM, Algérie, SAU, 2SAS65, Maison-Carrée, Chef de la SAU de Maison-Carrée, report, January 23, 1960.

125. On these questions, see Jim House, "Shantytowns and Rehousing in Late Colonial Algiers and Casablanca," in Naylor, *France's*, 133–63, esp. 150–54.

126. ANOM, Algérie, SAU, 2SAS52, Échelon de liaison d'Alger, *Rapport au sujet des populations des bidonvilles*, July 21, 1961.

127. AWA, SK85, 2ᵉ Bureau, Zone Nord Algérois, secteur Alger Sahel, *Fiche à l'attention de M. le Général Massu. Objet: Enquêtes sociologiques*, March 27, 1957.

128. These comments are based on the author's consultation of the majority of the district-based Algiers SAU archival boxes (ANOM).

129. See Torres, *Les bidonvilles*; Pierre Bourdieu, *Esquisses algériennes* (Paris: Seuil, 2008); Descloîtres et al., *L'Algérie*; Boumedine, *Bétonvilles*; Pelletier, *Alger 1955*.

130. See, in particular, Fanon's well-known description of segregation in *Les Damnés de la terre* (1961; Paris: Seuil, 1991), 127–29. For an overview, see Andrea Rapini, "Can Peasants Make a Revolution? Colonialism, Labor, and Power Relations in Pierre Bourdieu's Algerian Inquiries," *International Review of Social History* 61 (2016): 389–421.

131. Mathieu Rigouste, *Un seul héros le peuple* (Toulouse: PMN Éditions, 2020).

132. See Nadia Sariahmed Belhadj, "The December 1960 Demonstrations in Algiers: Spontaneity and Organisation of Mass Action," *Journal of North African Studies* 27, no. 1 (2022): 104–42.

133. ANOM, Algérie, SAU, 2SAS65, Maison-Carrée, *Rapport sur les événements de décembre 1960*, December 20, 1960, 2.

134. See Jim House, "Colonial Containment? Repression of Pro-Independence Street Demonstrations in Algiers, Casablanca and Paris, 1945–1962," *War in History* 25, no. 2 (2018): 172–201.

135. It was in Belcourt, where this spatial proximity was perhaps the closest, that shantytowns do feature in some press reports. See the Metropolitan French press reproduced in the FLN's publication *El Moudjahid*, no. 75, December 19, 1960.

136. See the press cuttings in ANOM, Algérie, 81K/137.

137. Original: *On sait bien que les troublions lors des émeutes ne viennent pas des bidonvilles.* AWA, 5K97, Département d'Alger, Arrondissement d'Alger, Affaires algériennes, *Rapport au sujet des populations des bidonvilles*, July 21, 1961.

138. ANOM, Algérie, SAU, 2SAS52, *Synthèse des rapports mensuels des SAS d'Alger*, January 31, 1961. See also 2SAS59, SAU Clos-Salembier, reports dated April, October, and November 1958, April and July 1959; 2SAS58, SAU Climat de France, report of August 24, 1959.

Index

Page numbers in italics refer to figures.

www.ingramcontent.com/pod-product-compliance
Lightning Source LLC
Chambersburg PA
CBHW022134020426
42334CB00015B/891